Facing Change in Health Care

Learning Faster in Tough Times

Winnie Schmeling, PhD, RN, FAAN
Tallahassee Memorial Regional
Medical Center

AHA AHA books are published by American Hospital Publishing, Inc.,
an American Hospital Association company

This publication is designed to provide accurate and authoritative information in regard to the subject matter covered. It is sold with the understanding that neither the author nor the publisher is engaged in rendering legal, accounting, or other professional service. If legal advice or other expert assistance is required, the services of a competent professional should be sought.

The views expressed in this publication are strictly those of the author; official endorsement by the Robert Wood Johnson Foundation, the Pew Charitable Trusts, or the American Hospital Association is not intended and should not be inferred.

Library of Congress Cataloging-in-Publication Data

Schmeling, Winnie.
    Facing change in health care : learning faster in tough times /
Winnie Schmeling.
        p.   cm.
    Includes bibliographical references.
    ISBN 1-55648-149-7
    1. Hospitals—Administration.   2. Organizational change.
3. Hospital care—Quality control.   I. Title.
    [DNLM: 1. Hospital Administration—United States.   2. Quality of
Health Care—organization & administration—United States.
3. Organizational Innovation.   4. Models, Organizational.   WX 153
S347f   1996]
RA971.S35   1996
362.1'1'068—dc20
DNLM/DLC
for Library of Congress   95-45010
                                                                            CIP

Catalog no. 174400

©1996 by American Hospital Publishing, Inc.,
an American Hospital Association company

Printed in the USA

Text set in English Times
3.5M—01/96—0430

Richard Hill, Senior Editor
Nancy Charpentier, Editor
Dennis Spaag, Editorial Assistant
Peggy DuMais, Production Coordinator
Marcia Bottoms, Executive Editor

To my sister,
Kathryn Hall Lange,

who has faced change with incredible courage,
and taught all those around her that every day is a gift.

Contents

List of Figures and Tables

Figures

Tables

About the Author

Winnie Schmeling, PhD, RN, FAAN, is project director for the Program to Improve Patient Care at Tallahassee Memorial Regional Medical Center in Tallahassee, Florida. The program is an organizational redesign project initiated as part of Strengthening Hospital Nursing: A Program to Improve Patient Care, a national program supported by the Robert Wood Johnson Foundation and the Pew Charitable Trusts.

Prior to joining TMRMC, Dr. Schmeling coordinated the research team that produced the Florida Nursing Shortage Study for the Florida Legislature and the Florida Health Care Cost Containment Board. In addition, she was executive vice-president at MGT of America, Inc., a Tallahassee-based management consulting firm with offices in Austin, Texas; Sacramento, California; and Olympia, Washington. She was with MGT for 10 years and established the firm's health care consulting practice.

Dr. Schmeling was elected a fellow of the American Academy of Nursing and was appointed by the governor of Florida to serve on the Board of Examiners for his statewide quality awards. She is cofounder and vice-chairman of the board of directors of Capital Health Plan, a 60,000-member, federally qualified, fully NCQA-accredited, not-for-profit HMO in Tallahassee.

Dr. Schmeling writes and speaks nationally on organizational change, organizational learning, work and role redesign, and performance improvement. She has consulted nationally for hospitals and health systems as well as local, state, and federal governments in the areas of managed care, integrated delivery systems, strategic planning, marketing, survey and opinion research, nurse recruitment and retention, and health policy and health care regulation. Dr. Schmeling received her bachelor's degree in nursing from the University of Delaware and her master's and doctorate degrees in health planning from Florida State University.

Foreword

Facing Change in Health Care: Learning Faster in Tough Times is a well-organized and insightful record of the learnings from the Robert Wood Johnson Foundation and the Pew Charitable Trusts national program entitled Strengthening Hospital Nursing: A Program to Improve Patient Care. The title of the 26.8 million dollar program references the need to deal with the systems issues facing nursing within the hospital work setting. While many perceived this to be a solely nursing initiative, the thoughtful leadership recognized that success would require a total organizational commitment to accomplish the desired outcome of improving patient care.

Over 600 grant applications, involving in excess of 1,000 hospitals, were submitted in 1989. This response reinforced the perception that the issues affecting patient care were of great concern and that hospitals were willing to accept the challenge to change—to accept the challenge to make systemic change in their organizations.

Learning was the critical component during the life of the six-year demonstration grant. Under the direction of the National Program Office, grantee project teams—including the CEO, nurse executive, medical staff and trustee representatives, and the project director— were exposed to recognized leaders in the field of organizational theory and organizational restructuring—leaders such as Russell Ackoff, Peter Senge, Don Lombardi, Tom Gilmore, Alan Barstow, and others from the Wharton School of Business in Philadelphia.

Exposure to knowledge and understanding of the concepts of change theory are only valuable to an institution when leadership puts that knowledge to use and makes something happen—in this instance changing the culture of the organization, addressing the systems that impact on the organization's ability to respond to the constantly changing environment, and developing an organization that can learn and has the capacity to change how work is done.

No one predicted the pressure on the hospitals and professionals that would become evident during the early 1990s, particularly during the first two years of the grant. Fiscal constraints, accelerated movement of care from hospitals to ambulatory care settings, increased pressures from managed care, and the multiple new configuration of hospitals into systems were some of the pressures experienced by the participating institutions. The grantees, as well as the total health care industry, were faced with demands for change that were more complex and rapid than anything in our history.

Dr. Schmeling, working with staffs of all the grantee organizations, has clustered their learnings in such a way that the reader will understand the relevance of each chapter to the whole—the relevance to accomplishing the desired outcome. This approach provides a very effective description of the approaches used by each of the grantee teams to develop and/or adapt their learnings from the experts. The reader can follow the logical sequence of the book and gain understanding and insights as to what must be accomplished if lasting change is going to occur in one of the most complex institutions in our society—the health care system. While each organization has approached the challenges of creating a learning organization with some uniqueness to their settings, the common critical themes are evident as the reader progresses through the book.

Dr. Schmeling and the contributing authors have shared their experiences and insights, all of which can help anyone who wants to start on the pathway toward change. The message that is continually reinforced is the necessity for ensuring leadership commitment, providing clear vision, understanding the complexities of learning and learners, providing people with tools and experiences, involving people from all levels of the organization, and always improving from the lessons learned. It is a cycle that never ends, and the institution that has made a commitment to be a learning organization is well positioned to deal with unknowns of the future because it has the capacity to learn and change.

Congratulations to Dr. Schmeling and all the contributing authors for making your work come alive. Your willingness to share your insights, your tools, and your learnings makes this book a very valuable resource for anyone interested in creating a strong organization for the future—because we must have the capacity to shape the future, and that requires individuals and organizations to have the capacity to change.

Barbara A. Donaho, BSN, MA, FAAN
Director, Strengthening Hospital Nursing Program
November 1995

Acknowledgments

This book is the result of the efforts of many, many people and organizations:

- The Robert Wood Johnson Foundation and the Pew Charitable Trusts saw the need for the Strengthening Hospital Nursing Program, and had the commitment to fund the program generously and the wisdom to place it in the capable hands of Barbara A. Donaho, director, and Mary K. Kohles, deputy director, transformational leaders by any definition.
- The Strengthening Hospital Nursing Program grantee organizations and others generously shared their learnings and contributed them to this book. Their contributions are particularly important because they offer hope that all things are possible. My thanks especially to the project directors who served as point people in gathering up these contributions, and who have been wonderful colleagues over the six years of the project.
- The late Brian Schenk of American Hospital Publishing, Inc., provided the initial vision and guidance for all of the books coming out of our projects. My thanks especially to Rick Hill for wonderful editorial advice and for mentoring me through this process. My thanks also to Janis Dutton, who skillfully edited the mountain of contributions (contributions were first edited by Judie Mulholland).
- None of this would have happened without the visionary leadership at Tallahassee Memorial Regional Medical Center. My thanks especially to Duncan Moore, president/CEO, for his support of the project and of this book, and to the project steering committee for their guidance over the years. Special thanks to Joan Futch, senior vice-president for nursing, who first saw the value of this project for our organization, and who has been a consistent and inspirational champion of change.
- The staff of the Program to Improve Patient Care deserve special thanks: DeeDee Lumpkin, Gina Kuperberg, Vivian Booth, Mary Bland, and Christy Harrison. They live and model the disciplines of the learning organization every day, and never fail to rise to the challenge of new opportunities. I am particularly grateful to DeeDee Lumpkin for her skill and patience in tracking contributions and preparing the manuscript.
- Finally, thank you to my family—my parents, who always believed I could do anything, and David, Amy, and Meg Schmeling, who have taught me what is really important in life.

Chapter 1

Embracing the Learning Imperative: Organizational Learning and Organizational Change

Five years ago, 20 project teams, representing more than 60 health care facilities, set out on a journey to redesign our organizations to improve patient care. These facilities were recipients of grants entitled "Strengthening Hospital Nursing: A Program to Improve Patient Care," a national program supported by the Robert Wood Johnson Foundation and the Pew Charitable Trusts. It was clear at the outset that this would mean involving our entire organizations in completely rethinking even the most basic roles, structures, and processes. What was not clear was exactly how we would accomplish this.

This book is about the journey so far—how we are learning to make organizational change. Though none of us would claim to have all the answers, we have learned a lot about how to get started and what it takes to create and sustain meaningful change. As a way of sharing what we have learned—our stories and programs, our frustrations and successes—voices of experience are sprinkled liberally throughout the book. One of those voices, from Beth Israel Hospital in Boston, frames the challenge that many of the project teams were to face to some degree:

> What would it take to get all 4,000 employees acting as if they owned the hospital? That was the question Beth Israel Hospital's senior management team began to explore in 1986, and the question that ultimately led to their commitment to create a work environment characterized by extensive employee involvement and organizational learning. Two key and interdependent facets of this strategy are education and participation. These two activities work together at Beth Israel to promote individual, team, and organizational learning.
>
> *Luanne Selk, manager, training and organization development, Beth Israel Hospital, Boston*

A great deal has been written about organizational change. Much of it has been extremely useful in helping us build our own models for change. But as Peter Senge warns in *The Fifth Discipline: The Art and Practice of the Learning Organization,*[1] receiving information—even understanding information—is not the same as learning. Learning is about changing how we think *and* what we do as a result of that understanding.

Thus it follows that organizational change—changing how we think and what we do—is fundamentally a learning process. In Senge's learning organizations, not only do individuals learn but so do organizations. Although individual learning is at the heart of organizational learning, it is not enough. To become a true learning organization, teams must learn as well; and what they learn must be incorporated into the organization's structures and processes to achieve the desired results.

Thanks to the work of Senge and others, we now know what a learning organization is. However, creating a learning organization is another matter altogether. This process of creation, what Senge calls moving from invention to innovation,[2] has been the substance of our work over the past three years. In many ways, our work is the work presented in Joel Barker's videotape *Paradigm Pioneers.*[3]

Barker defines *paradigm* as a set of rules and regulations that does two things:

1. It establishes or defines boundaries.
2. It directs us how to solve problems within those boundaries.

When a paradigm changes, or shifts, it fundamentally changes the way things are done. *Paradigm shifters* are those who create the new paradigm—the inventors. Barker reminds us that few will ever get the chance to be paradigm shifters. However, we do not have to create the new paradigm to be successful in it. We can *choose* to be paradigm pioneers. *Paradigm pioneers* are those people who make the new idea work, driving it from rough concept to practical application. Paradigm pioneers need these qualities:

- *Intuition:* The ability to make good decisions with limited information
- *Courage:* The willingness to move forward in the face of great risk
- *Commitment to time:* Accepting that it takes time to go from rough concept to working paradigm

The pioneer metaphor seems just right. After all, pioneers were those rugged individuals who set out to open up new territories so that settlers could follow.

Senge's work on the learning organization represents a paradigm shift—a new way of thinking about and creating organizational change. He has defined the concepts, described five necessary disciplines in some detail (discussed in the next section), and even thought through each discipline's essences, principles, and actions.

The central issue for those of us pioneering this paradigm is how to go about creating learning organizations—shifting the thinking *and* doing in our organizations. What are the key concepts to be learned, and are there ways to design what Senge calls *learningful experiences* to present those concepts so that they are compelling enough to fall on fertile ground. After all, people learn what they *want* to learn.

The Learning Organization

Senge defines *learning organizations* as those "where people continually expand their capacity to create the results they truly desire, where new and expansive patterns of thinking are nurtured, where collaborative aspiration is set free, and where people are continually learning to learn together."[4] An example of a learning organization is Mercy Health Services in Farmington Hills, Michigan. Marjorie Beyers, former associate vice-president for nursing, has observed the critical relationship between a learning organization and its staff:

Before an organization can become a learning organization, people have to become "learning people." They have to continue to grow. Only after individuals think of themselves as continually learning can the organization become a learning organization.

Five disciplines—sets of practices and principles—are necessary to the learning organization. The first three are individual disciplines, the last two are collective:

1. *Systems thinking:* A conceptual framework which recognizes that everything is related to everything else—that the world is made up of processes, not separate, unrelated events and actions.
2. *Personal mastery:* Personal commitment to our own lifelong learning, to the continuous process of personal visioning, to focusing on what we truly want, and to the truth, particularly about the current reality.

3. *Mental models:* How we see the world, including the ability to carry on "learningful" conversations in which people reveal their own mental models and open them to the influence of others.

4. *Shared vision:* A shared picture of the future we want to create. The gap between vision and current reality is the *creative tension,* the energy for change. A vision, no matter how "right," cannot be imposed.

5. *Team learning:* The process whereby a group becomes aligned (able to function as a whole) and develops the ability to create what its members really want. Teams, not individuals, are the fundamental learning unit in organizations. If teams cannot learn, organizations cannot learn. Team learning starts with dialogue that honestly and openly explores the issues before the team. Defensive routines are patterns of behavior that we learn to protect ourselves from threat or embarrassment. Teams must learn how to recognize and deal with defensive routines that shut down learning.

Senge believes that these five disciplines are necessary to the learning organization. However, not all learning is the same. He draws a distinction between adaptive learning and generative learning. *Adaptive learning* is about survival, allowing an organization to adapt quickly to change. On the other hand, *generative learning* is creative, allowing an organization to create its own future.

In a learning organization, people see themselves as part of a whole. They see life as a continuous change process. And they see themselves as continually changing—to create what they truly want.

A learning organization recognizes that individuals, teams, and even the organization itself must value and be committed to learning. Leaders model commitment to their own learning and to learning to learn together. Ultimately, what really matters is how each organization operationalizes the concept. Three health care organizations have defined what becoming a learning organization means in very different ways:

Learning organizations create a "community" in which participants develop a commitment to help each other in the learning process.

Learning facilitates the development of new and creative organizational solutions at those points in the organization where changes are most likely to succeed.

The learning organization integrates the following:

- Mission/vision/plans of the organization
- A measurement system to monitor progress toward the mission/vision/plans
- A structure for participative and collaborative interaction
- Innovation and continuous learning
- Celebration of accomplishments (reward results, not just efforts)
- Systems to support data-driven decision making

Vivian Booth, RN, project analyst, Work Redesign Program to Improve Patient Care, Tallahassee Memorial Regional Medical Center, Tallahassee, FL

Our greatest learning pertains to four interrelated areas: (1) an awareness of customer's needs and expectations, (2) an understanding of the nature of teams, (3) an appreciation of the inter-disciplinary efforts needed to provide patient care, and (4) an ability to achieve specified outcomes. Without these, none of it makes any difference.

Faye Gilbarg, regional director, medical management and quality, Providence Health System, Portland, OR

The purpose of the learning organization is to always question what is the effect of this action or that initiative and not to let "what you do" or "how your job is defined" rule what you do. Rather, you need to look at the reasons why you are doing something in the first place. A job that is critical in one period may not even be necessary in another, so the learning organization allows you to move into a different focus very easily with different people. The old organization held you pretty close to what it was you were supposed to do in your particular role. When change occurred, it was discrete rather than continuous; that is, you went from point A to point B and then you stood there. Whereas now, change is a moving target. As you continually improve the system, you change the ground rules as you go.

Marjorie Beyers, RN, PhD, FAAN, former associate vice-president, nursing, Mercy Health Services, Farmington Hills, MI

The Nature of Organizational Learning

Certainly, organizational learning involves individual learning. But organizational learning also involves team learning. Team learning is a totally different type of learning because it involves people learning together, a complex process full of pitfalls because of the added dimension of the need to deal with mental models—our own as well as those of others. However, the concept of the learning organization goes well beyond both individual and team learning. Remember, learning is changing how we think and what we do, and the organization cannot do that until individual and team learning is incorporated into even the most basic organizational structures and processes.

The metaphor of a tapestry best characterizes our experience with organizational learning. Many persons are weaving complex tableaux and in the process are honing and improving their skills. Individuals are learning from groups to the same extent that groups are learning from individuals.

Joan Lartin-Drake, PhD, RN, director, Center for Nursing Research, University Hospital/Penn State University Hershey, PA

We are all familiar with situations where individuals, even teams, seem to learn new ways of thinking and doing things but when those individuals are no longer involved, things just fall apart. Or, a new process has been put into place and works well until there is a crisis, then all bets are off.

In these situations, individuals and teams may have learned but the organization has not learned. The key to organizational learning lies in systems thinking—in understanding underlying structures. When placed in the same system, people tend to produce the same results. Until underlying structures are changed, thinking and behavior cannot consistently change.

Many of us have struggled with what organizational learning means. In some cases, the struggle has been within a single organization. In other cases, it has been between many organizations sharing a vision. In some cases, the struggle has been in large, academic medical centers with ample resources; in others, it has been in small, rural hospitals where resources are scarce. In all cases, the struggle has been to build a definition of organizational learning that works within a particular context.

Traditional organizations are built on the teachings of Max Weber, where rigid lines of authority exist and bureaucracy is king.[5] Until recently, hospitals and health care organizations as well as most businesses and government agencies have emulated this model. The organizational chart depicts the relationships and outlines prescribed roles and responsibilities. In a traditional organization, the boss is the boss and decisions are made top down. This model is comfortable because we know who is important and how to get things done. This is the model we learned while in school and the kind of organization where most of us have worked and functioned. The traditional organization is driven by a mission statement and a business plan. This model has not been all bad, but its effectiveness in our current environment is questionable.

The *learning organization,* or the *new-age organization,* is a new culture where the lines of authority and accountability are blurred—one where information exchange is king and getting information to the individual doing the work is the most important task. A matrix design with cross-functional teams rather than an organizational chart outlines the working relationships.

Teams are important because that is where decisions are made and the job gets done. In a learning organization, the "boss" is a partner and the leadership team is empowered and empowering. The learning organization is driven by vision but also has a mission and a business plan. The learning organization is alive with energy and creativity where the motto is "proceed until apprehended."

S. Ann Evans, RN, MS, MBA, FAAN, executive director, The Heart Institute at Tallahassee Memorial, Tallahassee Memorial Regional Medical Center, Tallahassee, FL

Vanderbilt University Hospital has operationalized organizational learning through objectives and expectations described in its mission statement and official policies. The practice of organizational learning is demonstrated in the creation of a decision support system that utilized data on corporate culture and key success measures to continually improve the quality of patient care and work life. Originally, the system was intended as a tool that top-level administrators would use to actively manage the corporate culture to create a more effective organization. The organizational learning reflected in this example soon appeared in the "trenches." After results from the system were disseminated, several managers of patient care units recognized that they could use the system to manage values and norms and key success measures at the unit level. Managers learned that by using the same tools as leadership, they could involve their staff in designing and implementing policies in their areas that were consistent with the institution's overall mission and direction. The result is greater horizontal and vertical integration within the institution, more staff involvement and ownership, and, ultimately, a more effective organization.

Oscar Miller, PhD, former consultant, research and evaluation, Center for Patient Care Innovation, Vanderbilt University Hospital and Vanderbilt Clinic, Nashville, TN

A learning organization has a shifting structure without the same hierarchy and same groundedness as before. In short, there is no right way or wrong way. For example, before, you had people in their fixed positions and, now, you have work teams that spin off to solve a problem or resolve an issue or create an innovation. When their work is completed, they may go out of business and/or a new team with different membership might take off in a new direction as new insights and new issues evolve.

Marjorie Beyers, RN, PhD, FAAN, former associate vice-president, nursing, Mercy Health Services, Farmington Hills, MI

Shifts in Thinking among Learning Organizations

Senge calls the shift in thinking in learning organizations *metanoia,* but cautions against using the word in public![6] Many of us have come to call this shift in thinking the "ah ha" experience. What happens is that the worldview literally changes, sometimes 180 degrees. The ah ha experience can happen to individuals, groups, organizations, and even groups of organizations. Our experience has been that once thinking shifts, perceptions are changed forever—and not only about work. We have seen this shift extend to all of life's relationships:

- *From seeing parts to seeing wholes:* Thinking inside the box—thinking only inside my position or department—ensures fragmented decision making that can never address key issues. Learning to make key decisions based on interrelationships and patterns improves our ability to learn where the leverage is for change.
- *From "arrows in" to "arrows out":* The arrows-in thinker sees obstacles, forces that mean things cannot be different. The arrows-out thinker sees opportunities and choices, the ways things can be influenced and changed.
- *From "what's wrong" to "what right would look like":* "Ain't it awful" is deeply embedded in many organizational cultures. Being the expert on what is wrong is a way to abdicate responsibility for what is. It takes courage to offer up your vision of what right would look like.

- *From events explanations to systems explanations:* Seeing life as a series of events, each with a cause, is linear cause–effect thinking. It is the longer-term patterns behind the events that offer the possibility of understanding underlying structures. Events explanations are reactive: They offer a way to react to the event. Systems explanations are generative: They address the underlying structure and allow us to generate or create change.

The following contributors reveal the degree to which shifts in thinking and doing have occurred in some health care organizations:

Among the eight vice-presidents, five of us have direct patient care accountability. Therefore, we really do need to cooperate and collaborate as we look at the processes and the outcomes that we want to achieve in this organization. We are doing that through patient care councils, which means that when we interact as a group, we try to maintain an understanding of the whole. For example, when I bring my group together (information systems, consultative nursing, social services, chaplaincy, medical education, Lifeflight [Emergency Medical Services and Flight Program] medical records, quality management, and the emergency center), we don't necessarily talk about individual needs but, rather, we talk about what is it that our organization needs in order to accomplish its strategic direction. For us, it is a whole different way of thinking and it makes the heretofore impossible, possible.

Evelyn Quigley, RN, MN, vice-president and nurse executive, MeritCare Hospital, Fargo, ND

The grant projects are encouraging the emergence of new paradigms for hospital organizational structures. Moving from the traditional hierarchies to circular or matrix designs with interdependent relationships, structures for the future will be flatter with fewer layers of management. These structural metamorphoses are intended to inspire and facilitate cultural change. Abandoning a provincial, territorial, departmental culture for one that is open to learning, one which values involvement of stakeholders at all levels, hospitals are striving for an ambience that supports continuous improvement. Such structural changes are rooted in the concept of the organization as a system, not a collection of independent parts.[7]

Mary K. Kohles, RN, MSW, deputy director; and Barbara Donaho, RN, MA, FAAN, director, Strengthening Hospital Nursing Program, All Children's Hospital, Inc., St. Petersburg, FL

Perceptions within health care are being altered by some additional changes in the ways learning organizations behave. The shift in thinking also creates a shift from:

- *Teaching to learning:* Too often, it is assumed that full responsibility for learning lies with the teacher. In other words, it is someone else's responsibility to teach us what we need to know. The fallacy is that no one can teach us what we do not want to learn. Thus, ultimately, we are responsible for our own learning.
- *Blame to shared responsibility:* Reactive thinking is built on the premise that when things go wrong, someone or something is to blame. Thus, correcting the problem requires fixing blame. In systems thinking, there is no blame. There are no bad people, only bad systems. We are all responsible for excellent systems.
- *"They" to "we":* The word *they* usually signals abdication of responsibility or an incomplete understanding of the pattern of relationships. Whatever happened had nothing to do with me; it happened outside me. Thinkers who use the word *we* include themselves in the pattern of relationships: There is no outside. We should eliminate *they* from our vocabularies; it is almost never a helpful concept.
- *Control to influence:* Traditionally, controlling has been seen as a function of managers (along with planning, budgeting, and so on). In the learning organization, managers do not control others but, rather, influence them. Organizational change is difficult for managers who believe that control is possible, particularly for those who have seen their work in terms of control. Systems thinkers see each of us as responsible for making

our own choices. It is probably impossible to *make* another person do anything. Thus, control is an illusion!

- *One right answer to no one right answer:* As children, we learn from our parents and teachers that there is a right answer to our questions and problems. As adults, we look to those in authority for the right answer. For example, "Just tell me what to do and I'll do it" or "You get paid the big bucks, you figure it out." But in complex systems, there are many right answers and, as continuous learners, we must and can find those answers together.

- *Training to learning:* Too often, our training programs have assumed that telling what to do and/or showing how to do results in learning. But learning requires practice. Thus, learning, practice, and action are kept together in a spiraling journey, with the focus on ultimate outcomes (in our case, for the patient).

There are endless variations on the shift-in-thinking theme. And in many ways, that is the whole point. Shifts in thinking have some underlying patterns, but organizations must define these shifts in ways that are meaningful to them in order to gain ownership of them. Following are examples showing how our organizations have developed a variety of operations to support shifts in thinking.

In 1990, our president, Lloyd Smith, laid out his vision of MeritCare as a learning organization. With the challenge of becoming a learning organization came the obligation to determine what the barriers to that goal were and then to remove them. It was found that in many services, productivity standards had long ago been developed without consideration for attendance at education opportunities. Associates felt that any classes offered were for managers only. This paradigm had to be changed if we were to achieve the goal set before us. With the support of our president, we were able to establish an education salaries account from which nonexempt associates could attend eight hours of education on paid time. The education salaries account allowed the organization to inspire associates across the organization to seek and value self-development. It created energy throughout the organization that was needed to begin the culture change process of becoming a place where learning was valued and expected.

Janet Feder, BSN, RN, education services manager, MeritCare Hospital, Fargo, ND

At District of Columbia General Hospital, we have shifted our thoughts and processes. Clinically, we have gone from individual decision making and care planning to multiple clinical departments making decisions together. Our collaborative care project teams were developed basically on the patient unit and they are multidisciplinary teams, composed of members from any and all areas of the hospital. They are usually cochaired by a physician and a nurse. Sitting on the team, there could be anyone from dietary to social work to a chaplain to housekeeping, to lab, to X ray. Just everyone. They conduct monthly meetings and they discuss patient and/or unit concerns. That approach has really worked well for us, and that is one of the ways in which we have shifted our thinking because now decisions about patients, which used to be made solely by physicians, are being made by a multidisciplinary team.

We are also in the process of a cultural shift in thinking. As a public hospital, we have always felt relatively safe because we believed that our patients would always be there. Now, with the potential for all patients to have a choice, we are really feeling and believing that what we do today will determine if we are our patient's choice tomorrow. Right now, we are trying to help our staff to constantly be cognizant of the reasons we are all here. We are trying to shift their thinking in that direction or, at least, to make sure they are thinking in the right way, that the patient must be the focus and the core reason for our hospital's existence.

Gloria Jacks, RN, project coordinator, Patient-Centered Care Delivery System, District of Columbia General Hospital, Washington, DC

Though the transition to a learning organization is occurring at all levels of the organization, the area in which this shift is particularly critical is the senior management team—the President's

Council. Previously, this group of vice-presidents advocated for their areas of responsibility, sometimes in competition for resources. The President's Council has evolved from an operations focus to that of leadership. The responsibilities of the President's Council are:

- To ensure the integration and alignment of the hospital's component parts to the whole organization
- To develop and implement strategic direction
  - Engage in strategic dialogue
  - Be stewards of the organization's resources
  - Be the eyes and ears for the organization in anticipating change
- To create, lead, perpetuate, and sustain a shared vision, values, and culture
- To be a living example of quality principles
  - Mentoring and teaching
  - Stewardship
- To make sure Abbott Northwestern has effective systems
  - Identify
  - Validate
  - Devote resources
- To consult and communicate as a partner and resource to each other and to the organization
- To keep customers and their requirements at the forefront of everything we do

This represents the systemic thinking, collaboration, and team-learning skills required. These elements did not come to the President's Council spontaneously; it is a discipline that they learned.

Julianne Morath, RN, MS, vice-president, patient care, Abbott Northwestern Hospital, Minneapolis

The Relationship between Organizational Learning and Continuous Change

We know that organizational change—changing how we think and what we do—is a fact of life and that it is fundamentally a learning process. We also know that in learning organizations, the organizations as well as the individuals in them learn. But what does this mean in terms of an organization's ability to survive and thrive?

The most successful organizations of the 1990s will be those that can change faster—which is to say, *learn* faster—than other organizations, particularly their competitors. As the world becomes more complex and interconnected, it is less and less likely that top-down, grand strategies will be successful. Instead, according to Senge, "the organizations that will truly excel in the future will be the organizations that discover how to tap people's commitment and ability to learn at all levels in the organization."[8] Duncan Moore, president/CEO of Tallahassee Memorial Regional Medical Center, in Tallahassee, Florida, communicated the urgency for change when he wrote:

Becoming a learning organization isn't just something nice to do when times are good and things are going pretty well. In fact, the tougher things get, the more important it is. Building organizational capacity for change—being able to learn faster than the competition—that's how an organization gains and keeps competitive advantage.

Yet, for most organizations the sad truth is that learning happens slowly, if at all. In many cases, individuals within the organization know there is trouble long before the organization as a whole figures it out and acts. Senge would say that the organization had a "learning disability."[9]

Certainly that has been the case for International Business Machines (IBM). IBM had neither creative tension nor energy for change because the company did not see its current reality accurately. IBM believed that the mainframe computer was the wave of the future and that customers would always be willing to pay a higher price for the IBM name and IBM service.[10]

In January 1993, IBM announced a loss of $4.7 billion, the biggest corporate loss ever recorded. What went wrong at Big Blue? Since the mid-1980s, the industry has been transformed by the popularity of the increasingly powerful and cheap personal computer (PC). Incredibly, IBM helped create this change but failed to respond adequately to it. In the 1960s, IBM had a corner on the mainframe market. The company had tremendous customer loyalty, largely because its products were good and were not compatible with other manufacturers' products. Then disaster struck in the form of standardization—PCs made with the same microprocessor chips, running the same software, tied together in networks as a cheap alternative to mainframes. Even IBM's entry into the PC market in 1981 just made the company's ultimate position worse. IBM went to Intel for the microprocessor and to Microsoft for the operating system. First dozens and then hundreds of firms jumped into the market with their IBM clones. IBM entirely missed out on the software market.

Why did it take IBM so long to react to the incredibly swift changes in its market? Perhaps it was blinded by its own success. In an effort to maintain its preeminent market position and protect its hugely profitable mainframe business, IBM failed to see the real threat of the PC. The company lost touch with what the customer wanted. But there was more. At the core of its corporate processes was a no-layoffs policy. It took eight years of losses to change that policy.

There are countless examples of organizations with learning disabilities, referring to organizations that cannot see impending disaster and once they do, do not react to it quickly enough. It is ironic that many of these organizations get into trouble by continuing to do well what made them successful in the past. Health care organizations are no exception. Hospitals must learn to see themselves as providers of health care across the entire continuum of patient care, not merely as providers of sick care within their own walls. Now more than ever, organizational learning is related to the ability to survive and thrive.

> Like IBM, hospitals and physicians have tended to believe that patients want quality and quality alone will be enough to maintain a market share. However, we are rapidly learning that quality is not enough. This premise is highly visible in the era of cardiac contracting for bypass surgery.
>
> Payers are no longer willing (if they ever were) to pay a premium for superior-quality care. Quality or quality outcomes are now the minimum threshold. Physicians and hospitals who are not competitive on prices, or at least in the same ballpark, cannot compete regardless of outcomes. Though high quality is not winning contracts, quality measures are used routinely to screen out subpar providers. The most important measure has become price and cost. This presents a difficult transition for health care providers who have been taught that quality is everything.
>
> *S. Ann Evans, RN, MS, MBA, FAAN, executive director, The Heart Institute at Tallahassee Memorial, Tallahassee Memorial Regional Medical Center, Tallahassee, FL*

> As caregivers, we tend to feel we know what is in the best interest of the patient. People are vulnerable and therefore expect to have someone provide service with appropriate expertise and knowledge. While we strive to meet the patient needs, and we do a good job of that, we may not truly understand all of the core needs and expectations of patients. Until the grant, we had not developed tools and methods to obtain in-depth knowledge of patient needs and expectations. A patient survey about patient satisfaction got us part way there, but it is the classic example of devising the questions from our perspective and not from the patient's perspective. Until the instruments are focused on the patient's needs and expectations, we can't be assured of getting useful and meaningful input from patients regarding the service we provide.
>
> *Dave Underriner, MHA, regional assistant administrator, clinical services, Providence Health System, Portland, OR*

Conclusion

Learning is about changing how we think and what we do as a result of the new thinking. It follows, then, that organizational change — changing what we think and what we do — is fundamentally a learning process. Individual learning is at the heart of organizational learning, but it is not enough. Organizations learn when what individuals have learned is integrated into organizational roles, structures, and processes. Senge invented the concept of the learning organization. Those of us who are trying to actually build learning organizations are taking his concepts and driving them up the learning curve to make them work for us as we go about improving patient care.

References and Notes

1. All of us have drawn heavily from Peter Senge's ideas, which he presented in the second annual meeting of all Strengthening Hospital Nursing Program project teams. These fascinating ideas can be found in his ground-breaking book *The Fifth Discipline: The Art and Practice of the Learning Organization.* New York City: Doubleday/Currency, 1990; and in Senge, P. M., Ross, R., Smith, B., Roberts, C., and Kleiner, A. *The Fifth Discipline Fieldbook.* New York City: Currency/Doubleday, 1994.

2. Senge, pp. 5–6.

3. Joel Barker is a futurist who has developed several videotapes that many of us have used to teach the ideas of visioning, paradigm shifts, and paradigm pioneering. The ideas mentioned here are presented in *Paradigm Pioneers* from the series *Discovering the Future,* produced by Charthouse International, Burnsville, MN, in 1992.

4. Senge, p. 3.

5. Gerth, H. H., and Wright-Mills, C. P., eds. *From Max Weber: Essays in Sociology.* New York City: Oxford University Press, 1946.

6. Senge, pp. 13–14.

7. *Strategies for Healthcare Excellence* 5(11):3, May 1992.

8. Senge, p. 4.

9. Senge, p. 18.

10. What went wrong at IBM. *The Economist* 326(1):23–26, Jan. 16, 1993; Big trouble for big blue. *U.S. News and World Report* 113(1):28–29, Jan. 4, 1993; and Managing. *Fortune* 127(5):37–42, May 3, 1993.

Chapter 2

Understanding How Organizations Learn

Organizational change—changing how we think and what we do—is fundamentally a learning process, made even more complex by the necessity for organizations to learn and change continuously. We are very early along in the struggle to learn how to actually create learning organizations.

In a recent article in *Harvard Business Review,* Garvin observes that "for learning to become a meaningful corporate goal, it must first be understood."[1] Learning is more than just knowledge acquisition; it also includes the ability to change—to improve—as a result of that knowledge. Garvin believes that the learning process must be actively managed in order for an organization to translate new knowledge into new practices. He sees organizational learning in terms of five building blocks:

1. *Systematic problem solving:* Includes the methods and tools of data-driven continuous improvement (reliance on data rather than guesswork) and the use of simple statistical tools to reveal patterns. It requires discipline and more attention to details. It also requires use of methods and tools first practiced in multilevel teams.
2. *Experimentation:* Includes "systematic searching for and testing of new knowledge," which may be through ongoing programs or demonstration projects. Both involve learning by doing and include knowing how as well as why.
3. *Learning from past experience:* Includes reviewing past successes and failures to "recognize the value of productive failure and unproductive success."
4. *Learning from others:* Includes looking outside one's own organization for new ideas—for example, SIS (steal ideas shamelessly) and benchmarking (finding and adapting best practices). Organizations that believe "they can't teach us anything" rarely learn very much from others.
5. *Transferring knowledge:* Includes spreading knowledge quickly throughout the organization using education and training programs, reports, tours, personnel rotation, and so on.

Finally, Garvin warns that we cannot manage what we cannot measure. The three stages of learning—cognitive, behavioral, performance improvement—must be measured. (See figure 2-1.) It is in the measurement and feedback of results that learning can be reinforced and accelerated. Learning is *reinforced* by measurement because seeing understandable results on a timely basis verifies that what we did is in fact producing the results we want. Learning is *accelerated* because when we learn how to learn, we can learn more quickly. (See chapter 8 for more on the three stages of learning.)

Figure 2-1. The Three Stages of Learning

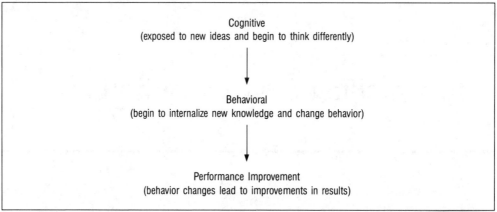

Source: Based on David A. Garvin. Building a learning organization. *Harvard Business Review* 71(4):90, July–Aug. 1993.

The Locus of Responsibility for Organizational Learning

Over the past five years, we have learned that responsibility for organizational learning must be shared throughout the organization. It is not the job of any one person or group of people, nor can it be accomplished alone. In a complex system, learning occurs at many levels simultaneously and interdependently, but the responsibilities are somewhat different given the learner's role in the organization.

Role of the Organization

The organizational environment must be conducive to learning. This starts with the organization's mission, which must include learning for individuals, teams, and the organization as a whole. Learning is most likely to take place when everyone in the organization understands that it is high on leadership's agenda.

According to Joan Lartin-Drake, director for the Center for Nursing Research, University Hospital/Penn State University, "In our experiences in the quest for organizational learning, we have discovered that while everyone in an organization is ultimately responsible for his or her learning, more responsibility is demanded on the part of leaders for setting a tone and/or climate that encourages and supports learning. This is particularly challenging in hospitals with their culture of perfectionism and many 'life and death' situations."

Leadership must value learning—their own, that of others, and that of the organization overall. The organization's leaders can open up boundaries and stimulate the exchange of ideas. They can create a forum to showcase learning, and help employees struggle with learning and applying new knowledge.

Joan Futch, senior vice-president of nursing services, Tallahassee Memorial Regional Medical Center, believes that "consistency is key to making learning work. Employees have seen new ideas come and go, and will be reluctant to devote time and energy to learning if they view it as just another fad. As new ways of thinking are taught, people in the organization will watch senior-level management carefully to see if they 'walk the talk.' The value of walking the talk—in other words, modeling continuous learning—cannot be overemphasized."

The organization also must provide support for learning. This means providing time for reflection and invention, as well as the financial resources necessary to support a continuous infusion of new ideas. Information is an important resource for learning. The organization cannot learn without a commitment to provide information when, where, and in the form in which it is needed to support continuous learning.[2]

Finally, the organization must recognize and reward learning. Desired behaviors should be clarified, widely communicated, and included in performance appraisal and reward and recognition programs. Risk taking must be rewarded—even when it results in failure.

Our colleagues provide three perspectives on creating an environment for organizational learning and how it has affected their organizations.

Ultimately, every member of the organization is responsible for learning. As we began our process of designing the service associate role, we needed a clear message that the organization was going to support our work. Once it was clear that executive management was supportive and that we as a group were committed to having our work driven by what was best for patient care, the task force started. Quickly, it was clear that this interdepartmental group knew no walls or major barriers in an organization that had always been compartmentalized. Executive support, commitment to patient care, appropriate representation of stakeholders, and knowledgeable staff all contributed to the success of this group.

Adrienne Ames, RN, MSN, associate hospital director and senior director, nursing, Vanderbilt University Hospital and Vanderbilt Clinic, Nashville, TN

We developed the following techniques to introduce gradually the idea and expectation of our organizationwide change, titled patient-centered redesign (PCR). They were useful in helping the staff in a traditional, successful organization understand that change would happen, that it would eventually apply to everyone, and that it would not (as some expected and would have liked) go away!

- Continuous change messages, both written and verbal
- Use of formal and informal communication channels for patient-centered redesign (PCR) messages
- Spreading the word about change through creation of new groups and integration of redesign communication into old groups
- Targeting of specific units/departments for change and widening to more and more such areas
- Constant reminders of the vision of PCR and its meaning

The CEO/president, who was highly supportive of the patient-centered redesign (PCR) project, was routinely involved in project meetings, and devoted a percentage of every week to deliberations and discussions about PCR-related change. Yet for many in the organization, this was not sufficient. They repeatedly requested validation of their efforts through direct communication from the CEO/president. Leadership staff, for example, expected the CEO/president to directly and routinely articulate PCR activity, progress, and goals in order to demonstrate that he truly believed in the program and was serious about its importance to the institution.

Cheryl B. Stetler, PhD, RN, FAAN, project director, patient-centered redesign, Hartford Hospital, Hartford, CT

Organizational learning starts with vision. Vision and the process of visioning are the catalysts for real organizational transformation. I was lucky enough to be part of the transformation from a traditional organization to a learning organization at the American Association of Critical Care Nurses (AACCN) in my role on the board of directors, as president-elect, president, and past president. This process began in 1988 with an examination of the organizational structure. The structural change led to a reexamination of mission and the development of a vision that is impacting every part of the organization. The change continues today. Creating the environment for organizational change is continual and is never complete, if you really are successful at creating the environment for a learning organization to flourish. It is similar to opening Pandora's box with creativity and innovation as the outcome. Once the box is open and empowerment of leadership teams occurs, there is no end to the synergy that develops. A learning organization is vision and mission in action. While acquisition of knowledge can be static, learning is an active process that puts knowledge to work.

S. Ann Evans, RN, MS, MBA, FAAN, executive director, The Heart Institute at Tallahassee Memorial, Tallahassee Memorial Regional Medical Center, Tallahassee, FL

Role of the Manager

Middle managers are in a pivotal position with regard to organizational learning. They have a clear opportunity to show they value learning by modeling continuous learning themselves. They also are in the position most frequently responsible for ensuring availability of the resources (particularly time) to support learning, because it is only through practice that cognitive learning can lead to change in behavior. They hold others accountable for their own learning through the performance appraisal system. Finally, they are responsible for providing the necessary measurement feedback to fuel continuous learning.

For example, at Abbott Northwestern Hospital in Minneapolis, Minnesota, managers support curiosity and risk taking even in how they approach those who have made mistakes. Managers are encouraged to think systemically and offer advice on how they would proceed if they had it to do over again. Ginger Malone, director, innovation and consultation, asks "If we had done this differently, how might it have turned out?" They have discovered that "when leaders understand that fear limits perception and narrows the field of vision, their interactions change to enable people to feel safe, increase their ability to perceive and discriminate and, thereby, learn. Learning occurs slowly over time and patience is necessary to let the process unfold, but there are unimaginable rewards."

The position of middle manager, more than any other, can shut down learning by behaving defensively. Managers at Vanderbilt University Medical Center, in Nashville, have shifted away from defensively managing "turf" to facilitative leadership and interactive planning involving several organizational levels. Through consensus building and open communication, department heads and managers of patient care services not only achieved patient/staff-focused roles in managing the quality and cost of care, but also have "built a bridge" that will be the route of choice as they grow and learn as an organization.

The models managers use to facilitate learning in their organizations vary according to organization, team, or individual. Following are some examples.

For starters, we changed titles and we began treating our employees as associates rather than subordinates. The use of the term *associates* sent the signal that we wanted to instill a feeling of collaboration and cooperation among all of us at MeritCare. Likewise, we abandoned titles such as directors, supervisors, and so on, and adopted terms such as managers, coordinators, and leaders. That same spirit holds true today as we move into the newly merged organization. It speaks to the vision of our CEO, Lloyd Smith, who has been decreasing the hierarchy and empowering the grass-roots level.

Evelyn Quigley, RN, MN, vice-president and nurse executive, MeritCare Hospital, Fargo, ND

I needed to establish trust with staff early because I walked into this change effort after it had already begun. I found one way of facilitating trust was through experiencing a "day on the unit," following a staff member for a day to see the organization from a staff person's perspective. So now as a leader, when I'm in meetings where we talk about all the changes, I can put in their slant and hook it to their reality. I feel one of my most important jobs is knowing the audience I'm working with—staff nurse, patient care manager, physician, and so on—and help them focus on the mission—one goal through many different paths. My role in organizational learning is constantly translating the mission of the hospital into the language of people with whom I work.

Terrell Smith, RN, MS, director, Children's Hospital, Vanderbilt University Medical Center, Nashville, TN

To help our teams learn the basics of work redesign, we offer a six-month start-up learning sequence. The multilevel team is unit based; each team member comes from the same organizational unit. In our model, the director of nursing plays a coordinator role for the team.

It was important to recognize the team's need to perform, and to compare with what other teams had done. The need to perform and the uneasiness with functioning in an ambiguous environment often resulted in frustration and a real desire to do a quick fix. As the coordinator, it was essential to deliver repeatedly the message [that] it's OK to be where you are. We found that percolation time is essential. We are learning a new language and a new way of being.

Sally Schlak, RN, MBA, nursing director, Tallahassee Memorial Regional Medical Center, Tallahassee, FL

Role of the Individual

Organizational learning begins with individual learning and achieving a sense of personal mastery. Senge defines *personal mastery* as "the discipline of continuously expanding your ability to create the results in life you truly seek, a quest for continual learning, a special sense of purpose, genuine caring, commitment."[3] In a learning organization, we recognize that an organization develops along with its people, yet no one can increase someone else's personal mastery.[4] Ultimately, we are each responsible for our own learning. To be committed to learning, the individual also must be committed to truth—to be honest with oneself and others—and to be able to balance his or her personal vision with current reality.

Practicing the discipline of personal mastery means not only learning to expand personal capacity but also "creating an organizational environment which encourages all its members to develop themselves toward the goals and purposes they choose."[5] Grantees in our program—in particular, Marjorie Beyers, a former nurse executive at Mercy Health Services in Farmington Hills, Michigan, and Julianne Morath, a nurse executive at Abbott Northwestern Hospital in Minneapolis—have experienced the importance of individual commitment to, and interest in, learning in order to come to the table as a functioning member of the team. There is a difference between people compliantly accepting training (which is often soon forgotten) and keeping learning alive through the energy of their own innate curiosity and enthusiasm.

Many of us have found the investment made in people returned many times over as their work inspires others in the organization, and have developed methods to encourage individual learning.

For almost four years, I've been part of a system that encourages continual learning. Three months after starting out as a patient escort, I was chosen to participate in a work redesign project. We transformed the orthopedic unit from a standard nursing unit to a *team* that delivered service and care in fresh, patient-focused ways. Lots of factors contributed to the success of the unit and to my personal and job-related growth as a service associate on the ortho team. For example, I learned to make and act on decisions appropriate to my areas of responsibility. By keeping the patient in focus, I learned to question tradition, to "slay a few sacred cows," and to trust my own feelings within the context of the team. Also on ortho, I developed a sense of trust in, and cooperation with, management and administration that I had never previously experienced. I was expected and encouraged to grow. The impetus was confirmed at all levels of the medical center. It was a fulfilling experience.

Jeff Sanders, former service associate coach, staff development, Vanderbilt University Hospital, Nashville, TN

MeritCare Hospital's commitment to become a learning organization paved the way for opportunities to support individual associates in determining and pursuing their personal development in the workplace. First, it was expected that each associate complete a self- and work team–assessment form. Based on this assessment, the associate developed a self-development plan. The goal of this plan was to enable the associates to identify skills which would enhance work performance. To assist associates in their self-development, a new peer role was implemented: the interpersonal relations (IPR) advisor. The IPR advisor was trained to be a role model, coach, and facilitator. Through the self-development concept, associates have gained greater appreciation for their contributions to the workplace.

Joy Bang, BSN, RN; and Penny Dale, MEd, educators, MeritCare Hospital, Fargo, ND

We are introducing the concept of learning–teaching contracts in conjunction with our regular performance review process. These contracts would encourage employees to identify the qualities they have which could be taught to others. By the same token, it would also help them determine what they would like to learn and how they can go about developing the requisite knowledge/skill base.

Ginger Malone, RN, MSN, director, innovation and consultation, Abbott Northwestern Hospital, Minneapolis

You cannot have organizational learning without a core of individuals who are committed to ongoing and continuous learning. The beauty of personal mastery is that it spreads into every part of a person's life. Growth at work does not occur in isolation; personal growth is a side benefit. Individual competence involves a daily commitment to learning. You cannot say "OK, I've got that done" or "I have learned that." We need to be ready for continual questioning and examining for new and alternative methods. Leo Buscaglia tells about his parents' commitment to learning. Each day at dinner, the children in this large Italian family had to report what new thing they had learned. What a way to start a staff meeting!

S. Ann Evans, RN, MS, MBA, FAAN, executive director, The Heart Institute at Tallahassee Memorial, Tallahassee Memorial Regional Medical Center, Tallahassee, FL

Role of the Facilitator

We have learned that people all over the organization can facilitate learning for individuals, teams, and the organization. Further, these people do not necessarily have to be formal leaders in the organization, nor do they have to be part of the formal structure traditionally responsible for learning.

One of the beauties of complex systems is that connections do not always have to be explicitly formed—they just are. When champions develop in the organization (wherever they officially "live"), find a way to use them! This role, often very challenging, can become a source of inspiration and enthusiasm for organizational change. The results will not always be perfectly predictable, but so long as we are learning from one another, we will be moving in the right direction.

Many of us have developed roles for facilitators. Here are some of the many ways in which they have been helpful.

The Quality Improvement Program at the University of Utah Hospital includes a formalized training program for the individuals within the interdisciplinary quality teams. Three roles have been defined: facilitator, team leader, and team member. The job of the facilitator is to support a number of team leaders in organizing and leading the interdisciplinary teams in quality improvement efforts. Facilitator training includes education and skill development in areas such as the quality improvement process, leadership, team building, launching and refueling teams, analyzing work processes, and problem solving. Depending on the needs of the team leader, the facilitator may, for example, provide feedback, reinforce training in process skills, assist in problem solving, or support the team leader in identifying data sources. Building leadership support into the structure of the Quality Improvement Program provides team leaders who may have had minimal leadership experience with a resource to help them move their teams to successful outcomes.

Cheryl Kinnear, RN, BSN, program manager, University Hospital's Program to Improve Patient Care, University of Utah Hospital, Salt Lake City

Process owners [a type of facilitator] have learned that their responsibilities are very different from those of the traditional team leader. Though they are both outside the organization's normal reporting structure, the process owner's principal mandate is to push people to new places and to try novel approaches. Although there has been considerable discomfort around the ambiguity associated with operationalizing their areas of influence, and the fact that there is no job description, the process owners themselves feel that this uncertainty fits well with their role as creative and innovative thinkers.

Concomitantly, process owners are having to deal with discomfort from their peers regarding the changes they are helping to precipitate. Those outside the loop are under the mistaken impression that organizational change happens quickly, that a master plan can be found outlining what to expect, and that the proposed changes are following a set agenda. As team members experience how the change process unfolds, they are making every effort to put others at ease about a process for which there is no road map but, as their commitment shows, will lead to success.

Ginger Malone, RN, MSN, director, innovation and consultation, Abbott Northwestern Hospital, Minneapolis

The role of the facilitator has been essential in meeting organizational learning needs when resources are limited and the scope is extremely large. Tallahassee Memorial Regional Medical Center (TMRMC) is confronted with the same universal constraints, that is, never enough resources (time, money, information, and knowledge), as most organizations attempting to create a learning organization.

By design, the facilitator functions rather like a conductor—getting all the instruments to play in unison. Hence, a facilitator is not defined by position.

The facilitator explains tasks, clarifies ground rules, includes all, helps groups deal with dominators, manages pace, helps refocus, catalyzes follow-up assignments, and ensures that everyone understands assignments.

The focus of the facilitator needs to be on the *learning needs of the learner* and not the *training needs of the trainer.*

Vivian Booth, RN, project analyst, Work Redesign Program to Improve Patient Care, Tallahassee Memorial Regional Medical Center, Tallahassee, FL

One of the challenges facilitators encounter is trying to help managers and leaders in an organization articulate the vision about where the organization is moving. Another challenge confronting facilitators concerns the ongoing need to help people move through new ideas, and the dynamics of changing how they think and work. Finally, most of the facilitators are challenged by the notion that they be, and help others become, as innovative and collegial as possible while at the same time they are expected to break down the boundaries and push the outer limits. Particularly in facilities that have a lot of history associated with them, the facilitators are especially challenged to help these people feel good about their work while at the same time not allowing themselves to become too attached.

Karen Logsdon, RN, MS, codirector, Strengthening Hospital Nursing Program, Providence Portland Medical Center, Portland, OR

Commitment versus Compliance

Ackoff's idealized design[6] and Senge's shared vision[7] are both defined as the future we are trying to create now. By either name, we cannot have a learning organization without it. It provides the pull toward what we truly want to achieve.

The *idealized design,* or *vision,* is a detailed picture of the ideal way to provide and continuously improve patient/family care. Moving toward this design requires large-scale organizational change, which requires large-scale organizational learning. However, there will be no movement toward the design or vision without commitment to, or enrollment in, the vision by many people in the organization. Senge's concept of commitment versus enrollment versus compliance is a useful distinction. (See figure 2-2.)

The committed person brings energy to the vision. People who are committed really want the vision to happen. People who are enrolled have chosen to become part of the process

Figure 2-2. Possible Attitudes toward a Vision

Commitment:	Wants it. Will make it happen. Creates whatever "laws" (structures) are needed.
Enrollment:	Wants it. Will do whatever can be done within the "spirit of the law."
Genuine Compliance:	Sees the benefits of the vision. Does everything expected and more. Follows the "letter of the law." "Good soldier."
Formal Compliance:	On the whole, sees the benefits of the vision. Does what's expected and no more. "Pretty good soldier."
Grudging Compliance:	Does not see the benefits of the vision. But, also, does not want to lose job. Does enough of what's expected because he has to, but also lets it be known that he is not really on board.
Noncompliance:	Does not see the benefits of the vision and will not do what's expected. "I won't do it; and you can't make me."
Apathy:	Neither for nor against the vision. No interest. No energy. "Is it 5:00 yet?"

Source: Reprinted, with permission, from Peter M. Senge. *The Fifth Discipline: The Art and Practice of the Learning Organization*. New York City: Doubleday/Currency, 1990, pp. 219–20.

but do not necessarily feel responsible for making the vision happen. Those who are compliant are just "going along" with the team. Commitment is seldom instantaneous, nor is it always easy to achieve. Most people in an organization start at some level of compliance and then, as they and the organization continue to learn, move toward commitment to building a shared vision.

Many of the organizations profiled in this book have used these ideas to encourage true commitment or enrollment with some interesting results.

Abbott Northwestern Hospital has never had any mandatory requirements for attendance at education programming, except for those things that are driven by regulatory agencies, yet we have never had difficulty filling our educational programs. Though we haven't completed a formal survey of why this is true, our impression is that staff members and managers at Abbott Northwestern recognize the importance of continuous learning and are genuinely interested in doing better and knowing more. As a group, employees have high standards and expectations for themselves and their colleagues.

The downside of this enthusiasm and interest in new things is that we can sometimes become distracted and lack focus in our approach. As a rule, we don't tolerate control well. In all honesty, our enthusiasm could be tempered by a touch of discipline. We're hoping that the recognition of this limitation will be the first step in our developing more focus and direction.

Ginger Malone, RN, MSN, director, innovation and consultation, Abbott Northwestern Hospital, Minneapolis

In the winter of 1993, Beth Israel completed four consecutive fiscal periods of low-patient volume. The problem was of such a magnitude that if it continued through the year, Beth Israel would show a sizable loss from operations. Senior management decided to take the problem to the work force. The executive vice-president asked every manager and supervisor to go back to their work teams, explain the problem, and ask for ideas about what could be done. In 10 days, the vice-presidents received over 3,000 ideas from employees and staff throughout the hospital. As a result of this level of influence and information, the vice-presidents were able to make decisions that resulted in an immediate $5 million savings. Additional savings were gained from the task forces that subsequently focused on particular themes from the ideas submitted. Importantly, the savings were sufficient to prevent layoffs or other damaging reductions that would have had long-term negative effects.

Overall, the senior management team was able to make better decisions than had they acted unilaterally, without the benefit of ideas and discussion throughout the hospital. As one vice-president said looking back on the event, "Five years ago, we wouldn't have been able to turn this situation around this quickly."

Luanne Selk, manager, training and organization development, Beth Israel Hospital, Boston

Team Learning: Learning to Learn Together

Organizations cannot learn unless teams can learn. When teams learn, they are aligned, they function as a whole, and they can produce the results they agree they want. And yet most of our experiences with learning, even our organizational learning experiences, focus on individual learning. No wonder it is so difficult for us to learn to learn together. Team learning is a skill; it requires practice.

There are significant barriers to learning to learn together that must be overcome. In multilevel teams, barriers are created by position in the hierarchy. In cross-functional teams, barriers are created by not sharing a common language or common mental models of how the system works. In all teams, challenging strongly held beliefs can cause defensive behavior. And defensive behavior is always a barrier to learning, which is the whole point of the behavior.

Furthermore, dynamics within learning teams are fluid and changing. In her work at Mercy Health Services, Marjorie Beyers noticed shifting interaction and leadership within teams on both the unit and executive levels. The teams relied on different people's talents, expertise, and charisma relative to the situation and methodology in use. They also learned that not every decision is a team decision.

> When a leader commits to learn simultaneously and in presence of those being led, the leader risks much. The organization could decide the leader is incompetent to lead because she or he doesn't know what she or he is doing.
>
> The leader also has much to gain by the opportunity to model the learning experience, admitting difficulty and struggling with the organization. More often than not, the leader gains respect by doing this.
>
> A sense of humor is vital. Laughing with fellow learners as you struggle to give up the old and learn the new builds bridges to a future of learning together.
>
> *Joan Futch, RN, MSHA, CNA, senior vice-president, nursing services, Tallahassee Memorial Regional Medical Center, Tallahassee, FL*

Critical Dimensions of Team Learning

What must teams learn? They must:

- Think deeply about very complex issues. The idea here is that the intelligence of the team is greater than the intelligence of even its brightest member.
- Learn how to behave in innovative, coordinated ways, rather like a jazz ensemble. Each member basically knows what the other will do, but there is still room for individual innovation within the basic framework.
- Develop a kind of operational trust so they can engage in true dialogue. (Trust and dialogue are discussed in more detail later.)

Vivian Booth, a project analyst at Tallahassee Memorial Regional Medical Center, has observed:

> Because teams are the fundamental learning unit of a learning organization, it is the way in which teams learn that becomes a microcosm for learning throughout the organization. Skills developed by teams cascade to other individuals and to other teams. The accomplishments of teams can set the tone and establish a standard for learning together for the larger organization.

All of us have struggled with team learning—how to put teams together, how to model team learning, and how to teach teams to learn together. Here is some of what we have learned so far.

Each time we set up a new team, we are almost back to square one, because even though team members have acquired requisite skills about group process, it is back to zero in developing a feeling of synergy or team spirit. Each team is different, each problem is different, and each response is different. You can't use the same stepwise progression with every issue. The hope would be that over time, each individual in our organization will develop an understanding of what it means to be part of a team and how it feels to solve problems as a member of a group.

It is always nice to have former team members in a new group because of the experience and skills they bring. It works both ways, though, because they end up learning new things.

Faye Gilbarg, regional director, medical management and quality, Providence Health System, Portland, OR

As a director of nursing, placing myself in the role of a learner was a difficult and sometimes uncomfortable position. Previously, I felt I was supposed to have all the answers and be in control. Now I was learning with the rest of the team and I felt very vulnerable. At times, it also seemed frustrating for the staff not to be able to rely on me for the answers. The director plays a critical role in creating a nonthreatening learning environment.

A difficult transition for me was the move from independence to interdependence, which is necessary for effective teams. I personally respected and valued my independent nature. It was a rude awakening to learn from Stephen Covey that interdependence was the more advanced, more mature concept.[8] For me, interdependence felt like a step backwards. However, the reward was beyond belief. It was exciting to see how much could be accomplished by a team who valued and modeled interdependent behaviors.

Kathy Holder, RN, MSN, director, nursing/quality, Tallahassee Memorial Regional Medical Center, Tallahassee, FL

One specific technique for reinforcing the idea that learning constitutes success is *critical incident analysis.* Every project and work environment experience critical incidents. Such events are often associated with emotional distress and behaviors such as being upset, guilty, or angry. The response to such incidents can manifest itself as internalizing, self-blame, and "beating yourself up"—or in terms of projection, blaming others and trashing the system. Critical incident analysis is a way to learn from our experiences. Listening and respecting the views of each team member is critical if each team member is to feel valued. The team collectively discusses what happened, why, and what could have been done differently. Even more important, they ask themselves: "What can we learn from this situation?" This type of analysis leads to a prescription for improving current efforts, plus averting similar problems in the future. In short, the process helps a team learn and model how to learn together.

Susan L. Beck, PhD, RN, project director, University Hospital's Program to Improve Patient Care, University of Utah Hospital, Salt Lake City

The primary means for promoting education and participation is the work team structure. Every employee belongs to at least one work team, a team headed by his or her supervisor and composed of all the employees who report to that supervisor. Employees may also belong to ad hoc work teams (teams that address a particular issue and then disband) and to interdisciplinary work groups (individuals who collaborate on an ongoing basis—for example, an operating room committee).

Work team leaders stay informed about the hospital's goals and results through a work team leaders' meeting held every four weeks. This meeting is not just a one-way information-sharing session: work team leaders have ample opportunity to ask questions and raise issues, and they do. Questions range from the factual ("What does case mix mean?") to those of a more analytical or probing nature ("Why is volume down in obstetrics, and what are we planning to do about it?"). The executive vice-president also seeks information from those attending the meeting—for example, "I'm hearing some problems about patients getting appointments. What are you hearing or seeing in your units?" In these ways, the work team leaders' meeting provides an opportunity for ongoing examination of the hospital's results and practices.

Although there are numerous centralized mechanisms that support education and participation (an idea review process, focus groups, town meetings), the work team leader remains central to building a learning organization. Whatever centralized forums exist, the bulk of an employee's experience of work is shaped in his or her own work area, by the leader of the work group. So it is key that these leaders have the skills to foster an environment where learning can flourish—where information is shared, new ideas are welcomed, issues are explored, and changes for the better are encouraged.

Given the pivotal role of work team leaders, Beth Israel has devoted considerable attention to supporting managers and supervisors in acquiring the skills to promote team learning. One example is the 40-hour management development course called the Leadership Track. In this course, work team leaders learn skills for creative problem solving, leading meetings, and facilitating group discussion. In particular, they learn how their behavior affects participation by members of their team and how emerging ideas can be nurtured so they are not "squashed" before they have been refined. Learning is highly experiential. Individuals bring real-life problems to work on, and group meetings are held in the classroom to explore these problems. The meetings are videotaped, and the videotapes reviewed for "lessons learned."

Luanne Selk, manager, training and organization development, Beth Israel Hospital, Boston

True Dialogue

As mentioned previously, dialogue is one of the critical dimensions of team learning. Senge says that it is the "free and creative exploration of complex and subtle issues."[9] In dialogue, each team member has access to the entire pool of thoughts created by the team, so the team can get well beyond any one member's understanding. However, another important thing happens in dialogue. Each person becomes an observer of his or her own thinking. This allows team members to move beyond their own assumptions.

In true dialogue, team members are willing to advocate and/or explain their own mental models (how they see the world) and inquire into each other's mental models. Further, mental models are presented in such a way as to encourage inquiry from other team members.

Charlotte Roberts of Innovation Associates explains true dialogue using the advocacy/inquiry matrix developed by Diana McLain Smith.[10] (See figure 2-3.) In the

Figure 2-3. The Advocacy/Inquiry Matrix

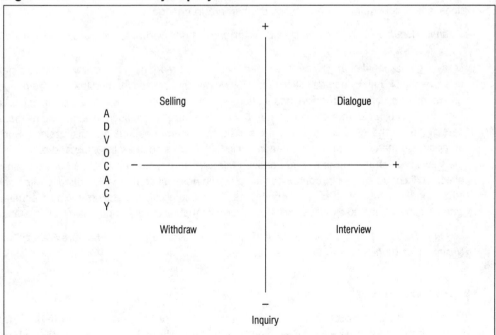

Source: Charlotte Roberts and Peter Senge of Innovation Associates, Framingham, MA.

low-advocacy, low-inquiry cell, nothing useful is happening. I do not explain my position and do not ask you about yours. In the low-advocacy, high-inquiry cell, I ask you lots of questions but do not tell you what I am thinking. You feel as if you are being "interviewed." In the low-inquiry, high-advocacy cell, I tell you all about what I think but never ask what you think. You feel as if I am "selling" my position. In the high-advocacy, high-inquiry cell, I tell you what I think and I ask you what you think, and thus true dialogue can occur.

Many of us have used these ideas to encourage true dialogue in our organizations. It is only through dialogue that we can come to agreement on shared values and directions. It is only then that we have the ability to build something together.

> Though sometimes we still have to go back and find some common ground, there appears to be more dialogue now in our organization. Dialogue is occurring between departments and people who have functions that affect one another. We have found the need for dialogue particularly important in data-driven decision making—to actually analyze the data as a group and not come with a predetermined solution. For example, one day, the laboratory people came and talked to the nursing people. They mentioned that they wanted to get rid of "the manilla file syndrome" and we said, "What on earth are you talking about?" To which they replied, "Well, you go to these interdepartmental meetings and the VP from nursing comes in with a file folder and says, 'Here's what's wrong and here's the data.' They are so intent on making their point and getting the thing solved that they already have a solution in mind." Constructive dialogue can't occur in this situation.
>
> *Marjorie Beyers, RN, PhD, FAAN, former assistant vice-president, nursing, Mercy Health Services, Farmington Hills, MI*

> Often, as relationships improve and people have a new way of looking at things, topics that previously were taboo—the "undiscussables"—begin to surface. One of the developmental tasks of the organization is to develop its resilience and strengthen its ability to deal with uncomfortable topics, without being overly threatening or threatened.
>
> By avoiding undiscussable subjects, an organization does not address or identify the real leverage of a situation. Embedded within the undiscussables are clues to the root causes of organizational dilemmas. As we begin to confront the mental models that each of us carries but may never express, we can explore the assumptions that underlie behavior. Those assumptions, when not explored, often represent barriers to change.
>
> *Julianne Morath, RN, MS, vice-president, patient care, Abbott Northwestern Hospital, Minneapolis*

> Many organizational changes are managed by a project management or work team. As part of University of Utah Hospital's initiative to improve patient care, we learned that this team must role-model the shifts in organizational culture that are needed for success. For example, in forming the project team, we discussed and then practiced norms such as including all members of the team, from the director to the secretary, in team meetings and discussions. Such an approach manifests the value of each individual. Norms such as listening and respecting the views of each team member are critical. Interrupting each other with the *but* word limits effective dialogue and is not condoned. Team members must communicate directly with each other about expectations, issues, or concerns. Complaining or "tattletaling" must be counteracted with a reminder to directly provide constructive feedback to the appropriate team member.
>
> *Susan L. Beck, PhD, RN, project director, University Hospital's Program to Improve Patient Care, University of Utah Hospital, Salt Lake City*

Learning versus Performance

We do some of our most spectacular learning before schools or teachers enter our lives. When we do start school, we learn at an early age that it is not about learning but, rather, about performance. There *is* a "right" answer and the teacher knows it. We learn that not knowing the answer is wrong. Further, we learn to associate opportunities for learning with threat and embarrassment. We learn not to sit in the front row and to look down so that we will not be called on by the teacher.

Every organization mentioned in this book has struggled with individuals and teams who were sure that there was a right answer and that the teacher or leader had it but was pretending not to because the exercise was good for them. We discovered that the alternative is to focus on learning, not performance.[11]

> We have recognized that it is as important to learn as it is to perform. Performance without learning is just that—a one-time demonstration for the benefit of someone else, required out of fear or judgment. The challenge is to inspire an intrinsic commitment to the expression of talent versus a performance to meet a required standard that is inspired by fear.
>
> *Julianne Morath, RN, MS, vice-president, patient care, Abbott Northwestern Hospital, Minneapolis*

> At Abbott Northwestern, the concepts of inquiry, dialogue, and lifelong learning are encouraged through classes, workshops, and daily interactions that encourage curiosity and risk taking. The promotion of these concepts is an ongoing process ranging from formal interventions to more subtle alterations in the way we've done business. For nurse managers, for example, a question has been included in their annual evaluations that asks what they have learned in the past year to increase their capacity to add value to the organization. In meetings, groups are asked what they have learned from recent experiences, whether or not they meet expected outcomes. *Success,* then, is redefined in terms of expanding our collective intelligence as an organization around critical issues.
>
> *Ginger Malone, RN, MSN, director, innovation and consultation, Abbott Northwestern Hospital, Minneapolis*

Trust

Team learning is essential to organizational learning, and true dialogue is required for team learning. However, dialogue requires revealing and advocating a position that makes us vulnerable. Therefore, not surprisingly, a high level of trust is required to engage in dialogue.

There are some significant organizational, cultural, and individual barriers to building trust. In our organizations, we function inside boundaries. We know little about what happens outside those boundaries, except that "they" (anyone who is not "us") are the cause of many of our problems, and if they would just correct their problems, our lives would be much better. The boundaries effectively keep us from working together, from learning about and from each other. Organizational memory is not always helpful either. Many things that should have been buried years ago live on to create distrust.

Joan Futch of Tallahassee Memorial Regional Medical Center has devised a particularly creative and effective exercise to break down barriers in her organization. She calls her exercise "the funeral."

> Creative ideas are often formed out of frustration. The managers in nursing services seemed buried in victim patterns of behavior. There was not a general willingness to try new things. They (whoever that was) would not let them try new things. In spite of all my prodding and pleading, there was no one who was willing to step forward and challenge change.
>
> I remember remarking that they were stuck in the past and that the past was dead and needed to be buried. This remark triggered an event which opened the way to change. We had a funeral.
>
> The funeral was staged to bury the past. We had a cardboard coffin, black candles, soft lights, and even some funeral music that was taped at a local funeral parlor.
>
> The funeral took place during one of our regularly scheduled administrative meetings. No one was allowed into the room until all had arrived so that latecomers would not spoil the effect. We sat quietly in the room listening to the music for several minutes before I explained the purpose of the meeting.

I gave each person present a stack of 3″ x 5″ cards. They were given instructions to write those things which were beliefs/ideas from the past that interfered with their ability to proceed with the future on the 3″ x 5″ cards. The cards were given to me, and we discussed each item listed. When there was consensus that it was indeed dead and could therefore be left behind, it went into the coffin.

I used the cards to provide anonymity, but as we talked, people began to take ownership of their cards and anonymity was not an issue. There were issues we could not agree to bury, but the burial list was impressively long and substantial.

I generated a list of burial items. The rule was that they could not be exhumed without written permission from me. If anyone brought up a buried item, they were to be reminded that it was buried and could not be considered without authorization.

This event was pivotal. I see it as the turning point that changed us from victims into proactive, creative patient care providers.

Joan Futch, RN, MSHA, CNA, senior vice-president, nursing services, Tallahassee Memorial Regional Medical Center, Tallahassee, FL

Although our culture is diverse, we have not yet learned to appreciate differences. Instead, we set up cultural boundaries that create opportunities for distrust—ethnic boundaries, age boundaries, income boundaries, gender boundaries, to name a few.

Even the way we think creates barriers to trust. When things go wrong, we usually assume someone is to blame. Still, when over time many people behave similarly in similar situations, we do not see patterns or underlying structural explanations. We see bad people, not bad systems.

But perhaps our biggest failing is our belief that we cannot be honest with one another. In our culture, organizations, and individual relationships, we are not very good at checking our egos at the door, looking each other in the eye, and saying, "Can we talk?" Trust develops when individuals believe they are understood and valued.

Some of us offer these thoughts on the importance of building trust and some techniques we have developed.

The trust issue is there at all levels, especially if you are moving away from a group ethic that has been competitive to one where sharing is the norm. In any group undertaking, there are all kinds of things that come up, and so I think trust at every level is a major issue. It is a question of taking the risk. But more important, you must trust that you will have all the information you need, all the resources you require to do the job, and that what you decide will be used in some meaningful way.

It is important not to give a group something to do and empower them to do it unless you really are going to let them do it. This is really the biggest trust issue. Its presence was felt in the traditional organization, but it will be front and center in the learning organization.

Marjorie Beyers, RN, PhD, FAAN, former assistant vice-president, nursing, Mercy Health Services, Farmington Hills, MI

Part of the barrier to any change process obviously is the fear factor and the need to drive out fear. In this institution, there has been a lot of fear. In some pockets, the fear has been driven out very effectively, and in other places, it hasn't; but as long as there is fear somewhere, anywhere, it is going to create a barrier for the organization as a whole. The whole issue of building trust within teams just takes so long. In fact, I think that the time requirement for people to process information has been a barrier because it is very difficult to maintain momentum during a change while time is elapsing. When members of a team change in midstream, it poses another barrier. New people have to get reoriented to the process and then that slows things down a little bit. I see a lot of that happening.

Jane Scharff, MN, RN, CNAA, project coordinator, Montana Consortium, Saint Vincent Hospital and Health Center, Billings, MT

Waseca Area Memorial Hospital developed a Staff Action Committee in the nursing department as a grass-roots approach to improving the delivery of nursing care and subsequent patient outcomes. This committee was made up of representatives of all nursing units and shifts. One of the projects the committee decided to start with was improving the working relationships and communication between nursing units. The Staff Action Committee decided to implement a Walk in My Shoes Program and have the nurses work in each other's units for a day so they would gain a better understanding of their colleague's work. The nurses who have experienced the program have had positive experiences. The Staff Action Committee plans to continue the program so that everyone in the hospital can participate. The "temperature reading" to date is positive. Communication is improving and trust levels have strengthened.

Shirley Raetz, RN, PCA, project director, Health Bond, Waseca Area Memorial Hospital, Waseca, MN

While successful partnering is created through agreements and shared experiences as nurses and care partners work together, it is the understanding about being accountable for emergent needs as well as the "dirty work" that forges a trusting relationship.

When two patients returned from the cath lab at the same time, each needing frequent vital signs [blood pressure and pulse reading], the care partner took one patient while the RN cared for the other. The RN later commented, "I was sure that the other patient was in good hands with the care partner. I felt as confident about the care he provided as the care I would have given to my patient." That sense of "getting it done for the patients" happens all the time. During a code, the care partner is authorized to begin CPR, but once a nurse takes over, the care partner immediately knows that he or she is responsible for making sure that the other patients experience no interruptions or discontinuities in care. No doubt, it would be easy to let "less desirable tasks" fall to the care partner. However, it is a measure of mutual trust and respect when the RN and care partner equally share in the unpleasant tasks of patient care.

Wendy Baker, RN, MS, former director, Center for Patient Care Innovation; and project director, Strengthening Hospital Nursing Program, Vanderbilt University Hospital and Vanderbilt Clinic, Nashville, TN

Defensive Routines

When faced with threat and embarrassment, people will behave very predictably—defensively. Argyris calls these habits *defensive routines,* ways we have learned to interact to protect ourselves from threat or embarrassment.[12] Senge warns that systems thinking is especially likely to call up defensive routines because of its "central message that we create our own reality."[13] It is much less threatening to see problems as caused outside ourselves, outside our control.

What causes us to behave defensively? Argyris believes that we are threatened most by the fear of critically examining ourselves. By constantly turning the focus away from ourselves toward others, we can shut down learning about ourselves. The key factor is the way we think about our behavior and that of others. Argyris says that the way we behave is rarely the way we think we behave. He calls the way we think we behave our "espoused theory of action" and the way we actually behave our "theory-in-use." "People consistently behave inconsistently, unaware of the contradiction between their espoused theory and their theory-in-use, between the way they think they act, and the way they really act."[14]

To avoid threat or embarrassment and to keep from feeling vulnerable or incompetent, Argyris says we design our actions according to four basic rules:[15]

1. To remain in unilateral control
2. To maximize winning and minimize losing
3. To suppress negative feelings
4. To be as rational as possible

Defensive routines encourage us to keep our reasoning private and avoid testing it. That is why they are so powerful and why they shut down learning. Turning this around means learning to examine our own reasoning and allowing others to examine it as well. Argyris suggests that we must create environments where questioning someone else's reasoning is an opportunity for learning, not a sign of mistrust.[16] People need to feel it is safe to participate without fear of repercussion or being branded a troublemaker for bringing issues to the table.

Organizations use defensive routines, too. And the same sort of productive reasoning can work at the organizational level. Argyris believes that this must start with the leadership group modeling the open examination of their theories-in-use, *often an uncomfortable process.*

> Keeping people happy is not a very good indicator of how well things are going. Having people say they are getting what they think they need to get may not be the pulse you want to take your readings from. Too many of us have been conditioned to give the knee-jerk (that is, expected) response. You need to get past the no-man's-zone in order to get at what really is happening. Sometimes when the staff gets uncomfortable about a proposed change or objects to something that is about to happen, you should say to yourself, "Oh, we must be going in the right direction, we've stretched them," instead of interpreting defensiveness to mean "We must have done something wrong." We try to have a lot of fun with conflict, and we feel that until we have pushed people's thinking to the edge of discomfort, we probably haven't pushed far enough.
>
> *Ginger Malone, RN, MSN, director, innovation and consultation; and Debra Waggoner, MA, MBA, director, consulting and development, Abbott Northwestern Hospital, Minneapolis*

The Need to Work with Assumptions

Two issues here are related to creating organizational change. One is the need to learn to work with assumptions; the other is to learn to recognize the assumptions we make and be willing to expose our reasoning to others.

The work of organizational change requires learning to work with assumptions, because early in change efforts there may be no hard data, no firm conclusions on which to base our actions. When we are, as Barker says, pioneering a new paradigm, we are by definition learning how to make it work.[17] We have all been in situations where people want to know conclusively that something will work before they will try it. Barker calls this "settler mentality" because the settlers were back at the ranch asking the pioneers, "Is it safe yet?" Sometimes in the work of organizational change, there is no substitute for intuition, the ability to make good decisions with limited information. We just have to trust our instincts, take a deep breath—and jump.

Senge argues that "suspending our assumptions" is an important dimension of dialogue where we become observers of our own thinking.[18] Suspending our assumptions is not the same as not making them. It just means that we are aware of them and hold them up for examination—by ourselves and others. In true dialogue, this is done collectively by the entire team.

Suspending assumptions can lead to surprising results. Our organizations have learned to examine their assumptions in all areas in order to achieve effective change.

> Assumptions are the boundaries which frame your mental models or paradigms. Whenever events are different than your expectations, it is most likely that your assumptions were incorrect. This lesson was brought home to one project team as they were trying to integrate their program into the regular budgeting process. They assumed that in the current health care environment, managers would want to effectively use resources and reduce costs. The reality was that budgets control a department's resources. More resources equal more potential to achieve your mission and more power. Thus the modus operandus was to maintain or increase your department's budget. There were no rewards for being cost-effective. This experience led the team to adopt a project motto: "assume nothing." Such an open-minded approach allows you to unveil the real operating assumptions and learn of the barriers to effective change.
>
> *Susan L. Beck, PhD, RN, project director, University Hospital's Program to Improve Patient Care, University of Utah Hospital, Salt Lake City*

We tend to say, "The physician doesn't want to be involved," and then make all kinds of assumptions. We never ask physicians, "When do you want to be involved, or how would you like to participate?" Next, we conclude, "No, they don't need this or don't value it"—but do we know that for sure? This miscommunication or lack of communication increases resistance and adversarial relations around the change. We must involve all key stakeholders.

Jeanette Ullery, RN, project director, The Rural Connection, St. Luke's Regional Medical Center, Boise, ID

One of the things we determined early on was that you can't make the assumption *this is how everybody has to do it.* There has to be some kind of openness. How things get implemented have to be bought into at the local level, and they have to be customized to the individual organization. Enabling that has created a much freer environment for people to share and try things out differently. I actually think it has helped our learning because there is no one right way to do anything, which heeds the canons of systemic thinking. We keep learning, each time somebody adds a new twist. I think that realization alone has helped to erode the barriers between the larger institutions and the smaller institutions. We have had leaders emerge from the smaller institutions who have been real creative and helpful. In fact, we are finding that the 1,000-bed hospital can learn a tremendous amount from the 100-bed community hospital. According to the old thinking, that would never have happened. Each of the principals would have had a mind-set and attitude that precluded those kind of exchanges.

Kathy Zelinsky, vice-president, patient care, Mercy Health Services North, Cadillac & Grayling, MI

What happens when you are changing systems is that you often encounter what Senge calls *counter-intuitive behavior.* That is, you are expecting a particular outcome but it plays out very differently. It forces you to challenge your own assumptions and mental models. I suppose the one that surprised me most, though it was not entirely unexpected, concerned the blending of titles. To discover just how near and dear titles had become to a person's identity and self-concept was a revelation for me. There was a lot of pain in the organization after we adopted that policy. In one initiative, we did away with three different management level titles and put them all under one title. The residual side effects of that action were more than I expected. I knew it would be difficult, but not to such a degree.

Lloyd Smith, MSA, president/CEO, MeritCare Hospital, Fargo, ND

Incremental Change versus the Quantum Leap

Organizational change takes time. This commitment to the long haul is difficult, because in our culture, we have learned to value big, quick, innovative change far more than small, slow, incremental change. Even in the case of small change, we like it to happen fast and are impatient when it takes time.

Staying inside our boundaries lulls us into the belief that the quick fix will work because we do not see the whole of which we are a part—our connectedness. Furthermore, when we do see all the connections, they seem too complicated to figure out. Therefore, rather than learn new ways of thinking, seeing patterns rather than events, we stay inside our boundaries where things seem somehow simpler.

Many organizations have discovered that in organizational change, there is a place for both incremental change and the quantum leap. Here are some observations on both.

On a routine basis, *incrementalism* was used as a strategy to facilitate unfreezing of the old culture and learning about the new, without major organizational upheaval. Although valuable, we also realized that such slow, gradual change had to be balanced by cataclysmic events (or quantum leaps). Such a periodic infusion, or *bolus of change,* helped to prevent disillusionment in those who had already become committed and who were thus looking for visible signs that change was really happening. It also served to jump-start a new level of learning, sometimes for those previously uninvolved.

Cheryl Stetler, PhD, RN, FAAN, project director, Patient-Centered Redesign Program, Hartford Hospital, Hartford, CT

One of the first things we did was a total restructuring, a large-scale change. The reason for that was, I had really come to the conclusion that we needed to get rid of a lot of the things that would inhibit and prevent us from moving forward with the objectives of the grant. If we didn't dissolve them literally, or resolve them up front, our task would be much more challenging and difficult. The traditional structure of hospitals is very narrow. It fosters mistrust in aligning organizations by occupation, by profession, and so forth. Plus, there are a lot of sacred cows you have to deal with, and so that is why I chose to really do the restructuring first, dealing with the structure part of Kilmann's model up front instead of later, as he recommends.

Lloyd Smith, MSA, president/CEO, MeritCare Hospital, Fargo, ND

Conflict

Conflict is a fact of life. The question is, What do we do with it? Do we avoid it, or do we use it to accelerate our learning? According to Senge, the difference between great and mediocre teams is how they face conflict. In great teams, conflict becomes productive because surfacing differences is the first step in building shared understanding. In mediocre teams, there is the appearance of no conflict, but everyone knows there is not really shared understanding.[19]

The issue of conflict is closely related to the earlier discussion of defensive routines. We say we want to avoid conflict to preserve our relationships (our espoused theory), but what we really want to avoid is a challenge to our thinking (our theory-in-use).

Conflict is an especially difficult issue for women in our culture who have been socialized to focus on relationships rather than issues. There also are geographic differences in how we surface and deal with conflict.

"Minnesota nice" is the phrase used to describe the tendency of many Minnesotans to appear outwardly agreeable while actually being resentful of what's happening. New staff members to the hospital, especially those from parts of the country where openness and honest emotion are encouraged, are often confused by the reactions Minnesotans have to certain experiences. A Minnesotan can construe a small disagreement as overwhelming conflict, for example. Those staff members accustomed to another experience are helping us learn that conflict is not a bad thing, that merely disagreeing doesn't mean you do or don't like someone, that differences among people are not bad things. In some instances, it has been helpful to have team members identify the driving and restraining forces around any decision or solution. This approach works well when team members are hesitant to disagree openly with other individuals but would feel more comfortable merely outlining the forces at play. At some levels of the organization, leaders are starting to use the principles of inquiry and advocacy, and pose questions in ways that are more solicitous of the contributions of others.

Ginger Malone, RN, MSN, director, innovation and consultation, Abbott Northwestern Hospital, Minneapolis

We are an organization that tends to avoid conflict. This creates difficulties because storming is a normal, healthy part of team learning. We quickly recognized that in order for us to continue with group growth, we had to address the issue of conflict in a positive manner.

We continue to experience conflict. Some conflicts we manage well and some conflicts we tend to avoid. We are not unique in this. There are still some issues we just don't confront. We have learned from our training and design teams that outstanding issues—specific issues about what they mean to them—need to be resolved as they move forward as a team.

Jeanette Ullery, RN, project director, The Rural Connection, St. Luke's Regional Medical Center, Boise, ID

Establishing an environment that enhances trust is critical to effective teams. In the past, we had been looking at what was best for efficient and effective operations of the specific departments and disciplines. When the patient/family was at the center, and we had to look at our work differently, we had to trust that the staff and affected stakeholders—the entire team— were looking at what was best for the patient/family. Sometimes this discussion of different viewpoints was difficult. Dealing with conflict is healthy for effective teams, but conflict was not always easy for us (particularly, we found, for women because we are more likely than men to focus on preserving relationships).

Kathy Holder, RN, MSN, director, nursing/quality, Tallahassee Memorial Regional Medical Center, Tallahassee, FL

There is a great desire in our organization for risk taking. However, when we had participants involved in Myers-Briggs, we learned that we really didn't have many iconoclasts. We didn't apply Myers-Briggs to everybody, but the sample size was large enough to confirm that we didn't have a lot of risk-takers, which meant that the ones who really are the risk-takers in our organization had more than their share of challenges. They were the ones sticking their necks out and not always being supported. We should have known better because of what we learned when we did away with all the military-like titles. We dismantled what used to be called a department head group (DHG), we discovered that when people would take the initiative by speaking out in the DHG meeting, they weren't chastised by administration, but by their colleagues. What we learned was that it was their peers who made them pay the price for displaying any kind of risk-taking behavior, not their leaders.

Evelyn Quigley, RN, MN, vice-president and nurse executive; and Lloyd Smith, MSA, president/CEO, MeritCare Hospital, Fargo, ND

Learning while Doing

Organizational change is a learning process that requires not only new information, but also practice in using that information. Most of us have never experienced this kind of learning before. Certainly, most of us have not been in situations where we are changing and learning while we are doing our work. For many, those who are used to change initiatives being handed down packaged with well-defined rules and through the routine structure, it is a very uncomfortable process. However, we have learned that it is worth the effort.

It used to be that joy came in knowing exactly what was expected of you and knowing how to do it. We learned how to do things and then we executed that knowledge of what we were doing in more of a sustained way. However, we weren't changing things to the degree that we are now, nor were we changing as fast. We had clearer rules to play by, and though we focused on the process and the relationships before, we worked within a routine structure that was fairly well defined and understood by everybody . . . and probably changed very little in the course of one's career.

Marjorie Beyers, RN, PhD, FAAN, former assistant vice-president, nursing, Mercy Health Services, Farmington Hills, MI

Tom Gilmore, organizational consultant, has described the continuous learning approach in creating change as similar "to trying to learn to ride a bicycle and build it at the same time." To learn as you go requires a willingness to take risks, learn, and move forward. It takes an understanding that all the answers are not known up front. It also means that it is okay to learn by trial and error. Not everything will be done right the first time, but it will be done better the second time. Not only is it possible to build that bicycle while you learn to ride it, this kind of approach is critical to a learning organization. By possessing the flexibility to fine-tune their efforts to transform a vision into reality, staff can learn and feel real ownership in their accomplishments.

Cheryl Kinnear, RN, BSN, program manager, University Hospital's Program to Improve Patient Care, University of Utah Hospital, Salt Lake City

Finding the time for reflection and analysis can be difficult. Finding the time, sometimes even the space, for developing collective thinking and skills can be even more frustrating when the pressures of everyday work are unrelenting. Sometimes we need to step back further to get a clear reflection, or listen to someone outside the team.

I walked in on a meeting in which team members were reflecting on their progress and how they thought they could improve in their care of a particular patient. The patient they were discussing, a woman with physical and behavioral problems as well as mental limitations, would have given everyone fits under our old system. Now I felt they were dealing with the challenge of her care very well. When the team encountered problems, they communicated well and found solutions. Yet in their analysis, I observed they were fairly hard on themselves. If they had stepped back far enough, they could have seen what I saw. They had lost perspective on the fact that what they routinely take for granted now, six months ago they wouldn't have been able to do at all.

Bill O'Dowd, PhD, director, rehabilitation programs, Sister Kenny Institute, Abbott Northwestern Hospital, Minneapolis

Conclusion

Organizational learning can be seen as a three-step process. First, we are exposed to new ideas and begin to think differently. Next, we begin to internalize this new knowledge and change our behavior. Finally, our behavior changes lead to improvements in organizational results.

Responsibility for organizational learning must be widely shared. The organization itself, managers, facilitators, and the individual, all are responsible for organizational learning.

Finally, learning to learn together is one of the biggest challenges in organizational learning. We define *learning* narrowly and believe that it is about knowing the right answer, about getting a good grade. Learning to learn together is at the heart of the learning organization. Only by learning how to break down defensive routines and engage in genuine dialogue can we truly learn together.

References and Notes

1. Garvin, D. A. Building a learning organization. *Harvard Business Review* 71(4):78–91, July–Aug. 1993.

2. Stata, R. Organizational learning—the key to management innovation. *Sloan Management Review* 30(3):70, Spring 1989.

3. Senge, P. M. *The Fifth Discipline: The Art and Practice of the Learning Organization.* New York City: Doubleday/Currency, 1990.

4. Senge, P. M., Ross, R., Smith, B., Roberts, C., and Kleiner, A. *The Fifth Discipline Fieldbook.* New York City: Currency/Doubleday, 1994, p. 193. This section provides a collection of exercises and discussions on working toward personal mastery.

5. Senge, Ross, Smith, Roberts, Kleiner, p. 6.

6. Ackoff, R. *Creating the Corporate Future.* New York City: John Wiley & Sons, 1981. Russell Ackoff, professor emeritus at The Wharton School, is the inventor of interactive planning/management. He sees it as the first systemically based planning/management methodology. His interactive process has been central in the work of the organizations profiled in this book.

7. Senge, p. 206.

8. Covey, S. R. *The Seven Habits of Highly Effective People.* New York City: Simon and Schuster, 1989, p. 48.

9. Senge, p. 237.

10. Presentation at the second annual meeting of the Strengthening Hospital Nursing Program, Tampa, Apr. 1991. Presenters Charlotte Roberts and Peter Senge of Innovation Associates, Framingham, MA, made their ideas available on videotape to all implementation grantees for use in our organizational learning experiences.

11. See: Argyris, C. Teaching smart people how to learn. *Harvard Business Review* 69(3):99–109, May–June 1991. In this article, Argyris proposes that every company faces a learning dilemma: The smartest people find it hardest to learn. His ideas on individual and organizational defensive routines and conflict have been particularly useful for many of us. See also: Argyris, C. *Overcoming Organizational Defenses: Facilitating Organizational Learning.* Boston: Allyn and Bacon, 1990.

12. Argyris, Teaching smart people how to learn, p. 103.

13. Senge, p. 237.

14. Argyris, p. 103.

15. Argyris, p. 103.

16. Argyris, p. 108.

17. Barker, J. *Paradigm Pioneers.* (Videotape.) Burnsville, MN: Charthouse International, 1992.

18. Senge, p. 243.

19. Senge, p. 249.

Chapter 3

Building a Model for Change

Although many things about organizational change are very difficult, one thing that is decidedly easy is to find ideas about it. There are ideas about restructuring, redesigning, reengineering; integrating, collaborating, and zapping; and shifting paradigms.

For many organizations, the question has been which model or set of ideas to use. All too often, an organization sets off down one path only to change direction when yet another new idea comes along. In such organizations, it is common to hear jaded discussions about the "flavor of the month." Little effort is made to integrate the old ideas with the new, although there frequently are many commonalities. There is little energy for change and learning within the organization because of the conviction that this new "flavor" too shall pass and that when all is said and done, "Nothing ever really changes."

Important new ideas almost always come from outside the organization. They may come from journals, books, videotapes, conference speakers—even the popular press. Or they may come into the organization via outside consultants. Wherever they come from, the critical issue is the fit between the ideas and the organization's vision. Bringing in consultants can be particularly tricky because it is too easy to ignore the importance of the work the organization can only do itself.

Avoiding the Lure of the Magic Bullet

Particularly in hospitals, there is a very strong selection bias for people who are trained to size up a situation and act quickly—jump in and fix it! And it is fortunate for many sick people that we can do just that. However, when it comes to organizational change, the quick fix is usually neither quick nor a fix. Usually, it is based on getting rid of what we do not want, which frequently results in something we want even less.

No one is more persuasive on the importance of focusing on getting what we want, rather than on getting rid of what we do not want, than Russell Ackoff.[1] Using the example of television, he goes so far as to suggest that it is possible to calculate the probability of getting a program he really wants to see. He points out that when he gets a program he does not like, it is very easy to get rid of it by simply changing the channel. However, the danger is that the next program will be even worse!

Even with a clear focus on getting what we want, we have learned that there is no magic bullet—no one approach, idea, strategy, or even consultant—that can create organizational change. Instead, commitment has been required over the long haul to patiently develop our own approaches, continuously blending bits and pieces from different models to fit our particular organizations. It is not a linear process with a beginning and an end. Rather, it is continuous—always examining new ideas, always integrating new concepts, always fitting the model to changing organizational initiatives and priorities.

Many of us have dealt with magic-bullet thinking and have struggled to integrate our models for change with important organizational initiatives such as quality, as well as with systemwide initiatives across many organizations.

We used four demonstration units as a way to learn about, and hopefully resolve, issues in care redesign. Central to our planning grant was the idea that we would encourage, promote, support each demonstration unit in its efforts to come up with the model of care that would best meet its patient population. Since then, we have learned that we have only begun to understand what it means to be population focused. Because patient populations move not only within the hospital but across settings to receive care from a variety of providers, we are trying to create an integrated care system for the Sisters of Providence Health System in Oregon. Managed care, dealing with populations whose needs change and how those needs are met in different settings, is what's driving how we are looking at redesign right now. That's very different from our focus in '89 and '90 when we first started. Even though we are still guided by the core premises, the context has changed how we look at and use those premises in redesigning and improving care delivery.

Marie J. Driever, PhD, RN, assistant director of nursing, quality/research; and codirector, Strengthening Hospital Nursing Program, Providence Portland Medical Center, Portland, OR

The appeal of the magic bullet is seductive, but it rarely provides any lasting change. As a 25-year critical care nurse, I am experienced with the quick fix and crisis management. I enjoy a fast-paced environment, and like the pace of rapid change and flux. Incremental change is hard for the impatient. My father always said, "I have plenty of patience; I haven't used any yet."

Organizational change is hard work and takes time. Commitment for the long haul is essential. It also requires the creation of teams of individuals from many professional disciplines who speak different languages and have different perspectives. We were also raised on the problem-solving method: Find out what's wrong and fix it. Now we are shifting to creating a new way rather than putting a bandage on the old. We have a new motto: "If it's not broken, find out why."

S. Ann Evans, RN, MS, MBA, FAAN, executive director, The Heart Institute at Tallahassee Memorial, Tallahassee Memorial Regional Medical Center, Tallahassee, FL

Developing Selection Criteria

Five years ago, each of us started in a similar place. We knew where we wanted to go but not how to get there. We faced the daunting task of creating large-scale organizational change to improve patient care, but none of us had cohesive models for how we would actually do it.

Now that we have learned how to build our models for change, it is clear that there are some criteria for selecting basic concepts as well as useful bits and pieces of concepts.

- *Focus:* The most useful basic concepts are broad in focus and fundamentally related to how we see and think about the world. For example, one such basic concept is systems thinking. Once basic concepts are in place, more narrowly focused concepts can be added for a more detailed understanding.
- *Clarity:* The most useful concepts are clear and easy to communicate, and can be understood by a wide range of people. They explain some common experience, strike a familiar chord with people, and provide a sense of direction for some common dilemma.
- *Alignment:* The more the concepts are aligned with the vision and organizational values, initiatives, and priorities, the more powerful they are in a model for organizational change. Important organizational initiatives might include strategic planning, quality planning, continuous quality improvement, work redesign, process reengineering, and integrated systems building.

  It is important to note that *alignment* means the fit between the ideas and the vision—in other words, what we want to create. Change and learning are never served by simply looking for ideas that support our own biases or justify where we presently are as good enough.

Following are two examples of how different concepts were included in our models for organizational change.

It became dramatically clear to us that if we were going to plan interactively (Ackoff), seek to learn together (Senge), and try to create an environment where staff could rebuild the organization (Gelinas and James), our fundamental structures, such as job descriptions and the way performance evaluations are conducted, would need to go through some profound change, too.

We used the Ackoff notion of idealized design to look at the job descriptions of patient care managers and department heads. By collaborating with key stakeholders, we began to design job descriptions based on the mission of our organization.

The mission accountability plan replaced our traditional performance evaluation rating system, and the "five practices" to achieve our mission became the guideposts in the job descriptions of our managers. The five practices were adapted from Senge's disciplines and include: (1) patient focus, (2) organizational systems, (3) facilitation/collaboration, (4) team learning, and (5) personal learning.

Soon it became obvious that these practices were not just for management-level staff but for everyone, regardless of role or title. To illustrate, the new job descriptions for service associates and care partners incorporate these practices and are now linked to our mission. Instead of being just lists of tasks to perform, these job descriptions now include quality standards which directly relate to our mission.

Karen L. Turner, EdD, training specialist; and Terry Minnen, MEd, shared governance liaison, Center for Patient Care Innovation, Vanderbilt University Hospital and Vanderbilt Clinic, Nashville, TN

Definitely, the area we emphasized in the structuring part of Kilmann's model was the blending of titles and functions so we could move away from provincialism and parochialism. This prior exposure really helped us absorb the tremendous changes that later accompanied our merger. Earlier, during the grant implementation, we had put together an executive group within the hospital which fostered teamwork, relationships, and interdependencies. Therefore, after the merger consolidation, when we put like in- and outpatient services together, we reordered all the portfolios or assignments among the vice-presidents and tried to combine functions so that there was no particular identity or a professional alignment, with the exception of finance and human resources. Interestingly, it turns out that this realignment was not difficult for those vice-presidents to step into because they had already been through a similar process with earlier structural changes we had implemented shortly after getting the grant.

Evelyn Quigley, RN, MN, vice-president and nurse executive; and Lloyd Smith, MSA, president/CEO, MeritCare Hospital, Fargo, ND

From the time of the planning grant year for the Robert Wood Johnson Foundation grant, we've spent time trying to develop our quality planning process. In the past year, a work group has been formed, which is made up of the planning and marketing vice-president, representatives from the Team Quality Planning and Measurement Committee, and representatives from finance, to see how we can integrate strategic planning, budget planning, and quality planning. The aim is to get consensus on a comprehensive plan that will guide everything we do on a yearly basis. To do so, they will be studying the work of six pilot groups that are currently determining ways to develop an integrated planning template that can be duplicated throughout the hospital. We hope that we'll be able to launch all departments on this kind of integrated planning effort by the end of 1994 to be implemented in 1995.

Ginger Malone, RN, MSN, director, innovation and consultation, Abbott Northwestern Hospital, Minneapolis

Understanding the Role of Leadership in Building the Model for Organizational Change

We have learned that leadership plays a key role in building the model for organizational change. It is the organization's leaders who set the expectation that the process of building the model is important because it ensures that the model fits organizational priorities. In our organizations, different levels of leadership have slightly different roles in building the model for organizational change.

The role of the board of trustees is to expect that there is a comprehensive model driving organizational change, to understand that model, and to hold leadership accountable for continuously refining the model and measuring results.

The role of the chief executive officer (CEO) is visionary. The CEO is expected to offer new ideas and concepts that could enhance the model; to continuously clarify organizational values, priorities, and initiatives that must be addressed by the model; and to continuously link the model for change to the vision—where the organization is going.

The role of senior management is to continuously integrate new concepts, ensure the fit of the model with organizational priorities, and have systems in place for measuring results. It is especially important that senior managers be flexible thinkers. They must see similarities between concepts and help others see them. In this way, leadership can help provide a clear sense of direction, rather than vacillating between concepts or giving the impression that old concepts are always being discarded for the flavor of the month.

Individuals from several organizations discuss the role that leadership played in building their models for organizational change.

A board member who takes the initiative in leading change is a tremendous asset to an organization. John Ashton is a member of the University of Utah Hospital Board of Trustees and the steering committee of the Program to Improve Patient Care. He has contributed valuable leadership to the program through his active involvement with internal and external stakeholders. Leading by example, Mr. Ashton consistently communicates the importance and validity of the vision through his actions. He initiates experiences to gain a clearer understanding of the goals of the program as well as the challenges. Mr. Ashton learned about one of the change efforts firsthand by spending time with the patient care coordinators in their work with patients. He conducted personal interviews with key stakeholders to better appreciate their perspective and communicate his belief in the vision. When it came time for the steering committee to address some difficult issues seriously, Mr. Ashton took an active role in organizing and leading an intense retreat. As a trustee, outside the organizational structure of the hospital, he is able to ask the difficult and sometimes threatening questions that must be explored. Mr. Ashton's involvement is sincere and consistent. In an effort to share our efforts with external stakeholders, Mr. Ashton organized a presentation of the program to the trustee and CEO members of the Utah Hospital Association. This kind of commitment and active involvement from the hospital board works to reinforce the support and value of our efforts to improve patient care. He reports that his involvement helps him in his role as a board member to better understand how the hospital operates and how the various disciplines interrelate.

Cheryl Kinnear, RN, BSN, program manager, University Hospital's Program to Improve Patient Care, University of Utah Hospital, Salt Lake City

There is a dichotomy between what we espouse—that is, what we say we are going to do—and what actually happens in practice. I really got caught in that quagmire inasmuch as I was moving ahead with empowering the vice-presidents and helping to push this principle throughout the organization, as were all of us, and all of a sudden, I realized that the board of directors wasn't there with me. Rather, they were continuing to expect the same level of disclosure and detailed knowledge base that I formerly practiced in responding to their queries. I no longer had immediate answers to some of the questions that board members required, so I would begin calling other people or bringing them to our meetings. The worst part is, if you don't educate the board members to what is going on, they get the feeling that you're losing touch with the organization. They might even develop a lack of confidence in you. Consequently, one of the things I learned firsthand was the need to communicate with the board of directors about where you are as you move your organization through a significant paradigm change.

Lloyd Smith, MSA, president/CEO, MeritCare Hospital, Fargo, ND

Lloyd Smith, our president and CEO, has certainly provided leadership. For example, on a monthly basis, he had us [the vice-presidents] meet with him for a morning breakfast so we could have a dialogue about certain chapters in *The Fifth Discipline*.[2] Looking back, those early morning sessions really helped us to understand the principles of a learning organization and how to apply them throughout the organization.

Evelyn Quigley, RN, MN, vice-president and nurse executive, MeritCare Hospital, Fargo, ND

Managers still have a unification function and a responsibility for the bottom line. We still have to have a top-management team vested with accountability that is mentoring, coaching, providing oversight, and keeping it all together. One of the unstated rules holds that everyone should be performing to a standard, and if they are not, it then becomes very hard, if not impossible, to lean on them. In the beginning, we attempted to avert this possibility through micro management. It is much easier to be a bean counter because you know what you are dealing with.

Since then, we have learned that the full value of a top-management team is to let it be a top-management team and not have it micro-manage the work. They have to truly be managers—that is, the art of delegation following the ideal of having hands off and letting go. We are poised for a new way of managing, and I think it's going to change how we function as individuals/groups, how we develop managers, and how we teach management in our academic institutions.

Marjorie Beyers, RN, PhD, FAAN, former associate vice-president, nursing, Mercy Health Services, Farmington Hills, MI

Any discussion of the role of leadership in building our model for organizational change always begins with hearing, seeing, experiencing Russell Ackoff at the first meeting of all 80 planning grantees in 1989. Unfortunately, the entire leadership team was not there, but we were well represented by a member of our board of directors, our CEO and COO [chief operating officer], and our senior vice-presidents for medical affairs and nursing. Had we known then how significant this event would be to us, we would have all been there!

Ackoff started talking at 7:00 p.m. on a Friday night—with a luau going on in the next room! In three hours, he covered the entire history of civilization, just him on the stage, sitting in a wicker chair, using the latest in audiovisual technology—an overhead projector with a roll of acetate and a felt-tip marker. What a communicator! His ideas held us spellbound. The next day, he spent the entire day telling us how to use these ideas to transform our organizations.

When we came home, we couldn't wait for the videotapes so we could share the experience with our colleagues. We bought his books, and began in earnest the process of reading and talking, discussing and testing ideas which would result in our own model—The Interactive Process.

The Leadership Team, Tallahassee Memorial Regional Medical Center, Tallahassee, FL

Integrating Several Models, Concepts, and Sets of Ideas

All of us have integrated many ideas to build our basic models for change. Even when we have used ideas from the same thinkers, we frequently have used them differently or put them together in different combinations.

There are many wonderful examples of model building from the SHNP organizations. At Harbor-UCLA Medical Center, in Torrance, California, their community design model is the catalyst for large-scale organizational change. This model is operationalized through the vision of a *community of patient care leaders*.[3] The community design model[4] is an organization design that emphasizes a spirit of community and individual leadership. The community design model identifies how people relate to each other, the environment, and the organization. The model has four key components: a conceptual framework, design values, strategic areas of focus, and change management processes. The conceptual framework is built on five major constructs with a coordinating focus on strategic management. The complementary constructs are:

1. Community
2. Transformational leadership
3. Harmony
4. Transitions
5. Learning organization

The model was developed in support of Harbor-UCLA's basic values—an internal sense of community and that every stakeholder is a leader.[5] (See figure 3-1.)

Nellie Robinson, former nurse executive at District of Columbia General Hospital, Washington, DC, has written about that organization's model for restructuring care, called the Patient-Centered Care Delivery System (PCCDS).[6] (See figure 3-2, p. 40.) It is based on a core value that the patient "provides the impetus for integration of healthcare services."[7] The model is based on four constructs:[8]

1. Patient-centered environment (patient is the focal point)
2. Organizational self-care (care and support for caregivers)
3. Partners in care (interdependence and collaboration among caregivers)
4. Masters of change (change is "inevitable and continuous," and "is the catalyst for organizational as well as self-development")

Although these ideas are identified separately, they are clearly dynamic and interrelated. Their integration, broad focus, and simplicity make a powerful statement about how change will happen at DC General.

At Abbott Northwestern Hospital, in Minneapolis, a great deal of attention has been paid to the process of organizational change. The hospital's model for change reflects that careful work. Change (desired performance) is seen as being related to the will to change, the capacity for change, and support for change. (See figure 3-3, p. 41.)

The people at Abbott Northwestern Hospital further define the pathway for developing the character necessary for the will to change, the capability necessary for the capacity for change, and the community necessary for the support for change. Their driving vision is breathtakingly simple and clear: *Patients are the reason we exist. People are the reason we excel. Systems support the work.* Their model powerfully integrates the work of Ackoff (interactive planning/management), Senge (learning organization), Hammer (process reengineering), Gelanis and James (collaborative organizational design), and Innovation Associates (facilitative leadership).

Over the past three years, one of the most significant things we have learned is the importance of each organization, or group of organizations, doing its own learning and building its own model for change. We were very fortunate to be introduced early on to the work of Ackoff and Senge. But the real lesson is how differently their ideas have been operationalized in each setting. Each organization has shaped its model for change to address its own values, priorities, and initiatives—in other words, its own vision. No one model or set of ideas has been enough. The greatest value to model building is the process of continuously seeking ideas and sifting through them, developing a common understanding of them, and integrating them into one powerful guiding force. In this way, new ideas can be added and used readily without creating the sense of constantly changing direction.

Figure 3-1. A Community Design Model

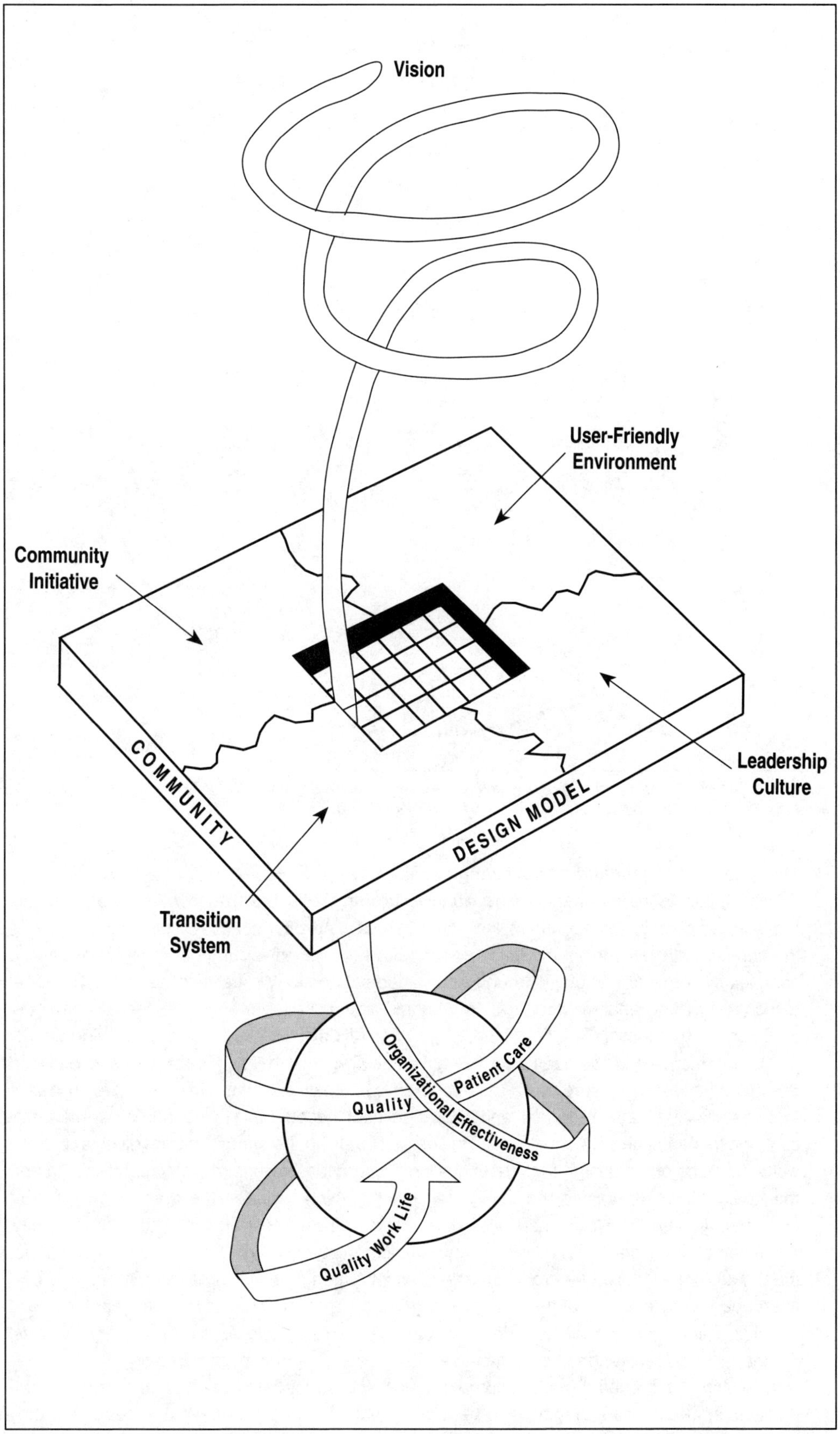

Source: Harbor-UCLA Medical Center, Department of Nursing, Torrance, CA. *Nursing Network* 6(4):2, 1994.

Figure 3-2. A Patient-Centered Care Model

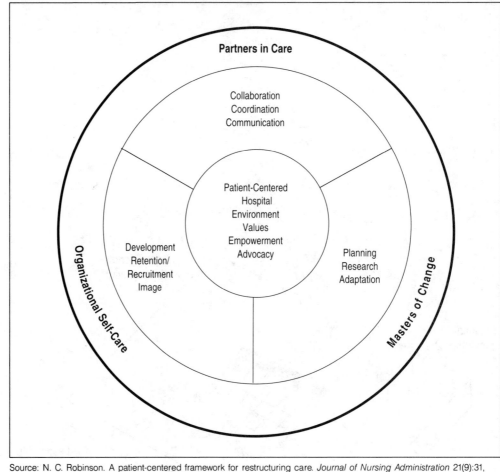

Source: N. C. Robinson. A patient-centered framework for restructuring care. *Journal of Nursing Administration* 21(9):31, Sept. 1991. Reprinted by permission of Lippincott-Raven Publishers, Philadelphia, PA.

The model driving organizational change at Tallahassee Memorial Regional Medical Center (TMRMC) addresses important organizational values and initiatives. The foundation of our model is interactive planning/management, invented by Russell Ackoff. Because systems thinking forms the conceptual base for his model, we have found it very powerful for creating change in a complex system such as our 771-bed tertiary medical center. We have refined Ackoff's model to focus on getting what we want, setting priorities, and doing more with less. We call our model the interactive process. (See figure 3-4, p. 42.) At TMRMC, it is how we do everything we do.

Our interactive process begins with idealized design. Figure 3-5 (p. 42) shows our idealized design for patient/family care. To us, the design says that patient/family care is what we do. It says that we are each equally important, and that we are each accountable for our role in patient/family care and for having the systems in place to see that quality patient/family care is given and given well. The parts of the design that are shaded represent the acute care institutional setting and the heavy circle represents the corporate setting, which includes the entire continuum of patient/family care. Each of the services extends beyond the corporate setting into our community.

As part of our interactive process, we have implemented Ackoff's interactive planning/management structure—the circular organization—in which planning boards plan simultaneously and interdependently throughout the organization. Our model is unit based, so the planning board belongs to the manager of the unit. The planning board also includes the manager's boss, the manager's direct reports, and affected stakeholders. Planning boards can do whatever they want so long as it does not affect someone else and so long as they have the resources. If it affects someone else, they have to get agreement. If they do not have the resources, they have to find them. Affected stakeholders must be included if they so desire. The definition of *affected* lies with the stakeholder, not the planning board. To get at issues that cross organizational boundaries, we are using Michael Hammer's ideas to reengineer important functions and key processes.

We have also integrated Peter Senge's model of the learning organization into our interactive process. We find that Senge's five disciplines add depth to the process. Ackoff deals with systems thinking at a fairly high conceptual level whereas Senge makes the ideas more real by introducing the idea of looking for underlying patterns. Ackoff's planning board structure is carefully crafted to put multiple levels and functions together in an organization. Again, Senge takes it further to help us deal with what needs to happen once they are at the table. Particularly helpful are his ideas about managing mental models (being honest about what you think), team learning (getting past defensiveness to learn together), and personal mastery (accepting responsibility for our own learning).

We have also integrated our interactive process with our continuous quality improvement efforts. All too often, continuous improvement methods ignore the issue of whether the process being improved is necessary in the first place. The interactive process eliminates this important deficiency by starting out with the ideal. The interactive process also addresses another limitation of traditional quality improvement methods—problem solving aimed at getting rid of what we *do not* want. The focus, instead, is on getting what we *do* want.

Finally, we have used Joel Barker's ideas about paradigms extensively.[9] He puts the whole idea of creating change in a larger context. Particularly useful have been his ideas

Figure 3-3.   A Model for Organizational Learning and Change

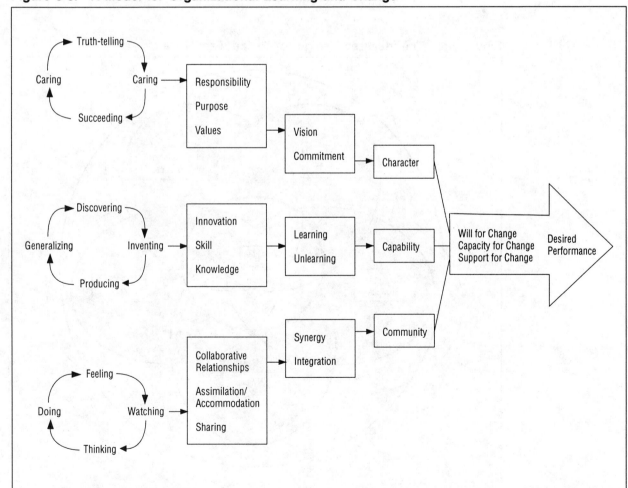

Source: Strengthening Hospital Nursing: A Program to Improve Patient Care. 1994 National Meetings, Oct. 17–18, 1994, Arlington, VA. Materials from Abbott Northwestern Hospital Presentation, p. 2.5.10.

Figure 3-4. The TMRMC Model: Interactive Planning

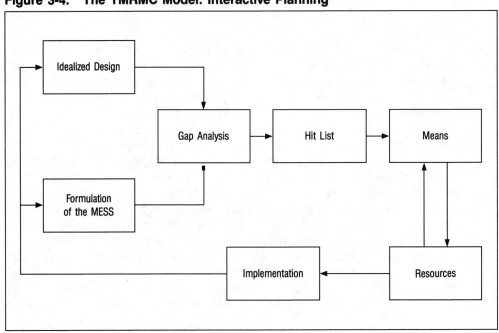

Source: Tallahassee Memorial Regional Medical Center, Tallahassee, FL.

Figure 3-5. The Idealized Design for Patient/Family Care

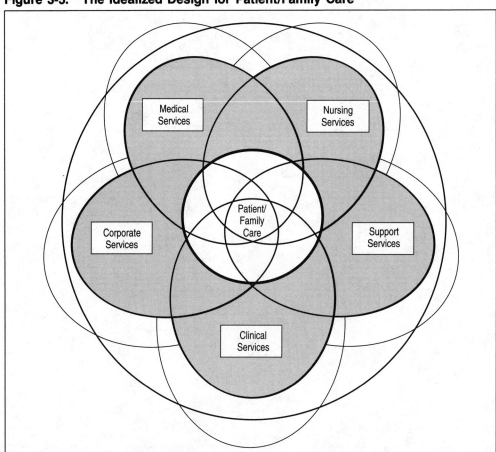

Source: Tallahassee Memorial Regional Medical Center, Tallahassee, FL.

about paradigm pioneers—those who take the new ideas and figure out how to make them work.

In many ways, we have been pioneering the Ackoff invention of interactive planning/management and the Senge invention of the learning organization. His pioneer metaphor has been especially helpful. Pioneers operate on intuition, courage, and persistence. They seldom have proof that the new ideas will work. Barker warns that too many people want too many numbers before they will make a decision. He calls that settler mentality and says that there can be no numbers until the pioneers generate them. This has been reassuring in our measurement efforts. We are indeed just now generating the numbers!

The Project Team, Program to Improve Patient Care, Tallahassee Memorial Regional Medical Center, Tallahassee, FL

Abbott Northwestern's model for organizational change uses a combination of the Gelinas/James and Hammer models as a basis for our model with modified concepts from Ackoff, Senge, and Barker incorporated into the design. From Ackoff, we use the concepts of idealized design and interactive planning. From Senge, we use the concepts of the five disciplines—personal mastery, team learning, systems thinking, mental models, and building a shared vision. From Barker, we use the concept of paradigm changes. From Hammer, we learned about business processes, the importance of identifying key organizational processes, the four-phased re-engineering road map, and we were taught how to use reengineering templates. Plus, we drew upon other tools and methods from continuous quality improvement theorists such as Deming and Juran. Mostly, however, we depended on the Gelinas and James integration of all the theorists' concepts (for example, systems thinking, quality improvement, the learning organization, reengineering, and visioning) as the foundation for our work.

Ginger Malone, RN, MSN, director, innovation and consultation, Abbott Northwestern Hospital, Minneapolis

In truth, no one model sufficed to guide our complex organizationwide project which targeted change in management, practice, systems, and roles within the context of our redesign vision. Except for Barker's concept of paradigms, Senge's systems thinking/learning organization, and Ackoff's idealized redesign, the names of authors, models, and related conceptual frameworks were used primarily by project staff. One reason was the decided difficulty that some individuals had with the "academic" nature of conceptual frameworks and the language of management and behavioral science.

An eclectic set of models and/or theories (including the Charns and Schaefer model for management in health care organizations) provided guidance in the planning, implementation, and management of change. No one framework, however, dominated; rather, multiple concepts provided a set of tools and mental models to facilitate forward movement at the right place and right time. For example, on occasion, idealized redesign was extremely valuable wherein people were effectively encouraged to shift paradigms, to stretch, and to think creatively.

Another invaluable resource was Hatten and Hatten's key principles for strategic management.[10] Although not designed for health care per se, their principles provided a context for thinking both about a visionary plan and about how and when to optimally push the system toward implementation. These principles describe nine strategies for enhancing the success of strategic management, which is a process that helps operationalize the "words" of a strategic plan into action. These principles suggest the following:[11]

- Use strategies that fit your environment or culture.
- Make certain that separate components of a strategy fit together.
- Focus rather than inefficiently spread resources out.
- Concentrate on organizational/departmental strengths rather than weaknesses.
- "Strategy is the art of the possible. Do what is feasible!"
- "A good strategy is controlled—surprises are failures of control."
- Build on successes.
- Get key stakeholder support.
- Do not take risks lightly.

Risk taking is, of course, required for visionary innovation, but the tenets of strategic management suggest that cost benefits need to be assessed and understood before moving full speed ahead. Finally, a recurring theme of Hatten and Hatten that applies within/across these principles is the concept of consistency. As strategies are used and redesign moves forward, make sure that everything is consistent with everything else!

Cheryl B. Stetler, PhD, RN, FAAN, project director, Patient-Centered Redesign Program, Hartford Hospital, Hartford, CT

Providers, administrators, faculty, and staff participating in the Health Bond Consortium are experiencing a mix/match of emergent models of organizational change from education and service which are mutually reinforcing. They flow from the paradigm of systems thinking which is gaining universal acceptance across the physical/social sciences, humanities, and other "new sciences" such as chaos theory, which further reinforces the importance of relationships and process.*

Health Bond has found that interactive planning and the disciplines of learning organizations are highly interrelated. Applying interactive planning processes creates an environment within which people in organizations can develop personal mastery (managing creative tension); the ability to critique mental models (empathize, walk in another's shoes, let new ideas in, let long-held biases out); develop a common ground of meaning through shared visioning and team learning (dialogue and discussion); and experience systems interdependencies and develop systems thinking abilities.

Through its service and education partnerships, Health Bond participants are experiencing parallels between Senge's and Ackoff's models for organizational change and that proffered by Em Bevis and Jean Watson for an "educationist" curriculum design in schools of nursing.[12-15] Rather than learning being the result of a student's achievement of specified behavioral objectives, learning is inherent in the relationship between people engaged in the learning endeavor (student–student, student–faculty, faculty–faculty, faculty–student). In this model, the emphasis switches from teaching to learning, from facts to discovery, from success/failure to continuous learning and improvement.

Ackoff's, Senge's, and Bevis and Watson's models of organizational change are process models. These models position Health Bond organizations to be very focused in the present on relationship management, communication, and on strategies for creating the future.

Coming to grips with the current reality of relationship management and communication patterns is only part of the recognized need. The other critical piece (using the interactive planning process) is developing skills for visioning the future. Leaders in Health Bond's consortium have heard Leland Kaiser speak and have read some of his writings over the past seven years.[16-19] Our thinking has been influenced and our "futuring bag of tricks" strengthened as a result. However, this does not mean Health Bond lacks a concern for outcomes or thinks that an emphasis on process without concern for structure is acceptable. We are aligning these change models with an action research model of evaluation, which emphasizes formative (continuous quality improvement) as well as summative assessments of the achievement of vision and objectives. Indeed, we are operationalizing a model for intersystem change.[20]

Sharon Aadalen, RN, PhD, director, Health Bond Consortium, South Central Minnesota, Mankato, MN

---

*In her ground-breaking book, *Leadership and the New Science: Learning about Organization from an Orderly Universe* (San Francisco: Berrett-Kohler Publishers, 1992), Margaret Wheatley describes the new science of chaos theory and relates it to organizations. She defines *chaos* as "the final state in a system's movement away from order—a period of total unpredictability" (p. 122). However, she points out that: "In chaotic systems, scientists can now observe movements that, though random and unpredictable, never exceed finite boundaries" (p. 123). *Chaos,* then, can be thought of as "order without predictability"—a paradoxical concept. Although a system may seem completely out of control, strange attractors seem to be responsible for shaping the patterns that exist even in chaotic systems. Wheatley sees vision, values, and meaning as the strange attractors in organizations that help individuals shape their behavior, bringing order, resilience, and self-renewal to the system (p. 133). See also von Bertalanffy, L. *General Systems Theory.* New York City: Braziller, 1969; and Lazlo, E. *Introduction to Systems Philosophy: Toward a New Paradigm of Contemporary Thought.* New York City: Gordon Breach, 1962.

At the University Hospitals of Cleveland, Everett Rogers's Diffusion of Innovation ideas and concepts have been central to the hospital's model for change. (See appendix A.) The following is a description of the hospital's curriculum:

Plan	Model
Curriculum to introduce collaborative care:	Rogers's *Adoption of Innovation* model: Description of individuals' reaction to change: Use of the model to team up with certain group types to implement change through the education process. The six behavioral pattern responses to change are listed below:
[Use of innovators] **Case Management** *Karen Zander, Center for Management* Fall 1991 A one-day presentation by an entrepreneur and leader in case management and development of critical paths.	Innovators: • Enthusiastic, energetic, thrive on change and are almost obsessed with adventure • Do not conform to established norms; viewed as successful but deviate from community norms due to progressive thinking • Often controversial, yet they influence change • Search out new ideas and spread them in their writing, travel, and networking
[Use of innovators/early adopters] **Shaping Health Care: Directions and Partnerships in the 90s** *Connie Curran, The Curran Group, Pilot Project Leaders, University Hospitals Network* A one-day seminar/workshop, including: 1. An update on health issues supporting adoption of case management and critical paths by a nationally recognized expert 2. Examples of local application of the concepts in pilot projects modeled by early adopters 3. Small group work (early majority) lead by pilot project leaders who used consultation and encouragement to foster adoption of change	Early adopters: • Opinion leaders who are sought out by peers for information and advice • Prefer to apply new ideas to their local situation • Facilitators of diffusion process during change • Regarded with high esteem for their success in application of ideas • Ideal role models • Excellent communication skills that can be used to reduce others' stress/conflict • Able to act as "troubleshooters" after implementation of change
[Use of early adopters] **Collaborative Care: Part I** *Pilot Project Leaders, University Hospitals Network* Series of half-day presentations featuring detailed technical approaches to the development of collaborative patient care pathways. Using modeling techniques, instructor presented participants with a detailed blueprint of process and product. A manual was distributed to provide specific steps, tools, and materials for groups planning to develop patient care pathways.	
[Use of early adopters and early majority] **Collaborative Care: Part II** *Pilot Project Leaders, University Hospitals Network* A half-day work session providing one-on-one consultation for ongoing groups. Leaders provided support, guidance, feedback, and reinforcement. Participants support and encourage each other.	Early majority: • Adopt new ideas shortly before the average person • Are careful and deliberate in adoption of change • Usually not the first to change and not seen as opinion leaders

(Continued on next page)

Plan	Model
Improving Your DRG Literacy Detailed explanations of recent changes in the reimbursement mechanisms and other environmental forces help to clarify and give support for improving the efficiency and effectiveness of patient care delivery systems. A panel of financial and clinical experts present examples of how the establishment of fiscal/clinical interfaces in collaborative care projects serves to improve patient care outcomes. A dictionary of reimbursement and financial terms is distributed and assists in providing a common language among participants.	Late majority: • Skeptical of innovation • Adopt change out of economic necessity and response to social/peer pressure • Openly resistive to change early in the diffusion process Laggard: • Last to adopt an innovation • Near isolates and dedicated to tradition using the past as their reference • Generally older, less educated, and on a lower socioeconomic level • Maintain status quo through ritualistic behaviors • Express resistance in negative terms related to innovation and innovators Rejecters: • Openly oppose innovation and actively encourage others to do likewise • May extend resistance to sabotaging an innovation

Nikki Polis, PhD, RN, project director, Strengthening Hospital Nursing Program, University Hospital of Cleveland, Cleveland, OH

From the beginning, we have said that we don't believe there is any one guru who exactly does it for us. All of them have certain similarities. We meshed our model with the SHNP change process, and we integrated that with our quality improvement processes so as to eliminate parallel processes. We have tried to integrate them into one program which we call Improving Quality through Patient-Focused Care. For the most part, we have pulled them together to suit our own purposes.

Jane Scharff, MN, RN, CNAA, project coordinator, Montana Consortium, Saint Vincent Hospital and Health Center, Billings, MT

We started with Ackoff's strategic planning process, but revised his work to specify the idealized end. It was, and is, our belief that a common focus of a set of patient outcomes to be achieved by the care that is delivered was one component of an idealized end people could use as an organizing focus. Then, of course, we heard about Senge during one annual meeting, and we have been trying to really understand and tie our experiences to what it means to be a learning organization. We like Gareth Morgan's ideas of shared understanding and the use of metaphors. Morgan proposes that, in any situation, people have only about 15 percent that they have control to change. Identifying that 15 percent creates leverage to bring about desired change. I think, in many ways, he has a way of dealing on a practical level with the issues that are inherent in Senge's learning organization concept. Morgan's concept of working toward a shared understanding is a way to operationalize some of Senge's dimensions of the learning organization.

Marie J. Driever, PhD, RN, assistant director of nursing, quality/research; and codirector, Strengthening Hospital Nursing Program, Providence Portland Medical Center, Portland, OR

Conclusion

It is fatally easy to fall into the flavor-of-the-month trap when it comes to organizational change. The easy part is that there are many great thinkers and ideas out there. The hard part is taking these ideas and testing their usefulness in your own organization. Useful ideas are broad enough in focus to offer help in understanding a wide range of issues and the relationships between them. They are clear; they make sense to those who will need to use them. Finally, they are aligned with organizational values, initiatives, and priorities, and provide a way to integrate all three.

The most important lesson has been that when all is said and done, there is no substitute for doing the hard work of building your own model to drive change in your own organization. "Cookie cutter" approaches have not been used in any of our organizations. This is not to say that our experiences are not useful for others. In many ways, our work has been the work of Barker's *Paradigm Pioneer,* taking new ideas and figuring out how to make them work. Pioneers seldom have proof that the new ideas will work. They operate on intuition, courage, and persistence to create the future they truly want.

Appendix A provides a detailed description of the key concepts used to build the models that are driving change in our organizations.

References and Notes

1. Ackoff, R. *Strengthening Hospital Nursing: A Program to Improve Patient Care.* (Series of six videotapes.) Presented at the Education Conference for SHNP Planning Grantees, Orlando, FL, Sept. 7–8, 1989.

2. Senge, P. *The Fifth Discipline: The Art and Practice of the Learning Organization.* New York City: Doubleday/Currency, 1990.

3. Strengthening Hospital Nursing: A Program to Improve Patient Care, 1994 National Meetings, Oct. 3–4, 1994, Louisville, KY (program, p. 5).

4. Nazarey, P., Siler, P., and Jordon-Marsh, M. Harbor-UCLA Medical Center: A Community of Patient Care Leaders Transitioning to a Culture of Empowerment. Grant proposal for Strengthening Hospital Nursing: A Program to Improve Patient Care. Sponsored by the Robert Wood Johnson Foundation/Pew Charitable Trusts. Torrance, CA: Harbor-UCLA Research and Education Institute, May 1990.

5. For a thorough understanding of the community design model, how it has been implemented, and the results, see: SONA 7 (Series on Nursing Administration). Nazarey, P., Siler, P., Jordan-Marsh, M., Goldsmith, S. R., and Sanchez, E. The community design model: a framework for restructuring. In: K. Kelly, editor. *Health Care Work Redesign.* Thousand Oaks, CA: Sage, 1995, pp. 131–149.

6. Robinson, N. C. A patient-centered framework for restructuring care. *Journal of Nursing Administration* 21(9):31, Sept. 1991.

7. Robinson, p. 30.

8. Robinson, p. 31.

9. Joel Barker's ideas are presented in *Paradigm Pioneers,* a videotape in the series *Discovering the Future,* produced by Charthouse International in 1992.

10. Armstrong, D. M., and Stetler, C. B. Strategic considerations in developing a delivery model. *Nursing Economic$* 9(2):112–15, Mar.–Apr. 1991.

11. Armstrong and Stetler.

12. Ackoff, R. *Creating the Corporate Future.* New York City: John Wiley & Sons, 1981.

13. Ackoff, R. The circular organization: an update. *Academy of Management Executives* 3(1):11–16, Feb. 1989.

14. Senge, P. M. *The Fifth Discipline: The Art and Practice of the Learning Organization.* New York City: Doubleday/Currency, 1990.

15. Bevis, E. O., and Watson, J. *Toward a Caring Curriculum: A New Pedagogy for Nursing.* New York City: National League for Nursing, 1989.

16. Kaiser, L. R. Planning for change. (Health care manager's notebook: a practical resource for all hospital managers.) *Healthcare Forum,* June 1980, pp. 35–38.

17. Kaiser, L. R. Inventing the future. Speech given at the Harpur Forum Breakfast, The Foundation of the State University of New York at Binghamton, Nov. 21, 1983.

18. Kaiser, L. R. Organizational mindset: ten ways to alter your world view. *Healthcare Forum,* Jan.-Feb. 1985, pp. 50-53.

19. Kaiser, L. R. The emerging hospital/employee relationship. *Healthcare Forum,* Jan.-Feb. 1986, pp. 17-18.

20. Chin, R. The utility of system models and developmental models for practitioners. In: W. G. Bennis, K. D. Benne, and R. Chin, editors. *The Planning of Change,* 2nd ed. New York City: Holt, Rinehart and Winston, 1968.

Chapter 4

Designing Compelling Learning Experiences

In the face of unprecedented change, the learning organization has captured our imagination. Although much of what is known about learning organizations has been known for years, not many learning organizations actually exist because building them requires such sweeping structural and systemic change over considerable time. We already have discussed the five disciplines of the learning organization: systems thinking, personal mastery, mental models, building shared vision, and team learning.[1] In their remarkable new book titled *Sculpting the Learning Organization,* Watkins and Marsick offer these thoughts. A learning organization:[2]

- Is not just a collection of individuals who are learning — instead, learning is also occurring simultaneously at various collective levels within business units and sometimes within the whole company
- Demonstrates organizational capacity for change
- Accelerates individual learning capacity but also redefines organizational structure, culture, job design, and mental models (assumptions about the way things are)
- Involves widespread participation of employees, and often customers, in decision making, dialogue, and information sharing
- Promotes systemic thinking and building of organizational memory

It is the organizational capacity for change that is of particular concern to us. Our people, teams, and organizations must be capable of not just change but, rather, continuous change. The challenge is enormous! This chapter discusses the elements that must be considered in the design of learning experiences that are necessary to build learning organizations.

The Challenge

Ray Stata, chief executive officer (CEO) of Analog Devices, believes that the only sustainable source of competitive advantage is learning faster than your competition.[3] Certainly, hospitals and hospital systems are faced with more competition than ever — and need to learn faster than ever. But there is so much to learn: learning new content, learning about learning, learning at new levels, learning to learn together, integrating work and learning, learning about learners, and, of course, finding the resources. We have learned that none of this is easy; it takes time and deep change. However, for us, it has been well worth the effort.

The project plan we committed to in 1989 could never have been realized without a massive educational effort. The goals and objectives of our project have moved out of the realm of *wouldn't it be nice to do for patient care* to *must do in order to survive.* In short, becoming and behaving as a fully integrated system of health care has affected each and every employee that functions within our boundaries. Therefore, designing effective educational experiences, although an incredible challenge, has become the driving force behind our organizational development.

Paula Delahanty, RN, project director, Strengthening Hospital Nursing Program, Penobscot Bay Medical Center, Rockland, ME

Learning to Learn

We need to learn new things, including new things about learning itself. Not only is the content new (systems thinking, continuous improvement, statistical techniques, and so on), but so is the thinking about learning itself. No longer are we talking about the simple transfer of information: There is a right answer and here it is. We now know the importance of learning how to learn together, particularly when there is no one right answer.

Much of what we know about learning is based on individual learning. However, we no longer are talking about just individual learning. To transform organizations into learning organizations and to develop the capacity for change, learning has to happen on three levels:

1. The level of the individual
2. The level of the team
3. The level of the organization

Some even suggest a fourth level—the societal level, or the level of the community.[4] Learning at this level supports the interdependence of organizations, families, and the community. For example, learning organizations create internal environments that support families and the community. They are family-friendly, supporting the balance of work and family life. Additionally, they are connected to the community—for example, they protect the environment and promote cultural diversity.

Although individual learning is absolutely necessary, it is not enough. For an organization to learn, teams also must be able to learn. For teams to learn, individual team members have to be able to learn the skills of dialogue—of advocacy and inquiry. They have to learn how to think deeply about their own mental models. They have to learn how to trade off the threat of embarrassment for the reward of learning how to accomplish something important together.

What we have done in the past no longer will work; the traditional active teacher-passive student methods fall woefully short. Unfortunately, much as with parenting, all too often we teach in our organizations the way we were taught in school. The usual pattern has been for the teacher to develop the content, tell it to the learner, and then test to see if the learner heard it. However, we are trying to teach things that have never been taught before, such as how to think differently and how to learn together. And we are not just dealing with the teacher's mental models; learners have mental models of learning, too. Frequently, they too believe it is the teacher's job to tell the learner the answer. Not having the answer is a failure, just as it was in school.

In building learning organizations, we are trying to move learners from dependence to independence to interdependence. Interdependence, the most highly evolved level, requires learning how to find answers together. Learners cannot learn interdependence with dependent (for example, lecture) or independent (for example, self-paced modules) teaching methods. However, we also are interested in learning personal mastery, individual responsibility for our own learning. Independent methods can work well for learning some of these skills. We have not found traditional dependent methods to be useful for much of anything.

Inherent in the design and delivery of any educational experience is the responsibility of the educator to speak the "language" of the participants. Our traditional nursing education service was given the leadership role of creating education opportunities to increase hospital associates' interpersonal communication skills. We served not only as the developers of the classes, but in some cases, the presenters too. As presenters, we called upon our personal experiences to illustrate the concepts we were teaching. However, our class evaluations quickly demonstrated that in many nonnursing associates' eyes, we were missing the mark. They either couldn't relate to our examples or they felt we were being insensitive to the complexity of issues they encountered in their respective services. In an effort to correct this, we spent time with members of nonnursing services to develop class examples that illustrated key learning concepts from their point of view. Class evaluations immediately demonstrated the effectiveness of *speaking the language* of our class participants.

Janet Feder, BSN, RN, education services manager, MeritCare Hospital, Fargo, ND

People need to have the opportunity to share the disappointment of giving something up in order to anticipate the joy of gaining something new. We try to have a time and place for the expression of those feelings. This helps to pave the way for productive discussions concerning change and the concrete steps that need to be taken in order to enable change.

Leslie Ajl, RN, MS, CS, psychiatric liaison nurse, Beth Israel Hospital, Boston

Ensuring Continuous Learning

Another common challenge in building a learning organization is that of ensuring that the organization is fully committed to the value of continuous learning and to the integration of learning with the work itself. But all too often, learning and working are seen as separate. For example, concentrating responsibility for teaching only in training departments can create firm boundaries between teaching and learning. The message is especially mixed when training is done away from the work setting only when there are no conflicting work demands. Workers see teaching and learning as something done in addition to work, not as part of it. A sad sign of this lack of integration—lack of commitment to the value of continuous learning—is that in the unenlightened organization, education is the first thing to go when times get tough. Ironically, cutbacks occur just when learning needs to be stepped up to increase capacity for change.

Working with Learners

Yet a third challenge in building learning organizations is that of working with the variety of learners. Most of our organizations are extremely diverse in terms of age, gender, ethnicity, language, and educational attainment, to name just a few dimensions. All these variables have ramifications for learning experiences. On the one hand, we are trying to keep the interest of a whole new generation of learners, raised on Sesame Street and MTV. Not surprisingly, many of these learners want to be passively entertained. On the other hand, we have more mature adult learners whose study skills may be rusty or may never have been good to start with. They may have little or no confidence in their ability to learn or be successful in learning situations.

When designing educational experiences in the old paradigm, we assumed that all learners shared a basic understanding or foundation; therefore, learning plans were designed to facilitate learning for the middle majority of learners. We didn't adapt learning or support learners who were at the extremes, those lagging behind the change or those with innovative views. Learners now come with diverse thinking around initiatives being explored, and learning plans need to reflect how an initiative fits into the larger vision of the organization. Part of my role is to honor many diverse ways of viewing issues while concurrently helping learners gain a focus without dampening innovative learning. Increasingly, the learning specialist helps bridge the gap between the organization's and the individual's readiness for change.

Mae McWeeny, MA, RN, learning specialist, Center for Professional and Clinical Development, Abbott Northwestern Hospital, Minneapolis

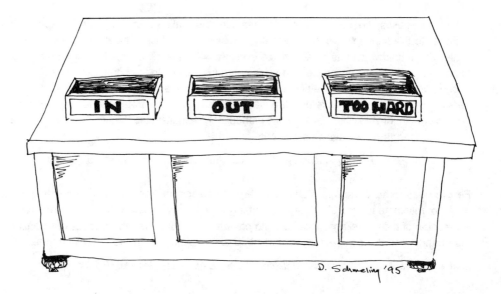

Workers bring to the workplace the best and worst of their past learning experiences. Adult educators suggest reducing learner anxiety by using individual self-paced learning methods. But could this attempt to protect the learner from anxiety in fact impede growth? We have learned that the greatest growth, for both individuals and teams, may happen when we find the courage to step outside our comfort zones. Protection only deprives people of this learning experience. Perhaps the best learning occurs when we help people cope with their anxiety—and move on. After all, the goal is for the learner to develop commitment to his or her own learning.

Finally, becoming a learning organization is difficult. Dean Atchison, former secretary of state under President Truman, was said to have three file baskets on his desk—IN, OUT, and TOO HARD! Learning organizations are in that third basket because we bump up against all three of the universal constraints: time, money, and knowledge. There is never enough of any of them. In these times of rapid change, which frequently necessitate quick strategic moves, building a learning organization seems to take too long. Time is a very precious resource in our flattened, downsized organizations. Additionally, learning to learn together can require significant resources. Interactive methods often are more expensive in terms of materials (for example, computer simulations, games, maybe even outside facilitators). However, it is important to recognize that our adherence to old linear mental models of change—isolate the problem, select the best solution, implement it—also increases the apparent difficulty of learning to learn together. The old model feels easier—and certainly faster. However, even though we arrive at a solution more quickly, we frequently do not get a good one, which in the long run makes the traditional approaches much more costly in terms of time and money.

Individual and Institutional Readiness for Change

Watkins and Marsick talk about "leverage learning," or learning that helps organizations achieve business objectives—in our case, learning that improves patient/family care.[5] They see individuals, teams, and organizations as ready for learning when three interacting components are present:

- *Focus:* Knowledge and understanding of the learning opportunity
- *Capability:* Skills and resources that enable learning
- *Will:* Motivation to carry learning forward (See figure 4-1.)

At the level of the individual, a new job opportunity (focus), a realization that new skills are necessary (capability), and a strong interest in advancement (will) might combine to produce

Figure 4-1. Readiness for Learning

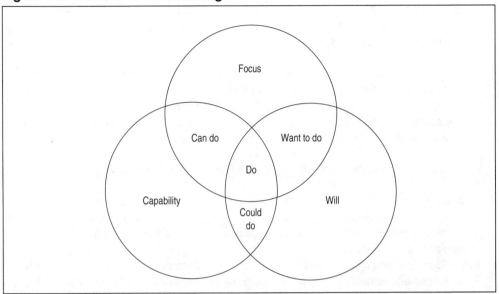

Source: Watkins, K. E., and Marsick, V. J. *Sculpting the Learning Organization: Lessons in the Art and Science of Systemic Change*. San Francisco: Jossey-Bass, 1993, p. 37.

individual readiness for learning. At the team level, a new organizational priority on continuous improvement (focus), a realization that new quality tools skills are necessary (capability), and a strong team value on learning together (will) would likely result in readiness for this team to learn statistical techniques. At the organizational level, a new competitor offering deep discounts, what Meyer calls the organizational "jolt" (focus), a concern that present cost/charge systems cannot adequately support cost/quality trade-off decisions (capability), and a need to respond rapidly or lose market share (will) can combine to heighten readiness to learn new ways to link clinical and financial systems.[6]

We have learned that a number of elements within organizations interact to contribute to organizational readiness for change: leadership, common vocabulary, management styles, skills for building trust, and analytic skills.

We have a couple of mottos here that we frequently use to remind ourselves of the influence of timing: "There will be no wine before its time" and "It's never real until you face the gallows." The lesson we seem to learn over and over is that timing is everything. There is a right time and a "ripe" time that contributes to the readiness of the organization as a whole, and the individual specifically, to be open to learning and change.

Wendy Baker, RN, MS, former director, Center for Patient Care Innovation; and project director, Strengthening Hospital Nursing Program, Vanderbilt University Hospital and Vanderbilt Clinic, Nashville, TN

Our key findings about organizational and individual readiness for change and learning may be summed up with the following observations:

External influences accelerate the readiness for change and learning.

We have been constructing new models of care delivery, implementing skill-mix changes, conducting health care finance and budgeting classes, and providing workshops on change and transition. All of these efforts, even if well designed, ring hollow for many individuals until they become bombarded with health care reform news on the radio, TV, and newspaper. When Peter Jennings from ABC News came to Vanderbilt to base a week-long series on health care reform, that got attention! Unfortunately, it takes that kind of emphasis for some individuals to make the connection between what is happening globally to what is happening locally. In our experience, readiness to learn is very much influenced by external influences.

A common vision accelerates learning and positions individuals for change.

There is a biblical reference that says: "Without a vision, the people perish." We have found that to be true. In our evaluation of several task forces for operations improvement, we critically examined our "lessons learned" by listing what worked and what did not. Consistently, what accelerated learning and tangible outcomes was clear vision. Where a clear vision was absent, readiness for change, learning, and action were inhibited.

Individuals can hold back the system; the system can hold back individuals.

We have discovered an age-old truth: Paradox is a way of life. Sometimes individuals are out ahead of the organization, poised and ready for change, but for various reasons, feel held back by a system. At other times, the organization is well ahead of individuals, pushing for change, saying you have permission—just do something! On the other hand, those willing to take risks, who identify learning needs and set about meeting them instead of waiting for permission, are still sometimes held back by old systems. We are discovering collaborative processes that will help us with designing systems where both the individuals and the organization can respond to change together.

Common skills can accelerate learning and change.

Although universal consistency in style is not our goal, it has been very useful to incorporate similar principles of facilitation and collaboration which have proven very productive in our organization and other institutions. The modeling and practice of these skills has accelerated the readiness of others to learn how to make work easier through facilitation and collaboration skills.

Just-in-time learning must become the way we do business.

We must continue to design learning experiences where learners can apply skills and concepts immediately and can be supported to do so. This is a cornerstone principle of adult learning. The challenge is designing just in time, or what we have come to affectionately call, "barely in time!" Gone are the days of tweaking things until they are perfect. This is requiring a major culture shift for us.

Karen L. Turner, EdD, training specialist, Center for Patient Care Innovation, Vanderbilt University Hospital and Vanderbilt Clinic, Nashville, TN

Obtaining Commitment from Leadership

A clear mandate from the leadership of the organization *must* be present. It is critical that leadership develop a vision for the learning organization and commit to it. Further, their commitment must be clearly formulated and articulated throughout the organization. It is not enough to have a general conceptual agreement; leadership must work out the specifics. They must agree that:

- Their commitment will be long term.
- They will walk the talk.
- Resources will be committed.
- Organizational structures and processes will be aligned with the vision.

Mixed messages are disastrous—for example, saying that individuals must be responsible for their own learning but dictating exactly what learning the organization will support, or saying that teams must learn to make decisions but building in checkpoints or sending messages about what can and cannot change.

The leader's job is to articulate the vision in order to make it a common vision in the organization. This means not only talking the talk but also walking the talk, modeling commitment to one's own learning, modeling the advocacy and inquiry skills necessary for team learning, and systematically integrating learning into organizational structures and processes to ensure organizational learning. In addition, leadership cannot expect to build a learning culture without rewarding learning. Most organizations will need to concentrate considerable attention on learning at the top to get this level of commitment.

Building a Common Vocabulary

An important effect of leadership clearly and repeatedly articulating the vision is that a common vocabulary begins to evolve that will accelerate learning in the organization. The vision contains the key concepts and words to build on. For example, Ackoff's interactive process begins with an idealized design of the future an organization wants to create.[7] Although *ideal* and *design* are clearly English words and English-speaking people have definitions for them, the phrase *idealized design* is not common to most vocabularies. Thus, a common definition must be developed. Another phrase in Ackoff's interactive vocabulary is "formulation of the MESS," the complex system of interacting problems. This phrase presents a slightly different problem. Most people have the word *mess* in their vocabularies, and there is even a common meaning. The problem here is developing a new common meaning.

A common vocabulary accelerates learning because once the basic terms are known and assimilated, learners can turn their attention to deeper understanding of the concepts. This is especially important to team learning. Most early team efforts include a struggle to develop shared meanings for words and concepts. We also have seen dysfunctional teams where usually just a member or two keep a team from moving forward by endlessly arguing over precise definitions of words.

Changing Management Style

A facilitative rather than a hierarchical management style accelerates learning, but often is one of the most difficult changes an organization must make. Managers using a facilitative style focus on getting excellent results through the involvement of others. This does not mean doing everything by consensus but, rather, through maximum appropriate involvement. Of course, many factors influence management style: age, gender, experience, personal style, tenure in the organization, and level in the organization. It is not uncommon for top-level, middle, and frontline managers to have different styles. The usual pattern we have seen is for top-level managers to make the shift to facilitative styles more easily than other levels. Middle-level managers, the target of many downsizing efforts, are a particularly beleaguered group in today's organizations. They also are frequently managers who have risen through the ranks and have more tenure in the organization. For managers who see their roles in terms of supervising, the shift to being a facilitative leader is very tough and very threatening.

Facilitative management styles accelerate learning because teams can more quickly get past issues such as who is in charge, what will the manager think, and can we really make these decisions ourselves. Even with facilitative leadership, at first, teams frequently do not believe they really can make decisions themselves. Practitioners at Beth Israel Hospital in Boston stress the importance of sharing information to get people involved.

The most important aspect of managing change involves helping people to feel a part of it. To feel left out of the planning stage spawns a feeling of resentment and resistance to change. Sharing information is empowering whereas lacking information is frightening. Change, even with information, involves uncertainty. We encourage managers to share all the information that they possibly can with their staff, despite the potential for a negative reaction. Managers are encouraged to ask their staff what they have heard so that they can dispel myths and rumors which frequently are more troublesome than the facts. Staff should be clear about what they have control over and what they do not. Managers are encouraged to take their staff along on their own journey of learning about potential changes that could affect them so that they can feel an integral part of the process. Our philosophy (under most circumstances) involves a "no-surprises" tactic.

Leslie Ajl, RN, MS, psychiatric liaison nurse, Beth Israel Hospital, Boston

Developing Skills for Building Trust

The advocacy and inquiry skills of true dialogue accelerate learning by building trust. There is little possibility for learning when key issues are undiscussable.[8] When team members protect themselves with defensive routines, learning is not happening for either the individual or the team. Briefly, *advocacy* is the ability to present your own mental models and your own rationale for proposed actions, whereas *inquiry* is the ability to inquire into the mental models and rationale of others and listen as an ally. Sometimes people say one thing and do another because they hold beliefs of which they are unaware. Surfacing hidden beliefs requires a level of trust that permits—and even invites—risk taking. Abbott Northwestern Hospital, in Minneapolis, measures gaps in trust and the effect on team performance.

> Abbott Northwestern uses an organizational effectiveness survey to assess employees' perception of the organization's performance as a whole. It is administered every other year to all employees. The survey was specifically designed to measure employee perceptions of how well the hospital was performing with respect to stated principles believed to be necessary for continued organizational success.
>
> One of the questions on the survey looks specifically at trust. The question is: To what extent do you have mutual trust and confidence with your boss? Responses on the survey are measured in terms of gap scores; the smaller the gap score, the more aligned employees are with the specific principles. The question about trust seems to be closely related to how effective various teams are in learning and engaging in true dialogue; the departments that have smaller gap scores experience better working relationships.
>
> *Ginger Malone, RN, MSN, director, innovation and consultation, Abbott Northwestern Hospital, Minneapolis*

Developing Analytic Skills

Common analytic skills accelerate learning at all levels. People learn best when they tackle real problems together in teams of peers. The statistical techniques of continuous improvement are particularly helpful because they provide data on the characteristics of problem situations as well as feedback on the effectiveness of various actions taken by the team. For example, flowcharting can be very useful in identifying all the pieces of a process as well as the interactions between the pieces. Using data to determine the effectiveness of team actions has the added advantage of integrating learning and work. People learn from their experience as they work when they reflect together on what they know about the problem and what has and has not worked to solve it.

Looking at Readiness for Change by Type of Learning

In the early stages of a large-scale organizational change effort, it is a safe assumption that readiness is not uniformly there, that it varies a great deal throughout the organization. Readiness varies by individual, level in the organization, department, and type of learning: individual, team, or organizational.

Individual Learning

Most professionals have navigated school successfully. They have had at least the success of completing their basic programs, many of them very rigorous. The more individuals have been involved in formal education, the better they are at it and the more confident they are in their own learning skills. But hospitals employ many, many individuals who have had minimal experience with school—or whose school experiences were not very successful.

Team Learning

Previous school success does not necessarily increase readiness for team learning. Argyris makes a strong case for why it may be even harder for smart people to learn because they are too invested in being right![9] Learning to learn together—what he calls *double-loop learning*—is more difficult because it involves learning to deal with threat and embarrassment, which call up defensive routines. When learners choose to protect themselves over learning, only single-loop learning can occur. Previous success in school also sets the learner up for looking for one right answer and for discounting the opinions of those without so much formal education, both of which are impediments to team learning.

Organizational Learning

Readiness builds with successes, although they may be small at first. Many teams start with small decisions that matter to them, but do not really challenge basic systems. As learners experience success, they are ready to take on bigger challenges. Organizational learning takes place when teams learn from one another and integrate learning into their work and the basic structures of the organization (for example, organizational systems for recognizing outstanding achievement).

Leebov's Willing and Able Matrix

Leebov provides another view of readiness, where people have the "right combination of attitude and abilities, enhanced skills, and the right mind-set."[10] (See figure 4-2.)

Obviously, the individual, team, or organization that is willing and able is most ready for change. Those who are willing but unable probably will respond well to learning opportunities. However, those who are unwilling, whether they are able or not, probably cannot make the transition to the culture of the learning organization. This matrix is particularly helpful in today's hospital environment which requires making tough downsizing and retooling decisions.

Using a Readiness Tool

Before embarking on large-scale organizational change, it may be useful to assess readiness within groups that will be involved. The Nursing Unit Cultural Assessment Tool (NUCAT-2) has been used successfully by several hospitals in the Vermont Nursing Initiative (VNI) and is shown in figure 4-3 (pp. 59–62). Carol Haraden of VNI explains how this tool is used.

> As part of the evaluation plan for the Vermont Nursing Initiative Project, three hospitals have used the Nursing Unit Cultural Analysis Tool: Version 2 (NUCAT-2) to assess a unit's readiness to embrace work redesign. The tool is administered to nurses from individual units, which allows a comparison both within and across hospital structures. The results are used to: (1) assess the staff's readiness for change, (2) identify potential pockets of resistance, and (3) target areas for change. Armed with this kind of information, the nursing leadership is better able to understand how variables affect and/or will be affected by implementation of new care delivery systems.
>
> Restructuring, designed to change the way we "do business," impacts the culture of a unit which is largely shaped by formal and informal rules governing day-to-day practices and procedures, well-established work habits/patterns, and preexisting attitudes of management and staff. Changes to any one or all of these "cultural elements" usually accompany a work redesign effort and often become the reason(s) why these kinds of efforts meet with resistance. Therefore, because the culture of a unit directly affects the outcome of work redesign efforts, it is

important to understand the culture of each unit both before and after the restructuring work is completed.*

Carol Haraden, PhD, RN, staff development coordinator, Medical Center Hospital of Vermont, Burlington, VT, Morrisville, VT

Content to Be Learned

As we have seen, readiness for learning is certainly an important consideration in designing compelling learning experiences. Another, and perhaps even more important, consideration is the content the learner needs to learn. Chapter 3 discussed in detail the necessity for building a model for change that fits the context of the particular organization. The model for change becomes the framework for the content that must be learned to implement the model.

The model for change is used to carefully identify new ideas, behaviors, and skills that must be learned to move the organization in the desired direction. Appendix A includes detailed descriptions of numerous models for change that have been used in our organizations. Each model includes a section on key concepts that had to be learned to implement the ideas. Chapter 5 provides a discussion on how to fit the content to appropriate approaches, methods, and tools.

However, before looking at approaches, methods, and tools, it is important to reflect on some important questions about the content:

- How different are the new ideas from current practices and beliefs?
- Do the ideas conflict with any deeply held organizational values?

Figure 4-2. The Willing and Able Matrix

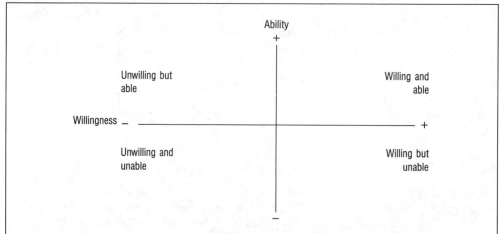

- *Willing and able managers* continuously develop their skills. They have a mind-set that motivates them to sharpen and use those skills in the service of solving real problems and making continuous improvements that result in increased customer satisfaction.

- *Willing but unable managers* lack the ability or persistence to acquire needed skills despite considerable drive to contribute to the organization's quality improvement.

- *Unwilling and unable managers* do not take steps to acquire the skills they need to improve quality. Also, they resist incorporating continuous improvement as an inherent part of their management responsibilities.

- *Unwilling but able managers* have the skills or the potential to learn the skills they need but lack the openness to incorporate these key skills into their everyday actions. Or the culture of the organization deflates their motivation and inclination to use the skills that they have.

Source: Leebov, W., and Ersoz, C. J. *The Health Care Manager's Guide to Continuous Quality Improvement.* Chicago: American Hospital Publishing, 1991, p. 19.

---

*The assessment of nursing unit culture is described more fully by Dr. Haraden in *Work and Role Redesign: Tools and Techniques for the Health Care Setting* (Chicago: American Hospital Publishing, 1995, pp. 141–46).

Figure 4-3. Nursing Unit Cultural Assessment Tool (NUCAT-2)

The primary purpose of this tool is to describe and understand your immediate work group in your practice setting. Your work group will likely consist of people who work the same hours on the same unit (section, department) as you do and with whom you have frequent contact. Many members of this work group will be members of the same profession as you are. However, there is no need to limit your work group to members of your profession. Think of your work group as consisting of all those who work closely with you, share your work-related values, and work with you to get the job done. These are the people you would describe as being "part of us."

The tool will describe your work group by picturing your group's culture. Culture has been defined as the set of solutions devised by a group of people to meet specific problems posed by the situations they face in common. In other words, it's "how we get things done around here."

There are no right or wrong answers for this tool. Rather, the primary goal of the tool is to understand how your group functions so that you can make the best decisions for the group.

The answers from all the members of your group will be added together to determine your group picture. In no way will anyone know the individual answers you give. Only group scores will be recorded.

You will notice the behaviors are listed down the center of the page. Please use the *left-hand column* to indicate your preferred behavior and the *right-hand column* to indicate your group's typical behavior. In each case, use the following scale to record your answers.

> 1 = not at all
> 2 = slightly
> 3 = quite
> 4 = extremely

Copyright © 1991 by Harriet Cooling

First, please circle and/or fill in the appropriate response:

(1) Unit _____

(2) Work status
   1. Full-time
   2. Part-time

(3) Age
   1. 18–30 years
   2. 31–40 years
   3. 41–50 years
   4. 51–60 years
   5. above 60

(4) Sex
   1. Female
   2. Male

(5) Years employed in nursing
   1. 0–1 years
   2. 2–4 years
   3. 5–9 years
   4. 10–15 years
   5. above 15 years

(6) Years in current job
   1. 0–1 years
   2. 2–4 years
   3. 5–9 years
   4. 10–15 years
   5. above 15 years

(7) Highest level of education
   1. Master's degree or higher
   2. Bachelor's degree
   3. RN diploma
   4. Associate degree
   5. LPN diploma
   6. Less than 1 year of training

(8) Type of practice pattern
   1. Functional
   2. Team
   3. Modular
   4. Primary
   5. Other: _____

(9) Position
   1. RN
   2. LPN
   3. Other: _____

(10) Shift
   1. Days—8 hours
   2. Evenings—8 hours
   3. Nights—8 hours
   4. Days—12 hours
   5. Nights—12 hours
   6. Days/evenings
   7. Days/nights
   8. Other: _____

My code number is:

_____

(Continued on next page)

Figure 4-3. (Continued)

Now please circle the appropriate number using this scale:

> 1 = not at all
> 2 = slightly
> 3 = quite
> 4 = extremely

My Preferred Behavior		My Group's Typical Behavior
1 2 3 4	(11) How important is it to understand the patient's feelings?	1 2 3 4
1 2 3 4	(12) How acceptable is it to refuse to help your coworkers when they ask for help?	1 2 3 4
1 2 3 4	(13) How important is it to work in an efficient manner?	1 2 3 4
1 2 3 4	(14) How important is it to follow nursing policies and procedures?	1 2 3 4
1 2 3 4	(15) How important is it to be competent?	1 2 3 4
1 2 3 4	(16) How important is it to promote group morale?	1 2 3 4
1 2 3 4	(17) How important is it to follow the organizational chain of command?	1 2 3 4
1 2 3 4	(18) How acceptable is it to tell others how to do something if they haven't asked for advice?	1 2 3 4
1 2 3 4	(19) How important is it to work hard?	1 2 3 4
1 2 3 4	(20) How important is it to attend in-service classes?	1 2 3 4
1 2 3 4	(21) How important is it to be creative in the nursing care you give?	1 2 3 4
1 2 3 4	(22) How acceptable is it to do your work by yourself rather than working together with others?	1 2 3 4
1 2 3 4	(23) How important is it to be comfortable handling emergencies?	1 2 3 4
1 2 3 4	(24) How acceptable is it to question a physician's orders?	1 2 3 4
1 2 3 4	(25) How important is it to take on added professional responsibility either on or off the unit?	1 2 3 4
1 2 3 4	(26) How acceptable is it to disagree with your manager?	1 2 3 4
1 2 3 4	(27) How acceptable is it to try to change people's behavior by joking about it?	1 2 3 4
1 2 3 4	(28) How important is it to get together with your coworkers outside the hospital?	1 2 3 4
1 2 3 4	(29) How acceptable is it to call in sick when you are physically ill?	1 2 3 4
1 2 3 4	(30) How important is it to offer to help others even before they ask for help?	1 2 3 4
1 2 3 4	(31) How acceptable is it to tell someone directly, rather than indirectly, that you dislike their behavior?	1 2 3 4
1 2 3 4	(32) How important is it to go along with peer pressure in giving nursing care?	1 2 3 4
1 2 3 4	(33) How important is it to be nonjudgmental of someone else's behavior?	1 2 3 4
1 2 3 4	(34) How acceptable is it to discuss new nursing care ideas you have read or heard about?	1 2 3 4

Figure 4-3. (Continued)

My Preferred Behavior		My Group's Typical Behavior

1 2 3 4	(35) How acceptable is it to compete with your coworkers?	1 2 3 4
1 2 3 4	(36) How important is it to have one person, rather than the whole group, decide what nursing care is needed for a particular patient?	1 2 3 4
1 2 3 4	(37) How important is it to act on the latest ideas?	1 2 3 4
1 2 3 4	(38) How important is professional growth and development?	1 2 3 4
1 2 3 4	(39) How important is it to have fun while you are working?	1 2 3 4
1 2 3 4	(40) How acceptable is it to focus on maintaining life, rather than enabling death to be comfortable, when death is inevitable?	1 2 3 4
1 2 3 4	(41) How acceptable is it to use your individual judgment in deciding what nursing care to give?	1 2 3 4
1 2 3 4	(42) How acceptable is it to achieve clinical advancement and promotion?	1 2 3 4
1 2 3 4	(43) How important is it to care for your coworkers?	1 2 3 4
1 2 3 4	(44) How acceptable is it to call in sick when you need a day off to rest up?	1 2 3 4
1 2 3 4	(45) How important is it to provide emotional support for your coworkers?	1 2 3 4
1 2 3 4	(46) How important is it to attend college classes for a degree?	1 2 3 4
1 2 3 4	(47) How important is it to spend a lot of time on paperwork?	1 2 3 4
1 2 3 4	(48) How important is it to meet patients' physical needs before their psychosocial needs?	1 2 3 4
1 2 3 4	(49) How acceptable is it to ask a coworker for help directly, rather than indirectly, when you are falling behind?	1 2 3 4
1 2 3 4	(50) How important is it to follow the directions your head nurse (unit manager) gives you regarding patient care?	1 2 3 4
1 2 3 4	(51) How important is it to be comfortable in watching for life-threatening complications?	1 2 3 4
1 2 3 4	(52) How important is it to become involved in the personal lives of patients and families?	1 2 3 4
1 2 3 4	(53) How acceptable is it to be assertive with your coworkers?	1 2 3 4
1 2 3 4	(54) How important is it to teach patients?	1 2 3 4
1 2 3 4	(55) How acceptable is it to tell others directly what to do, rather than give them ideas about what they could do?	1 2 3 4
1 2 3 4	(56) How important is it to make patients comfortable?	1 2 3 4
1 2 3 4	(57) How important is it to learn new techniques?	1 2 3 4
1 2 3 4	(58) How acceptable is it to prefer the old ways of doing things, rather than to look for new ways?	1 2 3 4
1 2 3 4	(59) How acceptable is it to stay angry with someone longer than a day?	1 2 3 4
1 2 3 4	(60) How acceptable is it to share your personal and/or family concerns with your coworkers?	1 2 3 4

Thank you for completing this tool.

(Continued on next page)

Figure 4-3.   (Continued)

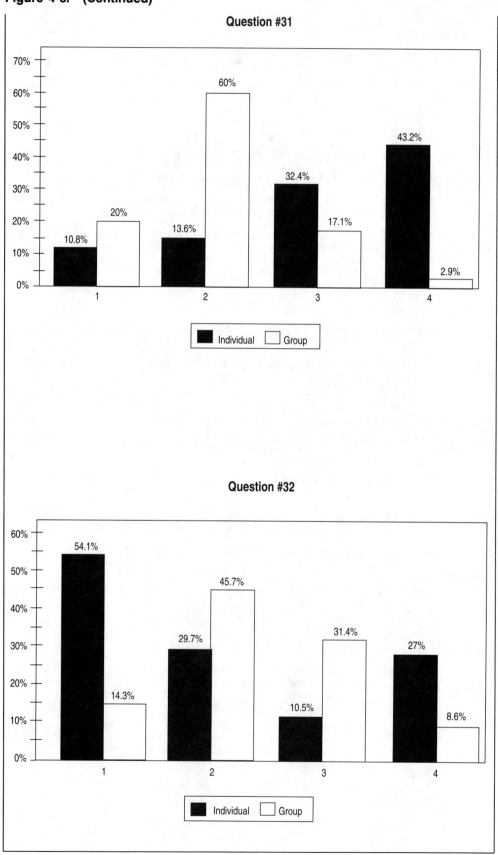

Source: Vermont Nursing Initiative.

- How abstract are the ideas?
- How do the ideas build on one another?
- What behaviors will need to change?
- Which ideas must be learned before behavior can change?
- Can ideas be learned independently?
- How long will it take to learn new ideas and behaviors?
- Who has to learn them?
- Do some have to learn them first?
- If everyone needs to learn them, does everyone need to learn them to the same extent?

These questions should help give some sense of the concepts, behaviors, and skills that need to be learned, by whom, and in what order.

Another element to consider is whether the content needs to be learned primarily at the individual, team, or organizational level. Although many concepts need to be learned at all levels, some are more appropriately learned at a particular level. Examples of content learning at one level might include:

- *Individual content:* Systems thinking, statistical process control skills
- *Team content:* Mental models, advocacy and inquiry skills
- *Organizational content:* Integration of learning and work, mechanisms for teams to learn from one another, reward and recognition structures

Only when it is clear what must be learned and by whom can learner characteristics of those particular groups be considered.

Learner Characteristics

The characteristics of the learner also must be considered in the design of learning experiences. This section discusses the influences of learning styles, characteristics of adult learners, and learner mix.

Learning Styles

In the not too distant past, discussions of learning styles referred only to individual differences. Now we know that individuals, teams, even organizations can have distinctive learning styles. An understanding of dominant styles and preferences is very important in designing learning experiences. There are a variety of models for describing and instruments for measuring learning styles. This subsection describes two of them: the Gregorc Style Delineator and the Myers-Briggs Type Indicator (MBTI).

The Gregorc Style Delineator is an instrument widely used in educational institutions. It is self-administered and results in an individual style profile called a Mind Style™. The two dimensions are concrete/abstract and sequential/random.[11] The four mediation channels are concrete/sequential, concrete/random, abstract/sequential, and abstract/random. The style characteristics of each are described in table 4-1.

The MBTI can be used by both individuals and teams, and is widely used in a variety of organizations. It uses 4 dimensions of human behavior to describe 16 personality types and 4 temperaments. These types are said to be a judgment-free way of explaining normal behavior. Using the MBTI is not so much a way of labeling people, but of understanding and celebrating differences.

The four dimensions are:

1. **E**xtroverted or **I**ntroverted
2. **S**ensing or i**N**tuitive

Table 4-1. Gregorc Style Comparisons

Frames of Reference	Mediation Channels			
	CS Concrete Sequential	AS Abstract Sequential	AR Abstract Random	CR Concrete Random
Key Words	Practical	Probable	Potential	Possible
World of Reality	Concrete world of the physical senses	Abstract world of the intellect based upon concrete world	Abstract world of feeling and emotion	Concrete world of activity and abstract world of intuition
Ordering Ability	Sequential step-by-step linear progression	Sequential and two-dimensional; treelike	Random weblike and multidimensional	Random three-dimensional patterns
View of Time	Discrete units of past, present, future	The present, historical past, and projected future	The moment: time is artificial and restrictive	Now: total of the past, interactive present, and seed for the future
Thinking Process	Instinctive, methodical, deliberate	Intellectual, logical, analytical, correlative	Emotional, psychic, perceptive, critical	Intuitive, instinctive, impulsive, independent
Validation Process	Personal proof via the senses; accredited experts	Personal intellectual formulae; conventionally accredited experts	Inner guidance system	Practical demonstration; personal proof; rarely accepting of outside authority
Focus of Attention	Material reality; physical objects	Knowledge, facts, documentation, concepts, ideas	Emotional attachments, relationships, and memories	Applications, methods, processes, and ideals
Creativity	Product, prototype, refinement, duplication	Synthesis, theories, models, and matrices	Imagination, the arts, refinement, relationships	Intuition, originality, inventive, and futuristic
Environmental Preference	Ordered, practical, quiet, stable	Mentally stimulating, ordered and quiet, nonauthoritative	Emotional and physical freedom; rich; active and colorful	Stimulus-rich, competitive, free from restriction
Use of Language	Literal meaning and labels, succinct, logical	Polysyllabic words, precise, rational; highly verbal	Metaphoric, uses gestures and body language; colorful	Informative, lively, colorful; "words do not convey true meaning"
Primary Evaluative Word(s)	Good, not bad	Excellent	Super, fantastic, marvelous	Great, superior
Negative Characteristics	Excessive conformity; unfeeling, possessive	Opinionated, sarcastic, aloof	Spacey, overly sensual, smothering	Deceitful, unscrupulous, egocentric

Source: Reprinted, with permission, from Gregorc Associates, Inc., Columbia, CT, 1982.

3. **T**hinking or **F**eeling
4. **J**udging or **P**erceiving

The 16 types are all the combinations of the above. (See figure 4-4.)

Two letters may be combined to produce four types, called temperaments, about which predictions can be made—in this case about teaching and learning. The four temperaments are related to observable behaviors and core values. They are: SJ, NF, SP, and NT. The first letter of temperament is S or N, meaning the preference for information gathering. The second letter refers to how you prefer to evaluate the data you have gathered (objective [T] or subjective [F]), or to what you prefer to do with the data (organize them [J] or continue to seek more [P]). (See figure 4-5.)

Recently, types and temperaments have been applied to teams and team learning.[12] Generally, team type and temperament are determined by looking at the types of the majority of the individuals on the team. Team types are described in figures 4-6 and 4-7 (pp. 67 and 68).

Figure 4-8 (p. 69) shows ways to introduce change grouped into four quadrants, each labeled by the first two letters of the type formula—IS, ES, IN, and EN. These quadrants reflect how a person or team might react to change. (Using this understanding of individual and team learning styles to design learning experiences is discussed in chapter 5.)

Characteristics of Adult Learners

In the past, much of what we knew about learning was based on how kids learned. And although some general principles may hold, adults are not much like kids. Adults bring so much more to the learning situation: more experience, more responsibilities, less time. They are dealing with more complexity in their lives than kids. Although adults are not necessarily less emotional, they hide their feelings better.

Thus, it is not surprising that adult learning has been a respected field for many years. However, what we know about adult learners is based on adult participation in formal learning experiences, not learning in the workplace or in learning organizations.

Nonetheless, we know that learning is a choice: People learn whatever they want to learn. The adult learner is particularly pragmatic, and usually will want to learn something he or she needs to know—for example, to solve a problem, advance a career, obtain a new position, or make more money.

Figure 4-4. Myers-Briggs Personality Types

ISTJ "Doing what should be done"	ISFJ "A high sense of duty"	INFJ "An inspiration to others"	INTJ "Everything has room for improvement"
ISTP "Ready to try anything once"	ISFP "Sees much but shares little"	INFP "Performing noble service to aid society"	INTP "A love of problem solving"
ESTP "The ultimate realists"	ESFP "You only go around once in life"	ENFP "Giving life an extra squeeze"	ENTP "One exciting challenge after another"
ESTJ "Life's administrators"	ESFJ "Hosts and hostesses of the world"	ENFJ "Smooth-talking persuaders"	ENTJ "Life's natural leaders"

Source: From *Type Talk: How to Determine Your Personality* by Otto Kroeger and Janet M. Thuesen. Copyright © 1988 by Otto Kroeger and Janet M. Thuesen. Used by permission of Dell Books, a division of Bantam Doubleday Dell Publishing Group, Inc.

Figure 4-5. Myers-Briggs Learning Temperaments

Everyone has the capacity to learn, but each type and Temperament has a unique style. Here are the learning profiles of the four Temperaments, courtesy of Dr. Keith Golay, a therapeutic counselor in Fullerton, California, who applies Temperament theory in matching methods and approaches to clients' types.

NFs

Will be most responsive when learning *about:*
1. The value the various species have to cultures
2. How to communicate to people about endangered species and their protection
3. The issue of humane treatment of captured and protected animals
4. The effects that laws and enforcement have on people; do they in turn infringe on the rights of people

Will be most responsive when learning *by:*
1. Writing letters to various people
2. Reading books on the subject and doing a paper
3. Doing role playing to display problems with people
4. Giving the class a speech on the subject
5. Working in small groups and sharing information
6. Designing a means to communicate about endangered species to the public, or setting up a campaign to inform the public about the needs of endangered species

NTs

Will be most responsive when learning *about:*
1. Problem solving—How to collect and analyze information related to endangered species
2. Ethology—How to collect and analyze information on the habits and needs of each species
3. Predicting—How to generate a prognosis for each species if various conditions do or don't exist
4. Explaining Why???

Will be most responsive when learning *by:*
1. Doing research in the library
2. Talking with an ethologist at a university
3. Reading books on the subject
4. Giving a lecture to the class
5. Having a debate on the pluses and minuses
6. Designing a test for students

SJs

Will be most responsive when learning *about:*
1. The laws, policies, and governmental agencies related to endangered species
2. How to care for animals once they are caught
3. How to collect and categorize the data related to the habits and needs of each type of animal
4. Keeping account of the various animals—collecting and storing information
5. How to disseminate information to others
6. New laws needed to enforce protection

Will be most responsive when learning *by:*
1. Writing for information
2. Going to the library and getting information
3. Interviewing people for information—designing an interview format to use, i.e., the questions to ask
4. Giving the class a talk on the subject
5. Collecting information from the government and putting it in a document

SPs

Will be most responsive when learning *about:*
1. Locating and capturing the animals
2. How to set up game reserves and build facilities to care for the various animals
3. People who locate and capture hunters and poachers
4. The current methods of enforcing laws

Will be most responsive when learning *by:*
1. Interviewing people
2. Viewing films on the subject
3. Visiting a game reserve, taking pictures to show in class, acquiring films to show to class on the subject
4. Drawing pictures to portray information
5. Constructing a reserve to display information

Why Adults Participate in Learning

In a classic book on adult learning, Cross explains her model for understanding adult participation in learning activities.[13] (See figure 4-9, p. 69.) The relevant variables and their interrelationships can be summarized as follows:

(A) *Self-evaluation:* If learners have self-confidence in their learning abilities, they will accept the risk in learning new things because they expect to succeed.[14]

(B) *Attitudes about education:* Learners are influenced by their own experience as well as the attitudes and opinions of others. Positive attitudes are contagious. Learners can "catch the interest from others around them."[15]

The bidirectional arrow between (A) and (B) suggests a reinforcing relationship; that is, adult learners who like learning and do well at it are likely to develop high self-confidence which in turn contributes to doing well in learning experiences.

(C) *Importance of goals and expectation that participation will meet goals:* "Participation must be successful" and "must accomplish the learner's goals," which suggests that goals must be apparent and that internal rewards may be the most important.[16] The reverse arrow suggests that expectancy is related to self-esteem; that is, learners with high self-esteem expect to be successful in learning experiences.

(D) *Life transitions:* The need to adapt to life changes is a powerful motivator for adults.[17]

Figure 4-6.   MBTI 4-Scale Team Questionnaire

Overuse of E			**Overuse of I**
This team talks and acts without much forethought.	There is a good balance of action and reflection on this team.		This team reflects too long before acting.
Overuse of S			**Overuse of N**
This team gets bogged down in details and misses the big picture.	This team has an appropriate balance of detail and big picture.		This team is too "pie in the sky" and overlooks reality.
Overuse of T			**Overuse of F**
This team overlooks the way that people react.	This team has an appropriate balance between tasks and people.		This team overlooks tasks that need to be done.
Overuse of J			**Overuse of P**
This team closes off options before giving them due consideration.	This team reaches a decision after appropriate consideration.		This team is unable to come to a conclusion and goes off on tangents.

(E) *Opportunities and barriers:* Opening up opportunities is just as important as removing barriers, but adults may not always be truthful about the importance of barriers; for example, not enough time may be an excuse.[18] The reverse arrow suggests that when motivation is weak, even small barriers may block participation.

(F) *Information:* The factors above may mean that the information about the learning opportunity is not actually received by the learner.[19]

(G) *Participation:* The chain of responses to the factors above determines whether the adult learner will participate in the learning opportunity.[20] The arrow from (G) to (AB) suggests that those who do participate are more likely to participate again.

This model reminds us of the importance of the learner's past experiences with learning as well as the importance of the learner's goals and life stage. Further, it reminds us that elimination of external barriers probably will not result in participation for those learners with low self-confidence and low expectations for success. For them, structuring successful learning experiences — even small successes — will be far more important.

Figure 4-7. MBTI Team Frustrations and Type Dialogue

ISTJ *Stop working so hard!*	**ISFJ** *Stop worrying about everyone!*	**INFJ** *Stop staring off into space!*	**INTJ** *Stop being so stubborn!*
Projects get done when we pay attention to facts and to what needs to happen now. Play comes later.	Each team member matters. Attention to each person's needs and wants helps us function well.	Thinking about the future and its implications for our team is vital to team productivity.	A team's vision that's well thought out is worth fighting for.
ISTP *Stop nit-picking!*	**ISFP** *Stop wearing your heart on your sleeve!*	**INFP** *Stop feeling hurt!*	**INTP** *Stop being so theoretical!*
Precision and accuracy of information allows our team to produce good work.	Caring for our teammates displays our humanity and can translate into increased team involvement.	Exploring our deeply held beliefs and values keeps this team on the right path.	Teams need to develop models and carefully analyze concepts before they can begin effective work.
ESTP *Stop being so blunt!*	**ESFP** *Stop playing!*	**ENFP** *Stop changing your mind and the team's direction!*	**ENTP** *Stop generating new actions!*
Sometimes this team needs a jolt to get it back to work.	Life should be lived; work should be enjoyed. Happy people are productive people.	This team needs to explore all options as it gets down to work.	Entrepreneurial teams keep business coming in.
ESTJ *Stop driving things so hard!*	**ESFJ** *Stop socializing!*	**ENFJ** *Stop talking!*	**ENTJ** *Stop trying to manage us!*
Some tough work needs to be done right now.	Friends and relationships keep people committed and loyal to the team.	Knowing each team member well is one of the things that holds this team together.	Someone needs to take charge.

Physical Issues

A great deal is known about the relationship between the physical changes of aging and their impact on the ability of the adult to learn. It now seems clear that if there is an age limit on learning performance, it probably is not until after age 75.[21]

The primary aging issues that influence learning are changes in reaction time, vision, and hearing. The time for learning new things increases with age. Vision, particularly in low-light situations, deteriorates with age. And hearing losses become apparent, especially in situations with background noise. In addition, women lose acuity for lower-pitch sounds and men for higher-pitch. Older women can hear women's voices better, older men can hear men's

Figure 4-8. Introducing Change to the MBTI Quadrants

Ways to introduce change to an IS	**Ways to introduce change to an IN**
• *Relate it to what I know* • Make practical sense to me • Change at a steady pace, step by step • Be careful and mindful of details • Give me time to think about it • Change "the way things are done around here" *only* from necessity	• *Relate it to new theories and concepts* • Let me work on change that has impact, especially conceptually and with ideas • Don't burden me with routines; let me change at my own pace, swiftly or slowly, as I think I need to • Let me set my own quality control and standards • Let me work with my own ideas • Change the ideas and concepts
Ways to introduce change to an ES	**Ways to introduce change to an EN**
• *Relate it to the work I do* • Show me the practical results change will bring • Offer a steady progression, step by step • Be realistic with the schedule and don't expect too much too soon • Let me "hash it over" with others • Show me that my work will be more effective if I make the change	• *Relate it to changing things in my world* • Challenge my imagination • Minimize the routine, maximize the variety • Let me work on the broad focus and overview of the change • Let me brainstorm with others and try out my ideas to see if they work and how people react to them • Let me try to change the world

Source: Modified and reproduced by special permission of the publisher, Consulting Psychologists Press, Inc., Palo Alto, CA 94303 from *MBTI Team Building Program* by Sandra K. Hirsh. Copyright 1992 by Consulting Psychologists Press, Inc. All rights reserved. Further reproduction is prohibited without the publisher's written consent.

Figure 4-9. Chain of Response (COR) Model for Understanding Adult Participation in Learning Activities

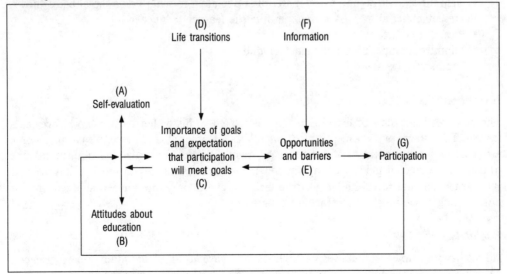

Source: Cross, K. P. *Adults as Learners: Increasing Participation and Facilitating Learning.* San Francisco: Jossey-Bass, 1981, p. 124.

voices better (something people in long-term marriages have known all along!). Fortunately, it is possible to compensate for these losses by:

- Increasing the time for learning
- Wearing glasses
- Increasing the amount of light
- Using hearing aids
- Decreasing background noise

Intellectual Issues

Learning ability—intelligence—probably remains stable throughout life. There are two generally recognized forms of intelligence: fluid and crystallized. *Fluid intelligence,* thought to be innate, plays an important role in problem solving and determines how well we see complex relationships, form concepts, and reason. It is relatively formless and is independent of experience and education. Tests for fluid intelligence include memory span, spatial perception, and adaptation to new or novel situations. Fluid intelligence peaks in adolescence. *Crystallized intelligence* is related to acquired abilities such as verbal comprehension, numerical skills and reasoning, judgment, knowledge, and experience. Tests for crystallized intelligence include vocabulary, general information, and experience. Crystallized intelligence increases up to about age 60, then what happens depends on what the person is doing. Active learners can increase their learning ability well into later life. Fortunately, the two forms of intelligence are complementary, with one decreasing as the other increases. Older learners also learn how to compensate. They are said to "substitute wisdom for brilliance." They also tend to compensate for less speed with more accuracy and fewer trial-and-error risks.[22]

It may be that different life stages require different learning abilities because "the greatest problems with memory occur with meaningless learning, complex learning and the learning of new things which require the reassessment of old learning."[23] Again, according to Cross, "complex learning and distraction are especially difficult for older learners because they have accumulated large stores of information, and scanning the stored information for recall takes longer, especially if the new information is inadequately associated with stored information. Older learners have the most difficulty with both initial learning and subsequent recall when learning tasks are fast paced, complex or unusual."[24]

Following are some suggested strategies to compensate for the intellectual issues of the adult learner:

- Make sure new material is meaningful.
- Help the learner organize new material and relate it to what he or she already knows.
- Present material at a pace that permits the learner to master it.
- Present one idea at a time.
- Minimize competing intellectual demands.
- Summarize frequently.

Emotional Issues

The adult learner's view of learning usually is related to his or her earlier experiences as a learner. They shape one's perceptions of oneself as a learner. These perceptions can become a barrier and could make the "difference between a lifetime of active learning versus one of isolated provincialism."[25] We may underestimate the importance of these barriers because the learner may not reveal his or her true feelings, giving only more acceptable reasons for not wanting to be involved in learning experiences.

Social Issues

Adults have multiple roles and responsibilities, and have accumulated many life experiences. They have passed through a number of physical, psychological, and social phases, and have experienced ambivalence and anxiety. And their diversity increases with age.

In his classic work on andragogy (the art and science of helping adults learn), Malcolm Knowles identifies the key characteristics of adult learners:[26]

- Adults are motivated to learn as they experience needs and interests that learning will satisfy; therefore, these are the appropriate points for organizing such activities.
- Adult orientation to learning is life centered; therefore, the appropriate units for organizing adult learning are life situations, not subjects.
- Experience is the richest resource for adult learning; therefore, the core methodology of adult education is the analysis of experience.
- Adults have a deep need to be self-directing; therefore, the role of the instructor is to engage in a process of mutual inquiry with them, rather than to transmit personal expert knowledge and then evaluate their acquisition of it.
- Individual differences among people increase with age; therefore, adult education must make optimal provision for differences in style, time, and place of learning.

The educational services staff at MeritCare Hospital have developed the matrix in table 4-2 to show the relationship between the concept to be learned, principles for children and adults, and practice implementations.

Learning occurs at a different pace depending on the learner. The adult learner will not soak up material the way a child will. He or she must assimilate new thinking until it fits with the old or until the old is rejected and replaced with the new. The individual can be caught in a struggle while this is in process. It is very important to individual and organizational learning

Table 4-2. Practice Implications for Adult Learning

Concept	Principles	Practice Implications
Self-concept	Child: Dependent Adult: Makes own decisions Self-directed Resents being talked down to, being judged, treated with lack of respect	1. Identify own learning needs. 2. Involved in planning process. 3. Teacher is advisor/resource. 4. Learner selects options. 5. Learner evaluates progress toward outcomes. 6. Teacher evaluates program.
Experience	Child: Little experience; one-way communication Adult: Vast experience contributes to self-identity and self-esteem	1. Retain and use information that can be integrated with past experience. 2. Information that conflicts with past is more slowly integrated. 3. Utilize teaching methods that incorporate past experiences. 4. Practice application to current life. 5. Utilize strategies that help become more open-minded.
Readiness to learn	Child: Basic skill building Adult: Ready to learn when encounter a problem or concern	1. Organize learning to coincide with identified needs rather than logical sequence. 2. Group learners with similar needs and interests. 3. Teacher must recognize existing concerns of learners.
Time perspective (orientation to learning)	Child: Subject centered, future oriented Adult: Problem centered, present oriented	1. Learners identify what they "need to know." 2. Content organized around identified needs.

Source: Developed by Educational Services, MeritCare Hospital, Fargo, ND.

to accept the individual at whatever level of learning he or she has achieved and allow verbalization of difficulty with understanding and acceptance. It's OK to be where you are. It's just not OK to stay there.

Joan Futch, RN, MSHA, CNAA, senior vice-president, nursing services, Tallahassee Memorial Regional Medical Center, Tallahassee, FL

Additional Learner Characteristics

A number of other learner characteristics must be taken into account in designing learning experiences in organizations. Based on our experiences in building learning organizations in hospitals and hospital systems, the characteristics we have found to be particularly important are limited reading, writing, and analytic skills, and cultural and ethnic diversity.

Limited Reading, Writing, and Analytic Skills

Many health care professionals working in hospitals have limited writing and analytic skills. Although some preparation is required in these areas, many professionals have little need to write anything other than short phrases describing observations. However, writing is important to learning from one another. Often the only way to know if there really is team agreement is to work at capturing the ideas in writing. Writing also is important to the transfer of learning between teams. When teams learn from one another and integrate that learning into organizational structures and processes, organizations can learn.

Most clinicians have very limited math and statistical skills, which are the foundation of continuous improvement. Further, in our culture, it is all too common for women to see themselves as not good at math. Statistical techniques and quality tools still are not part of the clinician's background, although they now are being taught in elementary school.

Adult literacy also is a serious issue for many hospitals. It is not uncommon to have a large percentage of workers who are not functionally literate—that is, who can neither read nor write. Many hospitals operate workplace literacy programs to give workers an opportunity to learn to read and write.

Cultural and Ethnic Diversity

Never has the work force in hospitals been more diverse on most any measure—different languages spoken, different cultures, different ethnicity. Hospitals reflect their communities. In many communities, the majority language is not English. At Harbor-UCLA Medical Center, in Los Angeles, they are building a community of patient care leaders despite the fact that 22 languages are spoken by their staff.

Different cultures have different mental models about learning. In some cultures, teachers are more likely to be seen as having the answers. In some cultures, gender role differences spill over to team learning situations, as do conflicts between ethnic groups. The key to keeping these differences from becoming barriers to learning is to help learners surface and deal effectively with their mental models.

The Mix of Learners

Another factor to consider in designing learning experiences is the mix of learners. Learners represent different disciplines, knowledge and skill bases, positions, departments, even old versus new organizational cultures. Certainly, there may be times when a learning experience is designed for a single department or a single discipline. But in a learning organization, it is important to learn to learn together—physicians and nurses, accountants and programmers, housekeepers and technicians. Our organizations have discovered the importance of learning together and understanding the wide range of diversity in learning styles and experiences.

There was some concern about the varying expertise among our first few clinical partner orientation groups. We were shifting FTEs [full-time equivalents] from various support areas to the bedside with the initiation of this new role. The class participants included phlebotomists, nurse assistants, EKG techs, nutrition techs, and others.

We decided to approach the development of this new role as an opportunity for adult learners to share their expertise with each other while learning to function as a clinical partner. The result was reflected in a cohesion among the learners and an atmosphere of collegial support in the classroom, lab, and on the clinical units. This approach acted to reduce some anxiety among the learners as well. Their valuable contribution to the group was both recognized and encouraged.

Fran La Monica, RN, MS, professional development and special projects coordinator, Mercy Hospital and Medical Center, Chicago

We have incorporated the use of the Myers-Briggs Type Indicator to help us with understanding differences in preferences for gathering information and making decisions, especially in teams. Personality type can have significant implications for communication and the design of learning experiences.

We have found that real-world application is very important for many types, especially sensing types. Understanding the background and the foundation of key concepts is important for many intuitive types. What we have realized, through general population statistics, is that many direct patient caregivers prefer sensing (a more practical, detailed, realistic, "now" approach), and generally, more administrators/executives prefer intuition (a more big picture, abstract, inventive, future-oriented approach). Many of the change efforts in which we have been engaged are ambiguous, broad systems changes, where we are literally discovering the answers as we go. Knowing that this sort of open-ended, big-picture approach is not appealing to all personality types, we have consciously tried to change the language of learning and incorporate a lot more application practice sessions to focus more specifically on everyday worklife issues.

Karen L. Turner, EdD, training specialist, Center for Patient Care Innovation, Vanderbilt University Hospital and Vanderbilt Clinic, Nashville, TN

We have found that the Myers-Briggs Type Indicator (MBTI) is an extraordinarily useful instrument at Abbott Northwestern. We have been using it primarily in personal mastery, a three-day retreat for nursing staff members, and in team learning endeavors. To date, more than 1,500 employees have taken the indicator, as well as our medical board members and their spouses. It provides a method for meaningful dialogue to better understand ourselves and appreciate differences in others. It has also helped to foster a sense of team learning. In addition, type watching, a by-product of the MBTI, provides a constructive response to the inevitable judgmental stereotyping that goes on in teams.

Ginger Malone, RN, MSN, director, innovation and consultation, Abbott Northwestern Hospital, Minneapolis

Our Multidisciplinary Apprentice Program includes people from different ethnic backgrounds: African-American, Hispanic, Asian-American, and Caucasian. As diverse as their backgrounds are, they have one common goal: They all want to better themselves through learning new skills. They have put themselves in a position where they can pursue a health care career, a goal which otherwise would have been impossible without their current resources. These apprentices are goal oriented, they know what it is they want although, at times, they need to be counseled on a better way of accomplishing their ends. They are also concrete learners; they learn best by direct experiences and want to be able to use and apply what they learn from the classroom to the clinical setting. They seek recognition of their different life experiences which they like to share. They are very aware of the learning environment and can quickly form their own opinions as to what qualities a good nurse should have and which types of caregiver–patient interactions work best. The RN [registered nurse] who works with each apprentice not only acts as a role model but as a mentor. Aside from supervising each apprentice, the RN care partner provides emotional support and helps the apprentice develop self-confidence.

Miriam O. Young, RN, MS, MAP facilitator/educator, University Hospital's Program to Improve Patient Care, University of Utah Hospital, Salt Lake City

Vermont has a high population of older nurses prepared in diploma programs or associate degree nursing programs. These nurses are also mothers and wives, and lack the assertive-culture characteristic of nurses in larger metropolitan areas. In addition, they possess a Yankee independence which makes it hard to address their needs. These nurses have learned to do with less but to expect more from themselves. They are generally hardworking, fiercely loyal to their patients, their communities, and institutions. And proud! Part of the work of the Vermont Network for Education has been to craft educational offerings to meet needs which staff didn't feel or even know they had, then help them gain access at a nearby location. When offered the opportunity for education through workshops, these nurses are not only eager to learn and share with each other, but they support each other in the learning, from one hospital to another.

Jane Hayward, RN, MSN, cochair, network for education, Vermont Nursing Initiative, Morrisville, VT

Learning Model Characteristics

The learning model selected is another important consideration in the design of learning experiences. The learning model is the translation of beliefs about how people, teams, and organizations learn in a systematic way to accomplish that learning. In our organizations, there are many variations: a dedicated staff of trainers, outside consultants, train the trainers, outside facilitators, facilitative leaders, just-in-time trainers, and neutral third-party facilitators. Some use one model for some types of learning and another model for other types: individual, team, and organizational. Many of these models are described in detail in appendix B.

The learning model is an important consideration in the design of learning experiences because it is so closely tied to approaches, methods, and tools. For example, a neutral third-party facilitator model probably would not fit well with lecture methods. If learning is to become a way of life for individuals and teams, and become integrated with work, the learning model must address how that would be expected to happen. The cascading model of learning is offered in this section, not as the one right way but as a promising approach for the learning organization.

The cascading model was developed at Xerox Business Products and Systems, which was the 1989 winner of the prestigious Malcolm Baldridge National Quality Award.[27] The most exciting thing about this model is that it is continuous. It also goes well beyond most models in that it includes what happens after the learner learns, integrating the learning into the work. The model has all the appropriate characteristics for building a learning organization. (See figure 4-10.)

The cascading model says that everyone in the organization is at some point learner, doer, teacher, and mentor. Where each person is depends on mastery of concepts and skill level, not on department, position, or level in the hierarchy. The commitment throughout the organization is that:

- Learners learn from teachers.
- Learners are mentored while they are using their new knowledge and skills in their work.
- When learners can successfully use the knowledge and skills in their work, they become teachers.
- Teachers teach learners.
- Teachers become mentors to the learner.
- Mentors help doers use the new knowledge and skills in their work.

Figure 4-10.   The Cascading Model of Learning

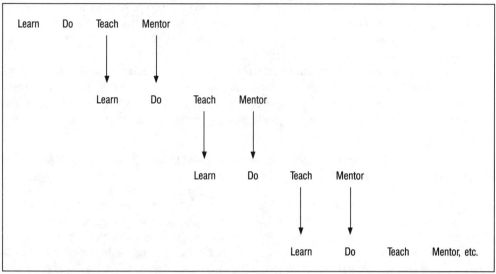

Source: Tallahassee Memorial Regional Medical Center. Based on J. Main. The people cascading through Xerox. In: *Quality Wars: The Triumphs and Defeats of American Business.* (A Juran Institute Report) New York City: The Free Press, 1994.

- Learners can be individuals or teams.
- Teacher teams teach learner teams.
- Mentor teams mentor doer teams.
- Learning, doing, teaching, and mentoring are integrated into the work or the organization.

The cascading model incorporates the idea of just-in-time, a philosophy of learning based on the notion of the teachable moment: The time when learners need to know is the time when they are most ready and therefore most likely to learn. Our organizations have used this model in their change efforts.

The cascading model of learning has worked very well for us. Learners tell us that they immediately sense the commitment of teachers who have been learners once, just like them. It all seems more possible when someone you know and respect has not only learned the material, but knows how to use it and can give you examples of improved results. Teachers tell us that they learn twice as much when they teach the material as they did when they were learners. Teaching reinforces the learning, and encourages the teacher to reflect on how learning has changed his or her work.

Vivian Booth, RN, project analyst, Work Redesign Program to Improve Patient Care, Tallahassee Memorial Regional Medical Center, Tallahassee, FL

We found that training with the basic continuous quality improvement tools and methods is an important prerequisite for larger organizational change efforts. Through trial and error, we discovered that much of our training/education is best done in a just-in-time mode—as groups encounter obstacles or find that they do not know what to do at a given time—that is the best teachable moment. Our new model for organizational change builds in this fact; our training is now offered when teams are most likely to need it.

Ginger Malone, RN, MSN, director, innovation and consultation, Abbott Northwestern Hospital, Minneapolis

When we chose the facilitative leadership course from Interaction Associates as a model for teaching and learning facilitative/collaborative processes for change and working together, we decided that the people charged with doing the most facilitation would logically be the ones trained and who, in turn, would then train others.

The Center for Patient Care Innovation has staff dedicated to consulting with individuals and groups in the organization to help facilitate and evaluate our changing culture. Four staff in the center were trained in the basic model of facilitation and then the advanced course, followed by a train-the-trainer course. Our instructor, then, cofacilitated and coached us through the first couple of courses that we implemented here.

Now, two years and many courses later, we have been able to tailor the course content to be "most fitting" for Vanderbilt and its changing issues. We have also developed an incredible network of people who coach and model for each other, and who continually call on us in the center for neutral facilitation, agenda planning, and consultation for meetings and team development.

Karen L. Turner, EdD, training specialist, Center for Patient Care Innovation, Vanderbilt University Hospital and Vanderbilt Clinic, Nashville, TN

Finally, the cascading model says that learning is not something we do when we can take time out from work, and teaching is not something done only by trainers in the training department. It says that knowing something is not enough, it must be used to make something better. It says that learners need mentors to effectively put new knowledge and skills to use. It is a powerful statement that continuous learning, doing, teaching, and mentoring is the way we work in a learning organization.

Organizational Characteristics

A number of organizational characteristics are important to consider when designing learning experiences. Among them are the organization's size, complexity, and physical configuration; its mission and priorities; and its available resources.

Size, Complexity, and Configuration

Size, complexity, and configuration are obvious issues to consider in designing learning experiences. Beyond the obvious issues of scale, however, are the interacting issues of small size, few resources, and isolated location. Many of us are building networks of small organizations that are hard-pressed to manage learning while doing. The organizations may be so isolated by distance or geography that face-to-face learning opportunities are impossible. There may be so few staff that each staff member is performing multiple roles, with little value on making time to reflect on work. Two organizations, the Vermont Nursing Initiative and the Montana Consortium, used collaborative models to overcome some of these obstacles. Interestingly, their methods and focus of collaboration are entirely different.

Having no corporate structure to draw on, the hospitals in the Vermont Nursing Initiative (VNI) developed their own networks to integrate services. As part of the VNI Network for Education, Vermont Interactive Television is an important tool where travel is difficult because of mountain ranges and unpredictable weather. Each television interaction site is within 30 minutes of most hospitals. The hospitals also work together to staff their services through a statewide staffing network. Project Director Toni H. Kaeding explains:

While most current health reform efforts are focused on the *vertical* integration of services, the Vermont Nursing Initiative provides a model for the *horizontal* integration of services based entirely on collaboration. True integration occurs on four levels: social, policy, issue, and system. We found that inattention to any one level compromises the effectiveness of the outcomes desired, and results in superficial products and services.

Also separated by long distances, organizations in the Montana Consortium have identified the need to focus their efforts outward into the communities they serve. Consortium Director Lynne Meredith Mattison says that in order for hospitals to survive, they need to shift paradigms from "we are the acute care hospital to we are a community health care provider working in collaboration with other organizations." The consortium is facilitating a community health planning process in six communities, and including citizens and public health officials in the process. According to Mattison, in the past, hospitals looked at one set of information and public health departments at another without ever understanding the overall health of the community. Through the planning process, the consortium also has discovered a gap in what the communities expect from their hospitals and what is offered, and are attempting to bridge that gap. The collaboration is then extended even further by bringing the six communities together to share what they have learned with each other and to generate new directions.

On the other end of the continuum, designing learning experiences in large organizations or those with multiple sites offers its own challenges. Just deciding where to start can be daunting. Integrating multiple sites, perhaps with different cultures, can be difficult. It is not uncommon for departments or programs located outside the main facility to feel isolated—outside the communication loop. A health care provider in rural Maine faced a similar set of challenges:

> The concept of systemwide education and shared educational resources was warmly received by our entire organization. However, applying the practice of systemwide education is not a simplistic function. Individuals across the system initially guarded their turf and their entity's issues. Plus, the challenge of multiple geographic sites, multiple variations in learning readiness, and multiple competing institutional specific initiatives seemed impossible to overcome. These obstacles, together with technical support from the National Office [of the Strengthening Hospital Nursing Project] moved us beyond the "one model of education" approach. We now have multiple educational designs including:
>
> * Large maximum-mix work sessions for heterogeneous groups
> * Retreat sessions for homogeneous work groups
> * Staff meetings/sessions bringing education to the point of service, utilizing multimedia resources
> * Slide presentations for broad audiences
> * Poster presentations for broad audiences
> * Inventory of guest editorials for local newspapers and publications
> * On-the-job training facilitated by project staff and interagency education staff
> * Systemwide adaptability to respond and sponsor a spontaneous educational opportunity or to meet the need of an urgent/crisis situation requiring educational support
>
> This multifaceted approach is allowing us to begin to meet needs otherwise constrained by time, money, turf guarding, scheduling, and variations in readiness.
>
> *Paula Delahanty, RN, project director, Strengthening Hospital Nursing Program, Penobscot Bay Medical Center, Rockland, ME*

In a consortium of health service and education organizations, learning occurs at all levels: at the team level as well as at the individual level, organizationally and interorganizationally. When organizations in a consortium desire to change from hierarchical, bureaucratic systems dominated by competition and individualistic concerns to collaborating interdependent systems, providers (faculty and professional staff) and employees need assistance and support in learning new ways of managing relationships and in establishing different means of communication. Expectations of shame, blame, and punishment need to be replaced with the expectation that problems and mistakes are opportunities for learning. The passivity which grows among personnel in hierarchical organizations needs to be replaced by energized individual initiatives and creative action. Novel structures or groupings need to be created which take people out of their usual interactions and work patterns, and place them with people from different departments, disciplines, organizations, and domains. In short, encouraging people to work together for a common purpose is a strategy the Health Bond Consortium has found to be very powerful. Examples of this strategy include:

- Cross-organizational shared-learning experiences with a strong emphasis on experiential learning related to commitment to coworkers, communication, leadership empowerment, care delivery system innovations
- Consortium interorganizational shared governance structure
- Program and service design/redesign using interdisciplinary service/education partnership teams and interdisciplinary innovation project proposals

Sharon Aadalen, RN, PhD, director, Health Bond Consortium, South Central Minnesota, Mankato, MN

Mission and Organizational Priorities

Mission is a key issue to consider in designing learning experiences. It is largely through learning experiences that the mission of the organization will be transmitted. Learning experiences provide an opportunity to communicate the mission and to explicitly integrate it into the work of the organization. For example, in the teaching hospital, the teaching mission is of utmost importance. In this environment, learning experiences are much more likely to include students, interns, and residents.

The influence of the academic environment on our design:

- Formal course content focuses on leading effective collaborative meetings, eliciting team participation, and managing complex projects. Participants then apply the tools in the manner best fitted to their setting.
- Any technique or course that is taught provides clear background on its conceptual origins.
- Clear links were built in our design to include school of nursing or medical school faculty either as course participants (in training programs) or as design participants (in projects).
- Clinical division chiefs were effective leaders for bringing together medical school clinical faculty and residents in their divisions to agree on clinical protocols.
- "Real-time" teaching of collaborative meeting and leadership skills pairs skilled facilitators as coaches for physician committee heads. Coaches sometimes serve as recorders in the meetings to keep current on the content and, thus, increase their coaching effectiveness.
- As physicians see the effectiveness of collaborative meeting and project management, they have requested help in learning these techniques.
- Residents were members of our perinatal planning project and played an active role through implementation where they participated in the interviews for the nurse case managers.

Wendy L. Baker, RN, MS, director, Center for Patient Care Innovation; and project director, Strengthening Hospital Nursing Program, Vanderbilt University Hospital and Vanderbilt Clinic, Nashville, TN

Organizational priorities also must be considered in the design of learning experiences. Of particular concern is a design that integrates these priorities so that they do not become compartmentalized—for example, the quality effort, the cost-saving effort, the leadership effort, and so on. Well-designed learning experiences can be the integrating force in the learning organization, as demonstrated by the following three hospitals.

In a project as multifaceted as redesigning an entire delivery system, education needs could be limitless. However, in a busy organization, it can be difficult to pull participants away from operations as frequently as an ideal educational curriculum would suggest, particularly when they are already being pulled away from their day-to-day duties by heavy, time-consuming involvement in related task force activity.

At Hartford Hospital, one strategy to deal with this issue was to use routine meetings and retreats for the business of redesign. Such retreats were, historically, highly valued and therefore could provide a targeted group of participants with a reasonable "readiness" to learn. This was particularly true as the agenda and participant list for such sessions were determined by top leadership. It is also important to note that leadership's presence at these sessions, and their role in program identification, afforded an opportunity to communicate their values about the redesign project to key members of the organization.

With such a format, formal educational programming was provided without the perception that "extra" time was required. The off-campus location and relaxed atmosphere also afforded an opportunity for networking and a degree of reflection; the latter, according to Beatty and Ulrich, is a significant component of increasing an organization's capacity for change.

Agendas for both traditional department head retreats and an annual meeting of the board and medical staff were thus developed around "patient-centered redesign" (PCR). Sample topics have included quality improvement, costs and managed care, and transformational leadership. Guest speakers were used; and success, of course, still related to the quality of their presentation. Such "external" agents, however, are at times able to more effectively communicate important messages than internal change agents.

Cheryl B. Stetler, PhD, RN, FAAN, project director, Patient-Centered Redesign Program, Hartford Hospital, Hartford, CT

We sent out a "call" for leadership development trainers to associates at MeritCare Hospital. Our vehicle was *daily rounds,* the official communication medium for MeritCare. We sought associates who demonstrated excellent interpersonal skills, ability to work well in groups or work teams, skills in leadership roles, and experience in teaching educational programs. As we began to shift the leadership paradigm at MeritCare, we were challenged to seek out individuals from all levels within the hospital to present the most current concepts in leadership.

The leadership trainers/facilitators role description was written, selection and training processes were determined. We had 15 associates take part in the trainers program—a mix of 8 from management positions, 7 nursing, 2 vice-presidents, 1 secretary, and 1 clerical lead.

During the leadership trainers' training, we saw firsthand the value of "leaving your title" at the door and coming together as "learners." The dynamics of the group created a rich educational experience where associates came together on the same level, learning and growing in an appreciation for each other and the organization for which they work. The passion for creating learning experiences for the whole organization was felt by the commitment each of them made to present the leadership component they had been asked to be responsible for.

Penny Dale, MEd, educator, MeritCare Hospital, Fargo, ND

The quality management department of our midsized community hospital had coordinated the development of an entirely new approach to patient care delivery. This new system involved many professions, all needing to be educated about the system prior to its implementation. The challenge was to design an education intervention that could be effectively used across departments and care settings.

Many options were considered before it was decided that video education would be the best medium for our culture and environment. Because of the diversity of health care providers, the variety of departments, and the number of shifts involved, it was of paramount importance that the message be consistent. The video provided viewers with an overview on the project presented by persons representing their department and explaining their roles The content included information on the system's goals, process, roles of the various professions, documentation formats, and the relationship of patient care pathways to quality improvement.

To ensure maximum accessibility to the information, the presentation was done on a looped continuous playback system. It was available on the staff development CCTV [closed-circuit television] channel every two hours for two months. To reach the physicians, the videotape was played in the medical staff office on their CCTV channel 24 hours a day, two days a week, for a month.

Jeanne Ann Tantlinger, BSN, RN, CCRN, former assistant director, quality management, Marymount Hospital, Garfield Heights, OH

Available Resources

Time, money, and knowledge—these are the universal constraints. There is never enough of any of them! Anyone can do more with more, our challenge is to do more with less. Obviously, the resources available must be a very important consideration in the design of learning experiences. The important question is not can we do it with what we have, but how can we do it? Available resources considerations should include at least facilities, equipment, materials, and staff.

Facilities, Equipment, and Materials

The physical space for learning experiences—the *facilities*—can be very important. Space for team learning should allow all team members to see and hear one another, permit writing on walls and other techniques, and be light and comfortable, with limited distractions. For many of us, space is at a premium, requiring advanced scheduling and superior negotiating skills!

Consider also the technology, or *equipment*, available for learning. Some organizations have invested in technology to support individual and team learning. Individual learning equipment might include VCRs, used with assisted self-paced modules, and computers, used with interactive computer-assisted programs. Team learning equipment might run the gamut from sophisticated computer learning labs for conducting complex simulations and equipment to project computer screens onto a larger screen making the computer output visible to an entire group, to simple equipment such as overhead projectors and flip charts.

Learning *materials* to be considered might include games, test materials, visual materials such as videotapes and color transparencies, and handouts for note taking. Materials are especially important in the cascading model of learning. When the learner becomes the teacher, the materials are all ready.

Staff

Available staff is another obvious consideration. Important considerations are how many staff, how much time they can devote, and their knowledge and skills. What is not so obvious is that the entire staff of a learning organization can be the teaching staff. When rolling out large-scale organizational change, it quickly becomes impossible for a small dedicated staff to meet all the learning needs. The choice becomes slowing down change—in effect, telling some it is not your turn to learn yet—or inventing a way to keep the change going. One way is to enlist additional teachers in the organization. Often a dedicated staff will find this difficult. They will be concerned that others will not do it "right," even that they themselves will not have a future role. We have learned that the only way to keep learning going is to give away the control. The dedicated staff can then move on to other critical issues, such as continuously improving learning experiences, integrating learning and work, and developing mechanisms for learning from one another.

The following examples of how two of our consortiums have coped with limited resources provide ideas that could be helpful in any organization:

Because of the limited resources in time, staff, and money of small hospitals, the Network for Education of the Vermont Nursing Initiative (VNI) was set up building on existing systems. These systems included the Vermont Inservice and Continuing Education Group (VICE). This group, made up of the in-service educators of Vermont hospitals, became the committee for the network. The VNI also contracted with the Center for Nursing, a collaborative model supported by the University of Vermont School of Nursing and the Medical Center Hospital of Vermont to develop professional initiatives for staff development and research, to provide the administrative work of the network. A "coop model" of education for Vermont hospitals developed out of these collaborative working relationships.

Ironically, a major problem which the Vermont Nursing Initiative and the Network for Education have grappled with has been the underspending of the money by the grass-roots portion of the system. These hospital staffs had become so used to doing without, they have needed help at the basic level just to learn what kind of resources are available and how to access these resources in order to facilitate the work of these projects. We have had to work hard to overcome a basic inertia in spending monies, a sense of whether or not it's a questionable justification for the expense.

Jane Hayward, RN, MSN, cochair, network for education, Vermont Nursing Initiative, Montpelier, VT

Patient care services personnel in rural hospitals often feel like Bartholomew Cubbins and his 10,000 hats. They perform so many role responsibilities and functions. The demands of multiple roles mean that the rural provider generalist has to have a very broad base of knowledge, competence, and skills. And it is very hard for this generalist to be able to have coverage so that he or she can leave the organization. The Health Bond Consortium has facilitated bringing consultation and education programming to staff in small rural hospitals by using the following strategies:

- Administrative/management exposure to consultation/educational/experiential learning opportunities (facilitates commitment to ensuring that staff are freed up to participate in similar learning opportunities)
- Teleconferencing (brings national programming to rural sites)
- Annual fall conference repeated at least two days (allows small hospitals to send half the staff one day, half the other)
- Fall conference registration opened to other service and education providers in southern Minnesota (enhances the opportunities for networking and accessing new colleague resource people)
- Obtaining grant monies supportive of computer system purchase, so that rural hospitals can access InterNet international communication networks and databases, as well as listings of audiovisual media and print resources available through the state library system and medical centers and area hospitals (increase the attractiveness of rural sites to baccalaureate faculty and students, further enhancing the rural hospitals resources)
- Development of a Regional Continuing Healthcare Education Council (ReCHEC), with membership representing nursing and allied health care providers from health care educational and service delivery settings (provides for quality cost-effective regional education planning, program implementation)

Sharon Aadalen, RN, PhD, director, Health Bond Consortium, South Central Minnesota, Mankato, MN

Continuous Design: A Shift in Thinking about Evaluation

The evaluation and continuous improvement of learning experiences is discussed in chapter 8. But while we are discussing design, it may be important to make the point that designing learning experiences is not something done only on the front end. Design must be continuous if learning is to be continuous and if the organizational capacity for change is to continuously increase.

There is a long tradition of determining the value of educational events, curricula, procedures, or individual performance level. The two main approaches today are formative and summative evaluation. *Formative evaluation* is that of evaluating the instructional process as it is happening, with the intent of making changes. It assesses how well the instructors and learners are doing so that any shortcomings or problems can be fixed. Examples of formative evaluation include end-of-session evaluation slips, most interesting/least interesting forms, and informal interviews. These techniques are discussed later in more detail in chapter 8, and examples are offered by many of us in appendix B. On the other hand, *summative evaluation* is done at the end of the learning experience. It is intended to assess learner performance, justify the worth of a program, or ensure that a course has been effective. Examples of summative evaluation include final exams, term projects, and oral presentations.[28]

The issue with traditional evaluation methods is not that they do not effectively evaluate individual performance or the effectiveness of various methods. The issue may be in the definition of *learn*. Does the word mean recognizing the concept, repeating the skill, or does it mean using the knowledge or skill to improve something, or solve a real-life problem?

> The current curriculum of the Multidisciplinary Apprentice Program (MAP) at University Hospital is set up so that apprentices are taught in the classroom, practice skills in the learning resource laboratory, and apply both knowledge and skills in the clinical setting. Apprentices attend classes twice a week and work in the clinical area three times a week. As soon as they learn a knowledge or skill in class, the opportunity to apply that skill or knowledge is provided. The learning is much more meaningful because apprentices are able to use what they learn almost immediately. This method helps apprentices to retain the information better because they can relate it to a concrete experience. The learning is more meaningful because they see its "use value" in providing patient care. The question Why do I have to know this? is answered almost immediately. If there are new procedures which the apprentice needs to have a chance to perform, he or she mentions it to the RN care partner, who will try to find a practice opportunity. The learning needs of apprentices are met in a timely manner. The clinical experiences also provide a basis for an interesting and lively discussion in the classroom. Apprentices ask very relevant questions and have a chance to share pleasant or unpleasant experiences with the class as each one adjusts to the hospital environment.
>
> *Miriam O. Young, RN, MS, facilitator/educator, Multidisciplinary Apprentice Program, University of Utah Hospital, Salt Lake City*

We may need to give up some of our linear cause-and-effect thinking in order to continuously improve learning experiences. Continuous improvement requires constant feedback and the willingness to continuously change. The continuous design is not neat; it must consider all the characteristics we have discussed *and the interaction between them!* It can't be compared as neatly over time, because the content changes.

On the other hand, should the evaluation criteria be how well the learner performed or how well the organization is performing? Perhaps the ultimate evaluation criteria for learning experiences in a learning organization should be:

- Are patients getting as well as they can get, are they getting better faster with fewer resources consumed, or are they staying well and avoiding getting sick in the first place?
- Are customers more satisfied with services?
- Are workers more satisfied with their work?

Organizational consultant Alan Barstow of Barstow & Associates, in Philadelphia, speaks of this process as a design spiral.[29]

> Successful organizational change happens in the hearts and minds of the members of an organization or it doesn't happen at all. Another name for it might be *learning*. But how can you tell if learning or change has happened? One noticeable outcome is change in the mental frame people have about how change should be planned and carried out. It happens when people recognize they have been restricting the range of their thought process and their course of action because of an assumption. When that assumption

is removed, change efforts are able to move forward in previously closed directions. These learnings are permanent, and they affect the way people will manage all future organizational change efforts. This learning, or *frame breaking,* is fundamental to successful organizational change. Let me describe one extremely common mental frame that hinders organizational change and how it can be effectively reframed.

Problem solving: A linear, plan–do frame. This is the classic problem-solving approach that is taught in virtually every discipline in every university. It is a step-by-step procedure in which you (1) specify your objective, (2) generate alternative courses of action to achieve the objective, (3) evaluate the courses of action with respect to their degree and likelihood of achieving the objective, (4) select the best course of action, and, finally, (5) execute it. In short, steps 1–4 are about *planning,* step 5 is about *doing,* and planning and doing are separated, even to the point where staff specialists *plan* and line managers *do.* This approach is so dominant in our culture that even those who don't follow it often attempt to recast their efforts in this frame when reporting them to others. Some people even think this approach is synonymous with rational thinking and can think of no alternative.

Many people try to apply this same model to organizational change, where the assumptions on which it is based do not hold. Often it is impossible to specify the objective because people disagree or they have multiple conflicting objectives or they do not know what they want except in very general terms. Frequently, the best course of action is not generated during the upfront planning stage, either because we are not aware of it, it has not been invented yet, or it has not yet become feasible because enabling events have not yet taken place. Evaluation is problematic because every course of action has unintended consequences besides the degree to which it achieves the specified objective, and one has to live with all the consequences tomorrow. Thus, selecting the best course of action, which in theory is almost as mechanical as solving a mathematical equation, places the problem solver in a dilemma. Either the problem must be trimmed to fit the methodology—a triumph of form over substance—or the method must be abandoned, usually in favor of a "gut-level" decision which may or may not be papered over with supporting analysis.

Caught in this dilemma, many planners call for more planning and analysis. Planning gets stuck in an *analysis paralysis* loop and nothing gets executed or done. Then comes step 5, execute, where book chapters become suddenly short and otherwise long-winded professors noticeably brief. Many plan–do change efforts don't get this far, and those that do disappear into an organizational black hole after a few months only to be replaced with a new "flavor-of-the-month" change effort. If you separate planning from doing, you make it impossible to modify plans based on what you learn when you put a plan into practice. This prevents you from learning and making change happen. It causes organizational change efforts to fail.

Given the complexity of organizational change, it is not surprising that the linear plan–do frame becomes unworkable. There is another frame: the design spiral. (See figure 4-11.)

Design: A spiral, learning frame. This frame recognized that successful organizational change is usually the result of iterative cycles of *action and reflection.* The journey along the spiral is driven by: (1) creating a vision (image), (2) presenting it to others and modifying it to achieve a shared vision (image), (3) testing it and putting it into practice, which results in (4) a revised vision (image) to be again presented to others, put into practice, and further revised, and so on.

The learning that takes place during these cycles can modify the objectives of the change effort as seen by any or all of the participants, and open up new possibilities for action that no one had considered before. This allows the organization to deal with the unintended and unforeseen consequences of its earlier efforts in a constructive way. Instead of trying to figure it out in advance and develop the perfect plan, the focus shifts to keeping the process moving forward and learning our way into effective performance and change.

Figure 4-11. The Design Spiral

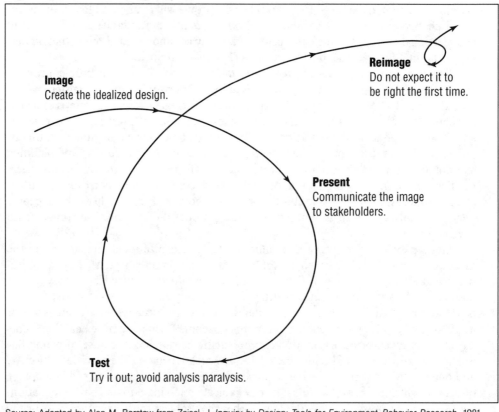

Source: Adapted by Alan M. Barstow from Zeisel, J. *Inquiry by Design: Tools for Environment–Behavior Research,* 1981.

The linear frame is most effective when we recognize a problem we or others have dealt with before and need to choose a solution based on its established track record. The spiral frame is more effective when we are searching and exploring for solutions in uncharted territory. The linear frame is about choosing between established courses of action; the spiral frame is about designing and inventing new ones.

By reframing the change process from a linear plan–do approach to a design spiral approach, people better enable themselves to execute and take action. This happens because people become less focused on whether their first efforts are correct and more [focused] on first efforts as approximations, and the necessary path to revised and refined second efforts. Lack of fit between intended and actual outcomes is reframed from mistakes, shortcomings, and problems toward valuable information, experience, and opportunity, which enables sustained learning. The shift of frame from linear plan–do to design spiral makes a difference in organizational change efforts—the difference between failure and success.

Conclusion

Any attempt to transform an organization into a learning organization requires adopting a new approach to the process of learning itself. This presents a number of challenges: rejecting old learning methodologies and learning new ways to learn, integrating learning with work so that learning is continuous, and adapting the learning process to the needs of a diverse work force. Any attempt to design new and compelling learning experiences involves a number of considerations: assessing individual and institutional readiness for change, determining the content that learners need to learn, understanding the influences on learning of myriad learner characteristics, selecting the appropriate learning model, assessing the organizational characteristics that affect learning, and determining an appropriate means of evaluating learning to ensure that it is ongoing.

References and Note

1. Senge, P. M. *The Fifth Discipline: The Art and Practice of the Learning Organization.* Doubleday/Currency: New York City, 1990.

2. Watkins, K. E., and Marsick, V. J. *Sculpting the Learning Organization: Lessons in the Art and Science of Systemic Change.* San Francisco: Jossey-Bass, 1993.

3. Senge, P. M. The leader's new work: building learning organizations. *Sloan Management Review* 32(1):7–23, Fall 1990.

4. Watkins and Marsick.

5. Watkins and Marsick, p. 36.

6. Meyer, A. Adapting to environmental jolts. *Administrative Science Quarterly* 27(4):515–37, 1982.

7. Ackoff, R. *Creating the Corporate Future.* New York City: John Wiley & Sons, 1981.

8. Watkins and Marsick, p. 84

9. Argyris, C. Teaching smart people how to learn. *Harvard Business Review* 69(3):99–109, May–June 1991.

10. Leebov, W. *The Health Care Manager's Guide to Continuous Quality Improvement.* Chicago: American Hospital Publishing, 1991, p. 19.

11. Gregorc, A. F. *An Adult's Guide to Style.* Columbia, CT: Gregorc Associates, 1982.

12. Hirsh, S. K. *MBTI Team Building Program: Leader's Resource Guide.* Stanford, CA: Consulting Psychologists Press, 1992.

13. Cross, K. P. *Adults as Learners: Increasing Participation and Facilitating Learning.* San Francisco: Jossey-Bass, 1981, p. 124.

14. Cross, p. 125.

15. Cross, p. 139.

16. Cross, p. 141.

17. Cross, p. 145.

18. Cross, p. 147.

19. Cross, p. 150.

20. Cross, p. 151.

21. Cross, p. 154

22. Heimstra, R., and Sisco, B. *Individualizing Instruction: Making Learning Personal, Empowering and Successful.* San Francisco: Jossey-Bass, 1990, p. 25.

23. Cross, p. 163.

24. Cross, p. 164.

25. Heimstra and Sisco, p. 29.

26. Knowles, M. *The Adult Learner: A Neglected Species.* 3rd ed. Houston: Gulf Publishing, 1984.

27. Main, J. The people cascading through Xerox. In: *Quality Wars: The Triumphs and Defeats of American Business.* (A Juran Institute Report) New York City: The Free Press, 1994.

28. Heimstra and Sisco, p. 122.

29. This frame was developed in collaboration with Kannard T. Wing from the author's own organizational change experience and from the action research of Kurt Lewin, the design spiral of John Zeisel, the plan-do-check-act cycles of Deming and Shewhart, Henry Mintzberg's emergent organizational strategy, and Donald Schon's "conversation with the situation."

Chapter 5

Fitting Content, Learner Characteristics, Learning Approach, and Learning Method

C hapter 4 discussed the elements that need to be considered in designing compelling learning experiences. These include:

- *Purpose:* What we want to accomplish—individual, team, and organizational learning to increase organizational capacity for change
- *Individual and organizational readiness for learning and change:* Leadership, common vocabulary, management style, skills for building trust, and analytic skills
- *Characteristics of the content to be learned:* Individual, team, and organizational content
- *Characteristics of learners:* Learning styles; characteristics of adult learners; limited reading, writing, and analytic skills; cultural and ethnic diversity; and learner mix
- *Characteristics of the learning model:* The way individuals, teams, and organizations learn to learn
- *Organizational characteristics:* Size, complexity, and configuration; and mission and organizational priorities
- *Available resources:* Facilities, equipment, materials, and staff

This chapter discusses the art of fitting all these considerations to a host of learning approaches, methods, and tools. It is important to note the word *art*. Although there is certainly a science of learning, the focus has been on learners in educational institutions and on evaluation of learner performance. We are breaking new ground here—the integration of learning and work in learning organizations to increase the capacity for change. There is no science yet—and even if there were, there probably is no substitute for making the best assumptions, giving it a try, staying close to the learners, and continuously improving the learning experience to achieve the best organizational outcomes.

Defining Approaches, Methods, and Tools

It may be helpful to establish some common meanings for words we will be using to describe the learning experiences we have designed. The language of education usually includes words such as *teacher, student, teaching approach, teaching method,* and *teaching tools.* The words we use are important. They should focus more on what we are trying to accomplish—learning—and less on active teacher–passive student roles.

Learning approach means the ways in which learners, or groups/teams of learners, are organized for the learning experience. Individual learning approaches might include independent study, correspondence study, internships, apprenticeships, and computer-assisted instruction. Group/team approaches might include classes, courses, seminars, workshops, team meetings, conferences, symposia, and retreats.

Learning method means the ways in which the teacher/trainer/facilitator/mentor establishes a relationship between him- or herself, the learners, and the learning task(s). Methods may be classified by purpose/function—for example, imparting knowledge/lecture or speech, learning a skill/demonstration or simulation, changing attitudes/role-play or facilitated group discussion, encouraging creativity/brainstorming or self-analysis and reflection. Obviously, some of these are better suited to individual learning and some to team learning.

Learning tools means learning aids that increase the effectiveness of approaches and methods. These too may be classified by purpose/function—for example, illustrative/overhead transparencies or flip charts, environmental/seating arrangements or sound systems.

Designing the Fit: The Challenge

Building learning organizations is an enormous challenge for hospitals and hospital systems. One of the reasons it is so difficult is because there is such a huge learning curve for the entire organization. At the same time, the point people for creating the change must deal with their own learning curves. For those with a specialized background in education and training, the rude awakening is that the paradigm shift to the learning organization takes us all back to zero. For those without a specialized background, the issue may be one of looking for help and the dawning realization that there are no right answers, no magic how-to formula. By whatever path, the challenge is that we all go back to zero. But even at zero, we know a good deal that is helpful in creatively designing the fit.

Instructional design literature abounds with advice on how to design instruction, including:

- Assessing the advantages and disadvantages of various approaches, methods, and tools
- Adjusting for reading and other skill levels
- Making instruction interesting
- Evaluating learner performance

Instructional designers focus mostly on individual instructional modules and training modules for groups. They specialize in designing materials that are used by individuals to learn alone or by teachers/trainers to work with groups. Most of these materials require a teacher/trainer in an active teacher role, with learners in relatively passive roles, although well-designed programs actively involve the learners to keep their interest. Well-designed programs also use specific examples to help the learner make applications in real-life situations. We are beginning to see the shift to materials for teams to use to learn together.

But we are in uncharted territory, trying to do something quite different: Individuals, teams, and the organization are learning to learn together, simultaneously and continuously. And we are systems thinkers! We know that the issue is not so much the approach selected but the relationship between content, approach, method, tools, learners, and so on. Therefore, there is no one right answer. The best mix may vary from individual to individual, team to team, day to day. Once again, this is not a neat, linear process.

What we now know about learning to learn together, we learned the same way we learned about building a model for organizational change and redesigning our organizations—by doing. And of course, we are not done. We continue to learn and improve our learning experiences.

These lessons are distilled into a way to use the interactive process to work through finding a good fit—one promising enough to try. Remember, teachers are learners too! We also offer a wealth of examples of approaches, methods, and tools that have worked in our budding learning organizations. In later chapters, we share what we have learned about how to manage, evaluate, and continuously improve learning experiences.

Designing the Fit: A Process

Most of us are using variations on the interactive process to redesign our organizations. This process is also useful in designing learning experiences, because designing a good fit is a systems issue requiring the simultaneous consideration of many elements and the relationships between them. The process consists of collaboratively working through answers to a series of questions:

- What are we trying to accomplish?
- What do we need to know to get there?
  - Specific concepts and skills?
  - How they build on one another?
- What is the best way to learn under available resource constraints?
- How can we best adapt the approaches, methods, and tools to fit the specific characteristics of our learning model, learners, and organization?
- What worked, and what did not work?
- How will we improve it?

Following are examples of five processes.

We have centered our curriculum design on caring as the essence of nursing practice. A foundational program is personal mastery: the nurse as person, colleague, and integrator of care. This is a three-day retreat where nurses have the time and environment to reflect on practice, support each other as colleagues, and dialogue about caring as an intentional and knowledge-based component of practice. On the second day of the retreat, we bring in patients and families to talk with us about what really matters to them in their care. Based on their stories and our interactions, we mutually strengthen our understanding and definitions of those caring processes that make a difference and facilitate healing.

Integral to the design of the personal mastery program is the principle that caring as the essence of practice is not something different from, or in addition to, but is an intentional component of what we do every day. It means that we systematically put into practice the values and beliefs that we articulate. It means that we acknowledge when there is dissonance between what we believe and what is occurring, and use this dissonance as a source of creative energy for change. It means we are committed to truth telling and walking the talk.

Mary Koloroutis, RN, MS, director, Center for Professional and Clinical Development, Abbott Northwestern Hospital, Minneapolis

When planning the redesign process for the women's health center, we recognized that health care providers tend to be doers and time is a valuable resource. We planned to use a change process that was unfamiliar to those on the design team. Rather than proceed in the traditional way, that is, provide extensive upfront teaching and preparation to the design team members, we chose to match our methods to the characteristics of these active learners and be cognizant of the organization's limited resources. Our goal was to model the change process versus teach it. We "kicked off" the redesign project by showing a brief video (about 30 minutes) that illustrated the process we planned to use. Education and training were provided on a need-to-know basis throughout the redesign process. "Just-in-time" education kept the group moving forward and allowed us to channel the group's energy toward *doing* the process of change, rather than *learning* about it. It is important when you use this learning-by-doing approach to regularly schedule time for reflecting on the process. Specifically, the group needs to assess what went well during the process, what was useful, what should be changed, what should be done differently, and what was learned.

Nikki S. Polis, PhD, RN, project director, Strengthening Hospital Nursing Program; and JoAnn Szwaczkowski, ND, MSN, RN, former director of nursing practice, University Hospitals of Cleveland, Cleveland, OH

At Boston's Beth Israel Hospital, a six-week competency-based orientation program assists the new clinical nurse in transitioning from academia to practice. The present health care environment is complex. The inpatient population in an acute care setting enters with a host of diverse care needs to be met comprehensively within a shortened length of stay. In order to successfully accomplish this objective, patients must be cared for by competent staff. Likewise, if a beginner nurse is to achieve mastery in patient care, he or she must be taught and developed by competent staff. The essence of competency-based orientation evolves around the learner and preceptor relationship. This pair is guided by objectives and subobjectives to be met fully to ensure safe, appropriate, and timely care to patients. The outcome of competency-based orientation is a new clinical nurse who is socialized to the institution and demonstrates safe practice, appropriate utilization of correct resources, and organization skills. However, the learning curve does not end after six weeks. Postorientation practice development is essential.

The nursing leadership group at Beth Israel Hospital has continued to develop and fine-tune a program of sponsorship called the Clinical Intern Nurse Residency Program. The major goal of this two-year program is to provide strong, consistent professional role modeling to the entry-level practitioner. As discussed by Kram,[1] there are several functions of sponsorship: role modeling, teaching, coaching, advocacy, facilitating access to information, counseling, risk taking, and creation and provision of opportunities. These facets collectively impact on the growth and development of the new nurse as well as that of the sponsor.

Selection of the sponsor is a critical responsibility for the nurse manager. Not only should the candidate consistently demonstrate professional practice behaviors, but he or she should also understand his or her role in achieving positive patient outcomes. In addition, the sponsor should possess excellent communication skills, particularly in the area of constructive feedback. Ongoing development of the sponsor is necessary as he or she expands his or her practice scope to not only affect patient care and patient teaching, but also to include consistently influencing the development of a peer. The sponsor should clearly understand the scope of the commitment over time.

It is crucial for the nurse manager to acknowledge that this transition to skillful influencing does not happen automatically. The elements inherent in the complex role of sponsor must be nurtured, supported, and evaluated as well. The holistic development of the sponsor is paramount to the success of the program. Thus, ongoing growth occurs simultaneously in both the beginner and in the sponsor. The nurse manager's commitment as mentor to the sponsor is similar to the sponsor's investment in the development of the new clinical nurse. Without this triad model in place, there is a risk that assumptions may be made around the logical and expected development of the new clinical nurse.

The nurse manager also creates and/or manipulates the environment for learning to occur. It is his or her responsibility to ensure that sponsorship activities will take place. This commitment may entail nurse manager interventions, such as covering shifts for staff members, seeking assistance for other units, and marketing the importance of the sponsorship program within the organization.

Michele McHugh, RN, MS, nurse manager, Beth Israel Hospital, Boston

Throughout this process of moving the innovation of the Network for Education over the life of the grant [Vermont Nursing Initiative], the challenge has been to identify content needs and match them to learner characteristics. This has been constantly changing with the growth process of the staff and leadership at each of the hospitals. Over time, individuals have become more creative and assertive, expecting more from the grant yet prepared to offer as much or more as well. Initially, workshops used a more didactic model with outside consultants. Increasingly, we are using each other as consultants as we have recognized the expertise of staff within our own facilities, some of which were already there. Our challenge in the network continues to be effectively using outside consultants, fostering our own resources, and then combining the two to provide challenging but stimulating learning opportunities to meet the continually changing needs of the population we serve. This growth in expertise and creativity has moved faster as the work has taken on a life of its own. Vermont now supports a growing system of nurses helping nurses, nurturing each other under the supportive umbrella of the Network for Education and the Vermont Nursing Initiative.

Jane Hayward, RN, MSN, cochair, Network for Education, Vermont Nursing Initiative, Morrisville, VT

From the very beginning of the innovation process, our strategies and tactics have been non-traditional. Once learning objectives have been identified, we've used nontraditional approaches. For example, rather than doing what we might call a lecturette and then have people apply that information, we have used games, skits, case studies, creative team activities, and personal experiences, a much more experiential type of learning than the traditional classroom approaches.

In the team learning concept, people end up teaching others and learning from others so that a lot of their learning becomes self-directed. This only happens after we've established ground rules and established trust, and after the team has become a group. This is important to group learning because it's very spontaneous, creative, and unpredictable. It defies the traditional educational approach of lesson planning, teaching methods, and content objectives.

Ginger Malone, RN, MSN, director, innovation and consultation, Abbott Northwestern Hospital, Minneapolis

What Are We Trying to Accomplish?

This is the first and potentially most important question in designing learning experiences, yet it is easy to overlook or take for granted. Usually, the design starts with the next question, What do we need to know? Choosing the latest superficial fad can be a real barrier to building organizational capacity for change. There are a number of reasons why what we are trying to accomplish is an important question. First, it focuses the design effort on the outcomes for the individual, teams, and the organization. If these desired outcomes for the organization have not been clearly articulated, they need to be or it will be impossible to know if they have been accomplished. Second, it probably is not possible to have meaningful leadership commitment to learning without a full understanding of what the commitment means, what the organization will look like, and what it will take in terms of time, money, and knowledge. Finally, and obviously, without clear knowledge of what we are trying to accomplish, it will be impossible to determine what we need to learn in order to reach our goal.

What *are* we trying to accomplish? The answer to this question needs to be at a high enough level to ensure meaningful answers to the next questions. Many of us have very specifically stated answers to this question. At Harbor-UCLA Medical Center, the answer would be creating a community of patient care leaders. At Tallahassee Memorial Regional Medical Center, the answer would be building a learning organization to ensure excellence in patient/family care, defined as optimal patient outcomes, outstanding service and value for customers, and a satisfying practice environment for employees while using scarce resources as efficiently as possible. At Abbott Northwestern, they describe their answer to this question as follows:

To be successful at our transition to the learning organization, we have identified five organizational competencies that are necessary. These five competencies include common focus, teamwork, effective change processes, continuous learning, and a customer-driven mentality. To ensure that these competencies align with the hospital's mission and strategic plan, a series of quality education/development programs have been developed.

Debra Waggoner, MA, MBA, director, consulting and development, Abbott Northwestern Hospital, Minneapolis

The more specific the answers to this question, the easier it will be to design effective learning experiences. Obviously, there are many versions of the learning organization and many ways to get there. But all these versions have some things in common. Spelling out and getting agreement on what the organization should look like is very important. Watkins and Marsick offer a description of their version:[2]

- A new way of thinking and working
- A commonality in systems thinking, decentralization, continuous learning, and empowerment

- Measurable change in the skill and innovation base in the organization
- Altered bureaucratic and hierarchical relationships
- Creation of collegial, problem-solving teams aligned around a globally understood mission
- Placement of mechanisms and systems through which at least the capacity to capture and share learning can exist across the entire organization

The authors' vision of what will be different in the learning organization is captured in figure 5-1. A thorough, shared understanding of what we are trying to accomplish will provide the necessary framework for moving on to the next question.

What Do We Need to Know to Get There?

There are really two important questions here:

1. What specific concepts and skills need to be learned?
2. How do the concepts and skills build on one another, or what is the sequence in which they can best be learned?

Mapping the concepts and skills is a way to begin, just as with trying to understand any systems issue. For example, Senge identifies five disciplines (systems thinking, personal mastery, mental models, shared vision, and team learning) as necessary to building a learning organization.[3] They might be mapped in a variety of ways, one of which is shown in figure 5-2.

Figure 5-1. What Will Be Different in Learning Organizations

From	To
Individual	
Learning that is canned, sporadic, and faddish	Learning that is continuous, strategically tied to future organizational needs
Learning that is not coherently integrated or sequential	Learning that is developmental
Learned helplessness	Personal mastery, learning to challenge assumptions and to inquire
Team	
Learning that is focused on task accomplishment with no attention to process	Learning that is focused on group development and on building collaborative skills
Rewards for individuals, not teams	Rewards for teams, whole divisions
Compartmentalization	Cross-functional, self-directed work teams
Organizational	
Learning that is superficial and unconnected to previous skills, truncated learning	Learning that builds over time on previous skill attainment
Learning through structural reorganizations without regard to learning barriers created; structural rigidity	Creation of flexible structures to enhance learning for everyone
Societal	
Unawareness of impact on society of policies; tunnel vision	Acknowledgment of interdependence and work to improve society generally
Attempts to control societal influence	Constant scanning and projecting of future trends while working to build a desirable future

Source: Watkins, K. E., and Marsick, V. J. *Sculpting the Learning Organization: Lessons in the Art and Science of Systemic Change.* San Francisco: Jossey-Bass, 1993, p. 259.

Figure 5-2. Mapping Concepts and Skills That Need to Be Learned Using Senge's Five Disciplines of the Learning Organization

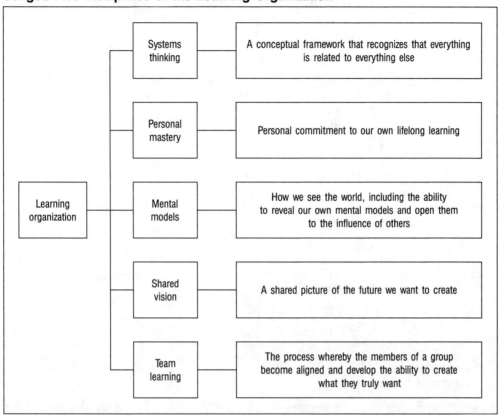

Next, concepts and skills necessary to each of the disciplines can be mapped. For example, mental models concepts might include inquiry, defensive routines, and single-loop and double-loop learning. Mental models skills might include advocacy and inquiry skills and surfacing mental models skills. (See figure 5-3.)

In many ways, sequencing is a chicken-and-egg issue. The answer as to which comes first is, it depends. Mapping provides some clues about sequencing. Concepts and skills that are common to many learning organization disciplines may need to be considered early. Another clue for sequencing involves readiness for individual, team, and organizational learning. Many organizations start with individual-level skills, under the assumption that the shift has to happen at that level first. But some individuals learn best from those around them. The best advice on sequencing is to try to identify and order the necessary concepts and skills and make the best assumptions as to how they fit. But it is a pretty safe bet that however it starts, it will change continuously—and improve.

Once sequencing has been addressed, the concepts and skills that will need to be learned now can be translated into learning objectives. These may be written to describe the desired resulting behavior or competency of the learner. The limitation of most learning objectives is that they do not clearly spell out how the learning experience is expected to result in outcomes for the organization. For example, learning process redesign concepts and skills results in a measurable reduction in first-dose antibiotic delivery time, a decrease in length of stay, and a decrease in deaths of pneumonia patients.

What Is the Best Way to Learn under Available Resource Constraints?

There are three distinct but interacting considerations in thinking through possible answers to this question. These are: the learning model, available resources, and learning approaches, methods, and tools.

Figure 5-3. Mapping Mental Models Concepts and Skills That Need to Be Learned

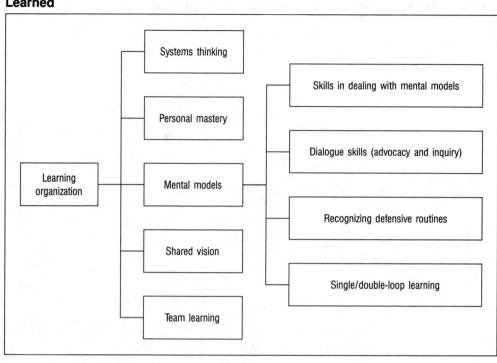

The Learning Model

As described in chapter 4, the learning model is the translation of the set of beliefs about how people, teams, and organizations learn into a systematic way to accomplish that learning. It is how the learning to support organizational change can best happen in your organization. In some organizations, the human resources department drives all these decisions. Frequently, distinct programs are planned for various levels in the organization—for example, leadership training. Sometimes a dedicated training staff is in place to do all training in the organization, or outside consultants may be used for particular concepts and skills, such as facilitative leadership. Frequently, consultants are combined with a train-the-trainer model to develop a cadre of trainers internally.

The learning model should account for the transfer of information and the learning of skills, in addition to integration of the knowledge and skills with work. It should be systematic, simultaneous, and continuous. To fit the requirements of the learning organization, it also should account for learning from and with one another, for accepting responsibility for one's own learning, and for teaching and mentoring others.

Bruce Joyce and Beverly Showers have studied the transfer of training to the work setting, and have been able to document much higher rates of transfer with strategies that include coaching in the work setting.[4] Figure 5-4 shows learner outcomes by training strategies.

Watkins and Marsick suggest that for organizational learning to occur, the learning model should account for "putting systems in place to imbed both learning outcomes and processes, information collection, widespread access to that information, rewards and recognition for learning and improvement, and widespread sharing of what is learned collectively and continuously through access to information."[5]

Finally, the learning model should enable learning at the organizational level. Watkins and Marsick identify four enablers: culture, structure, strategy, and slack.[6] (See figure 5-5.)

Available Resources

Because many approaches will work for most content, available resources should be considered at this point. We have already mentioned the universal constraints—time, money, and knowledge — and that there is never enough of any of them. The overriding question must be, What is the least resource-intensive way to do this effectively? For example, if a retreat is the best approach, can you afford Big Sky or will it be in your backyard? Both can be effective. The main issue is to be clear at this point about the resources that are available. We are all learning how to do more with less!

Learning Approaches, Methods, and Tools

Working through the approach to use is a logical next step — and an important one because it is so closely related to content. Earlier, we defined *learning approach* as the way individual learners or groups/teams of learners are organized for the learning experience. We also identified many approaches for individual and group/team learning.

Figure 5-4. Transfer of Training to the Work Setting

		Outcomes		
		Knowledge	Demonstration of Behavior	Transfer to Work Setting
T r a i n i n g S t r a t e g i e s	Presentation of concepts and theory	85	15	10
	Provides demonstration	85	18	10
	Practice with feedback	85	80	15
	Continuous follow-through Coaching and study groups in work setting	90	90	80

% = Number of trainees who reach level of competence

Source: Joyce, B., and Showers, B. Synthesis of research on staff development: a framework for future study and a state-of-the-art analysis. *Educational Leadership* 45(3):77–87, 1987. Reprinted by permission of the Association for Supervision and Curriculum Development. © 1987 by ASCO. All rights reserved.

Figure 5-5. Enablers of Learning at the Organizational Level

- Culture that is learning oriented, with beliefs, values, and policies that support learning—for example, tolerance for mistakes as opportunities for learning and problem solving (within well-defined financial limits), a surfacing of hitherto undiscussable topics, empowerment, and policies that reward knowledge and the sharing of knowledge as well as rewards for performance

- Structure that is decentralized, lean, and focused on team relationships

- Strategy that is entrepreneurial, focused on innovation and learning

- Enhanced slack or reserves in the form of employee knowledge, literacy, and willingness to learn and to solve problems; technology that frees people to learn and to work more productively; information systems that permit widespread collection and sharing of data and sharing of learning gained; and financial reserves dedicated to learning

Source: Watkins, K. E., and Marsick, V. J. *Sculpting the Learning Organization: Lessons in the Art and Science of Systemic Change.* San Francisco: Jossey-Bass, 1993, p. 166.

First, the content must be fit to the learning approach, considering the relationship between content (what needs to be learned) and learning approach (how learners are organized for the learning experience). Remember, what we are trying to become is a learning organization, so learning will need to happen simultaneously at many levels—individual, team, and organizational. The learning approach chosen must support the learning of the concepts identified in the previous step. Approaches that work wonderfully for individual learning may be abominable for team learning. It probably is impossible to effectively learn the inquiry skills that support team learning by listening to a lecture. On the other hand, the first step in learning inquiry skills may be simple acquisition of information about what they are and why they are important.

Heimstra and Sisco believe that "good instruction is a marriage between content and process," and that it is critical to "link mastery of subject matter with procedures that exploit the talents, capabilities, experiences, and characteristics of adult learners."[7]

In our organizations, we have used a variety of learning approaches: competency-based courses, reference manuals, training programs, even TV programming, and the Internet.

St. Luke's Hospitals/MeritCare used the concept of self-discovery retreats to promote self-awareness, self-healing, and team building. A design team was formed to create the retreat experience. Members for the design team were recruited through the hospital newspaper. The only requirements for serving on the team were an interest in the topic and a willingness to participate in all phases of the retreat development, including attendance at the retreats. Some members were recruited after the team had been meeting for several weeks. In fact, one member was recruited after he told the retreat design team that planned retreats would not appeal to the people in his service area. The team's response was, "Join our team and help us design something that they will want to attend!" He subsequently joined the team and become one of its most active members.

Many of the team members had little or no opportunity in their current position to create educational programs or work with associates outside their service area. As the team developed the format for the retreat, they discovered the importance of different coordination. They became leaders. Team members were valued for the skill and abilities they brought to the team, not for the position they held within the hospital. Through the process of creating the retreat for other hospital associates, the design team members learned not only about becoming a team but that a team is successful only if all the team members' talents are fully appreciated and utilized.

Trish Schrom, BSN, MBA, RN, educator, MeritCare Hospital, Fargo, ND

In an effort to bring together a previously fragmented, multidisciplinary group of care providers to function effectively as a team, the University of Utah Hospital organized one-day Goals and Roles Retreats. The main purpose of the retreats was to assist the team in "forming and norming." We wanted to provide team members with an opportunity to decide what needs to be in place for the team to function as a unit and to facilitate each individual's role as a member of the team.

In planning the retreat, it was important to acknowledge the varying and valuable perspective of each participant. Many of the individuals had never met, let alone functioned in an interdependent relationship. Drawing from the essential characteristics needed for an effective team, the objectives for the retreat centered around establishing a common vision and goals, identifying individual member contributions necessary for success, and defining roles, norms, and methods of communication.

A consultant with expertise in organizational change supported the retreat leaders in planning and facilitating the day. Varying activities were structured to achieve the objectives. The video *The Business of Paradigms*[8] was used to stimulate discussion about creating a new model of health care delivery. Other methods included short presentations, discussion, and individual and small group work.

Cheryl Kinnear, RN, BSN, program manager, University Hospital's Program to Improve Patient Care, University of Utah Hospital, Salt Lake City

When education services began designing learning experiences to increase organizational skills in interpersonal communication and leadership, we faced the challenge of inspiring support and interest across the organization. We knew that though we were talented and competent in many areas, there were many other associates who were equal or better. We also knew that people support what they invest in. Therefore, we determined that a key strategy would be to recruit and train as presenters, associates throughout the organization. We advertised through our hospital paper and took applications. Much to our surprise, we recruited candidates from all levels: frontline, middle management, and administration. We had representation from a variety of services: plant operations, medical records, dietary, customer relations, and many nursing services. We found this to be a wonderful opportunity to develop networks across the organization. The variety of experiences made the classes richer. It also produced for the organization new leaders who had previously been untapped. Drawing presenters from across the organization proved to be a key point of leverage enabling our success.

Janet Feder, BSN, RN, education services manager, MeritCare Hospital, Fargo, ND

Early in 1992, two representatives from the education department at Immanuel-St. Joseph's Hospital met with representatives from the school of nursing at Mankato State University (MSU) and from the health and safety division of South Central Technical College (SCTC). Our purpose was to develop a long-range plan to meet the educational needs of nurses in the region through an integrated network of service and education providers. After several brainstorming sessions, a three-phase plan for *ReCHEC*, a Regional Continuing Healthcare Education Council, was developed.

During phase I, we defined the organizational framework for the eventual development of an educational center. Then, in June of 1992, a regional advisory committee was formed, which added representatives from the nursing home facilities in the region, two rural hospitals, Minnesota Board of Health, and the regional state hospital for the mentally ill and retarded. It soon became apparent we needed to expand our role to include the education of all health care personnel (the largest group being nurses).

After many brainstorming sessions, and some interim projects of sponsoring workshops, we scheduled an eight-hour meeting to begin in-depth strategic planning. With our mission statement, values, and goal statements in writing, we were ready to spread the news of our presence to the region, which brought us into phase II, thereby giving us an identity and a sense of purpose.

One of our original goals—to plan and implement a physical center for nursing—may or may not happen in the near future. In the 18 months since beginning this initiative, other factors, such as the Healthcare Reform Plan, are impacting our discussions. For now, however, a regional council of service and education providers exists, and together we will continue to offer education to nursing and allied health personnel in the most efficient and cost-effective manner possible, with a degree of quality that few of us could accomplish working alone.

Norla Hesse, RN, director of education, Health Bond Consortium, South Central Minnesota, Mankato, MN

A model that has informed the design of compelling learning experiences is Don Blocher's seven learning environment conditions that provide for qualitative change and development:

1. *Involvement:* The learner must be psychologically engaged with the learning environment. This involvement represents the level at which some personal or material value is at risk. There are many ways to engender this kind of involvement. An environment that encourages curious and exploratory behaviors—and requires actions such as making decisions between competing priorities, assuming responsibility, relating to other people, and confronting one's own emotions and talents—is action-oriented involvement. Such involvement has more possibility of occurring in longer sessions such as workshops and retreats.

2. *Challenge:* Building in the condition of challenge means that an instructor/designer/facilitator creates a learning environment that promotes multiple levels of learning so that

the learner is in a moderate state of tension between old mental models and new ones. Therefore, multiple methods such as case studies, role-plays, structured exercises, readings, small group projects, dialogues, evaluation exercises, and so on can be used to introduce challenges between what a learner currently knows to be true and what are potentially different ways of thinking. This type of learning design allows for periodic recycling of concepts and experiences at successively greater depth.

3. *Support:* The presence of this condition implies that a learner experiences a degree of caring, honesty, and empathy from other significant individuals in the learning environment. Although this condition is hopefully part of any learning experience, retreats can offer an environment where usual patterns of interaction change, as inhibitions lower through the sharing of a meal or through the shear length of time that people spend together in this setting.

4. *Structure:* Within this condition, the learner has examples in the learning environment that are functioning slightly more advanced than his or her own present level of development. These examples are perceived to be more competent or adequate to meet the learning demands. That is why we sometimes choose to have a mixture of organizational levels and experience in retreats. The key is to provide some structure/strategies that will aid the learner in mastering the things that seem beyond his or her present capability.

5. *Feedback:* In these retreats or workshops, the design is to provide the learner opportunities to practice skills, behaviors, and competencies while receiving clear, accurate, and immediate feedback about the behaviors. This feedback may come from the instructor, or peers who serve as coaches.

6. *Application:* This developmental condition encourages the learner to actively test out new concepts, attitudes, and skills in a variety of real situations. These real situations may come through simulated activities in the retreat/workshop and through action projects afterward.

7. *Integration:* The learner, through this condition, reviews, critically examines, and evaluates the entire learning experience in a safe, reflective atmosphere. This allows time for personal and group reflection on specific learning insights. Many shorter class sessions do not allow for this period of integration in ways that extended workshops and retreats do.

Karen L. Turner, EdD, learning specialist, Center for Patient Care Innovation, Vanderbilt University Hospital and Vanderbilt Clinic, Nashville, TN

We had about 170 to 175 management personnel of all titles gathered at the local hotel for a two-day retreat and they, in essence, formulated the restructuring of the organization. At the grass roots, I wanted to develop ownership and commitment to a restructured environment, so we had max–mix groups throughout the day that really undertook the realignment of functions within the portfolios. We used big wall charts—huge walls of the hotel were plastered with these wall charts—and then we prioritized them. Afterward, both myself and the executive group took all of the material brought forward and made a promise that wherever we could not accept the recommendations of the group, we would share with them why not. However, there were very few of those instances. During that two-day retreat, we had one of the most telling days for management in terms of my sending a message that they were a team, they were to act on their own judgment, and they had been empowered to frame the environment however they wished.

Lloyd Smith, MSA, president/CEO, MeritCare Hospital, Fargo, ND

As health care institutions begin, and continue, to expand beyond the traditional hospital- or clinic-based services, the process by which we initiate and manage the change process must be rethought. Indeed, the challenge and opportunity of change takes on daunting proportions as we try to incorporate innovations into health care enterprises that are highly diverse in geography, organizational culture, goals, and even philosophy of service.

The introduction of care management to the University Hospitals of Cleveland and our network institutions posed just such an issue. Our implementation sites ranged from our main-campus academic health care center to four community-based hospitals and a multisite ambulatory practice, located over a four-county region of northeast Ohio. As each of these sites brought its own organizational culture, stakeholders, and issues to the care management process, it was clear that no single implementation strategy could be imposed on all the sites. Instead, what was required was an educational process which was sensitive to these issues and yet would produce individuals and teams who could be effective in their own institutions and yet have fidelity to the care management concepts. To meet these goals, we decided to create or grow local experts who could champion and guide the development of care management in each of the network sites.

Our first step in meeting these needs was the development of an integrated care management curriculum which provided didactic and small group work focused on practical how-to information gathered from our early experiences with care management. These sessions were targeted to all professions who were actively planning or in the process of developing care management protocols. This allowed us to focus support on those with a high interest and motivation and to identify evolving experts. Faculty from all professions were recruited from those involved in initial pilot programs. These experts could credibly address the issues, techniques, and successes of each of their projects.

In the first session, lecture and discussion were used to share the experiences gained by early adopters. In this session, content was provided on the development process, identifying and gathering a project team, developing shared goals within the team, potential pitfalls, and the types of data needed to begin and evaluate the project. The experiences of the experts were further leveraged in a written step-by-step guidebook on collaborative care that was distributed to all participants.

As a follow-up to these sessions, a set of consultation sessions were set up where the teams developing collaborative patient care pathways could discuss specific issues with the experts. During a typical session, four topic tables would be established. Topics included starting out, fiscal data, evaluation data, and facilitating the process. Special or particular needs could be addressed not only by the expert but by others in the discussion groups.

This sharing between project groups provided unexpected benefits. First was that it provided a broader base of experiences. This sharing gave an added richness to the discussions and promoted active problem solving among the participants, often leaving the consultant to the role of facilitator. The second benefit was a healthy sense of competition among the project teams, which appeared to spur on development.

The give and take inherent in these sessions permitted us to identify new leadership and experts from the session participants. These individuals were then recruited to serve as faculty and consultants for future collaborative care programs. In addition to providing expertise within the classroom, these individuals provided a high-profile presence within their practice environments by becoming the local expert. They became resources who could apply their knowledge and experiences with credibility and sensitivity to issues within their environments.

Growing our own experts in this way has been very successful in assisting us to build a critical mass of individuals knowledgeable in the process and products of collaborative care. Also, by incorporating these individuals into the educational session for collaborative care, we were able to keep the content fresh and relevant to the diverse populations within the enterprise.

John M. Sipin, RN, ND, data analyst, Strengthening Hospital Nursing Program, University Hospitals of Cleveland, Cleveland, OH

The next step in building the best learning experience for an organization is to fit the method to the approach. Consider the relationship between approach and method, keeping in mind the content. Earlier, we defined *learning method* as the ways the teacher/trainer/facilitator/mentor establishes a relationship between him- or herself, the learners, and the learning task(s). Methods may be classified by purpose/function—for example, imparting knowledge/lecture or speech, teaching a skill/demonstration or simulation, changing attitudes/role-play or facilitated group discussion, encouraging creativity/brainstorming or self-analysis and reflection.

Many methods will work with any one approach. For example, minilecture methods can work well as part of a workshop approach, as can brainstorming methods. What has worked best for us is to vary the methods to maintain interest and enthusiasm. The most effective learning actively involves the learner; most people find it difficult to be actively involved when being talked at. Many organizations use exercises or games to involve participants more actively.

The final step is to fit the tool(s) to the method. Earlier, we defined *learning tools* as learning aids that increase the effectiveness of learning approaches and methods. These, too, may be classified by purpose/function—for example, illustrative/overhead transparencies or flip charts, or environmental/seating arrangements or sound systems. In fitting the tools to the method, keep in mind the setting. For brainstorming, flip charts are very effective, unless the completed sheets cannot be stuck to the walls.

We have used many learning methods and tools in our organizations. The following examples come from three progressive organizations.

A game that we've found particularly useful is called Friday Night at the ER. It involves four people at a game board who act as employees in the ER, step-down unit, surgery, and ICU. The game teaches the importance of seeing the whole instead of just trying to do your best in your own particular area. We have also used the Star Ship Factory, a similar exercise in which a large group is broken up into teams and each team is assigned a particular role in the production of paper star ships. Abbott Northwestern did a modified star ship factory in which we built boats. This was a valuable exercise in terms of learning how processes work in a system and seeing how you're connected to the whole. If carried far enough, this game can take people through the redesign process and can simulate what the design/innovation process is about in ways that other learning activities would not.

Another game we play involves teams using various materials—feathers, paper bags, tinker toys, cotton swabs, pipe cleaners, play dough, and so on—to build the ideal patient experience. Teams work together in an animated session to produce their product of which, I might add, they are very proud. Teams representing other customers then come along, evaluate the product, and then change the design as they see fit. When faced with changes to their product, the groups usually go wild. We feel that this game teaches an incredibly useful lesson about what teams are likely to experience in the course of producing innovation projects themselves.

Ginger Malone, RN, MSN, director, innovation and consultation, Abbott Northwestern Hospital, Minneapolis, MN

Often a meeting or discussion can become the battleground of the few, where ideas with the loudest individual support are given the most consideration. Meetings also can be long and tiresome. Walk and Talk is a structured alternative used to minimize dominance in a discussion and allow all opinions to be heard. At the same time, it provides the participants the chance to relax, refocus, and dialogue.

The steps for Walk and Talk are simple. First, participants are paired and receive a set of questions or instructions designed to elicit individual ideas and thoughts on the topic of interest. Pairing can be done in several ways: color coding, matching numbers, or cards. Any two people with a match are a designated team. Next, team members are encouraged to walk (preferably outdoors) while they converse with one another. During this time, each member of the team will take turns being the interviewer. Either while walking or upon returning, each member records his or her partner's response to the given topics. At a designated time, the entire group reconvenes and each member reports his or her findings to the group for further discussion.

This team-building activity was arranged for the annual Program to Improve Patient Care Project staff retreat. It was found to be an effective way for everyone to communicate freely their expectations of the project, of the project team, and of themselves. Moreover, it was a fun alternative to the traditional sit-down discussion session.

Mimi Y. Liu, MBA, HSA, program coordinator, University Hospital's Program to Improve Patient Care, University of Utah Hospital, Salt Lake City

Collaborative care is an exciting method of coordinated patient care involving multiple professions working together to attain the best patient outcome. *Collaboration* and *coordination* are the key words in this process.

There is never an easy time to meet for collaborative care updates in our rehabilitation department of 40 full-time, part-time, and as-needed staff. In addition, we are a midsized community hospital with limited resources for education. We needed an education program on the collaborative care process that would be cost-effective and take advantage of self-directed learning. The solution was to design an education and information support structure, keeping the complicated schedules of our staff in mind. There are three components to the design; each addressed an expressed education or information support need.

First, a collaborative care bulletin board was designed for the staff office to provide basic information and guidelines related to the approach. Using a road map of Ohio as the backdrop theme, the definitions of *collaborative care,* the how-to's of working with a patient care pathway, and examples of specific patient pathways were graphically displayed. It was our own Trip-Tik® to collaborative care success.

Second, the staff developed a pathway manual that was intended to provide extensive, in-depth reference information related to each specific pathway. The manual included forms for each of the established pathways, related protocols, and guidelines. These documents were placed in a three-ring binder and updated on a regularly scheduled basis. The manual served as an immediate source of current information for staff working with patients on a patient care pathway.

Third, the department installed individual mailboxes for all the staff. In this way, the latest information could be disseminated to staff in a timely way, with the further assurance that all would consistently and simultaneously be informed of changes in plans.

Our staff has become very comfortable with the collaborative care pathway process. The staff can relate positive patient outcomes and care provider satisfaction to the team approach and to the planned staff education described here.

Mimi Pekarek, PT, clinical coordinator, rehabilitation services, Marymount Hospital, Garfield Heights, OH

We found that a particularly effective technique was based on "individual work." For example, in order to clarify roles and expectations, members worked alone and recorded their ideas on large poster board with markers. They then briefly shared with the group the following: their role in the care of the patient, their role as a team member, what they need from the team, and one norm they would like to see established in the group. This dialogue allowed members to learn about resources within their own team. Members asked each other to seriously commit to the continued development of their team. The group wanted a norm in which each individual had responsibility for "glitch control," identifying the glitches and dealing as soon as possible with the problems they may be causing. Retreat evaluations showed that STAR [service team with appropriate resources] members felt the retreat had succeeded in launching their work.

Cheryl Kinnear, RN, BSN, program manager, University Hospital's Program to Improve Patient Care, University of Utah Hospital, Salt Lake City

How Can We Best Adapt the Approaches, Methods, and Tools to Fit Our Organization?

It is at this point that the careful work described in chapter 4 really pays off. The learning experience now can become one that will work with your learning model, your learners, and your organization. Adaptations you might want to make to fit your learning model include:

- Making your learning experience participative
- Providing for continuous feedback
- Accounting for mentoring
- Making the participation max–mix (mixing departments, positions, disciplines, levels, and so on)
- Being sure to develop mechanisms to integrate the learning with the work of the organization

Adaptations to fit the characteristics of the learners might include:

- Being certain to make the best use of learner time
- Supporting the anxious learner
- Providing variety in the experience
- Using lots of examples to link up old and new learning
- Making the learning practical
- Adapting the setting to increase light and decrease distractions

Adaptations to fit organizational characteristics might be to make provisions for distance, inaccessibility, and multiple sites, and to integrate the organizational priorities for improvement.

For additional ideas on learning approaches, methods, and tools, we have found the following resources to be very helpful:

- *The Fifth Discipline Fieldbook: Strategies and Tools for Building a Learning Organization,* written by Peter M. Senge, Charlotte Roberts, Richard B. Ross, Bryan J. Smith, and Art Kleiner (New York City: Doubleday/Currency, 1994).
- *The Team Handbook,* written by Peter R. Scholtes (Madison, WI: Joiner Associates, 1988).
- *Facilitative Leadership,* by Interaction Associates, San Francisco, 1988.

What Worked, and What Did Not Work?

There are a wide variety of tools for staying in touch with the learner throughout the learning experience (discussed in more detail in chapter 8). But the most important issue may be the willingness to have everything on the table for change—to practice what we preach. Useful ideas include the plus/delta technique. This can be done during a session, at the end of a session, at the end of a program, and so on. Using a flip chart, two columns are headed + and Δ. In the + column, a facilitator writes what the group thought worked. In the Δ column, he or she writes what the group would change. When groups first start using this technique (discussed further in chapter 8), they will not be thinking deeply about the issues; that is, they will be giving acceptable answers or trivial ones (for example, the coffee was cold). But over time, facilitators and groups can learn to do this quickly and very effectively. Of course, the most meaningful understanding of what worked is developed by integrating learning experiences with work and looking at outcomes of that work (for example, did the patients get better?).

How Will We Improve It?

It is important for learners to see continuous improvement based on their feedback. Of course, what is really happening is that those in the teacher/trainer/mentor role are modeling continuous improvement. With experience, teachers/trainers/mentors can learn to adjust as they go along based on learner feedback, both verbal and nonverbal. Another helpful technique is for the group to decide what the parameters for change will be and to quantify the feedback. A technique for quantifying and analyzing learner responses is discussed in more detail in chapter 8. Debriefing at the end of the session and deciding what changes to make also is helpful. In this way, the learning experience can be reworked before the next session.

Appendix B provides detailed examples of learning approaches, methods, and tools that have worked in our organizations.

Conclusion

A systematic, interactive process is critical for fitting content, learner characteristics, learning approach, learning methods, and learning tools while considering organizational characteristics and available resources. The focus is on what are we trying to accomplish—the integration of learning and work to increase the capacity for change and produce excellent organizational outcomes. Of course, a learning model is needed that can accomplish this. The learning model cannot stop with individual learning or even team learning but, rather, must focus on how the learning is put to work to improve organizational results. The process urges careful attention to design considerations—characteristics of the content, learners, and organization, as well as available resources. Designing compelling learning experiences is a complex systems issue that requires setting aside old linear "if this, then that" thinking. Ultimately, the quality of the resulting learning experience is not so much due to the approach selected, but to the relationship between the content, approach, method, tools, learners, and so on. There truly is no one right answer. It is important to make assumptions based on the best information available, stay close to the learners, and continuously improve the learning experiences, focusing on outcomes in terms of organizational results (for example, did patients get better at less cost?). Continuous improvement should be a liberating concept. Remember the words of Joan Futch, nurse executive at Tallahassee Memorial Regional Medical Center, "Wherever you are is OK, so long as you don't stay there!"

References

1. Kram, B. I. *Mentoring at Work: Developmental Relationships in Organizational Life.* Glenview, IL, and London, England: Scott Foresman, 1985.

2. Watkins, K. E., and Marsick, V. J. *Sculpting the Learning Organization: Lessons in the Art and Science of Systemic Change.* San Francisco: Jossey-Bass, 1993, p. 192.

3. Senge, P. M. *The Fifth Discipline: The Art and Practice of the Learning Organization.* New York City: Doubleday/Currency, 1990.

4. Showers, B., and Joyce, B. Synthesis of research on staff development: a framework for future study and state-of-the-art analysis. *Educational Leadership* 45(3):77–87, 1987.

5. Watkins and Marsick, p. 157.

6. Watkins and Marsick, p. 166.

7. Heimstra, R., and Sisco, B. *Individualizing Instruction: Making Learning Personal, Empowering and Successful.* San Francisco: Jossey-Bass, 1990.

8. Charthouse International. *The Business of Paradigms.* (Videotape) Burnsville, MN: Charthouse International, 1990.

Chapter 6

Organizing and Managing Compelling Learning Experiences

Chapters 4 and 5 described many of the elements to be considered in the design of compelling learning experiences, including purpose; individual and organizational readiness; characteristics of the content, the learners, and the organization; the learning model; and available resources. They also suggested a process for fitting all these considerations to a variety of learning approaches, methods, and tools. In addition, appendix B includes a wealth of examples from our organizations that show how the fit has been effectively accomplished. With this chapter, our focus changes from design to delivery—to actually pulling it off!

Although many how-to materials are available that are designed to help teachers manage learning experiences, much of their content is based on the assumption that the learning experience ends at the close of the educational session or event. Teachers may be encouraged to make practical applications for the learner, and even include practice of the concepts and skills during the session or event. Additionally, teachers may be cautioned to consider, even measure, the transfer of knowledge or the ability of the learner to apply new knowledge and skills. However, in a learning organization, the definition of *learning* includes not only knowing the information and how it relates to work, but also *using* the information to improve the outcomes of the organization. Traditional materials treat learning as *separate* from work. In this chapter, we discuss what we have learned about managing learning experiences in an organization where (1) learning never stops (certainly not at the end of the session), (2) learning is integrated into the work of the organization, and (3) the effectiveness of learning is measured by organizational outcomes.

A number of factors must be considered in managing these new learning experiences effectively. We have found the following to be important:

- Getting and showing organizational commitment to a learning model that integrates learning with work
- Showing leadership commitment to learning experiences
- Recruiting and sequencing learners
- Sequencing and pacing the learning experiences
- Selecting and training teachers/mentors
- Using/aligning available internal expertise

Getting and Showing Organizational Commitment to the Learning Model

Getting commitment to the learning model is a function of:

- How well the case for the learning model is made and understood
- The degree to which stakeholders are involved in the design of the model and in the decisions about how it will be implemented
- Continuously asking for and effectively using stakeholder feedback

Making the Case for the Learning Model

Deep commitment cannot be expected unless the learning model is clearly defined and spells out why it matters to individuals and the organization. The learning model must include learning for everyone in the organization that is continuous. It must support learning from one another, with each individual at some point teacher or learner and each individual responsible for his or her own learning as well as for teaching others. Additionally, the learning model must require learning together, especially in uncharted territory where it is necessary to look for answers together. Finally, the learning model must include using knowledge to make a difference in what we do in our work. In hospitals, our work—our core business—is patient/family care. That is what everyone in the enterprise does, no matter the department or discipline. Each person must know to what outcomes he or she contributes, and how. The outcome of learning, then, is measured in terms of improvements in patient/family care. When the definition of *learning* in the learning model includes improved organizational outcomes, learning experiences by definition cannot stop at the end of the session, enabling the model to provide for how learning will be integrated with work. Most important, it means that the learning model is linked to key issues for the organization. Continuous learning at the individual, team, and organizational level is not just something nice to do; it builds organizational capacity for change, which is how organizations get and maintain competitive advantage. People can more readily commit to learning when it is so clearly important to them and their organization.

Defining Stakeholders and Getting Their Commitment

People commit to what they build, particularly to what they build together. This is the driving principle behind stakeholder involvement in the interactive process. Who are the stakeholders in the design and implementation of a learning model? In our organizations, the leadership of our projects and those tasked with designing and delivering the learning experiences were the initial stakeholders. But if the design is to include everyone, it is important to get involvement at all levels of the organization as it is implemented. Ideally, especially in the early stages of implementation, stakeholders are people who will commit the energy necessary for mentoring change, are opinion leaders, and have staying power to champion the implementation.

Asking for and Using Stakeholder Feedback

Stakeholder feedback used to drive continuous improvement is discussed in more detail in chapter 8. At this point, however, it is important to mention how essential this is to getting and using stakeholder feedback and keeping commitment to the learning model. As learning experiences are rolled out, ask for and use stakeholder feedback. Show stakeholders *how* feedback has been used and ask for it again. We have learned that it is not always apparent to stakeholders that their feedback was used. When they see how feedback is actually used, they will learn how to give useful feedback and come to recognize it as an important responsibility. They must understand that their feedback is more than just opinion giving. Unfortunately, in traditional organizations, there is a long history of asking for input with little feedback on whether or how it is used. Small wonder that so few stakeholders have a history of seeing ideas implemented and their effectiveness actually tested.

Certainly, getting stakeholder commitment to the learning model is important, but equally important is getting stakeholders to *show* their commitment. For example, learners should hear leaders voice their support of the learning model with comments that underscore its features, such as:

- "We are always learning."
- "Each of us is responsible for his or her own learning and for teaching others."

- "We haven't truly *learned* unless we *use* what we have learned to improve organizational outcomes."
- "Continuous learning is the secret to competitive advantage."

Those who effectively model being teacher and learner are important to showing commitment to the learning model; point them out. Use *many* teachers/mentors, not just a few and not always the same ones. Seeing a colleague teach and mentor is a powerful way to show commitment. Finally, ask for and use feedback from learners to show commitment to continuous learning.

> The potential for reaching outside rigidly defined boundaries is probably the most important lesson we have learned in this project. The patient's path through the care continuum includes a multitude of different stakeholders. For example, with older Medicare patients, our primary patient population, we have recognized that our area of influence extends far beyond the in-patient acute care setting. In community health care, I am dealing with a range of services provided by the acute care unit, a number of community-based agencies, home health care, skilled nursing, long-term care facilities, and so forth. Over time, I have learned that when working with various stakeholders, we not only need leadership commitment but also an understanding that broadens horizons by forcing us beyond "I am a nurse on an acute care unit" or "I am my position." My role has been to work with each of the stakeholders in expanding their knowledge base regarding the continuity of transitional care by organizing the learning experiences to put them into a broader context.
>
> *Lu Westoff, vice-president, Mercy Services for Aging, Sisters of Mercy Health Corporation, West Des Moines, IA*

> One of the early steps in Vanderbilt's change effort was to build collaborative and leadership skills among hospital and clinic administration and managers using Facilitative Leadership, a three-day leadership and meeting skills course. The executive director of Vanderbilt University Hospital and Vanderbilt Clinic, together with other members of the administration and various department heads, attended the third Facilitative Leadership course, conducted on-site by Interaction Associates. At the end of the course, he announced publicly that he not only wanted all administrators and department heads to attend, but he would fund internal staff training to become course faculty. Therefore, when a new director for the Vanderbilt Clinic was hired in 1993, part of his orientation was to attend Facilitative Leadership. Top administration has since approved a plan to support their direct reports to attend, and it is now standard practice to send each new department head a letter of invitation from the executive director. Since December of 1991, when the first course was offered, more than 500 faculty and staff have participated.
>
> *Wendy L. Baker, RN, MS, director, Center for Patient Care Innovation; and project director, Strengthening Hospital Nursing Program, Vanderbilt University Hospital and Vanderbilt Clinic, Nashville, TN*

Showing Leadership Commitment

As mentioned previously, showing commitment from leadership is key to successfully managing learning experiences. Their commitment must be visible, and it helps if leaders recognize learners for their accomplishments. However, it is important to use leaders' time wisely.

Ensuring Leadership Visibility

Our experience has been that leadership must be very visible. No matter how much learners hear about leadership's commitment from others, they still need to hear it directly from leadership. They want to *see* the leader learning with others and to see him or her as a teacher. We learned this dramatically at Tallahassee Memorial Regional Medical Center. Early in our learning process, we offered our department heads a two-day session on interactive planning/

management as a way to redesign our work to focus on patient/family care. Although several of the senior leadership team were presenters, the chief executive officer (CEO) was unavailable. Leadership commitment, including CEO commitment, to the interactive process was reinforced repeatedly. Still, at the end of the second day, the manager of a large department came up to the project director, looked around furtively as if to be sure no one could hear, and asked, "Does the CEO know about this?"

Still, for some learners, hearing—even seeing—is not believing. It is important to recognize that, for some, this may be a way to avoid full commitment: "I'll do it when my boss does it." Our experience has been that the learning sequence must deal very openly with whether someone has to give us *permission* to learn, and with the need to commit to our own learning whether or not others do. We have had to find a way to make these undiscussable issues discussable.

Leadership can be visible in the learning sequence in a variety of ways. We have found *vertical teams* to be effective because they include several levels of reporting relationships who are learning together. When the team continues learning in the work setting, the leaders have been an integral part of the whole learning process. Leaders model learning together and have an opportunity to walk the talk with their team. Vertical teams also mean that senior managers as well as middle managers are highly visible in the learning sessions.

A kickoff presentation by the CEO is another effective way to show leadership commitment. It is important that the CEO demonstrate a clear understanding of what is being asked of the teams and relate continuous learning to competitive advantage for the organization.

A presentation by the chief financial officer (CFO) showing how the competitive environment is changing also can be effective. The CFO usually symbolizes bottom-line concerns in the organization—and thus the need to learn to do more with less. The presentation might include how the changing competitive environment will place new demands on the organization for quality and efficiency, and can be related to specific teams, even specific jobs and departments. Such presentations show not only leadership commitment, but also the relationship between learning and the ability of the organization to survive and thrive.

Recognizing Learner Accomplishments

Leader recognition of learner accomplishments is a very effective way to show leadership commitment to learning. It may be formal or informal, ranging from a simple verbal "Nice presentation" to the learner or verbal recognition to the learner's peers, to formal memos to be included in performance appraisals. In many ways, effective recognition is quick and inexpensive, and requires no formal structure—only heightened awareness on the part of the leader.

However, recognition from the organization, another way to show leadership commitment, does require formal structures and processes. These show that the organization values learning by providing resources for learning, such as time. Teaching and learning expectations must be integrated into competency-based performance appraisal systems. There are many other ways to show organizational recognition of learning accomplishments—for example, holding an event to recognize mentors, staging awards ceremonies, even giving team bonuses.

Using Leadership Time to the Best Advantage

It is not news that there are many competing demands on a leader's time. When involving leaders in presentations in a learning sequence, it is important to have clear expectations about what is to be accomplished. Be specific about the length of the presentation and the amount of time the leader will need to be present. Schedule time on his or her calendar as far ahead as reasonably possible, and do excellent staff work on the presentation and materials to conserve leadership time. Write the presentation and prepare slides and handouts if necessary. Meet with the leader before the presentation to go over the materials and make final preparations. Finally, keep the learning event running smoothly and on time to minimize wait times for presenters.

Leaders can show commitment to the learning process in many ways, including taking time for rewards, recognition, and inspiration. Just as in our other efforts, we are learning as we go, creating new mental models or paradigms, and learning from each other.

In the literature, they talk a lot about the importance of the signal from the leadership team or top management in terms of the permission to change or the kind of conduciveness to change it sets up within the organization. We are sending a very clear signal throughout the organization as to what kind of behavior is being encouraged by top management. It says: This is how we want our organization to be. Ergo, these are the values we subscribe to—the blending, the integration, and the like as we integrate our initiatives throughout. There is no question that top leadership has to set both the tone and the example. Too often, all you get from top management is lip service or words to this effect: "It's okay. We will allow associates to go ahead and do this, but pretty much it is hands-off as far as we are concerned." Based on our experience, without a nod from top management, the mixed messages being sent as to what is important and what isn't important would likely culminate in enormous resistance on the part of staff.

The leadership team in a learning organization is like the hub of a wheel. They have an equal responsibility to communicate with the board and keep them up-to-date with what is happening and with the changes being implemented, and to the staff. This extends to stakeholders, too—that is, physicians and/or patients who are your customers—and likewise to any of the people who are connected to our business, such as suppliers outside the organization.

Evelyn Quigley, RN, MN, vice-president and nurse executive; and Lloyd Smith, MSA, president/CEO, MeritCare Hospital, Fargo, ND

Ideally, the reward structure needs to be changed to reflect the work of groups that are dedicated to accomplishing certain goals. A system that does not reward team behavior is a system that is working at cross-purposes. Yet rewards are not always tangible. In the old paradigm, an individual's status within the organization was an incentive, and people who were ambitious or highly motivated would often trade off financial gain for stature within the organization. Incentive, and the selection of individuals for positions, is different now that we have changed traditional position titles. We are struggling to recruit and to get the right kind of compensation structure in place. In the future, people will seek the position for the opportunity to develop their talents and to learn, as well as for the tangible rewards.

Marjorie Beyers, RN, PhD, FAAN, former associate vice-president, nursing, Mercy Health Services, Farmington Hills, MI

Managers need to maintain a balance by signaling occasional demands or expectations while at the same time allowing people to do what they need to do in order to learn. Our vision is to improve rehabilitative care. We have a highly interactive team-based model that we have moved toward, and several teams are learning—by doing, by working together, by attempting lots of things never even contemplated before. Sometimes it is very tedious to participate in a particular activity, or to fill out a certain batch of forms, or to collect data, or to sit through the meetings that are planning a project that may not immediately have a lot of payoff. It is part of my job, and the job of other program managers, to maintain the overarching vision and to know where the team is headed, so it is possible to get through those less-than-inspiring times. By providing some oversight and direction to that process, the overarching goals aren't compromised and the long-term vision doesn't get lost in the shuffle.

Bill O'Dowd, PhD, director, rehabilitation programs, Sister Kenny Institute, Abbott Northwestern Hospital, Minneapolis

Recruiting and Sequencing Learners

When implementing a large-scale organizational change, it is not uncommon to be faced with the daunting task of moving an entire organization up a very steep learning curve. There are many important issues to resolve with regard to learners, including: Who needs to learn? Who needs to learn first? Should we simply ask for volunteers, or should we select certain learners? In this section, we discuss what we have learned about recruiting and sequencing learners, getting alignment on participation in a large team, and dealing with those who either cannot or will not participate.

Recruiting Learners

In some cases, it will be necessary to create demand for learning experiences. For some individuals, it will be enough to simply offer the opportunity. However, for most, it will be important to clarify the purpose of the learning experience in terms of both why it is important to the organization, and what the experience will help the learner actually *do*. Clear expectations are helpful for a number of reasons, not the least of which is that volunteers will not have been misled.

The obvious strategies for recruiting learners are to ask for volunteers and to selectively invite participation. This usually is not an easy decision, especially in the beginning. Our experience has been that willing learners are more motivated to learn and more open to the learning experience. If the "right" people do not volunteer, keep in mind that we are not going for total consensus. Wherever learning starts, it is a giant step toward building critical mass from which change can grow.

Undoubtedly, there will be times when it will be important to select specific learners because they either are critical to some particular change or are important stakeholders in some important process. Although selecting specific learners can be very successful, it also can backfire if some of those selected are invested in blocking behavior.

> We learned an invaluable lesson from our original decision to pick people to be on a team because they were viewed as being obstinate. First off, a design team is meant to be creative and must act like a think tank. Therefore, in future, I would *not* recommend that somebody be selected because they are unreasonably obstinate and/or a potential obstacle downstream. We did that and it was a bad move on our part. In other words, don't make the mistake of choosing based on what you perceive to be *for their own good*. Such a strategy can backfire.
>
> *Ginger Malone, RN, MSN, director, innovation and consultation; and Debra Waggoner, director, consulting and development, Abbott Northwestern Hospital, Minneapolis*

Ideally, a vertical or family team will want to learn together because there will be far more support for integrating learning with work and for producing good outcomes as a result of the learning. Our belief is that learning is far less likely to occur without crystal-clear expectations that what is learned will make specific and lasting differences in organizational outcomes.

Developing Strategies for Sequencing Learners

If there is more demand for the learning experience than can be immediately met, it will be necessary to develop a strategy for sequencing learners. Again, it will be helpful to look for volunteers because they will be the most open and willing learners. Look for *vertical teams*—teams of individuals who work together and include at least three levels of reporting relationships. When vertical teams learn together, there is more support for using what was learned back in the workplace. Look for key players and opinion leaders. These are individuals who, down the road, can and will help as mentors, champions, and paradigm pioneers. Learning in a complex system is not a linear process. We have seen it demonstrated again and again that someday, some way, good things will happen when there are more true believers out there, even if it is not clear at the time how it will happen.

Find a way to use willing participants, particularly willing key players and opinion leaders. Even if they are not part of a team, create a role or opportunity for them. Early in our project at Tallahassee Memorial Regional Medical Center, our learning strategy was an intensive learning sequence for four vertical teams every six months, a start-up process for work re-design. Soon after the first group of teams began in the start-up learning sequence, the head of our employee assistance program, Keith Ivey, asked to participate. He had heard about it from one of the participating teams and quickly saw the value of reinforcing the inter-active process when he was called in to work with employees, usually to defuse a conflict situation. We worked together to create facilitator roles for those who were not really teams, but could help along the change process in some way. Since then, many facilitators have become important champions of the interactive process.

Sometimes it is even less clear how some willing person can be helpful. Shortly after Tallahassee Memorial's five-year implementation award was announced, a pulmonologist/intensivist physician, Dr. Ken Wasson, contacted the project director and expressed concern that he had not been informed of the project and needed to be brought up to speed so that he could become involved. At the time, our strategy for physician involvement was unit based. Physicians would be involved with work redesign in planning boards in the clinical area where they practiced. However, these would not be functioning for several months, and he wanted to be involved now—well, actually, yesterday! Here was a wonderful opportunity if we could invent a way to take advantage of it. The project director worked with the physician one-on-one to introduce the interactive process, which resulted in the first physician champion of the interactive process.

During this time, we learned that the physician also was a certified Apple developer and had a long-standing interest in clinical information systems. We formed a small team to develop the idealized design for a clinical information system that would support effective clinical decision making. This was the beginning of the total redesign of our information systems. The physician became chair of the Clinical Information Management Committee (CIMC) of the medical staff. He invited stakeholders from all over the hospital to participate as voting members, unprecedented for a medical staff committee. CIMC has become the keeper of the vision for integrated clinical information systems not just in the hospital, but across the entire continuum of patient/family care. Committee members have worked on defining the patient care process, helping with operational decisions on the fit between specialized departmental systems, developing a prototype for an automated patient record, and designing ways to link up community information systems.

When the demand for learning exceeds the supply of learning experiences, the learning model must support learning at the pace necessary for the organization. The question is not *whether* it can be done but, rather, *how* it can be done. The start-up learning sequence at Tallahassee Memorial is a good example of the demand-exceeding-supply dilemma. Early on, we had planned for four teams at a time in the start-up learning sequence. The plan was for one teacher/mentor, several guest presenters (mostly external consultants), and several grad students to help the teams with analytic work. The teacher mentored each team, which demanded a great deal of energy and time but was very effective. As we prepared for the next group of teams, it was apparent that demand was growing. Seven teams wanted to participate. We would need to either do it differently or tell people it was not their turn to learn. We decided that in a learning organization, it made no sense to put off willing learners. We totally revised our sequence, integrating previous learners as teachers and mentors. This was the beginning of our cascading learning model, where learners become teachers and doers become mentors. Needless to say, it required substantial adjustments. The single teacher/mentor had to learn to let go and recognize that others also could teach and mentor. And the learners had to learn to not feel slighted if they did not get the "real" teacher's attention.

Getting Alignment on Participation in a Large Team

Large teams may present a special learning challenge. To get alignment on participation in a large team, flexibility is the key. For example, the start-up learning sequence at Tallahassee Memorial included a vertical team of three who would cascade the learning back to the rest of the department. But large departments thought they needed more than one employee on the learning team in order to get a jump start on critical mass. So we moved to the auditorium and bought more flip charts for small group work! It became a vertical team responsibility to define its size based on the recruiting criteria discussed above. Team members also learned to find a way to include willing key players.

In any team, but particularly in large teams, it may be necessary to move ahead despite blocking behavior. For example, at Tallahassee Memorial, in one of our large departments, one entire shift refused to participate. They were very vocal about what was wrong with the planning board approach, even filing official complaints up the chain of command. All along the way, they were given the same message: If you don't like what is going on, participate. The spokesperson for the shift angrily told our employee relations person: "I've been here for 25 years. I've seen changes come and go. But you need to understand, this is frightening! It's not going away!" Eventually, we worked out a way for the staff to be involved, from a distance at first and then as full participants. The important thing was to keep moving ahead. Consensus does not have to mean 100 percent agreement. It can mean that we agree to disagree. Even though we all do not agree, we can agree to try some action, measure results, and revisit the issue at some specified time in the near future.

Dealing with Those Who Will Not or Cannot Participate

In the previous section, we discussed blocking behavior within teams. However, sometimes an entire team either cannot or will not participate. Often there are very real organizational priorities that may mean some teams cannot realistically be asked to take on an intense learning experience at a particular time. For example, it may be important to rearrange dates for those who are very involved in preparation for accreditation visits by the Joint Commission on Accreditation of Healthcare Organizations (JCAHO).

On the other hand, there are those for whom the time is never right. They may give an endless litany of reasons for why they would like to participate, but it is always the wrong time. In our experience, this is a leadership issue. In working together to find a way to work it out, it may be helpful to draw on Covey's example of the seventh habit of highly effective people called "sharpen the saw."[1] He gives this wonderful example:

Suppose you were to come upon someone in the woods working feverishly to saw down a tree.

"What are you doing?" you ask.

"Can't you see?" comes the impatient reply. "I'm sawing down this tree."

"You look exhausted!" you exclaim. "How long have you been at it?"

"Over five hours," he returns, "and I'm beat! This is hard work."

"Well, why don't you take a break for a few minutes and sharpen that saw?" you inquire. "I'm sure it would go a lot faster."

"I don't have time to sharpen the saw," the man says emphatically. "I'm too busy sawing!"

In his latest book *First Things First,*[2] Covey warns that we are driven by the wrong metaphor—the clock. As a result, we focus on time and keep trying to squeeze more and more of it into a day. He says that, instead, the driving metaphor should be the compass. Then our focus would be on where we are going and what we are trying to accomplish. He suggests categorizing our activities into four quadrants: Quadrant I—urgent and important; Quadrant II—not urgent and important; Quadrant III—urgent and not important; and Quadrant IV—not urgent and not important. (See figure 6-1.)

Covey sees sharpening the saw as an important Quadrant II activity. Most of us spend most of our time in Quadrants I and III. Covey calls this our addiction to urgency and says that "everywhere we turn, urgency addiction is reinforced in our lives and in our culture."[3] Figure 6-2 illustrates the addiction experience.

Few of us spend the necessary time in Quadrant II, although when asked what is really important to us, these are the things we would cite. So where do we get the time to spend on Quadrant II activities such as learning? Covey would suggest looking to Quadrant III—urgent but not important activities. "The key is learning to see all of our activities in terms of their importance."[4] In other words, think less about the clock and more about the compass.

But it is not always that simple. Learning while doing is not easy in our flattened, downsized, merged, stressed organizations. Dealing with the learning curve inevitably adds some inefficiencies. Even though it may be clear that work ultimately can be vastly improved, it is difficult to consciously choose the course that may make things worse before they are better.

For some, the issue may not be that they cannot participate but, rather, that they will not. It probably is important to have some clear leadership expectations at the outset about blocking. We have found it helpful to have a rule that individuals are not required to participate. However, an individual may not block someone else's participation. On the other hand, it probably is impossible to force someone to learn. Learning, as we have said before, is the ultimate personal choice.

It is important that leaders confront and deal with blocking behavior. However, confrontation is something most of us work hard to avoid. We would rather spend more time and energy going around the blocker and finding other ways to deal with issues. But what is really happening is that the blocker is being protected from learning. Blocking also can be a sabotage strategy (discussed in detail in a later section of this chapter).

Abbott Northwestern created a process to encourage participation in their change effort by identifying the many individual stakeholders involved in the system and recognizing the individual's desire for personal growth and contribution to the organization (Senge's personal mastery[5]).

We select our teams based on a request for a proposal (RFP) which provides an overview of the design configuration, criteria, format, process owners, the consultants and how they

Figure 6-1. The Covey Time Management Matrix

	Urgent	Not Urgent
	I • Crises • Pressing problems • Deadline-driven projects, meetings, preparations	**II** • Preparation • Prevention • Values clarification • Planning • Relationship building • True re-creation • Empowerment
	III • Interruptions, some phone calls • Some mail, some reports • Some meetings • Many proximate, pressing matters • Many popular activities	**IV** • Trivia, busywork • Junk mail • Some phone calls • Time wasters • "Escape" activities

Source: Covey, S. R. *First Things First: To Live, to Love, to Learn, to Leave a Legacy.* New York City: Simon and Schuster, 1994, p. 37.

Figure 6-2. The Addictive Experience

1. Creates predictable, reliable sensations
2. Becomes the primary focus and absorbs attention
3. Temporarily eradicates pain and other negative sensations
4. Provides artificial sense of self-worth, power, control, security, intimacy, accomplishment
5. Exacerbates the problems and feelings it is sought to remedy
6. Worsens functioning, creates loss of relationships

Source: Covey, S. R. *First Things First: To Live, to Love, to Learn, to Leave a Legacy.* New York City: Simon and Schuster, 1994, p. 35.

plan to be set up. In addition, we ask them to put on paper why they want to be a part of the change process, what is the support from their administrator and key physicians, and how broad is the investment up front. Securing this kind of buy-in a priori can prove invaluable later, if and when the level of support begins to falter, by reminding them: "Remember, it was your idea. You volunteered for this." Without this kind of impetus, the change initiative can stop abruptly. [For a sample of the RFP agreement and ground rules, see figure 6-3.]

While we have outlined some goals that all the teams are working with (in terms of creating explicit boundaries), we have refrained from saying: "You can't touch this department" or "You can't eliminate that job." Instead, we are really trying to get them to ask themselves: "What is the work, and who is the best person to do that work?" Our design team has about 10 to 12 people on it, and for each of the teams, there is an outer ring of consultants who are made up of stakeholders such as patients, families, outside agencies, board members, vendors, and physicians. These design teams can call on the consultants at any given time.

Ginger Malone, RN, MSN, director, innovation and consultation; and Debra Waggoner, MA, MBA, director, consulting and development, Abbott Northwestern Hospital, Minneapolis

Sequencing and Pacing the Learning Experiences

Effectively managing learning experiences requires careful attention to the order in which they are presented and the rate at which they proceed. Particularly for adult learners, experiences must build on one another with a chance to practice and reflect on what was learned. Experiences also must be managed so that the pace allows for learning a few concepts at a time while recognizing the adult learner's physical limitations (for example, vision, hearing, tolerance for sitting, and so forth).

Sequencing Considerations

Sequence refers to the order in which learning experiences proceed. In chapter 5, we suggested an interactive process for fitting design considerations (purpose; characteristics of the content, the learners, and the organization; organizational readiness; organizational priorities; and available resources) to learning approaches, methods, and tools. We proposed mapping the concepts and skills that need to be learned to answer two questions:

1. What concepts and skills need to be learned?
2. How do they build on one another, or what is the best sequence on which they can be learned? (See figures 5-1 and 5-2, pp. 92 and 93.)

If carefully done, these maps will provide the basis for sequencing the content. Hopefully, at this point, maps are continuously revisited and improved based on results—what works and what does not work—in terms of learner response *and* organizational outcomes.

However, concepts and skills are not the only sequence issues. Other considerations include see/hear–practice–do, varying activities and interaction, and just-in-time learning.

The See/Hear–Practice–Do Cycle

An important sequencing consideration is the see/hear–practice–do cycle. As we saw in chapter 2, the definition of *learning* includes cognitive (exposed to new ideas and begin to think differently), behavioral (begin to internalize new knowledge and change behavior), and performance improvement (behavior changes lead to improvements in results).[6] Thus, learning is more than simply receiving information, it is also using it to improve organizational outcomes. This can be accomplished most effectively when learners are exposed to the concepts and skills, and then have an opportunity to practice them in a learning environment before using them in the work environment. An effective learning sequence has been to see/hear

Figure 6-3. Sample Request for Proposals from Innovation Teams

As part of the joint team quality and grant efforts, we are seeking proposals from interested patient care units or program areas who would like to participate in a highly innovative venture.

The grant has been focusing on issues regarding how we "organize the work" to provide patient care. In order for innovative efforts to be successful, the focus needs to be on the patient, involve multiple disciplines, and the planning/design needs to occur at the "local" level rather than centrally.

Though innovation and creativity is the emphasis, there are some parameters or limits that teams would need to work within. For example, it would not be necessary to work within current job descriptions, but necessary to operate within state licensure laws and current contract considerations. Several other parameters are imperative: Work redesign efforts need to be multidisciplinary and result in positive patient outcomes.

The innovation teams will require intense evaluation as we study closely the process and outcomes. Teams will be provided with assistance through both a facilitator and a researcher.

These EPIC teams will emphasize the innovation component for patient care delivery/work redesign, incorporating the planning and measurement and improvement techniques.

Attached is a brief proposal that needs to be completed and returned to the grant office by September 20, 1991. Due to the anticipated magnitude of these projects, we will limit the selection to two to three areas.

Our hope is that eventually all units/programs will have the opportunity for work redesign.

Request for Proposals
EPIC Innovation Team

Unit/Program   Person(s) completing _____

_____   _____

1. What do patients need that is different or additional to what they currently receive?

2. Describe what opportunities exist in your area for:
   • Improving quality of care
   • Increasing care provider satisfaction
   • Enhancing collaborative efforts
   • Decreasing the cost of care
   • Increasing patient satisfaction

3. What issues/problems would you hope to overcome through innovation efforts?

4. Identify strengths of your unit/program that would provide a foundation to succeed in this endeavor.

5. Identify key health care team members who would be involved in, and essential to, the success of this project.

6. What outcomes would you be seeking as a result of exploring and implementing different health care delivery approaches?

7. Describe you unit/program's experience with change and innovation.

In addition to the above questions, please include a letter of support from the unit manager/program director, a physician, and an administrator.

Submit application to Grant Office on or before September 20, 1991.

(Continued on next page)

115

Figure 6-3.   (Continued)

NOVA/EPIC Innovation Team
Application Evaluation

Unit/Program _____   Evaluator _____

I. Criteria (Questions pertaining to application)	Exceeds (1)	Meets (2)	Does Not Meet (3)
1. Evidence of collaborative interest			
2. Clarity of reason to be chosen			
3. Evidence of patient-centered focus			
4. Evidence of improving care provider satisfaction			
5. Opportunity for improving patient satisfaction, clear about patient requirements			
6. Opportunity for improving costs of care			
7. Evidence of creative innovative thinking			
8. Evidence of commitment and appreciation for magnitude of change, realistic			
9. Acknowledgment of barriers to overcome			
10. Evidence of openness to experimentation or flexibility			
11. Evidence of ability to use consultation			

Endorsements

12. 3 letters present (Manager, Administration, and M.D.)

Unit/Program Pro Forma

13. Turnover rate

14. Vacancy rate (open positions)

15. Absenteeism

16. Budget performance

17. Quality management plan (attached)

18. Commitment/participation education (attached)

19. 1990 OES results (attached)

Leadership

20. Is there strong presence and support?

21. Evidence of continuing education/training

Other

22. Generalizability

23. Probability of success

24. Readiness

25. Summary of application:

26. Overall:

    Strengths   Limitations

Figure 6-3. (Continued)

NOVA/EPIC Innovation Team
Criteria

1. Clarity of reason to be chosen.

2. Evidence of commitment and appreciation for magnitude of change, realistic.

3. Readiness

4. Presence and support of leadership

5. Success of work redesign

The above criteria were considered most crucial on our review process.

the concepts and skills and practice them immediately in group exercises designed to reinforce them, and then provide direction and mentoring using them in the work setting.

It is particularly important that adult learners link the new to what they already know and have lots of opportunities to practice what they have learned. For example, at Tallahassee Memorial, when we teach systems modeling, we begin with a basic presentation of systems modeling concepts, using many examples from the organization. We then organize the participants into max–mix small groups for an exercise in which a systems model of a shoe store is built. Each group draws its model on a transparency and one member of each group presents it. The vertical teams then return to their planning boards and build systems models for their own areas, using the shoe store example to teach their planning boards about systems models. Each team is mentored by someone experienced in building systems models. When their model is complete, it is presented in the learning sequence to the other vertical teams.

Varying Activities and Interaction

An added benefit of see/hear–practice–do is that variety is very important to keep learners engaged. Consider varying active and passive learning activities and individual and group activities as in the systems modeling example above. An added benefit for adults is that varying activities fits well with the need to consider creature comforts.

Just-In-Time Learning

Another important sequencing consideration is just-in-time (JIT), or offering learning experiences at the time they are needed. The advantage to JIT learning is that learning experiences can be focused on particular issues and learners are very motivated to learn because they see the connection to some real issue. Many of us have noticed that learners are very motivated to learn about improving organizational performance just before the JCAHO survey! Taking advantage of the learning moment especially makes sense in these times of limited resources. In addition, use of what was learned may be more likely because improved results can be integrated quickly into the learning experience.

Pacing Considerations

Pace generally refers to the rate at which learning experiences proceed. Generally, pacing considerations include amount of content, length of sessions, need for percolation time, and desired level of detail. Learner response is the key indicator for determining the best pace.

Amount of Content

We have been most successful when we have focused on a few key concepts, linking them to what the learner already knows and offering specific help with applying them to the work setting. Particularly with new material, it is easy to lose people early in a session, which means that the whole session is a lost learning experience. It is helpful to present the same concepts in different ways to reinforce learning. Concepts should not be simply repeated. Adult learners believe they "already know that" if they have simply heard the words before. Slowing the pace with frequent summarizations also can be important. The old adage: "Tell what you will tell, tell, then tell what you told" works well. The slowest pace probably will be necessary for learning abstract, complex concepts that are perceived by the learner to be unrelated to what he or she already knows. For example, at Tallahassee Memorial, we have found consistently that measurement is a complex concept that is very anxiety provoking, probably because of the math involved.

Length of Sessions

Obviously, more content can be covered in longer sessions. The question is, How much can be absorbed of what was covered? All of us have offered learning experiences with sessions of different lengths. At Tallahassee Memorial, our experience is that adults start losing focus after about an hour. Consequently, we have designed shorter, more frequent sessions for ongoing learning experiences and have been most successful with two-hour sessions with a brief break midway. Midmorning, midweek sessions also have been successful.

Need for Percolation Time

If we really care about the integration of learning with work, it is important to allow for what we have come to call *percolation time,* that is, time for learners to reflect on what they are learning and to practice using the concepts and skills in their work. Even if they do not practice immediately, just the interval between sessions gives them time to reflect and deepen their learning by asking questions and probing the ideas. Appropriate pacing reinforces the concept that material has not been "learned" until it has been used in the work to improve outcomes. That takes time.

Desired Level of Detail

Obviously, the pace at which material can be introduced is directly related to the level of detail of the material. We have found that learners frequently want a level of detail that can slow the whole learning process to a snail's pace, particularly managers who feel they need to know more than their staff or those individuals with control issues. It is important to find ways to help people push past their comfort zones and move on, even if every last detail is not known. Some have a very hard time moving on and using the material unless they know exactly what will happen, and how. On the other hand, overly superficial treatment of complex material can make it very difficult for learners when they turn their attention to integrating the concepts with work. What has worked well for us is to have their colleagues tell their own stories about how the concepts and skills have been used to improve outcomes. Knowing that it *can* be done and that the outcomes are worthwhile helps reduce the need to master all the details.

Learner Response

The key indicator for determining the best pace is learner response. The key questions are: Are the learners engaged? What is their feedback? Learner response is discussed in more detail in chapter 8. However, at this point, it may be helpful to note that we have found that we need learner response during *and* after the session. During the session, we ask for feedback, checking on how clear concepts are. At the end of session, we ask for feedback again using the plus/delta format discussed in chapter 5, which allows for confidentiality. Of particular importance to this pacing discussion is to get the group to decide at what point the agenda will be suspended and previous material will be covered again. For example, the group might adopt a ground rule that if the Pareto analysis of their comments indicates that 50 percent or more thought the concepts/skills were muddy, the agenda would be suspended and the concepts/skills reviewed. This is particularly important because the concepts/skills have been mapped and it is clear how they build on one another.

Some learners will always have *lots* of questions, which can create pacing issues. We have invented ways to deal with them outside the group—for example, by assigning a mentor. Particularly at the beginning of the learning sequence, it is very tough for many learners because it takes time for the concepts to fall into place—for the "Ah ha" to happen. Using the experiences of others before them reassures learners that the "Ah ha" *will* happen if they push ahead.

Beth Israel Hospital has created a sequence of activities to carry out its mentor/sponsor program.

> Technology and science continue to be burgeoning areas of medicine and nursing. The curriculum within schools of nursing cannot keep pace with the rapid changes or the volume of information that must be taught to minimally prepare new practitioners for entry into the work force. Hospitals, as one of the employers of these new graduates, must provide an orientation experience which imparts the mission, values, and culture of the organization, while at the same time validating clinical competency. We have found the preceptor program which links the new clinical nurse with an experienced nurse in the practice setting for a six-week time frame to be an effective foundation for the successful transition from academia to practice. But the process can not stop there. The complexity of patient care needs coupled with increasingly abbreviated lengths of stay requires clinical nurses to have knowledge of a vast array of resources available to the patient and to be able to provide care in the most efficient, effective manner.
>
> We have formalized the postpreceptorship period into a planned program of sponsorship. Learning objectives have been developed to assure the public that well-prepared, professional nurses are available to meet and respond to dynamic societal health care needs. Toward this end, the objectives established focus upon the professional nurse's ability to: (1) demonstrate the centrality of the professional nurse–patient/family relationship in clinical practice; (2) demonstrate competence in providing high-quality, cost-effective nursing care; (3) demonstrate leadership skills in all aspects of professional practice; (4) formulate a plan for continued development and overall career goals; and (5) appreciate the larger context of the health care delivery system. For each objective, a variety of learning methods are used: clinical incidents, sponsor/new clinical nurse meetings, literature reviews, presentations at primary nurse rounds, patient reviews, attendance at workshops or forums, and maintaining a professional journal. In addition to their diversity, the range of activities reflects the various levels of involvement expected from the sponsor and the new clinical nurse.
>
> Pacing the information provided is critical to this type of learning process. It requires consideration of the individual needs of the learner while simultaneously moving him or her from more defined to more abstract methods of learning. During the first year of the Clinical Entry Nurse Residency Program, the focus is on hands-on clinical practice and establishing that the practitioner is competent. It is only after ensuring clinical competency that broader areas such as career planning and changes in the health care environment are addressed.
>
> Upon completion of this sponsorship program, the learner has met the objectives of the program, starting from the microcosm of the patient care unit and the provision of direct patient care to the larger sphere of career development and professional practice in the context of the health care system in which we practice. We anticipate that this program will prepare professional nurses to solidly assume their place within this ever-changing and increasingly challenging environment.
>
> *Heidi Alpert, RN, MS, nurse manager; and Susan Stengrevics, RN, MSN, nurse manager, Beth Israel Hospital, Boston*

Selecting and Training Teachers/Mentors

Teachers/mentors are critical in the learning organization because they are the key to the success with which learning will be integrated with work and improve organizational outcomes.

In the learning organization, teachers teach learners and mentors mentor doers. The roles of teacher and mentor are valued by the organization. Teaching and mentoring are integrated into the work and role of every worker, so teaching and mentoring are not necessarily separate jobs. By definition, learning experiences do not stop at the end of the training session! In this section, we discuss the selection and training of teachers/mentors, including the characteristics of effective teachers/mentors, as well as how teachers/mentors can be recruited and trained.

Characteristics of Effective Teachers/Mentors

Effective teachers/mentors have those characteristics that are traditionally associated with effective teachers: strong knowledge and skill base in some area, good presentation and listening skills, patience, enthusiasm, commitment, and caring. But in a learning organization, effective teachers/mentors also must be open to change, committed to their own learning and to modeling learning together as well as to the concepts taught. Effective teachers/mentors are opinion leaders. They are people with whom learners can readily identify, because they take the learner role too. They are comfortable with the notion that there frequently is no one right answer and are comfortable in uncharted territory. They model finding answers together. They live and breathe the pioneer mentality—intuition, courage, in it for the long haul. They are comfortable with differences; it does not have to be "My way or the highway." They have worked through control issues and believe that holding onto knowledge is not power, preferring instead to give it away and help people use it. Rather like Superman, the effective teacher/mentor walks on water and leaps tall buildings in a single bound!

Teacher/Mentor Recruitment

In traditional organizations, teaching and mentoring are usually distinct jobs found in distinct departments. In learning organizations, learning is continuous. All of us are at some point teachers/mentors and at other points learners/doers. Thus, teaching and mentoring are an important part of all jobs in the organization. Early in the transition to a learning organization, teaching and mentoring usually are seen as something extra that workers are asked to do. At this point, recruiting teachers/mentors will require a concentrated, persuasive effort. It is critical to be on the lookout all the time for those with the characteristics described earlier.

There are many methods for recruiting effective teachers/mentors. A call for volunteers usually yields some who are willing and, hopefully, able. Asking for suggestions from others such as managers, other teachers/mentors, or learners/doers can be effective, provided the characteristics of effective teachers/mentors are made clear. However, the most productive approach usually is face-to-face persuasion of those who in some way have demonstrated the necessary characteristics.

But sometimes even those who demonstrate the characteristics are reluctant to take on the role. In budding learning organizations, many are uncomfortable with the teacher/mentor role because they still have in mind the old paradigm where the teacher is always in the teacher role and has all the answers on many subjects. In the new paradigm, the teacher has many other roles and knows something he or she is willing to pass on to others and help them use to improve organizational outcomes. Usually, those who have the necessary characteristics are willing to try if they can be assured that they will be mentored in the role.

Teacher/Mentor Training

When taking on the teacher/mentor role, "just do it" is bad advice! Remember, these people are the key to integrating learning with work and improving organizational outcomes. It is critical to have very clear expectations for the role, including what the teacher/mentor will do, and for whom.

If the teaching role includes formal teaching, provide help with developing the content and materials. Team the new teacher with an experienced teacher until he or she is comfortable and deemed capable by the experienced teacher. Those new to the teaching role may have particular concerns about their presentation skills. Knowing that practice is the key usually eases those concerns.

Particularly in the mentoring role, the new mentor needs someone to model the role and provide support and helpful feedback. In this way, the experienced mentor shows how the new mentor can improve and at the same time models helping others improve. The mentor must focus on results, the outcome of what was learned. It will not be enough to simply help others apply what they learned. In a learning organization, what matters is that the learning actually results in measurable improvement.

The decision as to which individuals become teachers/mentors, and the level of training and support they receive in those roles, can determine the success or failure of a program.

Selecting and training trainers or teachers or mentors in our organization is based largely on whoever shows a desire or expresses an interest. If we spot someone who is enthusiastic and shows great interest in what we are doing, then we will ask them to join and become a cheerleader for us. We have found that when people are told by a supervisor, "I want you to go and sit on this committee," then that is basically what they do. They go and they sit on the committee. There is not a lot of input and certainly not a great deal of productivity. It is far better for someone to be on a committee because they're a "wannabe," rather than a "gottabe."

Gloria Jacks, RN, project coordinator, Patient-Centered Care Delivery System, District of Columbia General Hospital, Washington, DC

As much as possible, we try to make sure that enough of us have the knowledge and skill set to promulgate an idea. Individually, we all have a responsibility to train ourselves, educate ourselves, and study the concepts, but collectively, we try to make sure that we have actually understood the potential around them, and that is where the facilitators and others in leadership positions have really been helpful. Then, it is incumbent upon those of us who have had this exposure to disseminate information to the rest of the organization. This year and next, we are doing a really broad scope of training. Prior to this, we concentrated on just-in-time, which is very much a bubble-up activity.

We believe that the very best facilitators are the people who work themselves out of jobs. Over time, any given group should need less and less facilitation if what they have learned has become part of the culture. This strategy allows the facilitators to keep extending their reach throughout the organization—and throughout the region, if possible. It is our hope that someday, all teams will become self-facilitating, but it is fair to say, we aren't even close to accomplishing that yet.

Karen Logsdon, RN, MS, codirector, Strengthening Hospital Nursing Program, Providence Portland Medical Center, Portland, OR

In the majority of U.S. organizations, public speaking was listed second only to performance appraisals when employees were asked to identify what types of situations cause them the most anxiety on the job. So how do you get 34 employees to agree to speak in front of up to 100 people during the start-up and keeping-on educational sequences?

One of the obvious answers is simply to "ask" employees to participate. The answer to whom you should ask may not be so obvious. Asking everyone could be both labor-intensive (one of you and three thousand of them) and frustrating (people saying yes who are *willing* but not *able*). We have found that the "ideal" participants have the following characteristics:

- They are knowledgeable about the subject matter.
- They are well respected in the organization as a resource person.
- They have given successful presentations during previous start-up and keeping-on educational sequences.
- They are willing to learn/try new things.
- They don't turn and run away when they see you coming (smile).

At TMRMC, we strongly believe you must be supportive of others as they participate in things which may be outside their comfort zone, such as public speaking. We also feel the most important learning occurs outside the comfort zone of our "expertise." We mentor our presenters in many, many ways to make them feel comfortable with what they have agreed to do. A few important methods are listed below:

- Provide them with the training material to be covered in advance, so they know what is expected.
- Be flexible. Remember, it's OK to have people on different learning curves as long as they are headed in the right direction.
- Let the presenters know you will be meeting with them prior to the presentation to review the material and answer questions/concerns.
- Provide information about the audience (size, composition, climate/culture of the group).
- Provide them with honest "zaps" of encouragement (thank-you again for agreeing to . . .) as often as possible (on the phone, in the cafeteria, in the hallways, and before the meeting and/or after the meeting).
- Provide timely feedback after the presentation based on facilitator observations, reactionnaire/evaluation form, and individual comments.

Vivian Booth, RN, project analyst, Work Redesign Program to Improve Patient Care, Tallahassee Memorial Regional Medical Center, Tallahassee, FL

Using/Aligning Available Internal Expertise

One of the biggest challenges in a large-scale change effort is that of aligning other organizational initiatives and expertise with the change effort. Other important organizational initiatives might include strategic planning, quality, cost reduction, reengineering, or clinical pathways. We have learned that using available internal expertise as teachers/mentors in learning experiences can be an effective way to create alignment. In this section, we discuss the internal expertise that has been most helpful and how to create the needed alignment.

Identifying Available Internal Expertise

Although our organizations are quite different in terms of structure, there are some common themes in terms of the kinds of internal expertise that can be helpful. For most of us, it has been very useful to involve internal experts in quality, planning, innovation, organizational development, information, and education. It is very important to align the change effort with any existing quality improvement effort and to resolve any turf issues that may exist. Otherwise, they may be seen as separate—or even worse—conflicting efforts. Helpful quality expertise includes improvement processes, outcomes measurement, and quality tools. Planning efforts also must be aligned with the change effort. Helpful planning expertise includes knowledge of the changing competitive environment, interpretation of trend data, and project management skills. It is not always readily apparent how important it is to get alignment between information functions and the change effort. However, if data-driven continuous improvement is a core value of the change effort, access to information is obviously crucial. But even more important is the design of information systems to support the change effort. For example, clinicians spend the majority of their time processing information. Unless the information systems focus on patient/family care and support clinical decision making, improvements in clinical and service outcomes are unlikely.

Aligning Available Internal Resources with Organizational Change

In most of our organizations, a number of plans, by whatever name, spell out organizational direction in the near term—for example, the strategic plan, the quality improvement plan, the management development program, the cost reduction program, the plan for developing and using clinical pathways. Desired change is also often articulated in organizational priorities that are driven by customer needs. Ideally, these plans are integrated and form a clear picture of where the organization needs to go—and the way it needs to change to get there. However, it may be that each plan comes out of a separate department and the documents are not integrated with one another or with the change effort. Most of us have designed ways to bring the necessary stakeholders to the table to hammer out the differences and align the efforts. In the following examples, note the involvement of stakeholders in designing the change process and the learning sequence. Particularly at MeritCare, involving "information providers" has been an effective way to break down barriers and link the efforts.

The imperative to convene all primary providers of data/information within MeritCare Hospital came from multiple sources. As the organization embarked simultaneously on many change efforts, numerous project teams involved in work and role design, case management, and TQM [total quality management] became increasingly frustrated with the maze they encountered when they sought pertinent information. As real-time management of resources became the expectation of administration, the need to access especially financial and clinical data in a timely, user-friendly manner became critical. Representatives from medical records, information systems, business office, financial services, quality and utilization management, nursing operations, admitting, hospital education, and planning and research were brought together to focus on the following issue statement:

As work and role redesign projects, case management teams, and TQM teams expand and *all* managers become increasingly accountable to improve efficiency, the need for timely information to evaluate effectiveness and efficiency is critical. Future organizational success will depend on information providers integrating core competencies and capabilities to diagnose efficiencies and inefficiencies. As key information providers, you are the appropriate group to begin addressing these issues.

Among the representatives' short-term goals were to:

- Produce a resource listing the information and consulting sources, including when and how to access these resources.
- Decrease duplication of effort in providing and seeking information in support of such projects as work and role redesign, case management, and TQM projects.
- Increase access to the appropriate information and consulting services relative to using, interpreting, and collecting information.

The long-term goals were to:

- Create an integrated approach and methodology to information flows, similar to an interdisciplinary team approach, to serve all customers better as a team of information providers.
- Design and provide education opportunities relative to information and its efficient use in the organization.
- Develop panels of providers and users to work toward better use of information in the organization.

During the initial four-hour session, the group created a beginning resource list for users, identified over 70 barriers and issues related to the current system, and also identified over 20 present or potential bridges that could improve the system. Among the common "barrier" issues were:

- Territorial behavior
- Resistance to and fear of change
- Lack of trust/data integrity
- Limitations in computer system capabilities
- Duplication

- Inadequate time and money
- Lack of common definitions
- Inadequate user skills in data interpretation

These themes emerged across the identified "bridges":

- Education
- Interfaces between providers, users, and data bases
- Tools

For the first time, all of the information providers were brought together to pool their collective knowledge and perspectives. The second four-hour meeting proved to be even more enlightening. The entire session was consumed by one mission: to agree on common definitions for seven terms that often were interpreted in multiple ways. They included length of stay (LOS), admission, discharge, census, patient day, bed capacity, and short-term stay. Not only were the participants amazed at the variety of calculation methods used, they also learned about one another's professions and their national guidelines, which helped explain why some groups (for example, medical records) use the definitions and calculations that they do. One instance that exemplifies the confusion is how newborns (bassinets) are counted. "Inborn" babies (delivered at the hospital) are counted one way and infants transferred in after birth are counted another way.

"Eye-opening!" "Very necessary!" "Much better appreciation for the user's maze!" "Greater respect for, and understanding of, national requirements and individual department needs!" These were some of the evaluation comments offered by the participants at the end of the second session.

The journey toward an integrated approach that streamlines information flows, improves access and user-friendliness, and provides relevant training to information users in the use and interpretation of data has begun. Early outcomes include a published resource directory that identifies who provides what types of information, common definitions as well as variations for each of seven terms, and a standardized data set for the development and implementation and monitoring phases of clinical pathways.

Ruth B. Hanson, MSEd, RN, project director, Strengthening Hospital Nursing Program, Merit-Care Hospital, Fargo, ND

In the early part of 1990, the management team of University MEDNET began to realize that we would have to change the way health care was delivered in our organization in order to fulfill our mission and remain competitive in the 1990s. Although most agreed that change was necessary and inevitable, no one was sure how to make it happen.

Two major events occurred at approximately the same time which simultaneously supported our implementation of change:

Our chief executive officer began to hold focus groups with physicians and staff to develop key values for the organization. The development process took approximately one year. After they were finalized, the management team began a process of preparing training for themselves and the other members of the organization on how to implement and live the values.

The management team set a goal to implement continuous quality improvement. A training program was developed and implemented for physicians and staff throughout the organization. Following the training, participants were asked to identify processes needing improvement and set up teams to address these issues.

During the same time these events were occurring, we were invited to participate as part of the University Hospitals of Cleveland Network and the Robert Wood Johnson Foundation/Pew Charitable Trusts "Program to Improve Patient Care" grant. In August 1991, MEDNET grant leaders formed an Innovation, Development and Evaluation Assistance (IDEA) Committee. The goal was to assemble a cross-functional group of nurses, physicians, administrators, medical assistants, a consumer, and others to begin generating innovative ideas and plans which would change the ambulatory care delivery system at University MEDNET. The committee met approximately once per month and named themselves the "Dream Team." Their goal was to identify the characteristics that would create the ideal University MEDNET.

The creation and existence of the IDEA Committee fit with and exemplified the kind of changes the management team wanted to make in the organization. The committee was an excellent example of how our values could be implemented. One of our values is "We value innovation and the open discussion of new ideas." The group's purpose embodied this concept, and its existence served as an example to the organization of how participation on the committee was living the values. During the training presented by the managers for the physicians and staff, the IDEA Committee was often cited as an example of the kind of behavior we were attempting to promote in the organization.

The IDEA Committee also served as a catalyst for the implementation of our continuous quality improvement [CQI] program. At the time we began educating our staff in CQI principles and the use of teams to improve processes and solve problems, several subgroups of the IDEA Committee were already functioning as cross-functional teams. Many were using techniques such as brainstorming, Pareto diagrams, and benchmarking. It was often said by IDEA Committee members who were also going through the training, "We're already doing CQI, we just didn't know that's what it was called." This realization made the new concepts being taught easier to understand and less difficult to envision.

Because we experienced successes from the IDEA Committee, it provided an example to the organization that the use of cross-functional teams to improve processes could be successful. One of the successful projects of a subgroup of the IDEA Committee was the development of an ambulatory patient care pathway for OB [obstetric] patients. The project was successful because all stakeholders involved in the care of our OB patients participated and were willing to take ownership in the project. It set an example for the organization of how powerful collaboration could be and paved the way for other similar groups to form and develop pathways and practice parameters.

As we moved through our process of designating process improvement teams, members of the IDEA Committee who had experience were used as leaders/facilitators for the new teams. They provided an invaluable resource for the new teams forming in the organization.

The implementation of the grant at University MEDNET came at a perfect time in our organization. People involved with the grant were developed as leaders and innovators in the organization. They were pioneers in implementing the new ideals the management team was seeking to instill in the organization. The presence of the committee and the successes were invaluable resources in implementing change at University MEDNET.

Sally Young, vice-president, quality assurance/risk management, University MEDNET, Cleveland, OH

The idea for the Center for Patient Care Innovation was born during the planning year for the Robert Wood Johnson/Pew Charitable Trusts Improving Patient Care grant. Based on an institutional needs assessment, planning committee members concurred that practicing physicians and nurses knew what was needed to improve patient care in their area. What they did not have, was an armamentarium of skills to manage projects, think differently about familiar work, do complex work analysis or in-depth evaluation. Started as an office with the project director and an administrative assistant, the following individuals have become part of the staff (in chronological order):

- The center director, who is also the grant project director. She provides overall administrative support and integration with the larger organization. She also consults primarily with administration on collaborative change initiatives. Her preparation is in nursing with a master's degree.
- An administrative assistant coordinates office activities, manages the budget, and provides customized graphics for planning activities. She oversees the work of two technical secretaries, one whose work includes formatting and upgrading collaborative pathways.

- A liaison for shared governance. This position initially focused on implementing a unit board or unit-based interdisciplinary planning group system in patient care services based on Russell Ackoff's circular organization. The individual in this role has a master's degree in education.
- A training and design consultant. This position focused on leadership development in the midst of profound organizational change. This person is the course director for facilitative leadership and consults widely in the organization on teams, off-site meeting planning, and ensuring that training approaches in redesign reflect and model organizational values. Our design consultant has a doctoral degree in education.
- An evaluation consultant was the third position hired to track organizational culture changes and to work with individual project teams on their evaluations. This position was filled with a doctorally prepared sociologist.
- A leader for the perinatal redesign project and collaborative care/case management projects. She is a registered nurse with a master's degree in public health.
- A sixth member of our team was hired in 1993 to implement, systemwide, the documentation-by-exception system perfected in several pilot units. She also supports the development of a computerized collaborative care system. Prior to joining the center staff, the documentation specialist was a staff nurse in surgical services and had been elected Staff Nurse of the Year for the hospital. She has a BS in nursing.

Discrete services/products offered by the center include:

- Consulting services:
  - How to create a more integrated system
  - Project management
  - Training/learning (design)
  - Team building
  - Transitions
  - Planning and running collaborative meetings/retreats
  - Program evaluation and/or research methodology
  - Case management/managed care
  - Shared governance
  - Work redesign
  - Myers-Briggs Personality Inventory Tool analysis
- Tools (including development, revision, and maintenance):
  - Pathways
  - Meeting techniques
  - Questionnaires
  - Graphics development
- Products:
  - Performance evaluation tools/support
  - Strategic coaching
    - With managers
    - Institutional or organizational change
  - Neutral facilitation
  - Identify/be conduit for available resources/networking
  - Tracking and influencing organizational culture

Wendy L. Baker, RN, MS, director, Center for Patient Care Innovation; and project director, Strengthening Hospital Nursing Program, Vanderbilt University Hospital and Vanderbilt Clinic, Nashville, TN

Confronting and Dealing with Sabotage

We have already discussed defensive routines, and we know that when faced with threat or embarrassment, people respond defensively. But beyond defensiveness, for a variety of reasons, a few will be very vested in preventing change and may resort to sabotage in an effort to block or undo change.

Blocking behavior must be confronted, but most of us will avoid confrontation because it is uncomfortable. Allowing the blocking behavior to work protects the blocker from a learning experience. For some, confrontation stimulates the necessary learning. For others, there is no change. Some of those in our existing organizations will not be able to make the transition to the learning organization. There will be no place for those who will not learn and grow.

In the meantime, it has been very liberating to learn that total consensus is not required for change to happen. What is required is critical mass from which change can grow! Through an educational program on sabotage, participants in the Vermont Nursing Initiative learned to identify obstructive behavior and develop ways to overcome such behavior.

Support for the hospital restructuring projects has been a primary focus of the Vermont Nursing Initiative (VNI) staff for the past three years. Bimonthly meetings for hospital project coordinators serve as a vehicle of support. They provide an opportunity for discussion, dialogue, and education. The educational experiences are organized around topics of immediate interest to the members of the group. As the projects moved from planning to the implementation stage, the topics for learning varied from interactive planning and change theory to continuous quality improvement and project management. During year three, the staff of the VNI identified a widening gap among projects in their ability to maintain the momentum of change. A search for indicators causing the variation began in earnest.

Discussions between VNI staff and consultant Dr. Martin Charns led to the realization that sabotage was a barrier to change in some of our hospitals. So in an attempt to raise the consciousness of the entire coordinator group, an educational program on sabotage was developed.

The first type of sabotage described was the *senior executive soft pedal.* In this situation, the executive vocalizes a desire to have a particular change occur but takes no real action. When others in the organization act in ways that are counter to the change, the senior executive accepts the behavior without confronting these individuals that such acts are no longer acceptable. Another example of the soft pedal is the executive's nonattendance at meetings where planning for the implementation of change is the focus. The executive may send a substitute to this meeting, but typically the person she or he sends will be unable to convey the same level of commitment. Alternatively, support may not be provided or other people are not encouraged to participate strongly enough to ensure their commitment. Hope Is Not a Plan is applicable to this example. To succeed, the senior executive must support change through action. This behavior ensures against rewarding for nonchange while hoping for change to occur.

Senior executive action speaks louder than words behavior can do much to unravel a change process. This example deals with actions related to the commitment of time. This sabotage includes verbalization of support for change followed by such contradictory activities as cancellation of important meetings to discuss planning or implementing change, diffusion of project deadlines and milestones, or no follow-up on assignments. These executive actions could include committing to other major activities unrelated to the change, or sending ideas to committee for further unnecessary deliberation. The result of such deliberation may be analysis, paralysis, or death of the idea. It must be recognized that resources are essential to change implementation. These resources need to be managed well over the time required for change to occur.

Senior executive action speaks louder than words regarding leadership is a separate category of sabotage. Project leadership is the focus. The key leader of members of the change group may have so many other responsibilities, it is impossible for him or her to work on the change process. The leadership responsibilities may then be given to a junior person who doesn't have the established base of influence or to a part-time person who has no time to adequately execute the work. The solution to the task of leadership selection is to assign project leadership to people who are highly respected and who can influence others.

The *senior executive abdicates leadership* scenario can occur when, in the name of empowerment, the executive allows the project leadership to work independently when support and guidance are needed. True empowerment does not mean abandonment by the senior executive.

Senior executive expressed doubts is a sabotage example that illustrates this executive's power to influence change. Others in the organization will be reluctant to believe in and support the change if the leader expresses doubt. Visits to other successful sites of change may help to develop commitment from this senior executive. One project coordinator used this strategy to influence a key member of a multidisciplinary team. This member consistently expressed doubts and had effectively blocked the process of change. After a visit to a nationally recognized success story, this key member became an advocate for the change.

In the *abilene paradox,* the senior executive or the change task force itself picks a project which no one really wants but everyone goes along with it. The consequences of this decision can be multiple. No energy is really directed at the project. It is difficult to keep involvement or interest. Participants are frustrated with the change project. Finally, there is detraction from the momentum of change. These consequences emphasize the significance of strategically selecting the initial focus of change. The selection should not be made simply because something must be done. In Vermont, the VNI was a million dollar motivator to create change. The hospitals that initially rushed ahead with a poorly chosen effort eventually found themselves with a project that became undone.

The language of change must be used as a vehicle for communication, not confusion. If a careful communication strategy is not developed, *project babble* may result. If the language about change is global and general, people can't engage in dialogue or know what they're agreeing to do. Use of jargon from the organizational literature that others do not understand may cause participants to tune out. Confusion can also occur when terms are used that people think they understand but which actually have different meanings. Several steps were taken by the VNI to avoid the confusion of project babble. Project coordinators were the focus of numerous educational offerings to familiarize themselves with the language of the nursing and organizational literature. Topics for these sessions included interactive planning, change theory, project management, and total quality management. The Network for Education component of the VNI scheduled interactive television programs and day-long sessions on case management, shared governance, and role restructuring in order to update hospital staff to the language of these selected innovations. Literature reviews were conducted on these topics and were made available through the VNI office.

The final type of sabotage described by Dr. Charns was entitled *the missing member.* This occurs when people key to the implementation effort are not included in planning and change. The strongest factor in securing commitment to an idea is participation in the development of the idea. Thus, identification of the key stakeholders in the change needs to occur early in the planning process, and energy needs to be expended to engage them. Physicians were identified as one of the key stakeholders in all the VNI projects. Their actual participation in the development of the idea varied. For example, several case management projects included physicians in the initial development of clinical pathways while others developed the first clinical pathways and then included physicians. All these VNI hospitals have enjoyed a level of success in implementing clinical pathways. The lessons learned from this experience are that the physician's role in the proposed change project needs to be carefully evaluated. Then, strategies can be developed to engage the physician at the most appropriate time for the unique culture of each organization.

The Vermont Nursing Initiative project coordinator group was not surprised by the types of sabotage presented by Dr. Charns, because several members had already experienced some form of it. The project coordinators who had planned strategically for proposed changes learned of potential barriers to change, previously ignored or avoided. In hospitals where the effects of sabotage are minimal, change has already resulted in measurable outcomes; whereas obstructive behavior can usually be identified in projects where change has yet to occur. In hospitals where sabotage has less of an impact, a critical mass of individuals, committed to the change project from the beginning, are able to overcome the barriers presented by this type of behavior.

Ellen Ceppetelli, RNC, MS, assistant project director, Vermont Nursing Initiative, Montpelier, VT

Conclusion

In a learning organization, it is important to expand our definition of *learning* from knowing the necessary information and how it relates to our work to knowing how to use the information to improve organizational outcomes. Learning is continuous and is integrated with work. Effectively managing learning experiences means getting and showing commitment to the learning model. It means that we learn together, and we all teach and mentor others.

Leadership must be visible in the learning experiences, as both presenters and learners in vertical teams. And it is important to pay attention to the sequence of learners, to who learns when. Although it may be important to select particular learners, never let a chance go by to involve the willing because they will become the champions. Pace also is important. Roll out the learning sequence at a rate that meets organizational and learner demand and allows for excellent learning outcomes. Finally, it is essential to recruit teachers/mentors shamelessly and actively, and always to use existing expertise.

For those who cannot participate, keep arrangements flexible and emphasize the value of Quadrant II (important-but-not-urgent) activities. For those who will not participate, always confront blocking behavior. Avoiding the issues, or working around them, just deprives the blocker of a learning experience.

References

1. Covey, S. R. *The Seven Habits of Highly Effective People.* New York City: Simon and Schuster, 1990, p. 287.

2. Covey, S. R. *First Things First: To Live, to Love, to Learn, to Leave a Legacy.* New York City: Simon and Schuster, 1994, p. 37.

3. Covey, *First Things First,* p. 35.

4. Covey, *First Things First,* p. 41.

5. Senge, P. M. *The Fifth Discipline: The Art and Science of the Learning Organization.* New York City: Doubleday/Currency, 1990.

6. Garvin, D. A. Building a learning organization. *Harvard Business Review* 71(4):90, July–Aug. 1993.

Chapter 7

Using Consultants to Accelerate Learning

On our journey to becoming learning organizations, we all have learned the value of bringing in new knowledge from outside the organization. As Joel Barker says, "the best ideas frequently come from an outsider—someone who doesn't really understand the prevailing paradigm in all its subtleties—who doesn't understand that it can't be done!"[1] Insularity can be very self-defeating. It probably is impossible to solve problems with the same ideas that created the problems in the first place.

On the other hand, no one else can do your learning for you. The focus of this chapter is on using consultants to accelerate your own learning. Consultants abound in the field of organizational change, and if an organization has the necessary financial resources and has carefully designed the right circumstances, they can be extremely helpful. In this chapter, we discuss several types of consultation as well as a process for learning from consultants. There are many good reasons for using a consultant. We describe those reasons that are good and those that might lead to an ineffective consulting experience. Selection of the consultant is a key issue. It is very important that agreement be reached on the criteria to be used in the selection process. Effectively managing the consultation requires a clear understanding of what the consultant will do, as well as reasonable expectations about what he or she is to accomplish. Clear objectives, time lines, and costs are essential for successful consulting engagements. Good consultants welcome clarity and continuous feedback on how well they are meeting the agreed-on objectives.

Consultants need not always be from outside the organization. Many of us have found internal consultation to be an extremely effective strategy for accelerating organizational learning. In addition to discussing internal consultation, this chapter describes some of our organizations' successful external and internal consulting experiences.

Using a Process for Learning from Consultants

There are many ways to structure a successful consulting experience. Our experiences with consultants run the gamut—from a one-time consultation to an ongoing relationship, from one consultant to a team of consultants, from the consultant coming to the organization to selected individuals from the organization going to the consultant. However the experience is structured, the focus should be on organizational learning, that is, on integrating learning with the work of the organization. Structures and processes will be necessary for ensuring that individuals learn, and that what they learn is embedded in the organization. For example, if selected individuals are sent off to hear a consultant, what they learn must cascade to others in the organization. In a learning organization, willingness to teach and mentor others is a condition of being selected to attend outside meetings. Too often, there are situations such as the one reported by a colleague who works with an educational organization undergoing restructuring. One individual on the staff was a perennial conference attendee. She had been trained by the top consultants in organizational change. Her colleagues called her the Teflon™ Lady because none of the training seemed to "stick." What a waste! Many of us have seen situations where consultants are brought into an organization, several presentations are made for managers, and that is the end of it. No attempts are made to help the managers make the necessary applications to their work, or to help them use the new ideas to improve organizational outcomes.

Basically, regardless of how the consultation is structured, we want to avoid the consultant having the only learning experience! For this reason, it is helpful to see learning from consultants as a process that includes:

- Identifying the organizational need for a consultant
- Selecting the consultant
- Assessing the fit between consultant and organization
- Managing the consultation

Identifying the Organizational Need for a Consultant

Before considering the need for a consultant, it is important to have completed the process of identifying the learning needs and mapping the concepts to be learned in terms of how they build on one another. (See chapter 5.)

Keeping in mind what is to be learned, it now is possible to identify the organizational need for a consultant in terms of how a consultant can accelerate learning. The need for a consultant can then be compared to available organizational resources in terms of knowledge, time, and money. The following subsections discuss the reasons for learning from a consultant and the types of consultation that may meet the organizational need.

Reasons for Learning from a Consultant

There are many good, legitimate reasons for learning from a consultant. For example, a consultant may:

- Have new knowledge and skills needed by the organization. He or she can be particularly helpful early in a change effort when individuals in the organization have not yet learned to think outside the boundaries of their departments and disciplines.
- Bring added credibility to an organization that already has the necessary expertise (the expert from out of town phenomenon). In some cases, he or she comes from a company with the necessary credibility, for example, a Big Six accounting firm or a successful organization being benchmarked.
- Have notoriety in addition to new ideas. Perhaps he or she has authored a best-selling book.
- Bring objectivity or impartiality to an organization that has the necessary expertise but needs an outsider who can absorb the fallout from any unpleasantness or collateral damage.
- Save time for an organization that may have the necessary expertise but not the staff to devote to an issue.

The important thing is that good reasons all accelerate the organization's own learning.

There also are some bad reasons for hiring consultants, ranging in seriousness from merely a waste of money to long-term damage resulting from avoiding a learning experience. Some organizations cannot resist being trendy. They must work directly with the hottest new author, giving little thought to integrating the concepts with the work of the organization. Or an organization may place too high a value on the expert from out of town, failing to recognize its own internal expertise. Some organizations are looking for the magic bullet—the perfect solution. Too often, the solution is a cookie cutter approach, imported from elsewhere, with little thought given to the fit with the organization and its people.

A number of bad reasons are related to avoiding a learning experience. For example, costs may need to be reduced but rather than involving the organization in the learning necessary for systemic change, an outside firm may be brought in so that the blame for downsizing decisions can be shifted to it. Another variation is bringing in an outside consultant to avoid involvement in the issues or to get a quick fix. Still another variation is to avoid the necessary internal work to get agreement and commitment. In all these scenarios, the organization is being protected from the learning essential to its survival. Organizational learning is how organizations build capacity for change.

Types of Consultation

Robinson and Robinson[2] identify three types of consultation: expert, pair-of-hands, and collaborator. In the *expert type,* the organization looks to the consultant for the definition of the problem and the solution. In the *pair-of-hands type,* the organization has identified the problem and the solution, and looks to the consultant to implement the solution—to become, in effect, another pair of hands. In the *collaborator type,* the organization and the consultant are partners in identifying the problem and implementing the solution.

In another look at types of consultation, Berger and others[3] identify the expert and the process consultant. The *expert* is the more detached type of consultant. He or she is asked to "fix" the problem—in other words, to identify problems, make decisions, and implement strategies without involving the organization in the process to any great extent. On the other hand, the *process consultant* is asked to help the organization "fix" the problem.

In our organizations, we have combined these roles and invented some of our own. In terms of our organizational change efforts, we have used consultants in three roles:

1. *Expert:* The organization needs the consultant to expand its knowledge base.
2. *Supplier:* The organization has the necessary expertise and knows what it needs, but needs the consultant to supply it.
3. *Partner:* The organization partners with the consultant to work out together what is needed and how it will be done.

Michael Hammer's consultation with Abbott Northwestern Hospital is a good example of the expert role. Like many others, people at Abbott Northwestern had read Hammer and Champy's best-seller *Re-engineering the Corporation: A Manifesto for Business Revolution.*[4] When they wanted the organization to learn more about reengineering, they invited Hammer to speak to their managers.

Later, as they made plans for implementing the reengineering concepts, they selected several managers and sent them to his seminar to receive more extensive training. In this example, Hammer is in the supplier role.

Al Barstow's consultation with Tallahassee Memorial Regional Medical Center is a good example of a consultant in a partner role. Working within the mission, values, and culture of the organization, and within the framework of what we were trying to achieve in terms of organizational change, Barstow became what he calls a *thinking partner,*[5] an ongoing collaborator with the leadership of the organization to come up with ideas together to accelerate learning and change. This is what he has to say about using consultants wisely.

There are many reasons why organizations hire consultants, and many of them are bad. Hiring consultants to do the work so managers and employees won't have to do it is one example. Another is hiring consultants to get things done quickly.

Consultants can help you solve problems, but they can't solve problems for you. Why? Because the organization is a system with complex interactions of all of its parts, people, and problems. Effective solutions have to take these complex interactions under consideration in order to fit. A consultant hired to solve a problem for the organization typically does not know, or have the time or access required to learn about, the interactions specific to the client organization. Consequently, the problem is treated as discrete and separate from the rest of the system, and a solution is then imparted and installed. Most solutions don't solve problems; they only shift them to other parts of the system.

A consultant's *outside* perspective and expertise is often valuable, but it does not replace the managers' *inside* perspective and expertise. Consultants should be viewed as collaborators and thinking partners, rather than outside suppliers of management expertise. This is a good example of the design or learning spiral discussed in chapter 4. Hiring a consultant to do the work so managers and employees won't have to do it is a good example of the linear plan–do frame.

Using consultants to get things done quickly has all the drawbacks of most quick-fix solutions. That is to say, a quick fix treats the symptoms, not the real problem or root cause. Furthermore, a quick fix has unintended consequences; it undermines the system's fundamental and internal abilities to fix itself. The quick fix is attractive because the fundamental solutions and corrective actions take longer.

Consider the following example: An organization faced with a problem decides "We don't know how to deal with this, and it will take too much time to learn." The organization then hires a consultant to solve the problem quickly, and let's say the consultant succeeds in solving the problem, or relieving the symptoms, for a while at least. Guess what happens the next time the problem reappears? Right. They call a consultant. The organization has developed a dependency on calling in consultants to fix the problem. Will the problem reappear? Yes. Remember the organization didn't have time to learn how to better deal with the problem, so it called in a consultant. Consequently, the managers and employees haven't increased their understanding of the problem and its root cause. They continue to act and make decisions as they did before and, *voilà*, the problem reappears. It is unlikely the consultant will be able to effect a fundamental solution for the reasons discussed above (that is, consultants can't solve problems for you). Moreover, in many cases, the root cause is lack of knowledge and understanding of the problem by the organization's managers and employees ("We don't know how to deal with this"). The quick-fix solution of hiring a consultant doesn't solve this problem; it only makes it worse because the necessary learning process is short-circuited. Over time, the capacity of the organization to take corrective action and fix itself is undermined.

Does this imply that you should not hire consultants? No, just that you shouldn't hire them to solve your problems for you, nor should you expect to achieve fundamental solutions quickly. Using consultants wisely means intensive collaboration between organizational personnel and consultants, rather than replacement of organizational personnel by consultants. And it means focusing on increasing the organization's capacity to learn and fix itself, rather than the quick fix.

Alan M. Barstow, PhD, executive director, Barstow & Associates, Philadelphia

Selecting a Consultant

The next step in the process of learning from a consultant is selecting whom you want to work with. Keep in mind that this is about looking for a thinking partner, about looking for help.

Years ago, Marlo Thomas produced a wonderful album of songs for children called *Free to Be You and Me.*[6] One of the songs, "Helping," written by Shel Silverstein and sung by Tom Smothers, has some excellent advice for those looking for the right consultant:

Some kind of help is the kind of help that helping's all about.
And some kind of help is the kind of help we all can do without!

We have learned that the consultant must fit the organizational context. Cookie cutter approaches are a waste of time and money, the kind of help we all can do without!

Basically, there are two ways to go about identifying consultants with whom you may want to work: looking at consultants who seek you out, or seeking out consultants who you have reason to believe would be helpful. All of our organizations are routinely approached by consultants who want to work with us. Most of them offer written information about their credentials and client base that can be reviewed. Another approach is to issue a formal request for proposals (RFP). The RFP should specify exactly what the organization wants to accomplish, and by when. It is helpful to consultants to know the available resources so that the proposal can be properly sized. Often organizations believe that the amount available should not be disclosed because some consultants might do the work for less money than others. However, specifying the resources available probably will result in proposals that can be compared more readily.

Although all of us have used consultants in our change efforts, none of us selected consultants who came to us. Instead, we sought out consultants who we believed had the necessary credentials and experience to meet the learning need. There are a number of ways to identify potential consultants. Most frequently, we identified potential consultants through reading and networking with other organizations, particularly other grantee organizations, the National Program Office, and the funding organizations—the Robert Wood Johnson Foundation and the Pew Charitable Trusts. Of particular importance were the learning opportunities provided by the National Program Office which exposed all of us to a variety of writers and thinkers who many of us subsequently used as consultants—Russell Ackoff, Alan Barstow, Peter Senge, Don Lombardi, and Tom Gilmore. Another important resource has been professional organizations, particularly the American Hospital Association (AHA). Its Society for Healthcare Planning and Marketing publishes a consultant directory yearly that is very helpful. In addition, AHA staff are very familiar with particular consultants and can give feedback on presentation skills as well as the response of other organizations who have used them.

Our most important advice on identifying consultants is to have a crystal-clear shared understanding about the organizational need and the resources available. Once the need is clear, the next question should be: Can the need be met with a one-time expert-type consultation, or will a longer-term thinking partner be necessary? If the organizational need is for a one-time infusion of ideas, an expert consultant will be helpful. However, if the need is for an expert who will work with the organization over time to think through issues and approaches, a thinking partner will be more helpful.

The next question is: Can the consultation be done within the available resources? Of course, it has been established before embarking on the search for a consultant that resources were available. Now the challenge is to size the consultation to the resources. For example, if the daily fee is too high, would half a day work? Can you get by with fewer visits? Will other organizations share the cost? Are there others who work with the consultant who might be available at a lower cost?

Finally, *never, never* get past this step in the process without knowing how the consultant works and something about his or her track record. This is particularly important if all you know about the consultant is through his or her writing. It would be most helpful to actually see the consultant present and interact with others, perhaps at a conference. If that is not possible, talk to people who have worked with the consultant on similar engagements. If he or she will be making presentations, ask detailed questions about presentation and facilitation skills, and participant response. If the consultant will be a thinking partner, ask about personal style, how well prepared he or she is for each meeting, and how well the consultation stays on track.

Assessing the Fit between Consultant and Organization

Assuming you have identified consultants who can meet the identified need within the available resources and have done so capably in other organizations, you now are ready to look at the fit between the consultant and your own organization. The important issues include:

- Logistics
- Personal style
- Fit with organizational culture and values
- Mutual importance of the work
- Mutually defined expectations and outcomes

Logistics can be a show-stopper, so it is important to deal with them early in the process. For example, one of the well-known change gurus, in great demand, will only come to organizations that can be reached without changing planes and where he can accomplish what needs to be done in a single day with no overnight stay. Obviously, many organizations are ruled out, although some could send the helicopter! Other logistic issues might include meeting space. Another popular consultant only works in settings where small group work is possible, including the ability to write on the walls. For some, the added cost of outside meeting space may be an issue.

The *personal style* of the consultant is an important selection consideration, particularly when large numbers of people in the organization will be affected. The consultant should be believable and should model the concepts communicated. For example, a consultant presenting a session on learning to learn together should not come off as an egotistical lone ranger. Obviously, the most effective interpersonal style will vary with the organization. What works in Boston might not work in Billings.

Another important issue is that of the consultant's *fit with organizational culture and values*. Does his or her philosophy and values fit with the organization's model for change? Hopefully, some of the fit will be apparent from available writings, but again, there is no substitute for talking with other organizations and for talking frankly with the consultant. The greatest danger would be to select a consultant whose philosophy and values contradict those imbedded in the model for change. For example, our models for change place a high value on there being no one right answer. However, it would be very easy to find consultants who have the one right answer and will show you exactly how to impose it on the organization.

In talking to the consultant, there should be a clear sense that your *work together is mutually important*. The consultant should show genuine concern for how the work will affect the organization. Ask detailed questions about how his or her work was used in other organizations, and for results in terms of organizational outcomes. Good consultants want to be a positive influence and accept responsibility for outcomes. They never blame the organization for less than positive results. Although talking with the consultant is essential, talking with other organizations with whom the consultant has worked will provide the best information for making a good judgment about fit.

Assuming we have successfully negotiated the process so far, we are now ready for the most important issue—*agreement on mutually defined expectations and outcomes*. Up to this point, a good consultant will have developed a good sense for organizational readiness for change and organizational context in terms of culture, values, barriers, and commitment to change. At this point, a good consultant will be extremely concerned with reasonableness of client expectations and will work with the organization to clarify expectations as well as outcomes.

There should be concrete evidence of this mutual agreement in the form of a written work plan with time frames, designated responsibilities, a budget and payment schedule, and defined outcomes for the engagement. These are particularly important because they will become the mechanisms for effectively managing the consulting engagement. Usually, these are part of the contracting process that also should include assurances about confidentiality, and ownership of materials developed and publication rights. Obviously, contracting for a single seminar is far less detailed than for a long-term thinking partner.

A good consultant will invest the time necessary to get agreement, and will listen carefully. He or she does not have all the answers, and will not do the work *for* you. Finally, a good consultant will make reasonable commitments and will be clear about exactly who in the firm will be doing the work, which principals and which associates.

Julianne Morath at Abbott Northwestern Hospital says, "Choosing a consultant is a decision that is directly affected by an organization's culture and what the organization is attempting to accomplish."

When deciding whether or not to hire a consultant, individuals within the organization need to determine if the organization has the expertise or the potential for developing that expertise internally.

One of the things that we at Abbott Northwestern Hospital are concerned about is helping the people who work here develop the capacity to learn so that, as new challenges confront us, we'll be able to respond. In this time of never-ending change, we want to have internal resources to call upon for support and assistance. We want to ensure that we are continually improving the quality of our thinking and our relationships as we confront new challenges.

We have worked with consultants who have taught us what we needed to know to respond to specific challenges. We also have sent staff members outside the hospital so that they could develop new ideas, establish networks, discover new technologies and methods, and bring them back.

At Abbott Northwestern, we are fortunate to have a consultation and development department, a branch of human resources, that includes quality process experts who support teams engaged in work redesign projects and change management. To reinforce the expertise and guidance they provide our staff members, we invest in continuing their development as experts within our organization. By sharing what they have learned in their experiences outside the organization, they replicate it through other staff. They are constantly preparing themselves — and us — for the next wave of change. The knowledge they gain cascades through the organization.

Julianne Morath, RN, MS, vice-president, patient care, Abbott Northwestern Hospital, Minneapolis

Susan Beck, of the University of Utah Hospital, shares some of that organization's experiences and offers some advice.

Selecting and effectively working with a consultant requires careful consideration and planning. Yet in reality, many organizations select consultants based on the notoriety of the individual or the organization with which the consultant is affiliated, a personal recommendation, availability, and cost. Indeed, we were influenced by these factors in our work with consultants in the Program to Improve Patient Care, and we learned that they may not be the critical indicators of a successful consultant–client relationship.

Although someone may have led a very successful and acclaimed project, such an individual may be very nearsighted and operate under a belief that his or her organization's way or model is the best — and perhaps only — way to do things. Such a consultant may come in and try to take you somewhere without seeing where you really want to go. Thus, rather than bringing ideas and assuming they apply to your situation, a good consultant listens and tries to understand your vision and operation clearly. The consultant then draws upon his or her own experience and expertise to provide individualized guidance to your work.

A personal recommendation to use a particular consultant also can backfire. If the person making the recommendation worked with this consultant before, it is important to inquire about the purpose of the relationship and the type of expertise that was actually provided. If the consultant is a personal friend of "the recommender," the judgment as to the quality of the consultant's work may not be objective. Furthermore, if "the recommender" is an internal stakeholder, there is the risk that the consultant may enter the organization with a biased perspective gleaned from the view of this one individual.

One common mistake is to contract with someone for a one- or two-day consulting visit without allowing for adequate planning and follow-up time. Yet the use of consultants in a one-shot deal can be effective for certain activities, especially workshops and retreats. For example, we used the services of Mr. Tom Gilmore from the Wharton Center for Applied Research, University of Pennsylvania, Philadelphia, to both teach and guide us in using the interactive planning process.

For support in organizational development, there is a distinct advantage in developing an ongoing relationship with a consultant, especially given the time it takes for an outsider to really grasp the culture and concerns of your organization. At the University Hospital, we were able to work with Dr. Arnold (Oz) Rothermich, a consultant in organizational development from the University of Utah. There was a tremendous advantage in developing a trusting, working relationship with someone locally available and willing to jump in and troubleshoot when the process of change became especially difficult.

In the real world, the cost of the consultant always influences the selection process. The most highly paid consultant is not always the best. The real success factor is matching the expertise and style of the consultant to the needs of your organization. Are you looking for someone to be a neutral facilitator of a group process, or do you need someone with specific knowledge or experience to guide your design or implementation? Clarify your needs, find the best match, and set clear expectations and boundaries with the consultant. In the long run, these steps will strongly influence a productive consultant–client relationship. Such an approach will promote an experience where the consultant is working to serve you, the client, rather than the other way around.

Susan L. Beck, PhD, RN, project director, University Hospital's Program to Improve Patient Care, University of Utah Hospital, Salt Lake City

Managing the Consultation

This is the last, and perhaps the most frequently overlooked, point in the process of learning from consultants. Effective management, of course, requires its own structure and process. The structure must include a single person charged with responsibility for managing the consultation, as well as the tools described earlier—the work plan and the budget. The structure also may include a larger group, for example, a steering committee, to which the single person is accountable. It may be helpful to look at managing consultants in terms of the phase of the consultation: planning, implementation, or wrap-up.

Planning Phase

The planning phase of the consultation builds on the agreements made during the selection process. At this point, there should be a clear understanding of what the outcomes of the consultation are to be. Keep in mind that the purpose of the consultation is to accelerate learning and that learning must happen at the individual, team, and organizational level. Therefore, there should be clear expectations at all three levels.

It will be most helpful to work with the consultant to develop a more detailed work plan. The work plan should include all activities necessary for the consultation, as well as those activities necessary to integrate what has been learned with the work of the organization, including measuring results. It is here in the work plan step that many consultations go awry. Too frequently, little thought is given to what the consultant will do, what will be necessary to support the consultation, and how what is learned will be integrated with the work to improve organizational outcomes.

It goes without saying that the work plan must fit with the budget. But it can be tricky to work out the hours or days spent on various tasks, keeping in mind time on-site and travel expenses. Most consultants also charge for telephone consultation time. We have found it useful for the work plan to include at least three columns: activities, person responsible, and time frame. The bottom line is to develop a work plan with enough detail so that it can be an effective tool for managing the consultation. It must clearly state what will be done, by whom, and when. It is extremely important to use time wisely, particularly expensive consulting time. Be sure to periodically build in planning time for the person managing the consultation to spend with the consultant to give and get feedback on how the consultation is going, and to update the work plan.

Implementation Phase

The management challenge during this phase of the consultation is to keep the process on track and to be attentive to changes that might be necessary to ensure, or even improve, the expected outcomes. Using the consultant's time wisely may mean preparing carefully for consultant visits, reconstituting work groups so that they are more effective, and working behind the scenes with these groups to prepare them to take advantage of time with the consultant. Information flow also may be important—getting materials to the consultant to review prior to the visit, preparing materials for distribution during the visit, and so on. A common time waster for consultants is to be prepared to work on an issue, but the client is not ready with the background information when it was promised. Most consultants are juggling many engagements simultaneously, so it is important to meet the time frames in the agreement insofar as possible.

It is rare that a consultation proceeds exactly as planned — and there is good reason to question whether it should. Particularly when working with a thinking partner, it is very important to build on what has been learned as the consultation goes along. Equally important are changes and revisions that reflect a widely shared understanding of how the expected outcomes can best be achieved. Making these periodic adjustments is a way to ensure that organizational learning results from the consultation.

Wrap-Up Phase

Too often, when the consultation is over, the consultant leaves, taking all the learning out the door. Wrap-up is the most often neglected phase of a consultation. Yet it is the most important way to prevent the phenomenon of the consultant having the best learning experience.

The transfer of knowledge and how it will be imbedded in organizational structures and processes should have been addressed in the planning phase, and included in the work plan in the implementation phase. In this phase, we look back over the consultation to make certain that nothing was unintentionally left undone.

It also is important in this phase to make certain that final billing arrangements are clear, that all contractual obligations have been met, and that there is a clear understanding as to ownership of materials. At this point, the consultant should return working documents owned by the organization, and the organization should return materials owned by the consultant. Agreements to use materials should be finalized as well. Also, publication plans of both parties should be discussed and agreement reached on authorship, copyrights, trademarks, and so on. This will be necessary to avoid the unpleasantness of seeing organizational materials published by the consultant, or worse, having your materials used by the consultant in another organization. Always retain ownership of your materials and allow publication only if you have the right to approve anything published about your organization.

A key to success is recognizing the interaction between the organization and the consultant, and clearly defining the roles of each.

In times of intense change, we tend to underestimate and mistrust our own wisdom. We must learn to take advantage of our organization's collective wisdom and unleash the talent at our disposal. Unexpected and powerful solutions emerge when we look to those closest to the work for the answers.

When outside consultants are engaged, it is important that we retain ownership of the change process. We must be sure that we are not just looking for a one-time, outside intervention but, instead, will use the consultant's expertise to build for the future. The old maxim You Can Feed the People or You Can Teach Them How to Feed Themselves has never rung more true as it pertains to the consultant–client relationship. The onus is on consultants to teach their clients to become self-supporting, to create a jumping-off point from the knowledge and expertise they share. Often organizations use consultants so that they can avoid dealing with sensitive subjects within their organization or for affirmation of their current approach to a situation. In today's world of change, it is only through truth-telling and by dealing with the sensitive subjects that we are able to learn and develop the capacity for effective collective action.

Julianne Morath, RN, MS, vice-president, patient care, Abbott Northwestern Hospital, Minneapolis

When dealing with consultants, it is vital to facilitate their success in the organization. One way to facilitate this success is to have a key person give the consultant information about the organization. It is not only helpful to share facts such as organizational tree, mission, goals, background on why we want this consultation, but also to share thoughts and feelings about the environment and atmosphere of the hospital. As a facilitator of the consultant, I am up front that this is my intuitive assessment and may not be reflective of the hospital as a whole. It does give intimate perspective of the current outline.

One of the qualities of a consultant that benefits us is flexibility and availability to communicate. When our hospital used a consultant for change management education, I was able to meet her face-to-face a few times. Though that is not always possible, I find it valuable to have that level of communication. She was willing to conduct several conference calls, even though we were still in the brainstorming phase. As the date of the targeted consultation drew nearer, I kept her informed as to last-minute changes. Our organization was in the middle of reorganization when the relationship started and "language" was changing overnight. It was important to have her use our language. For example, we went from departments to services. Having consultants use the organization's current lingo offers them immediate credibility with target audiences. Credibility is directly related to their success.

In summary, it is important to work hard with a consultant so he or she can be successful. It is important to share as much of the organization as possible. This means providing enough of the right information and then trusting the consultant with it. Communication also needs to occur so that joint expectations and parameters of the consultant's involvement are clear. Ultimately, the organization needs to take accountability for its own learning and behavior changes. An organization cannot expect a consultant to work a miracle. Resources also need to be well allocated.

Roberta Young, educator, MeritCare Hospital, Fargo, ND

Ken Boutwell is president of a very successful national management consulting firm based in Tallahassee with offices in Austin, Texas; Sacramento, California; and Olympia, Washington. He is in an excellent position to offer advice on how to get the most value from consultants.

Outside consultants can provide very valuable services for organizations, particularly in one of the following situations:

- An objective outside evaluation is needed.
- Specialized skills are needed to address an important issue.
- Highly skilled assistance is needed for only a short time period.

However, many organizations fail to get the most from their outside consultants because they do not adequately plan and prepare for the consultant's work. To get the most from a consultant, an organization should:

- Make sure that the selected consultant has had prior relevant experience and has no conflicts of interest.
- Check references and ask for and review copies of previous work before contracting with the selected consultant.
- Clearly define the consultant's responsibilities (and expected deliverables) before hiring the consultant so that there is a clear, mutual understanding as to what is to be accomplished.
- Require that the consultant prepare, and submit for your approval, a detailed project work plan and time schedule so that you will have a basis for monitoring the consultant's progress.
- Make all needed information available to the consultant early in the process so he or she can be fully informed about the issues of concern.
- Be open and honest with the consultant about any factors that may affect his or her work.
- Be responsive and timely to consultant's requests for reviews of work plans and products.

Ken Boutwell, PhD, president, MGT of America, Inc., Tallahassee, FL

Using Internal Consultation

Increasingly, internal consultation is being recognized as effective in organizational change efforts. Not surprisingly, internal consulting works much the same as external consulting, except that internal consultants are members of the organization.

To understand the *value* of internal consultants, Gilley and Coffern[7] list eight fundamental purposes, ranking them from highest to lowest in terms of their influence on organizational change:

1. Providing information
2. Solving problems
3. Conducting an effective diagnosis
4. Providing recommendations
5. Implementing change
6. Building consensus and commitment
7. Facilitating client learning
8. Improving organizational effectiveness

They consider the first five as more traditional purposes of consulting, with the last three emerging as important as we move toward learning organizations where the bottom line is improving organizational effectiveness.

Most of the project directors in our organizations have functioned primarily as internal consultants as we have guided the change efforts in our organizations. Although our projects have been organized quite differently, for most, there has been some value in not being readily identified with any one organizational entity—in other words, in being seen as impartial and objective. Most of us also have been able to extend the efforts of the small project staff by recruiting and training others as facilitators and mentors, building a cadre of internal consultants.

The consultant perspective seems just right for building learning organizations. The good consultant meets you where you are, offering the necessary help to accelerate learning but not doing it for you. The good consultant is a thinking partner who works with you to find answers, rather than imposing the one right answer. And the good consultant focuses on results in terms of organizational outcomes!

> When one of my clients brings a new or diverse idea to me that I haven't worked with before, I try to become as knowledgeable as I can about their vision and direction. Sometimes this is the hardest part of the consulting relationship because often clients cannot articulate how an idea could be operationalized. Dialogue encourages them to more clearly articulate their innovative ideas. During this time, I try to ascertain how their idea fits familiar conceptual frameworks or models. For example, a nurse leader and consultant called me to help her design a survey she could use to measure leadership behaviors with her managers. Our initial conversation attempted to determine the feasibility of measuring leadership in this way. I asked her to share with me some of her heros in leadership development. Using the list she generated and a more comprehensive literature review, I discovered references to the Kouzes and Posner leadership model. I shared this with her and we explored if it could accomplish what she envisioned as a leadership development model. Much of what I do as an internal consultant is to help clients more clearly articulate their ideas, to help them consider how their idea fits within the organization or how it supports ongoing nursing department initiatives.
>
> *Mae McWeeny, MA, RN, learning specialist, Center for Professional and Clinical Development, Abbott Northwestern Hospital, Minneapolis*
>
> In our experience, there is an unwritten bias which says, "We don't believe that the information a group can come up with internally is as thorough or as professional as you would get from an outside consultant." It goes without saying that outsiders usually bring in new ways of doing things, databases, comparative information that maybe isn't available in-house. Still, that doesn't

mean that we have to undervalue the contributions made by internal people or to assume that their decisions won't be as good as they should be. Sometimes that may be true, but it largely depends on how dedicated those people are to coming up with alternative ways of doing things. Historically, we tended to look outside for more answers and now, we look within.

Our belief is that the answers lie within if we just learn to ask the right questions, and it is our responsibility to figure out what those questions are. Some of our potential internal consultants have gone off, for example, to Hammer's re-engineering program, and they are trying to develop themselves into resident resources, comparable in quality and expertise to anything we'd find externally.

Ginger Malone, RN, MSN, director, innovation and consultation; Elaine Slocumb, RN, PhD, nurse leader and consultant, information systems, evaluation and measurement; and Debra Waggoner, MA, MBA, director, consulting and development, Abbott Northwestern Hospital, Minneapolis

We, like so many organizations across the country, have been dealing with issues of productivity and downsizing. It is no secret that we are trying to get the biggest bang for the buck while keeping in mind that we need to hang onto quality indicators at the same time. The trade-offs between these two issues have yet to be resolved, which brings to mind an incident that happened here a year ago.

Our administrative team decided that they were going to hire consultants to come in and help us look at where we needed to make cuts, specifically trimming our FTEs [full-time equivalents]. At the same time, there was a productivity task force, made up mostly of managers, a few other key people, along with several of the administrators who were working together on how to deal with the issue of productivity. When the decision came to their attention that the administrative team had decided to hire a group of consultants for a six-figure consulting fee, this group said, "Absolutely not! We won't stand for it. We think that we can look at these problems in our own way."

A group of middle managers put together a proposal for creating a Position Review Committee that would take responsibility for reviewing all FTE requests and for dealing with the fallout from any of the requests that were either approved or denied. As a group, everyone promised to get this place trimmed down by a 100 FTEs through attrition over the period of one year, to which the Administrative Council said, "If you think you can do it, go for it." To make a long story short, this group of middle mangers was able to get overstaffed departments closer to benchmark and, overall, in the organization, they were able to bring us in line. We didn't quite make 100 FTEs in a year's time, but they didn't quit. At this point, we are vastly trimmer and there have been no layoffs.

Jane Scharff, MN, RN, CNAA, project coordinator, Montana Consortium, Saint Vincent Hospital and Health Center, Billings, MT

Sharing Examples of Successful Consulting Experiences

Many of us have had successful consulting experiences. Some of them, and the elements that made them successful, are described in this section. Note particularly how MeritCare talks about carefully preparing one of its consultants so that she could use their language, how Vanderbilt looked at their consultants' successes in other organizations, how Health Bond looked for a shared vision, and how Tallahassee Memorial structured its thinking partnerships.

At MeritCare, we prepare consultants in advance so that they have an accurate view of the organizational context. Barbara Hanley is a good example of a consultant whom we prepared thoroughly. She was able to come in, use our language and not impose new jargon. Combining her expertise and external perspective with our thorough insider briefing enabled her to build on work we were doing. We have learned that if you can blend a new process or concept into what you are presently using, resistance to change is less, and effectiveness is enhanced.

Our relationship with Barbara Hanley has persevered over time. I think that effective consulting relationships in a learning organization exist over time and require up-front investment on the part of the organization. The consultant isn't there to provide answers but, rather, to bring expertise and knowledge about "best practices" across the nation, and to help you discover your own opportunities and options.

Ruth B. Hanson, MSEd, RN, project director, Strengthening Hospital Nursing Program, Merit-Care Hospital, Fargo, ND

More than 500 Vanderbilt staff and faculty have attended Facilitative Leadership (FL), a three-day course on leadership and effective meeting management developed by Interaction Associates (IA). An IA trainer first delivered the course on-site in 1989 for a group of administrators in patient care services. After two successful courses for hospital and clinic administrators and executive managers, also delivered by IA trainers, the executive director of Vanderbilt University Hospital and Clinic decided to offer the course to all Vanderbilt administrators and managers. He requested that the course be delivered by internal faculty.

Four staff members from the Center for Patient Care Innovation were designated to become the internal faculty. All staff members had completed a basic FL course. A senior trainer from Interaction Associates delivered the on-site course to train the internal Vanderbilt faculty. He also was available the first few times that Vanderbilt delivered the course.

We talk regularly with our initial contact at Interaction Associates. She is a resource to us and informs us of new course offerings.

Wendy L. Baker, RN, MS, director, Center for Patient Care Innovation; project director, Strengthening Hospital Nursing Program, Vanderbilt University Hospital and Vanderbilt Clinic, Nashville, TN

Several factors made Gelinas and James attractive consultant candidates to assist us in our organizational reengineering effort:

- Mary Gelinas, a principal in the firm, had been one of the designers of Facilitative Leadership, a course developed by Interaction Associates but adapted by our Center for Patient Care Innovation faculty. More than 200 of Vanderbilt's managers have attended.
- The Collaborative Organization Design model developed by Mary Gelinas and Roger James had been used successfully in a variety of corporate and service sector change initiatives.
- Most important, the model built on the numerous preceding change efforts at Vanderbilt and assumes that the only sustainable change is collaborative change.

The working model of two internal consultants together with Gelinas and James reflects the value that was put on building and developing the expertise of the organization and internal consultants. Executive management and the two internal consultants agreed on a shadow consulting relationship for our collaborative change initiative.

The project ran from late October 1993 through June 30, 1994, when the design phase was complete. Ten design team members spent approximately two to three days weekly on the project. The internal consultants spent at least this much time, usually three to three and a half days weekly. Gelinas and James coached the internal consultants on strategic points of the model and had some regular interaction with executive management. One of them was on-site twice monthly, for three to four days. There were two- to three-hour conference calls weekly with all four consultants. Regular feedback on how the four-way consulting relationship was working was essential to its success.

Wendy L. Baker, RN, MS, director, Center for Patient Care Innovation; and Marilyn Dubree, RN, MSN, director, patient care services, and chief nursing officer, Vanderbilt University Hospital and Vanderbilt Clinic, Nashville, TN

Health Bond's consulting relationship with Creative Nursing Management (CNM), Marie Manthey, president, was enhanced by involving Marie and vice-president Susan Forstrom in day-long service/education strategic planning sessions, in October of 1991, January 1992, and again in February 1995. In May of 1993, Susan Forstrom and Diane Miller participated in another strategic planning session related to service/education partnership development. Shared visioning over time between representatives of Health Bond's member hospital and partner schools and CNM consultants has created a rich mosaic and context for creating a preferred future.

Creative Nursing Management's programming emphasis on empowerment of patient care services personnel focuses on experiential learning for direct communication relationship management, problem solving, and risk taking. Health Bond has accessed nursing education faculty to these learnings. The programs and consultations which Health Bond has made available to hospital members and partner schools related to leadership empowerment and care delivery systems innovations are grounded in relationship and process emphasis.

Coming to grips honestly with the current reality of relationship management and communication patterns is only part of the recognized need. The other critical pieces are developing skills for shared visioning and encouraging employees to lean into the creative tension between "what is" and a preferred future.

Sharon Aadalen, RN, PhD, director, Health Bond Consortium, South Central Minnesota, Mankato, MN

Our project features a thinking partnership with the Florida State University, which is designed to bring a wide variety of the best possible thinking to bear on our project. The purpose of the thinking partnership is to provide us with ever-increasing knowledge of, and access to, resource people and ongoing research which would benefit the project.

We had expected that this strategy would result in a group of faculty resource people who would solicit papers to be presented in a symposium. The thinking partnership is now taking the form of resource people being made available to our project teams on a case-by-case basis to work on particular issues. University resource people include:

- Dr. Robert Zmud, College of Business, the eminent scholar in Management Information Sciences at FSU. He has taught systems modeling and other business concepts in our educational sequences. He is also working with our technology impact study helping the research team collect and analyze data related to change-of-shift report and implementation of the electronic Kardex™.
- Dr. Michael Showalter, College of Business, an expert in work measurement and operations research, has taught work measurement and quality improvement concepts in our educational sequences. He is working with several teams, particularly the orthopedic nursing unit team as they develop clinical paths. He has helped them conduct patient focus groups to determine how patients measure quality. He has also helped as they form interdepartmental teams to deal with managing processes.
- Dr. Gary Heald, College of Communication, an expert in survey and opinion research and in research design and statistical analysis, assists us in conducting project surveys (employee satisfaction, physician satisfaction, and physician office staff satisfaction). Dr. Heald provides special analysis of employee satisfaction surveys, participates on the career development planning board, and facilitated focus groups for both start-up and keeping-on educational sequences. In addition, Dr. Heald teaches a six-week course in statistics during our educational sequence, providing the necessary statistical foundation for continuous improvement.
- Dr. Fred Seamon, Department of Public Administration, an expert in human resources and cultural diversity, has worked with teams in environmental services and dietary services to redesign our start-up staff interview process. In these areas, the staff is large and there are few staff with interviewing skills. We designed a group interview process, starting with managers, to get the information necessary for the start-up team to work with. Dr. Seamon continues to work with both departments as they redesign their "interpersonal environment." In addition, Dr. Seamon teaches a segment in celebrating differences in our educational sequence, providing team members with the opportunity to identify both similarities and differences, and how to take advantage of diversity in the workplace.

- Dr. Duane Meeter, Department of Statistics, an expert in quality tools and methods, taught a course in how to improve a process in our educational sequences, and is available to project staff to consult on quality issues.

In summary, we have been very fortunate to have a cadre of resource people from FSU who are committed to our project and willing to work with our teams on specific redesign issues.

Vivian D. Booth, RN, project analyst, Work Redesign Program to Improve Patient Care, Tallahassee Memorial Regional Medical Center, Tallahassee, FL

Conclusion

Consultants may be used to *accelerate* learning. It is very important to be clear about the organizational need to be addressed by the consultant, to select a consultant who fits with your need and your organization, and to do your own learning! Look for a consultant who will be a thinking partner, not one with a cookie cutter approach that is imposed on the organization. Plan carefully and manage the consultation using the work plan as a tool. Carefully integrate what has been learned into the work of the organization so that organizational effectiveness is improved.

The key factors of a successful consultation are a shared vision of where the consultation is going, a shared understanding of how and when you will get where you want to go, and a shared belief in the importance of the work. The best consultations fit the organizational context and are focused on improving organizational outcomes—the kind of help that helping's all about!

References

1. Barker, J. A. *Future Edge: Discovering the New Paradigms of Success.* New York City: William Morrow and Company, 1992, p. 55.

2. Robinson, D. G., and Robinson, J. C. *Training for Impact: How to Link Training to Business Needs and Measure the Results.* San Francisco: Jossey-Bass, 1989.

3. Berger, M. C., Ray, L. N., and Tonga-Armarasco, V. D. The effective use of consultants. *JONA* 23(7/8):65–69, July–Aug. 1993.

4. Hammer, M., and Champy, J. *Re-Engineering the Corporation: A Manifesto for Business Revolution.* New York City: HarperCollins, 1993.

5. Barstow, A. M. Unpublished manuscript. Philadelphia: Barstow & Associates.

6. Silverstein, S. Helping. In: *Free to Be You and Me.* New York City: Bell Records, a Division of Columbia Pictures Industries, 1972.

7. Gilley, J. W., and Coffern, A. J. *Consulting for HRD Professionals: Tools, Techniques, and Strategies for Improving Organizational Effectiveness.* Burr Ridge, IL: Irwin Professional Publishing, 1994.

Chapter 8

Rethinking Evaluation: Continuously Improving Learning Experiences

Much of what we presently know about evaluating learning experiences comes from the study of children in schools, which offers a rich science of learning as well as of evaluation, tests, and measurement. In this chapter, we stretch our assumptions about learning and evaluation, and describe the challenge of evaluating learning experiences, particularly in learning organizations. We also present some traditional approaches to evaluation as well as some of what we have learned about evaluating learning experiences in our organizations. Next, we suggest that continuous improvement is a more systemic model for evaluating and improving learning experiences. Finally, we present a model for rethinking learning that describes the breadth and depth of learning necessary for an organization to learn, which is how organizations build capacity for continuous change.

Facing the Challenge of Focusing on Organizational Outcomes

Because evaluation of learning and learning experiences has focused primarily on children and on learning in school settings, the evaluation methods traditionally used in schools also have been used to evaluate the effectiveness of learning in the workplace. However, attempting to apply traditional evaluation methods to learning organizations presents a number of challenges. First, and most obviously, workers are adult learners. Unlike children, adult learners must unlearn obsolete concepts and link new ones to what is already known to solve real-world workplace problems. Second, the best measure of workplace learning effectiveness is not an individual test score—or even a team test score. The best measure is organizational outcomes.

The most significant challenge we face in learning organizations is that any evaluation method must account for two key concepts—the *depth* and *breadth* of learning necessary in a learning organization. In chapter 2, we discussed Garvin's ideas on building learning organizations.[1] He sees learning as occurring in three overlapping stages: cognitive, behavioral, and performance approval. (See figure 2-1, p. 12.)

Later in this chapter, we propose that these stages reflect the *depth* of learning in a learning organization. The first stage, cognitive, begins with exposure to new ideas and ends in a shift in thinking as a result of the new ideas. The second stage, behavioral, begins with internalizing the new ideas and ends with a change in behavior. In the third stage, performance improvement, behavior change is directed toward some issue and is used to produce measurable improvement in results. It makes sense that the first two stages are necessary for organizational learning to occur: "I need to know about something before I can do it." But the deepest learning takes place when organizational performance is improved: "I know it, I know how to do it, and I *use* it to measurably improve organizational results."

Most evaluation tools test only the cognitive stage of learning (what we know). However, increasingly, evaluation tools are being developed to look at how well learners can demonstrate the concepts they have learned in practice settings. These tools test the effectiveness of the behavioral stage of learning. Still, for most of us, it is a huge leap to see organizational outcomes as measures of the effectiveness of learning experiences. Although we measure organizational effectiveness as part of our improvement programs, learning and improvement—or training and quality—are usually separate efforts. In the learning organization, the whole point of learning is change. It is not enough to know something or even to know how to do it; rather, the concepts must be used to get results! The depth of learning is achieved by integrating learning with work.

The second key learning organization concept is *breadth* of learning. In chapter 2, we also discussed many of Senge's ideas on building learning organizations.[2] Among them is the idea that certainly individuals must learn, but organizations cannot learn unless individuals can learn to learn together, in teams. The breadth of learning can be seen as a continuum from individual learning to team learning to organizational learning. Most evaluation methods focus on individual learning, although we are beginning to consider how team learning can be evaluated. Traditional evaluation techniques have not focused on the effectiveness of organizational learning.

In the learning organization, individuals must be committed to their own learning. But individual learning alone is not enough, because people come and go and take their knowledge with them. Organizations cannot learn unless people can learn together and embed what they learn into organizational structures and processes to improve organizational results.

Moving Away from Traditional Evaluation

As mentioned previously, what we know about learning is based largely on individual learning and on kids learning in school. And what we know about evaluation is based largely on evaluating individual achievement in some discrete lesson or course of study.

Traditional evaluation is relatively static. Students are tested on particular content, and may or may not be tested on how well they can relate new content to previously learned content. However, some of this is changing as many school improvement programs now are focusing on critical thinking skills that test how well students can synthesize information and put together the most important concepts.

Most evaluation assumes an essentially linear model. The pieces of content add up to a course and are tested. Interaction between the content of different courses is not considered because the courses usually are taught by different teachers.

In traditional evaluation, learning effectiveness is measured according to individual performance. Further, the individual performance is independent. Students rarely learn together—that is, learn from one another to come up with an answer or solve a problem. However, schools are beginning to shift their focus to more experiential learning, with students working in groups to solve real problems. These learning approaches get more at the behavioral stage of learning and at team learning. When these students get to the workplace, they will be far better prepared to learn together, particularly if schools also shift their thinking about evaluation from measuring performance to measuring learning.

Barbara Shapley of the Florida Department of Education describes new approaches to evaluation that foster lifelong learning:

> Machiavelli wrote that "There is nothing more difficult to take in hand, more perilous to conduct, or more uncertain in its success, than to take the lead in a new order of things." No organization in 20th-century society is more deeply rooted in the past than American schools. To change schools, to transform them to communities of learning, will take more than "educational reform," it will take rethinking the way we educate our people. In 1990, the U.S. Department of Labor published the Secretary's Commission on Achieving Necessary Skills (SCANS) Report, establishing a framework of competencies students will need to live and work in the 21st century.
>
> If we are to succeed in creating a new way of thinking, the focus must go beyond teaching practices. The school cannot separate itself from learning. The organizations we call schools

must become learning communities that prepare students for lifelong learning. Graduates must be prepared for postsecondary education *and* (not *or*) the workplace. Focusing more on the needs of the learner and tailoring learning events for student success, teachers become facilitators and students become active in their own learning.

To improve learning experiences, we need to align curriculum, instruction assessment, and evaluation as part of, and not separate from, the process. This requires a shift in thinking about:

- How people learn
- The structure of learning events
- Evaluation of learning events in terms of alternative/authentic assessments, with the role of standardized tests as only one element of the total evaluation

How people learn: Recent studies in "brain-based learning" reveal new understandings of how the brain works. Research in the neurosciences summarizes that the brain processes and organizes many things simultaneously; learning is a psychological experience and much more than just a mental exercise; patterns of experience help determine the significance of content; the relationship between one's emotional state and learning is critical; and the brain responds to challenges but is less effective when threatened. Though the emphasis may be on understanding how children learn, these principles relate to adult learners' cognitive development, as well. Cognitive complexity has the potential to develop throughout one's life, even to late adulthood. The implications of brain-based learning theory for staff development are immense. Teachers need to know effective elements of good instruction, for their students and themselves. The power and attraction of staff development lies in the opportunity to talk to other teachers. Through coaching and mentoring, teachers can take charge of their own profession. By redesigning staff development to involve the teacher-learner, teachers reflect and talk about their own thinking; initiate change in the school environment; contribute to the knowledge base of their own profession; design new roles for themselves; and, most important, transfer these same skills to their students.

Learning events: Learning must be centered on ideas and problems, not fragmented into discrete subject areas controlled by a seven-period day. Futurists advocate personalized education based on the idea that the many differences that exist among people should be cherished as a major source of creativity and diversity. This means that students and teachers themselves must plan their own learning events providing a variety of options for intellectual growth. Effective methods of instruction should be carried out over a sustained period; should include an adequate theory base, modeling and demonstration, and opportunity for practice; followed by a system for providing feedback, evaluation, and refinement. Assessments should be ongoing and embedded within the learning activity. This is the essence of collaborative learning.

Evaluation tools: The evolution of information technology has profound implications for curriculum and instruction in the learning organization. The concept of *cognition enhancers* defined as technology providing empowering environments and hypermedia will have significant impact for schools and the workplace. An example of a cognition enhancer is the division of labor that occurs when the machine (computer) handles the routine mechanics of a task while the person is immersed in its higher-order meanings. Data bases for information management can provide the empowering environments for standardized tests, statistical data comparisons measuring student progress in different ways. Hypermedia, the most sophisticated framework for creating interconnected, weblike representations of symbols (text, graphics, images, software codes) is the most exciting development in assessing and evaluating learning. This development will make it possible to have on a 3.5″ diskette a student's portfolio of work. Text files on the hyperstack can disclose test scores, writing samples, and other written products; graphics files can show pictures, video clips, drawings, and the like. The concept of a digital portfolio makes possible what was only a futurist's dream in transforming education.

The future of public schooling is ours to create. We have the tools and the minds to shape authentic learning organizations. The task ahead is to provide information to all stakeholders—

students, teachers, administrators, parents, the business community—regarding new roles in the dynamic transformation of schools.

Barbara Shapley, MS, school improvement team leader, Florida Department of Education, Talla-hassee, FL

Hiemstra and Sisco define *evaluation* as "appraising the value or worth of some educational undertaking such as a curriculum, a particular instructional procedure, or an individual performance in some area of learning."[3] Evaluation is based on learning goals and objectives—what is to be learned or accomplished. Goals and objectives must be measurable, and should be stated in behavioral terms that describe minimal or optimal competencies.

The two prevailing approaches to evaluating learning experiences are formative and summative evaluation. *Formative evaluation* is done during the learning experience for the purpose of making changes and improvements during the experience. Examples of formative evaluation include end-of-session feedback slips, formal interviews, and most interesting/least interesting feedback techniques. These are used to assess how well teachers and learners are doing as the learning experience rolls out. *Summative evaluation* is done at the end of the learning experience to assess learner performance or the effectiveness of the experience. Examples of summative evaluation include tests, term papers, projects, presentations, or ratings.

These are both excellent methods for evaluating learning experiences. But it is important to recognize their limitations when applied to organizational learning. As these techniques typically are applied, they evaluate individual cognitive and possibly behavioral learning. Although they also could be applied to team learning, the measurement tools are only now being developed. However, the most serious limitation is the assumption that evaluation is somehow a separate effort that ends at the end of the learning event. In the learning organization, learning is continuous and is integrated with the work of the organization.

In becoming learning organizations, we are breaking the mold of traditional thinking in designing our organizations. It stands to reason that we also need to break with traditional methods of evaluation. Lloyd Smith, president and CEO of MeritCare Hospital, credits the learning organization principles with unleashing a creative energy in his hospitals that has led to the in-house development of a unique performance review and development system. Four other organizations have experienced firsthand the challenge of evaluating learning experiences.

We are becoming more intentional about the outcomes we want to occur with major initiatives requiring our involvement. We need to attend to the evaluation of the process of change and innovation. As people go through change, it affects each individual within that process very differently because of who they are, their values, beliefs, and past experiences. We need to begin to attend to this as the learning organization moves to the next level. Clearly, we need to be able to demonstrate outcomes in order to ensure our own viability. But are innovations moving so fast and so fluidly that we need to ask if our current ways of thinking are standing in the way of identifying what and how to measure?

Mae McWeeny, MA, RN, learning specialist, Center for Professional and Clinical Development, Abbott Northwestern Hospital, Minneapolis

Until we begin linking the outcome of work to the organization or groups within the organization, as opposed to individuals, I don't know how we can take full advantage of the learning organization. Too often, we tend to credit one individual in an organization with making things happen and then, when that person leaves or moves on, people have such a strong association with that individual, they fail to see that the project can go on, with or without them. If a project gets too tied to one individual and the individual for whatever reason leaves the organization, what happens? The whole thing just collapses because no one feels they can continue with it. Rather than acknowledging the contributions within the organization that that person greatly facilitated, we tend to focus on the big hole or void their leaving creates. No matter who comes and who goes, as long as the vision remains the same and as long as it is supported by the head of the institution, the work can continue.

Carolyn Hunt, RN, MS, former project director, Patient-Centered Care Delivery System, District of Columbia General Hospital, Washington, DC

As part of our implementation strategy for professional practice, there is a quality and evaluation work team that is developing formative and summative evaluations of practice. The formative evaluation focuses on measures to determine if the outcome that was expected is achieved. This is ongoing, and the data feed back into our planning process and affect the next stages of our implementation plan. The summative evaluation focuses on a longer-term research design which will measure how caring processes affect the patient's experience and outcomes of care.

Mary Koloroutis, RN, MS, director, Center for Professional and Clinical Development, Abbott Northwestern Hospital, Minneapolis

Evaluating Learning Experiences

In our organizations, we have used a number of formative and summative evaluation techniques, and have found them to be helpful in evaluating learning experiences. The plus/delta ($+/\Delta$) technique is a formative evaluation tool that is simple and quick, but powerful in terms of involving learners in the design of the learning experience and giving useful direction to the teacher/mentor. It can be used with individual learners, teams of learners, or the group of learners as a whole. For our purposes, we will assume the entire group will participate and that the facilitator will use a flip chart and markers. The exercise begins with dividing the page into two columns with the headings $+$ and Δ as shown in figure 8-1. The $+$ represents what learners think was effective in terms of their learning; the Δ represents the changes learners would suggest. The exercise can be done quickly, usually just before a break or when there is a natural break in the topics. The facilitator asks first for what has been effective, then for suggested changes for making the learning experience more effective. Each response is written clearly on the flip chart. The pages are saved and used to make any necessary adjustments in the learning experience. The entire exercise can be done in under 10 minutes. Our experience has been that it takes practice for learners to participate effectively. At first, they are inclined to give "safe" feedback—for example, the room was hot, the coffee was cold. But with practice, they see how the information is used and accept responsibility for giving useful feedback.

All of us have used summative evaluation techniques. The most typical is the commonly accepted format for evaluating programs for which continuing education credit will be earned. First, behavioral objectives are developed for the learning experience. *Behavioral objectives* specify those learner behaviors that will demonstrate competence in terms of what is to be learned. Learners are asked for their perceptions of how well the learning objectives were met, usually on a 5-point Lickert-type scale. Next, they are asked open-ended questions about what did and did not work in the learning experience, and about how they will use what they learned in the workplace. Finally, learners are asked how they think the learning experience could be improved. Sometimes they also are asked to rate the teacher in terms of a number of factors such as knowledge, organization, and presentation style.

A particularly good example of summative evaluation is the University Hospital (University of Utah) evaluation of its Multidisciplinary Apprentice Program (MAP).[4] The MAP "proactively recruits and trains versatile and diverse workers for the Workforce of 2000."[5] Apprentices function as assistive workers for direct and indirect patient care activities. They are recruited from specific target groups, including high school youth, minorities, displaced, and nontraditional workers. The training program lasts six months, and includes course work and work experiences.

The summative evaluation was conducted at the end of the training experience and was intended to determine, from the perspective of the apprentice, best/worst aspects of the MAP

Figure 8-1. The +/Δ Format

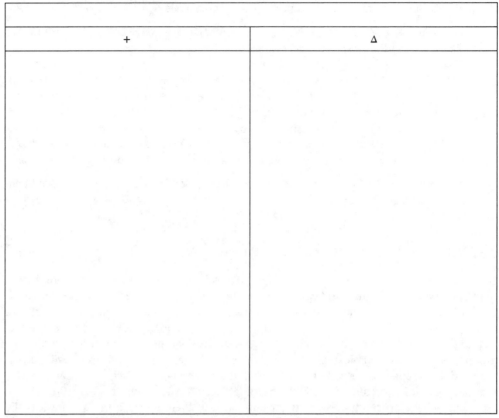

Source: Program to Improve Patient Care, Tallahassee Memorial Regional Medical Center, Tallahassee, FL.

as well as to solicit their suggestions for improvements in the program. Three areas were evaluated: class experience, work experience, and counseling. Each apprentice also was asked to indicate his or her confidence level with each of a list of specific skills learned in the course.

The evaluation found high levels of satisfaction with class experience and work experience. The participants also identified counseling by the program facilitator as being critical to apprentice success.

The University of Utah Hospital's formative evaluation of its service teams with appropriate resources (STARs) program also provides a good example. According to Cheryl Kinnear, "In order to successfully implement a program with a high level of change and complexity, formative evaluation is critical. If evaluation is done along the way, those involved are able to appreciate a sense of accomplishment, evaluate their readiness to move forward in development, and redesign existing systems or future plans before a tremendous amount of time and energy are wasted."[6]

Critical components to successfully maintain continuous quality improvement are ongoing evaluation of improvement efforts and timely feedback of information to the team about how they are doing. This information gives the staff a sense of accomplishment and helps to complete the circle of continuous learning. The team is able to evaluate discrepancies between *real* and *desired* performance and target problems or other improvement opportunities.

One aspect of University Hospital's Program to Improve Patient Care is the restructuring of patient services from a functional, hierarchical structure into service teams with appropriate resources (STARs). The STARs approach works to coordinate care across boundaries that frequently have led to fragmentation of services. Inpatient, outpatient, and home care providers are all a part of the interdisciplinary team. This organizational structure facilitates interdisciplinary cooperation and communication; consistency of caregivers and care; and coordination of services—aspects of care determined to be important to our patients. Four demonstration

STARs were implemented in February 1993. The first year of development was focused on establishing the structure and processes by which the STAR would function, defining goals, and clarifying team member roles.

A telephone survey was conducted in June 1993 as part of the year one evaluation of STARs. The focus of the survey was to assess the perspective of those directly involved in development and implementation of the program regarding progress to date, impact on patients and providers, and suggested future directions. The phone interviews were conducted by trained staff not directly involved in the program. Core, consultative, and support members from each STAR were represented in the sample. Of the total sample, 33 percent were nurses, 12 percent were physicians, 25 percent were other STAR members, and 22 percent were in management positions. Eighty-two percent of the respondents rated themselves as somewhat or extremely knowledgeable about the STARs program.

The first part of the survey evaluated to what extent we have actually created STARs in terms of structure and process. Questions were worded and organized to evaluate separately whether an aspect of the STAR (for example, STAR communication method) was (1) *defined* and (2) if it was actually happening in practice. The second section of the survey assessed members' perceptions regarding the impact of the STARs approach on quality and cost of patient care. Open-ended questions were used to solicit specific examples. The final part of the survey asked STAR members to evaluate the effectiveness of specific project support strategies (for example, retreats), identify priority aspects of the STAR to be developed or "fixed," and provide general suggestions.

The information gleaned from the survey has been used in multiple ways to support the continued development of STARs. The survey results seemed to give STAR members a sense of progress to date and provided future direction. Upper management was able to appreciate the steady progress and staff level support for the program. Such a perspective is limited when dealing with the larger organizational barriers.

The survey results indicated clearly that STAR members were ready to begin quality and cost improvement activities. Areas of role ambiguity were pinpointed. These and other areas of importance were acted upon quickly as the plan for the second phase of STAR development was revised and finalized. The approach used to share the results was to share various aspects in differing formats depending on the information needs of the group. A comprehensive report was distributed at a later time. It was important to begin sharing and utilizing the information provided by the survey as soon as possible, rather than waiting until a formal report could be distributed.

When staff are engaged in the process of measuring progress and performance in improving the quality of care, their sense of participation and interest is strengthened. The survey provided a valuable checkpoint early in STAR development to evaluate and adjust our approach to a very complex endeavor.

Cheryl L. Kinnear, RN, BSN, program manager, University Hospital's Program to Improve Patient Care, University of Utah Hospital, Salt Lake City

Teachers at Tallahassee Memorial Regional Medical Center (TMRMC) frequently use class projects for both teaching and evaluation. The projects allow individuals and teams to use the information they have been taught and to sharpen their team skills. According to Vivian Booth, project analyst, the practical assignments provide valuable feedback to the teachers by allowing them to evaluate the learning experience to see how much of the information has been retained by participants. TMRMC also uses participant reactions ("reactionnaires"), interviews, and open discussions as sources of rapid and detailed information for evaluation of their learning sequences.

There are three aspects of the learning program than can be examined by evaluating participants' reactions. One aspect is the program's content: how useful, interesting, and clear it is; the speed of delivery; the auxiliary materials; and the guest speakers. Another area has to do with the instructor, including credibility, humor, communication skills, enthusiasm, and interpersonal appeal. Finally, the logistical concerns, such as the room, the temperature, and the test or other performance measures.

Reactionnaires are one of the most common forms of participation feedback. These forms are completed at the end of each session. At TMRMC, we use a reactionnaire at the end of each session.

Interviews provide us with highly individualized feedback using predetermined closed- and open-ended questions, or they can be informal discussions. We use an informal focus group at the end of the start-up and keeping-on educational sequences, facilitated—and reports issued—by one of five internal consultants. Information is gathered from both the most recent teams completing start-up and the teams now in the keeping-on phase, on issues such as ways to improve the program. This information is used to make continuous improvement in the start-up educational learning sequence content and to determine how to meet the need of the keeping-on teams.

Open discussions enhance the participants' sense of partnership in the design process and are an excellent closure activity. These discussions usually ask questions such as: What part of the program was most useful to you? Was the level of the program and speed of the delivery appropriate for you? What part of the program was least useful to you? What part of the program seemed the slowest? Did any part of the program bother or annoy you? How could participants be more involved or active in the program? At TMRMC, we use our graduation ceremony as a more positive and learning-oriented approach for a closure activity. The teams are asked to spend approximately five (5) minutes sharing the most important things they learned, how their unit has changed as a result of the learning, and what they plan to do in the future with what they have learned.

Vivian Booth, RN, BS, project analyst, Work Redesign Program to Improve Patient Care, Tallahassee Memorial Regional Medical Center, Tallahassee, FL

Doris Armstrong and Cheryl Stetler of Hartford Hospital propose specific criteria for evaluating an innovative design. The purpose of these criteria is not to rule out risk taking and adoption but, rather, to provide a systematic and realistic view of the model and expected outcome. The criteria include:[7]

1. *Substantiating findings:* How much information is there in the literature or through conference proceedings on this innovation? How much of the information is research or evaluation or purely experiential reporting? How widely has it been tested/supported? Are there any threads of support or problems throughout all the writings/reports?
2. *Fit of setting:* Is there similarity between your own environment and that of the original innovation? Does it fit the goals/values of not only your department but the institution. Is there a philosophical as well as a pragmatic fit? Were the patients the same? What was the staffing mix/nurse–patient ratio and level of education of the staff? Will the innovation deal with the critical issues that must be faced within your environment? Will it fit the type and number of nurses or personnel you will have available in three to five years?
3. *Current basis for practice:* What are you doing now? Do you really know how well it does, doesn't work? What is your basis for current evaluation? Do you routinely collect nurse satisfaction and/or patient satisfaction or patient outcome or cost data?
4. *Feasibility (resources + readiness + risk):* In terms of *readiness,* how willing are key stakeholders to participate in this particular change/innovation? Will they buy a "ready-made" package? Does a common set of values exist to support this type of change? What types of *resources* will be required? What will it cost? What kind of *risks* are involved, including risks to significant relationships, credibility, and recruitment?

Evaluating performance in practice is another challenge our organizations face. Beth Israel Hospital has found use of narrative descriptions of patient care situations to be a meaningful component in evaluating their practice.

One important role of a nurse manager is the provision of a meaningful and effective forum for the evaluation of a professional nursing practice. Evaluation of practice has had to evolve as experienced nurses, many with advanced degrees, have chosen to remain in direct patient care roles. Standard evaluation tools, skills checklists, and other context-free standards of performance appraisal fail to capture the more salient aspects of expert practice, and leave the participants feeling dispassionate about the evaluation process.

A unit-based expert practice forum was formed and meets monthly to provide recognition and support for nurses with five or more years of experience. Clinical narratives and minutes reflecting the groups' discussions are kept on the unit and are read by all nursing staff. Currently, nurses are asked to write one or two narratives that describe important events in the care of patients that occurred within the year. The narratives are submitted to the nurse manager one month before the scheduled evaluation meeting. What constitutes *important* is highly individual, but resembles the criteria that Benner[8] uses in describing guidelines for writing critical incidents. The nurse manager and the clinical nurse being evaluated discuss the critical incident and why the experience had importance for the nurse's practice. The nurse's narrative is incorporated into the final written evaluation.

The first group of clinical nurses that participated in the use of clinical narratives expressed concern over being judged by their writing skills and focused on the details of the *assignment:* Does the critical incident need to be typed? Many nurses had difficulty recalling an important patient care incident in their own practice, although they could clearly identify their peers' important patient care moments. The nurses reluctantly cooperated, but thereafter were vocal advocates for the new process.

Suggestions from this group were used to modify the process so that all critical incidents are now shared with staff at regular meetings. The discussions generated by the presentation of the exemplar to a group provides the nurse with valued recognition of his or her contribution to patient care. By asking such questions as "Would you do anything differently in your patient care situation?" and "Were there any surprises in the patient's outcome or the outcome of your interaction?" nurses gain valuable insight into their own practice and can identify goals for continued development. The group invariably gives constructive feedback which incorporates an element of peer review that is flexible and ongoing.

Other positive outcomes of using patient narratives as part of the evaluation process include: assisting the nurse manager to identify obstacles to care on the unit; providing insight to staff in the areas of effective communication and conflict resolution; and sharing clinical expertise which contributes to the body of knowledge of nurses on the unit.

As the group developed and the process of writing and presenting critical incidents became more sophisticated and refined, members acknowledged the role it played in creating an environment that supports the nurse in providing constructive feedback to, and receiving and utilizing feedback from, peers. They appreciated this sanctioned forum where feelings of confusion, ambivalence, frustration, and grief could be discussed within the context of a patient care experience. Members expressed an improvement in their willingness and skill in providing feedback to their peers in their daily practice. Enhanced clinical knowledge and a genuine respect for the diversity of peers' styles and creative approaches to patient care were natural outcomes.

The expert practice forum has laid the foundation for self-evaluation which encourages a critical look at performance and clinical practice. What started out as an effort to develop a more useful method of evaluation of expert nursing practice has evolved into a vehicle for growth and development for the entire clinical nursing staff.

Judy Silva, RN, MSN, nurse manager, cardiology specialty unit, Beth Israel Hospital, Boston

The results of learning organization efforts, especially personal mastery, are particularly difficult to quantify. According to Mae McWeeny and Mary Koloroutis of Abbott Northwestern Hospital, one measure is the sustained interest in, and demand for, training programs. If people feel that their learning efforts are helping them grow and are making a difference in their practice, enthusiasm will spread throughout the organization.

Moving toward Continuous Improvement

As we have rolled out learning sequences in our organizations, we have seen the limitations of traditional evaluation methods. As we push for depth and breadth of learning in our organizations, we believe that continuous improvement is a more promising model for evaluating and continuously improving learning experiences.

Certainly, continuous improvement is not a new idea. One would be hard-pressed to find a hospital today that does not have continuous improvement at the heart of its quality efforts. But our experience has been that the concept of continuous improvement is not widely applied to learning experiences.

Because a wealth of materials on continuous improvement is available, we will not describe the concepts in detail here. However, for an excellent overview of continuous improvement, as well as for specific descriptions of the necessary tools, read *The Health Care Manager's Guide to Continuous Quality Improvement,* by Leebov and Ersoz.[9] Leebov and Ersoz call their continuous improvement process the customer-driven management model. (See figure 8-2.) The process begins with identifying customers and their expectations, and then translates them into requirements. Next, outcome measures are developed and performance is measured. Results are reported, conclusions drawn, and improvements pursued, which leads back to performance measured in a closed loop, indicating that the process is continuous. Improvements are pursued through the plan–do–check–act (PDCA) cycle. (See figure 8-3, p. 158.)

There are many models for data-driven continuous improvement, several of which are described in appendix A, including Deming's 14 points, PDCA, and Ackoff's interactive planning/management process. Although the language varies from model to model, all the models share some important features: They are systemic, dynamic, driven by measurement, and focused on outcomes. It is precisely these features that make continuous improvement such a powerful model for improving learning experiences.

Systemic and Dynamic

Continuous improvement is based firmly in systems thinking. It is not a linear cause-and-effect model. Instead, it helps us look at the parts and their relationships—the many interacting causes and effects. Systems thinking also helps us focus on underlying processes, looking for patterns and leverage for change rather than seeing only discrete events or individuals.

Continuous improvement is dynamic. Traditional evaluation ends with the learning event. The feedback loop in every continuous improvement process ensures that what is learned will be fed back to the beginning to improve the next iteration of the entire process. Static evaluation models depend on no unplanned changes during the experience, so that assumptions can be tested for what accounts for the results. Continuous improvement means *everything* is on the table for change *all the time*. When it is clear that a change is needed to improve results, it is made immediately.

Abbott Northwestern Hospital has had firsthand experience with the difference between traditional evaluation processes and continuous improvement.

> Our model calls for visioning based on various customer requirements. Once we've identified customer requirements and come up with a vision based on those requirements, then it is time to think about how we are going to evaluate the vision and how we will know when we have achieved it. Traditional evaluation tends to wait until the process is complete. With continuous redesign, we're constantly going in a loop, knowing what the requirements and the vision are, assessing current reality, identifying our performance targets, reiterating that process as times goes by, and making changes based on new input. You never get to the endpoint because it's a continuous process. It's very different from the traditional rigors of evaluation in which you can clearly determine cause and effect.
>
> *Ginger Malone, RN, MSN, director, innovation and consultation, Abbott Northwestern Hospital, Minneapolis*

What we love about Hammer and systems thinking is that we are actually looking at our business according to a process, not a department. To us, as a grant-funded hospital, changing the fundamental organizational structure has to be around what is a patient and what is the ideal patient experience and for sure it is not solely around departments. The only way we could get at it, from the patient's experience, is to look at it in more of a business sense, which hospitals are not all that comfortable doing. It is hard for us to live in all of this ambiguity and uncertainty and unknowing when the entire infrastructure is not designed to look at things as processes. Let's face it, a hospital is a very traditional, pretty hierarchical, vertically designed organization, but processes are horizontal. Finally, just to illustrate how far we've come in our thinking: One day we heard our CFO [chief financial officer] say, "What are you trying to tell me? You mean, it is the process that should get funded, not the department?" and in unison, we replied, "Yes! Yes! Yes!"

Ginger Malone, RN, MSN, director, innovation and consultation; and Debra Waggoner, MA, MBA, director, consulting and development, Abbott Northwestern Hospital, Minneapolis

Figure 8-2. The Customer-Driven Management Model

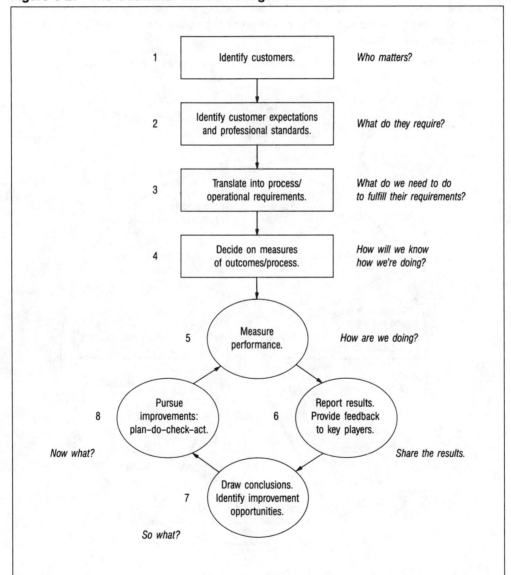

Source: Leebov, W., and Ersoz, C. J. *The Health Care Manager's Guide to Continuous Quality Improvement*. Chicago: American Hospital Publishing, 1991, p. 31. Reprinted, with permission, from the Einstein Consulting Group, Philadelphia.

Driven by Measurement

For far too long, health care has dodged the rigors of measurement. We have had plenty of good reasons. It is hard, both conceptually and technically. There is a lot of individual variation. Our present information systems do not easily capture important measures. And, of course, probably the most common reason of all: We could be sued for less-than-perfect results.

Improvement without measurement is a random event. It is like trying to increase your speed by 5 mph without a speedometer! The only way to hit the mark is through continuous feedback of data that tell you the result of your actions. Two of our organizations offer their insights into outcomes measurement.

Information systems are emerging as one of the most critical, yet underrated, factors in our learning process. A good information system can get timely information to the people making the decisions and/or have the same information simultaneously broadcast to the entire organization. One of the biggest drawbacks in our innovation effort is not having an information system that supports this kind of work, that's responsive enough to inform the task. Consequently, we are having to go back a few steps and re-create our own communication and information system linkages. It is not easy, but that is what has to be done if we want to continue to move ahead with our initiatives.

Marjorie Beyers, RN, PhD, FAAN, former associate vice-president, nursing, Mercy Health Services, Farmington Hills, MI

Figure 8-3.   The PDCA Model

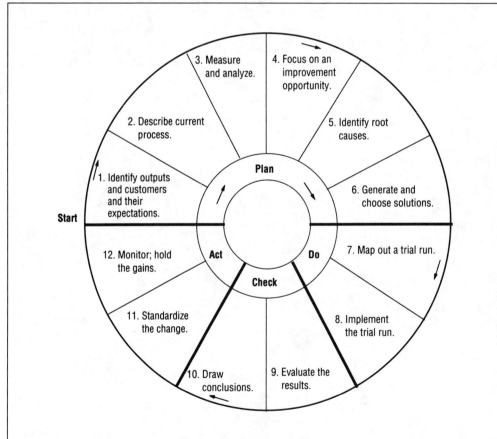

Source: Leebov, W., and Ersoz, C. J. *The Health Care Manager's Guide to Continuous Quality Improvement.* Chicago: American Hospital Publishing, 1991, p. 21. Reprinted, with permission, from the Einstein Consulting Group, Philadelphia.

Three years ago we formed a clinical information management committee consisting of physicians, senior staff, department heads and representatives from clinical and business-related areas, to select a user-defined patient-focused clinical information system. What we have discovered is that the process of getting together to get *agreement* on what we do (the delivery of health care services), and what an ideal clinical information system would look like, has been quite a revelation with many exciting and anxious moments. There were many definitions of clinical information systems, numerous language barriers, and lots of turf issues. Tremendous redundancies were identified, and many of us did not have a clue as to what other committee members do as it relates to the patient care process.

As we began to describe the ideal patient care process model we learned that: (1) delivering high-quality, cost-efficient patient care across the entire continuum of care must be outcome driven, (2) a focus on departmental systems can result in suboptimization, of other departments negatively impacting the outcomes, (3) some of our biggest efficiencies or gains can be from the reduction or elimination of "handoffs" or delays between departments, and (4) we do not want to simply automate what is—doing the wrong thing faster!

Recognizing that information systems are a vital strategy in the pursuit of excellence in health care, I think it is a mistake to implement clinical information systems before streamlining key processes that can impact quality, costs, and outcomes. With health care evolving from a transaction-oriented industry, and managed care in a capitated environment becoming the dominant form of health care delivery, focusing only on departmental needs (for example, creating islands of information) is no longer compatible with organizational viability. Information technology should be evaluated and selected based on how it supports *well-defined* organizational initiatives, and improves organizational effectiveness.

Mary Bland, RN, director, clinical informatics, Tallahassee Memorial Regional Medical Center, Tallahassee, FL

We are looking at a number of evaluation procedures in a continuous fashion that should give us some notion as to whether we are on target. We have been participating in a universal data system program for a number of years which allows us: (1) to compare our outcome data, called FIM (functional independent measures) scores, with other hospitals within the state, the region, and the nation, and (2) to compare ourselves to our own historical performance. In addition, we have a well-established baseline of patient satisfaction data which we have been collecting for many years through postdischarge surveys. Early in the planning of our reengineering effort, we conducted focus groups with staff, former patients, and family members, and will conduct more in the future. All of these procedures come into play in the measurement and monitoring of outcomes.

Bill O'Dowd, PhD, director, rehabilitation programs, Sister Kenny Institute, Abbott Northwestern Hospital, Minneapolis

Focused on Outcomes

Finally, continuous improvement is focused on outcomes. We frequently caution our teams not to confuse effort with results. It is very easy to get caught up in the busy day-to-day events and lose sight of the end result of our work. It is likewise easy to feel that things must be better because we are working so hard.

This is related to the previous point about measurement—with an important difference. *What* we measure is important. Outcomes are the end results we are looking for because they are the requirements of our customers. For example, at Tallahassee Memorial, we believe that excellence in patient/family care means optimal outcomes for our patients, outstanding service and value for our customers, and a satisfying practice environment for our employees, while using our scarce resources as effectively as possible. As a result, we have grouped our outcome measures into five categories: patient outcomes, service excellence, cost, productivity, and staff satisfaction.

Following are more examples of outcomes measurement:

For many of us, learning to focus on outcomes is a change in the rules. In the past we have been rewarded by the successful completion of tasks. Now the rules say to survive in this new highly competitive health care market, purchasers of our service will be focused primarily on three outcomes: (1) patient satisfaction with care, (2) efficiency of care, and (3) effectiveness of care.

To be outcome driven, we must work furiously to shift our organization from a task orientation to a process orientation. We must identify key processes (medication administration, admission/registration, diagnostic testing, and so forth) and define the ideal flow for these key processes at an enterprise level to achieve the desired outcome. For example, how the medication administration process flow should look from the time the medication is ordered to the time the patient receives the appropriate medication (enterprise view).

Key process flows defined by a department can look very different from the same key process flow defined at the enterprise level. Process flow defined by department also increases the potential for bottlenecks or hand-offs where processes can break down and negatively impact outcomes. For example, the pharmacy department defines the medication administration process from the time they receive the order until the medication is dispensed to the unit. Nursing defines it from the time the physician writes the order (then it is handed off to the pharmacy and picked up again when the medication is delivered to the unit) until it is administered to the patient.

Everyone, regardless of department, needs to be accountable for the outcome. This changes the incentive from the performance of the department to the performance of the organization. Clinical pathways are an excellent example of being outcome driven. Clinical pathway outcomes have been identified based on best practice at TMRMC and nationally. Inefficient key processes, easily identified as variances to the pathway, are tracked and can be targeted for reengineering to ensure excellent outcomes.

Mary Bland, RN, director, clinical informatics, Tallahassee Memorial Regional Medical Center, Tallahassee, FL

The objectives we are trying to reach must meet standards of excellence in five different domains. They must help to (1) improve patient outcomes, (2) decrease cost, (3) reduce complexity or simplify systems, (4) create more meaningful work, and (5) increase patient satisfaction. All of our teams, including consultants, are held accountable for obtaining exacting measurements on each dimension.

As for the exact nature of their work and how it is operationalized, it is different depending on the scope and the area of inquiry. All the teams have autonomy within the framework of meeting the five criteria. How they choose to function is up to them. We have a general model that guides the process of work. It was developed through the influence of *The Fifth Discipline*, authored by Peter Senge, coupled with the methodology of reengineering, developed by Michael Hammer. We are using the learning model and change management model as the two processes that cut through all manner of processes, as the teams experience different phases of change.

Julianne Morath, RN, MS, vice-president, patient care, Abbott Northwestern Hospital, Minneapolis

Our teams are trying to improve the process that patients experience as part of the care received. For example, in orthopedics, from the outset the team is expected to identify the outcomes to be achieved at the end of the patient stay in the inpatient setting and 30 to 60 days out, after the stay with a monitoring system set up to identify and collect relevant information. Six years ago, prior to the grant, there wouldn't have been a focus on the outcomes after the inpatient stay. As soon as the patient left, end of story. It was up to the physician to worry about what happened next. Now, as a result of that 30-day survey, the team made some changes in how they prepare a patient for discharge, not just in terms of equipment but also in terms of very specific questions they ask the family or patient about their living situation that go beyond the usual do-you-live-alone line of questioning.

Faye Gilbarg, regional director, medical management and quality, Providence Health System, Portland, OR

Mary K. Kohles and Barbara Donaho write in *Strategies for Healthcare Excellence* that a complicating factor the hospitals have found is that rational scientific research methods are not intended to adapt as change evolves. Although the hospitals are using a variety of evaluation designs, action research is the primary format. This method relies on case studies, interview surveys, meeting minutes, anecdotal stories, and operational data as tools for reporting results. Once work teams define what it is they want to achieve by their efforts, they develop indicators by which to gauge their work and its results. For example, for a project involved in designing preadmission teaching kits for orthopedic total-knee patients, the unit would monitor the time, degree of postsurgical ambulation possible, and amount of pain medication required to maintain comfort. The data are compared to retrospective review figures from medical records of patients who did not receive preadmission teaching. After comparisons are made, any adjustments deemed necessary are made in collaboration with the patient care team.[10]

A Powerful Model for Improving Learning Experiences

As discussed in the previous section, the continuous improvement model is a systemic, dynamic model that has the formative and summative features of the traditional evaluation approaches but adds the important feature that it is continuous. In addition, continuous improvement is driven by measurement and focuses on outcomes. For all these reasons, it fits extremely well with the concepts of the learning organization, particularly in terms of the need for integrating learning with the work of the organization. Further, the purpose of both individual and team learning is for organizations to learn how to improve their outcomes continuously. Thus, it is logical that the best measure of organizational learning is whether results improve continuously. Are patient outcomes improving? Are customer expectations met and even exceeded? Are costs decreasing? The continuous improvement model has the added advantage that it will serve us well in the capitated environment. We can expect that purchasers of care will require measures of effectiveness, efficiency, and satisfaction by patient population—and that we will need to continuously improve on these measures in order to survive and thrive.

The continuous improvement model has some limitations that are due largely to how the model is implemented. As sometimes practiced, the focus may be on interim process measures that are assumed to affect outcomes, without actually tracking outcome measures. In addition, there is the temptation to focus on fixing things and, in the process, getting rid of what you do not want. However, the focus should be on getting what you *do* want. Unless opportunities for improvement are selected carefully, there is a danger that improvement efforts could be focused on doing the wrong thing right, rather than on doing the right thing right. Peter Drucker expressed it best by saying there is nothing as counterproductive as trying to improve something that does not need to be done at all.

In talking about bringing about change and continuous improvement, we have to ask ourselves: Is work redesign really innovation, or is it just rearranging the deck chairs on the Titanic? What's the point of redesigning the wrong thing? The [Montana] consortium was set up with the sole purpose of helping organizations change. The original focus made a lot of sense at the time when there was a serious nursing shortage. Plus, there were a lot of internal kinds of issues pertinent to hospitals. Now, five years later, the health care environment is changing and technology is going to move patients out of hospitals faster than you can blink an eye. If we really see our role as helping organizations change, then we need to really be pretty aggressive about how we go about our business. We have had to seriously question our modus operandi.

Lynne Meredith Mattison, MHA, director, Montana Consortium, Saint Vincent Hospital and Health Center, Billings, MT

To continuously improve learning experiences, the greatest need is for a model that does not stop the evaluation process at the individual level. In order for individual learning to lead to team and organizational learning, a model is needed for improving the integration of learning with work across the breadth of learning (individual, team, and organizational) and to the depths of learning (cognitive, behavioral, and performance improvement). Continuous improvement is such a model.

Kohles and Donaho offer the following guidelines for organizational learning and change:[11]

- Plan for significant up-front development time.
- Develop a common language that all stakeholders can understand.
- Involve physicians early on, especially as change impacts their work.
- Involve the financial department in planning and implementation.
- Develop community linkages, emphasizing the continuum of patient care services.
- Include payers and policymakers in a timely manner, extending the change to impact health care policy and regulations.
- Understand the competencies of all disciplines, recognizing the unique talents that each person brings to the change process.
- Integrate restructuring and quality management/continuous improvement early.
- Integrate restructuring as a part of the strategic plan (approved by the board of trustees).
- Develop measurements to demonstrate the cost impact of institutionwide restructuring, understanding the return on the organization's investment.

Continuously Improving Learning Experiences

It has not been uncommon for teachers to teach continuous improvement concepts and tools without, themselves, applying them to improving learning experiences. At Tallahassee Memorial, we were fortunate to see this opportunity for improvement early in our change efforts through the work of Dr. Doug Zahn, professor of statistics at Florida State University. For several years, he has used an end-of-session feedback technique he calls the *minute paper* to continuously improve his statistics courses. In an article on this improvement technique, he talks about breaking through his own resistance to using the minute paper.[12] His resistance was in the form of concerns about losing respect or power, about students complaining about everything (making it too painful for him), and about losing control of the course and having students sabotage the pace of the course. As a result of persevering with the minute papers, Zahn reports that he now has a firm data-based sense of where the class is at all times during the course and that student ratings of the course and the teacher have increased continuously.

We use a variation of the minute paper in our learning sequences and have written about the technique in more detail in appendix B. (Our instrument is shown in figure 8-4.) At the end of a learning session, we ask all participants to complete the comment form. Signing one's name is optional, but participants who do sign their names are assured of receiving individual feedback. The questions are related to whether we met learner expectations, whether the material was clear, and whether there are things that can be improved.

At the end of the session, the teacher/mentor(s) together review the comment forms while the session is still fresh in their minds. They make comments directly on the forms. Before the next session, they address any specific requests for help or clarification. The comment forms are then analyzed and Pareto charts are developed for each question. (See figure 8-5, p. 165.)

At the next session, the comment forms, along with teacher/mentor responses, are available to be picked up with other materials for the session. Forms are available in an expandable file, filed by the first letter of the learner's last name. The first five minutes of the next session are devoted to a review of the comment forms, using Pareto analyses. The group uses the data to decide at what point the agenda should be suspended and to clear up points that are vague. Our experience is that unless almost half the group is unclear on some point,

Figure 8-4.   Start-Up VIII Comment Form: TMRMC Program to Improve Patient Care

---

Start-Up VIII Comments—April 5, 1995

1. Did you get what you came for today?   YES   NO

    If yes, what did you get?

    If no, what was missing?

2. What was the muddiest point remaining at the end of today's meeting?

3. What single change could we have made to have improved this meeting?

4. Any other comments or questions?

Name: _____
                        (Optional)

Source: Program to Improve Patient Care, Tallahassee Memorial Regional Medical Center, Tallahassee, FL, 1995.

the group will want to press on. In any case, the group decides and the teacher/mentor models responding to the comments. When changes are suggested, they are addressed specifically. If the change cannot be made, reasons are given. For example, at the beginning of a learning sequence, our groups consistently ask for coffee to be served. Because we have no catering budget, we treat this as a serious issue and use it to model coming up with alternatives. Eventually, group members come up with alternatives and move on to more substantive issues. It is extremely important to openly address changes that are made in the learning sequence and to specifically state that they are being made as a result of learner comments. In this way, the teacher/mentor models openness and willingness to change, and the learner experiences change as a result of his or her feedback. It is important not to overreact to single comments, even if they are loud and persistent. The Pareto analysis is an especially helpful tool in this regard because it helps keep focus on the vital few comments (rather than the trivial many), modeling data-driven decision making.

Many of our organizations have used continuous improvement techniques to improve learning experiences.

> Through the influence of faculty in the School of Nursing at Mankato State University and through experiences with colleagues at Creative Nursing Management, Health Bond Consortium participants have been learning mindmapping skills.[13] *Mindmapping* is a tool and a technique for developing more creative and innovative approaches to thinking.
>
> Mindmapping is assisting us to develop creativity, enhance team learning, and strengthen problem-solving competencies among consortium participants. As Wycoff states, it is "a powerful information processing, idea generating technique."[14]
>
> Faculty have demonstrated the use of this technique to students for their use in note taking, developing the plan for a writing project, and in doing presentations. Diane Miller of Creative Nursing Management mindmaps continuously as she works with participants in leadership development education. The use of multicolor, multiscented marking pens further stimulates creativity and the engagement of the whole brain.
>
> Health Bond's efforts to improve and/or design consumer-responsive health care systems are focused on maximizing our human resources. Health care organizations have traditionally valued "left-brain" thinking (language, logic, numbers, sequence, details, linear, symbolic

Figure 8-5. Pareto Analysis of Comment Forms

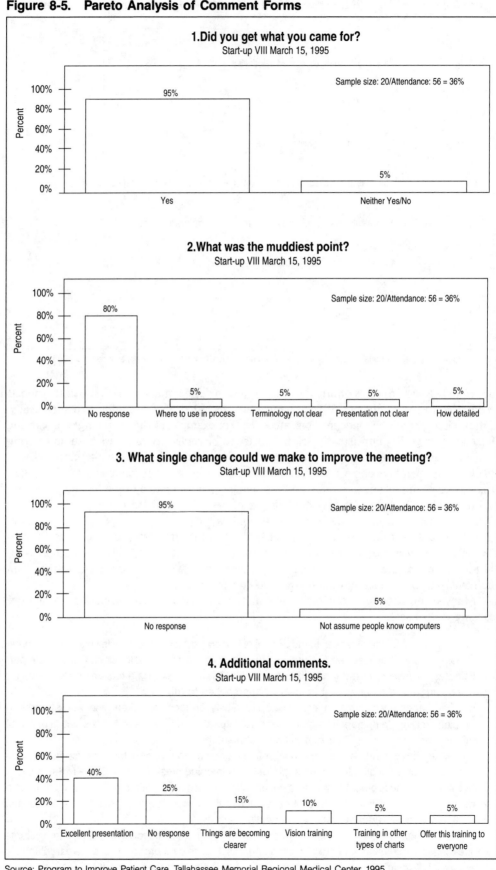

Source: Program to Improve Patient Care, Tallahassee Memorial Regional Medical Center, 1995

representation, judging) and distrusted "right-brain" thinking (imaging, rhythm, music, imagination, color, wholes, patterns, emotions, nonjudgmental approach). For "whole-brain" learning, teams need to think most creatively and effectively by encouraging interactions between the two hemispheres.

When participants in leadership development education have worked in groups to draw with pictures only (not words) their group's view of current reality and vision of the future, it has been possible to identify commonalities or patterns across groups in the resulting pictures, as well as identifying unique learning team perspectives. More important, it is possible to identify changes in the themes depicted by group pictures over time. The result is a picture story of organizational and interorganizational culture change over time.

Sharon Aadalen, RN, PhD, director, Health Bond Consortium, South Central Minnesota, Mankato, MN

TMRMC [Tallahassee Memorial Regional Medical Center] uses unit-specific results of the entire team to determine how the learner changed because of the learning experience. Team performance depends both on individual excellence and on how well each member of the team works together. When a group of people function as a whole, it is a phenomenon called *alignment*. Alignment empowers the whole team, which is necessary before the individual can be empowered. Empowering the individual when there is a relatively low level of alignment worsens the chaos and makes managing the team even more difficult.

Our start-up and keeping-on teams are continuing to develop unit-specific performance measures in all five of our measurement categories (quality [patient outcomes], quality [service excellence], job satisfaction, cost, and productivity), key process measures (high-volume, high-risk, and problem-prone) as well as quality control measures. Our vision is that each unit and team would be able to track its own improvement on the ongoing measures, as well as priority improvement opportunities that each is working on. Data would be available in a form which would be both simple and highly visual so that all workers could understand their outcomes—that is, how redesign is influencing their measures.

Vivian Booth, RN, project analyst, Work Redesign Program to Improve Patient Care, Tallahassee Memorial Regional Medical Center, Tallahassee, FL

Boards identify areas for further attention at the close of each session when they publicly "evaluate" the meeting's process and their functioning as a group. This group-generated public feedback becomes the basis for improvements such as more usable data and timely information, greater meeting efficiency, balanced participation, and the inclusion of additional stakeholders.

Annual or semiannual reviews of unit board accomplishments/outcomes provide both a point of closure and a picture of just how much the boards are able to improve patient care and work life satisfaction. Based on this type of feedback, many boards have noted that not only have they had great success in planning and implementing changes on their units, but they have evolved to a point where they are addressing greater challenges and becoming increasingly multidisciplinary in their initiatives. "Looking back" provides a clear context for the future work of the board. Equally important, it affirms the contribution that both staff and leadership make toward improving the unit through collaborative efforts.

Terry G. Minnen, MEd, shared governance liaison, Center for Patient Care Innovation, Vanderbilt University Hospital and Vanderbilt Clinic, Nashville, TN

The role of the clinical education specialist was redefined in view of the changing health care environment and the need to focus on added value to patient care and practice. As a result, the nursing education department evolved into the Center for Professional Development, with a more clearly defined focus on improving clinical and professional practice while at the same time reducing costs.

The center provides leadership and consultations for the improvement of patient care for individuals and units/communities of care to facilitate learning to strengthen practice. This is accomplished through three service areas:

- *Professional development:* Professional practice model, managed care, leadership, innovation, individual consultation, and practice support
- *Clinical development:* Orientation, competency-based practice, in-services, mandatory education requirements, individual consultation, and practice support
- *Learning services:* Conferences, recognition programs, outreach, writing and publishing, career guidance, academic alliances, individual consultation, and practice support

Mae McWeeny, operations manager, Center for Professional and Clinical Development, Abbott Northwestern Hospital, Minneapolis

Holding the gains of continuous improvement implies that organizations will continue to measure their success with change.[15] The formula for success, and failure for that matter, is often buried in the experience of doing. The way to improve is to evaluate each experience. That is, watch teams work and learn from them! Take the opportunity to define the change process, celebrate success, and learn from your mistakes.

Improvement teams at Boston's Beth Israel Hospital used quality improvement theory to improve patient care systems. We applied the theory to health care processes and learned to improve the process across the system. This is what we know.

Education and team building: Team building breaks down barriers of resentment and builds trust. It is a powerful exercise that transforms a group into a working team. It is the stuff that breeds commitment and the energy of success. Team building is time well spent.

Problem identification and organization: Know the problem exists! Avoid creating a team to solve a problem because this will invite fear and skepticism. Bring the team together when the process owner has data to show there is a process worth improving. Use the data to focus on the process, not the performance of people. (This will lessen the initial defensiveness among team members.) In addition, hold the entire team accountable for getting the work done between each meeting because this will sustain momentum. And set time limits on the length of the project.

Diagnostic journey: Develop facilitators for priority projects because they empower the team to improve the process. Facilitators help the team understand work as a process, use data for continuous improvement, and create innovative solutions. They manage the project! Provide data management support for teams so that feedback and decisions are timely. This will maintain enthusiasm.

Remedial journey: Establish a mechanism for recognizing the accomplishments and recommendations of the team. The subtle essence of respect and open-mindedness among team members is a continuing source of energy for the team and intrigue for the organization.

Nancy Miller, RN, MS, nurse specialist, quality assurance and special projects, Beth Israel Hospital, Boston

Putting It All Together: A Model for Rethinking Learning in a Learning Organization

In the course of our journey toward becoming learning organizations, it has become clear that we have had to shift our thinking about what learning is and about the purpose of learning. Wendy Baker at Vanderbilt University Hospital calls this a BFO, a blinding flash of the obvious! However, it is important to note that it usually is only obvious after a lot of careful thinking and work.

The first shift of thinking builds on the work of Garvin in which he sees learning in three overlapping stages—cognitive, behavioral, and performance improvement.[16] The cognitive stage is about changing thinking, the behavioral stage is about changing behavior, and the performance improvement stage is about using knowledge to improve outcomes. We refer to this as the *depth* of learning that is necessary in a learning organization. This rethinking of learning requires us to ask the question, Has the concept been learned if nothing improves? Expanding our thinking about the depth of learning gets at a major limitation in our present learning experiences: translating cognitive learning into new behavior that results in improved organizational outcomes. The depth of learning is achieved through integrating learning with work.

The second shift of thinking builds on the work of Senge[17] in which he sees organizational learning requiring individual learning but, more important, team learning where individuals learn to learn together. We refer to this as the *breadth* of learning that is necessary in a learning organization. Rethinking the breadth of learning requires us to ask the question, How can we push individual learning to team learning to organizational learning? Team learning is a systems concept, Senge's fifth discipline of the learning organization. A system is not the sum of its parts but, rather, the product of its parts and their interactions. Team learning is not the sum of what individuals have learned but, rather, the product of what each team has learned as a result of the interactions between them. Likewise, organizational learning is not the sum of what each team in the organization has learned but, rather, the product of what each has learned as a result of the interactions between them. The breadth of learning is achieved by learning together.

Putting depth and breadth together in a single model helps us see how learning experiences can build on one another to get us where we truly want and need to be—the corner that combines organizational learning and performance improvement. This is the organization that has capacity for change, the organization that can learn fast and continuously improve its results. (See figure 8-6.)

This framework of organizational learning also can help us rethink evaluation and continuous improvement of learning experiences because it requires us to ask the question, What is the measure of learning in each section of the model? Tests and competency checklists may be good measures of the cognitive or behavioral stage, but the only true measure of the performance improvement stage—the ability to create improved results—is organizational outcomes. We can never get to improved organizational outcomes if our learning experiences are mostly in the corner that combines individual and cognitive learning. Thus, the best measures of learning experience effectiveness are organizational outcomes—patient outcomes, customer service, cost, productivity, and staff satisfaction. This represents an enormous shift in thinking about evaluating learning experiences.

We close with an important observation about learning organizations, the organizations that have achieved depth and breadth of learning. It may seem too daunting a task. Does

Figure 8-6. A Model for Learning in a Learning Organization

Depth of Learning	Breadth of Learning		
	Individual	**Team**	**Organizational**
Cognitive	Individuals change their thinking.	Teams change their thinking.	Teams throughout the organization change their thinking.
Behavioral	Individuals change their behavior.	Teams change their behavior.	Teams throughout the organization change their behavior.
Performance Improvement	Individuals improve organizational results.	Teams improve organizational results.	Teams throughout the organization improve organizational results.

it mean that every single person in the organization is in the corner box combining organizational learning and performance improvement? Fortunately, our experience has been that total consensus is not necessary. It is really about developing critical mass from which change can grow. Margaret Mead said it best: "Never doubt that a small group of thoughtful, committed people can change the world. Indeed, it is the only thing that ever has!"

References

1. Garvin, D. A. Building a learning organization. *Harvard Business Review* 71(4):90, July–Aug. 1993.

2. Senge, P. M. *The Fifth Discipline: The Art and Science of the Learning Organization.* New York City: Doubleday/Currency, 1990, p. 236.

3. Hiemstra, R., and Sisco, B. *Individualizing Instruction: Making Learning Personal, Empowering and Successful.* San Francisco: Jossey-Bass, 1990, p. 123.

4. Program to Improve Patient Care. Evaluation of the Multidisciplinary Apprentice Program: Part II. *Evaluation Reports,* Report No. 4. Salt Lake City: University Hospital, University of Utah, Dec. 1993.

5. Strengthening Hospital Nursing: A Program to Improve Patient Care. Project description, University of Utah/University of Utah Health Science Center, 1994 National Meetings, Portland, OR, November 3–4, 1994, p.8.

6. Kinnear, C. L., ed. Service teams with appropriate resources (STARs): telephone survey of STAR members. *Evaluation Reports: University Hospital's Program to Improve Patient Care* 5:19, May 1994.

7. Armstrong, D. M., and Stetler, C. B. Strategic considerations in developing a delivery model. *Nursing Economic$* 9(2):114, Mar.–Apr. 1991.

8. Benner, P. *From Novice to Expert.* Menlo Park, CA: Addison-Wesley Publishing, 1984.

9. Leebov, W., and Ersoz, C. *The Health Care Manager's Guide to Continuous Quality Improvement.* Chicago: American Hospital Publishing, 1991.

10. Kohles, M. D., and Donaho, B. Strengthening Hospital Nursing: Program to Improve Patient Care. *Strategies for Healthcare Excellence* 5(11):3, 1992.

11. Kohles and Donaho.

12. Zahn, D. A. Getting started on quality improvement in statistics education. In: *Proceedings of the Section on Statistical Education of the American Statistical Association.* Alexandria, VA: American Statistical Association, 1991, pp. 135–40.

13. Wycoff, J. *Mindmapping: Your Personal Guide to Exploring Creativity and Problem-Solving.* New York City: Berkeley Books, 1991.

14. Wycoff.

15. Plsek, P. E., and Arturo, O. Quality Improvement Tools. Data Collection. Juran Institute, 1989.

16. Garvin, p. 90.

17. Senge, p. 10.

Appendix A

Models Driving Change at Grantee Organizations of the Strengthening Hospital Nursing Program

In chapter 3, we offered many examples of how we built our models for organizational change. In this appendix, we offer more detailed information on the models, theories, and sets of ideas that we found particularly useful. For each model, theory, or set of ideas, a summary includes some or all of the following:

Name of model/concept: Usually the name by which the model/theory/set of ideas is known in the literature.

Name of key author(s)/thinker(s): Usually the name of the author/inventor of the model/theory/set of ideas. Sometimes it is the name of the consulting firm that holds the copyright or trademark on the model/theory/set of ideas.

Affiliation of key author(s)/thinker(s): Usually the name of the organization (for example, university or firm) with which the author/inventor is affiliated.

Key features of model/theory/set of ideas: Explanations of the most important ideas included in the model or theory. It is important to note that the contributing organization defines what is key based on its own model for change. Although in some cases several organizations have written about the same ideas, each organization selected different key concepts.

Definition(s) of concepts that had to be learned: Definitions of concepts that needed further explanation so they could be learned in the organization.

How the model/theory/set of ideas was used: Explanation of how the ideas were implemented in the organization.

Key publications/references: Citations necessary for readily accessing published materials.

Contributor(s): Name and position of the person(s) writing the description.

Contributor affiliation(s): Organization of the person(s) writing the description.

A note of caution: The intent of this appendix is not to summarize the models driving change in each of the SHNP organizations but, rather, the key features and important ideas we have used to build our own models. For more information on the various SHNP grantees and their models for change, contact the contributor or see the proceedings of the 1994 national meetings available from the National Program Office.

Appendix A is organized as shown in table A-1.

Table A-1. Models Driving Change in SHNP Organizations

Page Number	Organization	Model/Theory/Set of Ideas	Author
171	Tallahassee Memorial Regional Medical Center	Interactive Planning/Management	Russell Ackoff
		The Learning Organization	Peter Senge
		Managing Mental Models	Peter Senge
		Paradigm Pioneers	Joel Barker
		The Maturity Continuum	Stephen Covey
		Deming's 14 Points	W. Edwards Deming
179	Health Bond	Systems Thinking	Leland Kaiser
		The Caring Curriculum	Bevis and Watson
		Leading an Empowered Organization	Manthey and Miller
		Visioning Health Futures: Storytech	Arthur Harkins
185	Hartford Hospital	Strategic Management	Hatten and Hatten
187	MeritCare Hospital	5 Track Model for Organizational Change	Ralph Kilmann
		Leading for the Situation	Kenneth Blanchard
		The Five Leadership Practices of Exemplary Leaders	Kouzes and Posner
192	Vanderbilt University Hospital and Vanderbilt Clinic	Interactive Planning	Russell Ackoff
		The Learning Organization	Peter Senge
		Collaborative Organization Design	Gelinas and James
196	Harbor-UCLA Medical Center	Principle-Centered Leadership: Empowerment	Stephen Covey
		Harmony Principle	David Boje
200	University Hospital/ University of Utah	Stages of School Improvement	Matthew Miles
		Force-Field Analysis	Kurt Lewin
202	University Hospital/ Penn State University	Interactive Planning/Idealized Design	Russell Ackoff
		Sociotechnical Systems	Eric Trist
		Group Relations	Eric Trist
207	Vermont Nursing Initiative	Continuous Quality Improvement	Deming and Juran
210	Northeast Health Consortium	Team Learning	Peter Scholtes
211	Mercy Hospital and Medical Center	Inquiry Mode of Learning	Cyril Houle
212	University Hospitals of Cleveland	Diffusion of Innovation Model	Everett Rogers
214	Beth Israel Hospital	Clinical Narratives	Benner and Tanner
217	Abbott Northwestern Hospital	Reengineering	Michael Hammer
		Interactive Planning	Russell Ackoff
218	Providence Portland Medical Center	Finding Your 15%	Gareth Morgan

Models Driving Change at Tallahassee Memorial Regional Medical Center

Name of model/concept: Interactive Planning/Management

Name of key author(s)/thinker(s): Russell Ackoff

Affiliation(s) of key author(s)/thinker(s): Professor emeritus, The Wharton School at the University of Pennsylvania, Philadelphia, PA; Principal, Interact, Inc., the Institute for Interactive Management, Bala Cynwood, PA.

Key features of model/theory/set of ideas: Ackoff is the inventor of interactive planning/ management. (See figure A-1.) He calls it the first systemically based planning process, that is, incorporating systems theory. Interactive planning/management is a process for creating the desired future and inventing the means to bring it about. It begins with formulation of the "mess," the system of interlocking threats and opportunities—in other words, the future being created now. Next, the idealized design is created. This is the idealized present, the best ideal-seeking system that can be conceived of now. Gaps between the mess and the design are identified, and means are invented for closing them. Resource requirements are determined for the means, and the implementation and control plan is developed. The means are implemented and results fed back to the beginning of the process.

Interactive planning/management is a continuous process. Ackoff's structure for implementing interactive planning/management is the planning board. The planning board belongs to the manager and is composed of the manager, the manager's boss, the manager's direct reports, and affected stakeholder(s). Planning boards can do whatever they want so long as they have the resources and what they do does not affect someone else. If it does affect someone else, they have to get agreement. If they do not have the resources, they have to find them. Planning boards throughout the organization are planning simultaneously and interdependently, creating what Ackoff calls the *circular organization.*

Definition(s) of concepts that had to be learned:

- Focus on getting what you want, not on getting rid of what you do not want. They are not the same thing! Ackoff illustrates this point with the television dial. It is easy to get rid of what you do not want by just changing the channel. But the probability is great that you will get something you want even less!
- Plan backward from where you want to be. Knowing where you want to go limits the possible alternatives that must be considered and makes it easier to get there.
- Distinguish machine-age thinking from systems thinking. In *machine-age thinking,* we try to understand problems by taking them apart, understanding the parts, and putting them back together. In *systems thinking,* we understand problems by looking at the pieces and their interrelationships, and aggregating that understanding up to the whole. When a system is taken apart, it loses its essential properties, and so do the parts.
- Stakeholders are those persons affected by a system or process. In interactive planning/ management, they are always included. Ackoff's advice is never to plan *for* someone else.

How the model/theory/set of ideas was used: At TMRMC, we have implemented interactive planning/management with a few refinements. (See figure A-2, p. 173.) We start with idealized design to reinforce the point that we should focus on getting what we want. We have created a separate step for gap analysis and for determining the priority gaps that will be focused on—the "hit list." Finally, we have created a loop between means and resources to reinforce the point that means cannot be selected for which resources are not available.

Figure A-1. Ackoff's Interactive Planning/Management Model

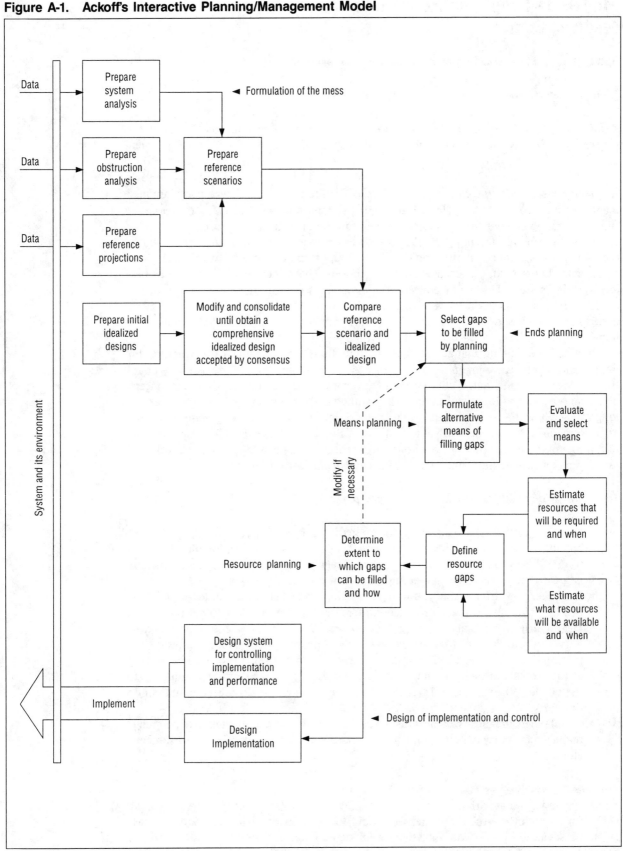

Source: Ackoff, R. L. *Creating the Corporate Future*. New York City: John Wiley and Sons, 1981, p. 75. Copyright © 1981. Reprinted by permission of John Wiley and Sons, Inc.

Figure A-2. The Interactive Process at TMRMC

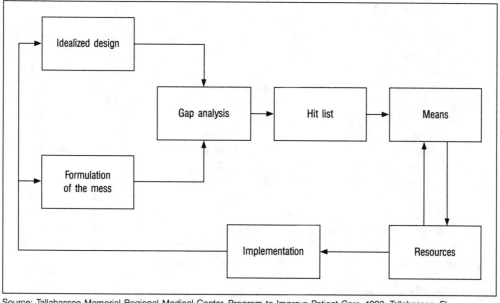

Source: Tallahassee Memorial Regional Medical Center. Program to Improve Patient Care, 1993, Tallahassee, FL.

The interactive process is used throughout our organization. It is our work redesign process, starting on specific work units and spreading to cross-functional teams. Our model is called Interactive Unit-based Work Redesign. It also is our quality improvement process. Performance measures are developed in the formulation of the mess step, and data-driven continuous improvement is the purpose of the whole process. Our model is called Interactive Quality Management. We also use the interactive process in our organizational strategic planning process, which includes the board of directors, the medical staff, and TMRMC leadership.

Key publications/references:

Ackoff, R. *Creating the Corporate Future.* New York City: John Wiley and Sons, 1981.

Contributor(s): Program to Improve Patient Care Project Team

Contributor affiliation(s): Tallahassee Memorial Regional Medical Center, Tallahassee, FL

Name of model/concept: The Learning Organization

Name of key author(s)/thinker(s): Peter M. Senge

Affiliation(s) of key author(s)/thinker(s): Director of the Systems Thinking and Organizational Learning Program at the Sloan School of Management at Massachusetts Institute of Technology (MIT), Cambridge, MA, and a founding partner of Innovation Associates in Framingham, MA.

Key features of model/theory/set of ideas: When we give up the illusion that the world is created of separate, unrelated forces, we can build learning organizations. These are organizations "where people continually expand their capability to create the results they truly desire, where new and expansive patterns of thinking are nurtured, where collective aspiration is set free, and where people are continually learning how to learn together" (Senge, p. 3).

The five disciplines of the learning organization are:

1. *Systems thinking:* A conceptual framework that recognizes the interconnectedness of events and actions.
2. *Personal mastery:* The discipline of continually clarifying and deepening our personal vision, of focusing our energies, of developing patience, of seeing reality objectively, and of commitment to our own lifelong learning.
3. *Mental models:* Deeply ingrained assumptions, generalizations, or even pictures or images that influence how we understand the world and how we take action. This includes the ability to carry on "learningful" conversations that balance advocacy and inquiry, where people expose their own thinking effectively and make that thinking open to the influence of others.
4. *Building shared vision:* The capacity to hold a shared picture of the future we seek to create. A vision, no matter how heartfelt, cannot be imposed.
5. *Team learning:* The intelligence of the team exceeds the intelligence of the individuals within the team. When teams are truly learning, not only are they producing extraordinary results but also the individual members are growing. Teams, not individuals, are the fundamental learning unit in organizations. If teams cannot learn, organizations cannot learn. Team learning starts with dialogue. Teams must learn how to recognize patterns of defensiveness that undermine learning.

Definition(s) of concepts that had to be learned:

- *Creative tension:* The energy for change created by the difference between the vision and the current reality.
- *Dialogue:* Balancing advocacy (revealing your own thinking) with inquiry (asking questions to understand someone else's thinking).
- *Systems archetypes:* Patterns of structure that recur again and again. Understanding the structure means knowing where the leverage is for change in the system. "Structure influences behavior," Senge has written. "When placed in the same system, people, no matter how different, tend to produce similar results" (Senge, p. 42). In other words, there are no bad people, only bad systems.

How the model/theory/set of ideas was used: We believe that organizational change—changing how we think and what we do—is fundamentally a learning process. We have used Senge's concepts to begin to build a learning organization. We have particularly emphasized the concepts of system thinking, team learning, dialogue, and creative tension in our two learning sequences: start-up (for new teams) and keeping-on (for experienced teams). One of Senge's most powerful ideas is the difference between learning and performance, and how difficult it is for us to learn to learn together.

Key publications/references:

Senge, P. M. *The Fifth Discipline: The Art and Practice of the Learning Organization.* New York City: Doubleday/Currency, 1990.

Contributor(s): Program to Improve Patient Care Project Team

Contributor affiliation(s): Tallahassee Memorial Regional Medical Center, Tallahassee, FL

Name of model/concept: Managing Mental Models

Name of key author(s)/thinker(s): Peter M. Senge

Affiliation(s) of key author(s)/thinker(s): Director of the Systems Thinking and Organizational Learning Program at the Sloan School of Management at Massachusetts Institute of

Technology (MIT), Cambridge, MA, and a founding partner of Innovation Associates in Framingham, MA.

Key features of model/theory/set of ideas: "Many of the best ideas never get put into practice," Senge has written. Usually, this failure "stems not from weak intentions, wavering will or even nonsystemic understanding, but from *mental models*." New ideas fail because "they conflict with deeply held internal images of how the world works, images that limit us to familiar ways of thinking and acting" (Senge, p. 176).

Mental models are active; they shape how we act! Although people do not always behave congruently with their espoused theories (what they say), they do behave congruently with their theories-in-use (their mental models).

The problem with mental models arises when they are tacit, that is, when they exist below the level of awareness. "We trap ourselves, say [Chris] Argyris and his colleagues, in 'defensive routines' that insulate our mental models from examination, and we consequently develop 'skilled incompetence'—a marvelous oxymoron that Argyris uses to describe most adult learners, who are 'highly skillful at protecting themselves from pain and threat posed by learning situations,' but consequently fail to learn how to produce the results they really want" (Senge, p. 182).

Traditional organizations are characterized by managing, organizing, and controlling. Learning organizations are characterized by visions, values, and mental models. Their core values include merit (doing what is right) and openness (telling the truth).

Skills needed to manage mental models include (Senge, p. 186):

1. Recognizing leaps of abstraction (jumping from observation to generalization)
2. Exposing the "left-hand column" (saying what we usually do not say)
3. Balancing advocacy and inquiry (skills for honest investigation)
4. Facing up to the distinction between espoused theories and theories-in-use

Most of us can deal with differences so long as the learning process is open and people act with integrity. Systems thinkers shift from mental models dominated by events to mental models that recognize longer-term patterns of change and the underlying structures producing those patterns.

Definition(s) of concepts that had to be learned:

- *Defensive routines:* Behavior intended to protect ourselves from threat or embarrassment.
- *Dialogue:* Balancing advocacy (revealing your own thinking) with inquiry (asking questions to understand someone else's thinking).
- *Espoused theory:* What we *say* we believe about how the world works.
- *Mental models:* Deeply ingrained assumptions and beliefs about how we understand the world and how we take action.
- *Theory-in-use:* What our actions say we believe about how the world works.

How the model/theory/set of ideas was used: We have found that one of the hardest things for us to do is to look at ourselves and how we think. This is an individual-level skill and is critical to engaging in dialogue, which is necessary for team learning to occur.

We use these ideas to challenge ourselves to look at our own mental models, the ones we say we believe (espoused theories) and the ones we seem to believe based on how we act (theories-in-use). The ideas about the core values of doing what is right and telling the truth are helpful in challenging us to think deeply about trust. The important questions for each of us are: Do I trust? Am I trustworthy?

These discussions are very difficult when teams are first forming and learning to learn together. We have incorporated these ideas into an exercise that is described more fully in appendix B.

Key publications/references:

Senge, P. M. *The Fifth Discipline: The Art and Practice of the Learning Organization.* New York City: Doubleday/Currency, 1990.

Contributor(s): Program to Improve Patient Care Project Team

Contributor affiliation(s): Tallahassee Memorial Regional Medical Center, Tallahassee, FL

Name of model/concept: Paradigm Pioneers

Name of key author(s)/thinker(s): Joel Barker

Affiliation(s) of key author(s)/thinker(s): Founder of Infinity Limited, Inc., Lake Elmo, MN

Key features of model/theory/set of ideas: Change can be frustrating. Just as we master one change, along comes another. Some people have learned to deal with change, to move from one change to another with relative ease. Barker calls these people *paradigm pioneers.* When a paradigm changes or shifts, it fundamentally alters the way things are done.

You do not have to create the new rules to be successful, if you understand the role of a special group of people who drive the new paradigm from rough concept to practical application. The new concept cannot emerge without the paradigm pioneer who is willing to accept risks to open up the new way. Pioneers open up the territory; settlers follow when it is safe.

Key characteristics of paradigm pioneers:

- *Intuition:* The ability to make good decisions with incomplete information
- *Courage:* The willingness to move forward in the face of great risk
- *Commitment to time:* Understanding that it takes time to go from rough concept to a working paradigm

Too many people want too many numbers before they are willing to make a decision. That's *settler mentality.* There can be no numbers until the pioneer generates them. Pioneering a paradigm in combination with continuous improvement yields competitive advantage. Later, when settlers come into the market, there is nothing left for them.

Paradigm pioneering + continuous improvement = never give the settler an even break

To become a paradigm pioneer:

1. Get outside your boundaries; see what others are doing.
2. Be willing to break your own rules of past success and to recognize that the new rules probably will be brought to you by someone from outside your organization.
3. Develop new reading habits.
4. Be prepared for failure, but don't let that stop you!

Remember, you can *choose* the pioneer pathway. There will always be a new idea to make the world a better place.

Definition(s) of concepts that had to be learned:

- *Kaizen:* The Japanese concept of continuous improvement through small incremental change.
- *Paradigm:* A set of rules and regulations that does two things: (1) establishes or defines boundaries, and (2) directs us how to solve problems that lie within these boundaries.

- *Paradigm shift:* A fundamental change, an invention or discovery that completely changes the rules. When a paradigm shifts, everything goes back to zero. Past success guarantees nothing!
- *Pioneer:* One who chooses to take the new paradigm and drive it from rough concept to practical application.
- *Settler:* One who chooses to wait to adopt the new idea until its practical application has been well established.

How the model/theory/set of ideas was used: In our organization, we have used Barker's concept of the paradigm pioneer to help build a learning organization. We believe that Senge's learning organization concepts represent a paradigm shift; that is, they completely change how we think about organizational change. Senge himself believes that his concepts are an invention and others will learn how to put them into practice. We have found that it is very helpful for teams to see themselves as choosing the pioneer pathway. This is indeed new territory; there are no easy answers out there. It is up to us to learn the answers that will work for each of us.

Key publications/references:

Barker, J. *Paradigm Pioneers.* From the videotape series *Discovering the Future.* Burnsville, MN: Charthouse International, 1992.

Contributor(s): Program to Improve Patient Care Project Team

Contributor affiliation(s): Tallahassee Memorial Regional Medical Center, Tallahassee, FL

Name of model/concept: The Maturity Continuum

Name of key author(s)/thinker(s): Stephen R. Covey

Affiliation(s) of key author(s)/thinker(s): Founder and chairman of the Covey Leadership Center and the nonprofit Institute for Principle-Centered Leadership, Provo, UT, which publishes *Executive Excellence* magazine.

Key features of model/theory/set of ideas: Covey sees the maturity continuum as beginning with dependence, moving through independence, and moving on to interdependence—the most highly evolved relationships. In our culture, most of us have learned that the most highly evolved relationships are independent; we place a very high value on independence.

Dependence ——————————→ Independence ——————————→ Interdependence

Dependence is the paradigm of you: *You* take care of me. *You* come through for me. *You* didn't come through for me. I blame *you* for the results. *Independence* is the paradigm of I: *I* can do it. *I* am responsible. *I* am self-reliant. *I* can choose. *Interdependence* is the paradigm of we: *We* can do it. *We* can cooperate. *We* can combine our talents and abilities to create something greater together.

Interdependence is the more mature, more advanced concept. It is a choice only independent people can make. According to Covey, dependent people cannot choose to be interdependent. They do not have the character to do it; they do not own enough of themselves.

Definition(s) of concepts that had to be learned:

- *Dependent people:* People who need (depend on) others to get what they want.
- *Independent people:* People who can get what they want through their own effort (depend only on themselves).

- *Interdependent people:* People who can combine their own efforts with the efforts of others to achieve their greatest success.

How the model/theory/set of ideas was used: We have used Covey's ideas about maturity to look at how we view working together in teams and working with stakeholders. Most of us have learned to value independence above all other relationships. In our culture, this is particularly true among men. To work with others to accomplish something feels too much like dependence; it is uncomfortable. It feels like needing others when you should be able to just do it yourself. Many clinicians also highly value independence. Clinicians see themselves as practicing independently and strongly resist working with others if they feel that others might have the ability to influence how they do their work.

Key publications/references:

Covey, S. R. *Principle-Centered Leadership.* New York City: Summit Books, 1991.

Covey, S. R. *The Seven Habits of Highly Effective People.* New York City: Simon & Schuster, 1989.

Contributor(s): Program to Improve Patient Care Project Team

Contributor affiliation(s): Tallahassee Memorial Regional Medical Center, Tallahassee, FL

Name of the model: Deming's 14 Points

Name of key author(s)/thinker(s): W. Edwards Deming

Key features of model/theory/set of ideas: The 14 Points for Management were put forward by Deming after he realized that use of statistical methods alone was not enough to ensure an organization's survival. His mission was to seek greater sources of quality and improvement; however, when statistical methods failed to live up to their potential, he began what became a lifelong investigation, encapsulated in the following:

1. Create constancy of purpose for improvement of product and service.
2. Adopt the new philosophy.
3. Cease dependence on mass inspection.
4. End the practice of awarding business on price tag alone.
5. Improve constantly and forever the system of production and service.
6. Institute training.
7. Institute leadership.
8. Drive out fear.
9. Break down barriers between staff areas.
10. Eliminate slogans, exhortations, and targets for the workplace.
11. Eliminate numerical quotas.
12. Remove barriers to pride of workmanship.
13. Institute a rigorous program of education and retraining.
14. Take action to accomplish the transformation.

How the model/theory/set of ideas was used: At TMRMC, we used some of Deming's ideas in helping to:

- Build a shared vision for the organization (idealized design for patient/family care).
- Inculcate a "proceed until apprehended" mentality, assuming that forgiveness will be there (for example, it's okay to make mistakes).

- Implement a circular design (that is, never-ending), always upping the ante.
- Set up planning boards, utilizing an all-on-one-team approach (for example, the Joiner Triangle).
- Encourage stakeholder involvement (a stakeholder is one, if he or she thinks he or she is).
- Establish that a planning board can do anything it wants as long as it does not affect anyone else and the requisite level of resources are available. If a proposed decision affects someone else, his or her approval must be obtained; if resources are unavailable, they must be found.
- Guide the creation of multidisciplinary team(s) (for example, the patient meal work group).
- Establish the *How to Improve a Process* education sequence (for course outline, refer to figure A-3, pp. 180–81).

Key publications/references:

Deming, W. E. *Out of the Crisis.* Boston: MIT Center for Advanced Engineering Study, 1986.

Joiner, B. L. *Fourth Generation Management.* New York City: McGraw-Hill, 1994.

Contributor(s): R. Darrell Lee, MS, former project analyst (currently, quality process facilitator)

Contributor affiliation(s): Tallahassee Memorial Regional Medical Center, Tallahassee, FL (currently, All Children's Hospital, St. Petersburg, FL)

Models Driving Change at Health Bond

Name of model: Systems Thinking

Name of key author(s)/thinker(s): Leland R. Kaiser

Affiliation(s) of key author(s)/thinker(s): President of Kaiser & Associates, a health care consulting firm, located in Brighton, Colorado, and associate professor, graduate program in health administration, Graduate School of Business, University of Colorado, Denver.

Key features of model/theory/set of ideas: Leland Kaiser is an expert at assisting organizations to change the way they think and at catalyzing individuals to become visionary leaders of visionary organizations. He asks his audience to think beyond the boundaries of conventional wisdom and to play with outrageous ideas as the road to creating a healthful future for health care organizations. For example, in 1985, Kaiser encouraged children's hospitals to connect with senior citizens. Throughout his career, he has goaded audiences to think in terms of interdependent systems and to use electronic telecommunications for distance learning. By 1992, he was challenging hospitals to directly contribute financial support to, and invest in, the health and well-being of the community in which they are located.

Definition(s) of concepts that had to be learned:

- It takes a crisis to become more conscious: learn to dismantle old forms, liberate their energy, and build new structures better suited to the future (Kaiser, 1983).
- Consciousness which is inclusive provides the platform for imagining and implementing a more extensive future, improving current awareness and creating a larger destiny (Kaiser, 1983).
- Winning organizations will be the ones which can think in the biggest terms and imagine the greatest possibilities: The future is one of invention, not adaptation (Kaiser, 1985).

Figure A-3. Keeping-On Educational Sequence (August to December 1995)

August

August 3, Meeting

    Thursday (10:30–12:30 Auditorium)

    Welcome new Keeping-On teams

    Idealized design for Keeping-On

    Keeping-On educational sequence

    Quality or Else videotape

August 17, Workshop

    Thursday (10:30–12:30 Auditorium)

    • Help with identifying a process from hit list

    • Help with forming groups

Things to do:

• Bring your hit list for this planning cycle

September

September 7, Meeting

    Thursday (10:30–12:30 Auditorium)

    Overview of improvement process

    • Developing a project work plan presentation

    • Identify a critical process flow from original idealized design and from hit list

    • Process flowcharting

September 14, Workshop

    Thursday (10:30–12:30 Auditorium)

    • Help with developing work plans

    • Help with flowcharting your process

Things to do:

• Identify a process from your hit list that your want to work on this planning cycle.

October

October 5, Meeting

    Thursday (10:30–12:30 Auditorium)

    Project measures and baselines for the process

    • Project specific

    • Data collection of elements of process (determine delays, etc.)

    • Explanation of variation in data

    • Graphical methods (data presentations)

    • Review work plan

October 12, Workshop

    Thursday (10:30–12:30 Auditorium)

    • Help with data collection

    • Help with graphical methods

Things to do:

• Bring flowcharted process

• Bring completed work plan

November

November 2, Meeting

    Thursday (10:30–12:30 Auditorium)

    Analysis of idealized design factors (understanding how this process can contribute to the work unit's idealized design)

    • Cause-and-effect diagram

    • Data collection

    • Review work plan

Things to do:

• Bring completed graphs of data collected

Figure A-3. (Continued)

November (continued)

November 2 Meeting (continued)

Develop idealized design for this process
- Idealized process flowchart
- Factors influencing project measures
- Review work plan

November 16, Workshop
Thursday (10:30–12:30 Auditorium)
- Help with cause-and-effect diagram
- Help with idealized flowchart

December

December 7, Meeting
Thursday (10:30–12:30 Auditorium)
Alternative means (more than one solution)
Implementation work plan
- Implementation schedule
- Resource requirements
- Review work plan

Materials:
- Bring cause-and-effect diagram
- Bring idealized flowchart
- Bring draft of poster plan

December 14, Workshop
Thursday (10:30–12:30 Auditorium)
- Help with alternative means
- Help with your project work plan for January–June
- Help with poster presentation planning

December 21, Thursday

- Poster plan due in project office
- Implementation plan for January to June 1996 due in project office

---

January

January 4, Workshop
Thursday (10:30–12:30 Auditorium)
- Poster construction

Things to do:
- Bring your supplies and poster plan

January 11, Poster Presentation
Thursday (7:30–4:00 Auditorium)

How the model/theory/set of ideas was used: Executives of Health Bond's service–education partnership have heard presentations by Leland Kaiser several times during the 1980s and early 1990s. He was featured at a meeting for the Minnesota business community related to health care reform in November 1993. His provocative communications (presentations and publications) have had a significant impact on these executives, who have since developed a shared meaning around visioning and inventing the future, issues and strategies related to planned change, and changing hospital–employee, hospital–provider, and hospital–community relationships.

Key publications/references:

Kaiser, L. R. The emerging hospital/employee relationship. *Healthcare Forum,* Jan.–Feb. 1985, pp. 17–18. (Human resource management)

Kaiser, L. R. Inventing the future. Speech given at the Harpur Forum Breakfast, The Foundation of the State University of New York at Binghamton, Nov. 21, 1983.

Kaiser, L. R. Organizational mindset: ten ways to alter your world view. *Healthcare Forum,* Jan.–Feb. 1986, pp. 50–53.

Kaiser, L. R. Planning for change. *Healthcare Forum,* June 1980, pp. 35–38. (A practical resource for all hospital managers)

Contributor(s): Sharon Aadalen, RN, PhD, consortium director

Contributor affiliation(s): Health Bond Consortium, south central Minnesota, and Mankato State University School of Nursing, Mankato, MN

Name of model: The Caring Curriculum

Name of key author(s)/thinker(s): Em Olivia Bevis EdD, RN, FAAN, and Jean Watson, PhD, RN, FAAN

Affiliation(s) of key author(s)/thinker(s): Em O. Bevis, nursing education consultant, Bluffton, SC, and adjunct professor of research, Georgia Southern College, Statesboro, GA; and Jean Watson, professor, school of nursing, University of Colorado Health Sciences Center, Denver.

Key features of model/theory/set of ideas: In the preface to Bevis and Watson's book *Toward a Caring Curriculum: A New Pedagogy for Nursing,* Patricia Moccia, CEO and executive vice-president of the National League for Nursing, wrote: ". . . education for the new age is not about content (old Tylerian behaviorist paradigm), it is about soul, it is about process." And this education creates and extends, Moccia asserts, ". . . an educational community that will foster three fundamental feelings for all involved: a sense of agency, a sense of responsibility and accountability, and a sense of connection" (p. xi).

The *caring curriculum,* as defined by Bevis and Watson, represents the tradition in which education is "an emancipatory project." These nursing leaders set out to create a new curriculum development paradigm for nursing education that will provide the public with skilled, compassionate scholar-clinicians into the 21st century. Key features of this new paradigm are:

1. Liberate students and faculty from authoritarian restraints of empiricist/behaviorist models (eliminate behavioral objectives and teacher roles/behaviors necessitated by these objectives).
2. Acknowledge students as equal partners in the educational enterprise (restructure the way faculty and students relate to each other).
3. Define curriculum as interactions between and among students and teachers (clear intent that learning takes place).
4. Facilitate structuring of learning differently (engage learner in scholarly pursuits; abandon dominance of lecture in nursing education).
5. Help faculty humanize educational process (change content domination of current curricula).
6. Support alliance of students, teachers, and clinicians.
7. Restructure focus of learning (ground learning experiences in clinical practice).
8. Provide practical guidelines for faculty (eliminate restrictions on faculty expression of individuality, creativity, and style).

9. Acknowledge wide variety of ways of knowing (legitimize those things that are not empirically verifiable).
10. Eliminate education-based class and caste system in nursing (acknowledge and value contributions of all nurses and make career progression education accessible).
11. Offer a criticism model for assessing learning—in addition to empiricist/behaviorist model appropriate to training (Bevis and Watson, pp. 1–2).

Definition(s) of concepts that had to be learned:

- *Active learning:* Learning that engages the intellectual effort of both students and teachers; necessary for development of creative thinking that is the mark of the educated person (Bevis and Watson, pp. 5–6).
- *Curriculum:* Interactions and transactions that occur between and among students and teachers with the intent that learning occurs (Bevis and Watson, p. 5).
- *Learning:* Change in human disposition or capability, which can be retained and which is not simply ascribable to the process of growth (Bevis and Watson, p. 265).

How the model/theory/set of ideas was used: Bevis and Watson's work, along with the American Association of Colleges of Nursing's publication *Essentials of College and University Education for Professional Nursing,* has guided development of a new curriculum in the school of nursing at Mankato State University, and has affected faculty collaborative development at South Central Technical College's practical nursing program. The emphasis on Senge's work of building learning organizations within consortium member hospitals and partner schools has been reinforced by Bevis and Watson's emphasis on an educationist approach. Through Health Bond's service–education partnership, these models of organizational change are nurtured. Senge nudges health care organizations to develop the disciplines of personal mastery, mental models, shared vision, team learning, and systems thinking through true dialogue (interactions leading to shared meaning). Similarly, Bevis and Watson urge a model of caring in learning: a shift from teaching to learning, from an emphasis on facts to an emphasis on discovery, from an emphasis on success or failure to an emphasis on continuous learning and improvement. Faculty are to role-model healthful behaviors; to encourage continuous, lifelong, active, and critical learning, exposing their own ideas to self- and other constructive critique; and to foster belief in the power of interactive partnerships in learning.

Key publications/references:

American Association of Colleges of Nursing. *Essentials of College and University Education for Professional Nursing.* Washington, DC: AACN, 1986.

Bevis, E. O., and Watson, J. *Toward a Caring Curriculum: A New Pedagogy for Nursing.* New York City: National League for Nursing, 1989.

Contributor(s): Sharon Aadalen, RN, PhD, consortium director; Kathryn Schweer, dean, school of nursing; Mary Huntley, RN, PhD, acting associate dean; Mary Kay Hohenstein, RN, MEd, instructional dean

Contributor affiliation(s): Health Bond Consortium, south central Minnesota; School of Nursing, Mankato State University, Mankato, MN; Health and Safety Division, South Central Technical College, Mankato, MN.

Name of model: Leading an Empowered Organization

Name of key author(s)/thinker(s): Marie Manthey, MNA, RN, president, and Diane Miller, BSN, RN, consultant

Affiliation(s) of key author(s)/thinker(s): Creative Nursing Management, Minneapolis, MN

Key features of model/theory/set of ideas: One of the more notable trends in the past several years is introduction of the term *empowerment* into the vernacular of health care organizations. The word sometimes indicates giving power to others. In some organizations, it means that managers are delegating portions of their role to employees. The issues with empowerment begin, in part, because of the term's diversity of meaning.

As the path to empowerment begins, one challenge is to identify tangible evidence that something has changed. Three key mind-set changes are necessary to achieve empowerment, and these are delineated and put into the daily operations of an organization as the first measurable step is taken. These mind-set changes are:

1. Decentralization
2. Managers adopting leadership styles that facilitate growth
3. Adherence to a process that moves the organization along a continuum with the conscious awareness that this transformation occurs over many years

These three mind-set changes alter the way people think about themselves and their roles, and indicate that the organization is willing to begin a transformative journey.

Definition(s) of concepts that had to be learned: Participants in situational leadership for empowerment change processes gain an understanding of critical concepts through new information and experiential learning. These concepts are: (1) relationship management, (2) problem solving, and (3) risk taking.

Relationship management is based on interpersonal integrity and assumes each individual in an interaction takes responsibility for his or her part in relationships. Learning about articulating and negotiating expectations among personnel, and appropriate delegation of responsibility, authority, and accountability are important related concepts. Healthy relationships are characterized by open communication, trust, and respect.

Effective problem solving is defined as using a sequential and methodological approach to focus on results or desired outcomes. It also involves using consensus decision-making processes.

Risk taking is acting on creative ideas to accomplish desired ends. An environment that supports risk taking must be characterized by discipline without punishment and discipline that is positive.

How the model/theory/set of ideas was used: Administrators, managers, faculty, supervisors, and expanded role personnel (for example, nurse clinicians) within Health Bond's member hospitals and partner schools all have had the opportunity to participate in leadership empowerment experiential education. The initial program, Leaders Empower Staff (LES), lasts for three days. Three to six months later, a one-day "shot-in-the-arm" follow-up program is held to facilitate participant movement along the path dedicated to gaining new knowledge, raising consciousness, and changing individual and group behavior.

Contributor(s): Diane Miller, RN, BSN, consultant; Sharon Aadalen, RN, PhD, consortium director

Contributor affiliation(s): Creative Nursing Management, Minneapolis, and Health Bond Consortium, south central Minnesota

Name of model: Visioning Health Futures: StoryTech

Name of key author(s)/thinker(s): Arthur Harkins, PhD

Affiliation(s) of key author(s)/thinker(s): Professor in educational administration at the University of Minnesota, Minneapolis.

Key features of model/theory/set of ideas: StoryTech is a narrative futuring technique, a process for creating a preferred future that Health Bond participants have had a chance to learn along with staff from other providers and educational groups in south central Minnesota. It is a story-writing process that enables individuals and groups to redefine themselves, their goals, and their purposes congruent with a positive vision of future change.

The tension created between *classical reality* in this model and *virtual reality* is similar to the creative tension described by Robert Fritz in *The Path of Least Resistance* (New York City: Fawcett-Columbine, 1989) and developed by Peter M. Senge in *The Fifth Discipline: The Art and Practice of the Learning Organization* (New York City: Doubleday/Currency, 1990), and the first steps of the interactive planning process as described by Russell Ackoff (The circular organization: an update. *The Academy of Management Executives* 3(1):11–16, 1989).

Definition(s) of concepts that had to be learned:

- *Classical reality:* The everyday perceived world
- *Virtual reality:* Any future world in which the participant defines self positively

How the model/theory/set of ideas was used: The StoryTech Model/Theory has been used in two major ways within Health Bond: (1) as a clinical intervention called One Day Plus, a service–education joint venture between Waseca Area Memorial Hospital's Family Focus Outpatient Chemical Dependency Clinics (1991–1993), and (2) as a visioning process within the Health Bond Consortium (1992–1993). When used as a clinical intervention in groups of chemically dependent people, positive attitudinal and behavioral changes were shown. In addition, a variety of client-centered manuals were developed reflecting this storytelling intervention. The school of nursing at Mankato State University featured Harkins as a speaker at its 1993 interagency meeting. In 1993, he facilitated two identical day-long fall conferences for personnel in Health Bond's three member hospitals and two partner schools, as well as an evening dinner meeting for the three hospital boards of directors and representatives of their respective medical staffs. The visioning processes for these events are called Envisioning Tomorrow's Health Care. These events occurred in October 1993 at the end of year three of the grant and set the direction for Health Bond's leadership for future health care reform within south central Minnesota for the final two years.

Key publications/references:

Harkins, A., and Gordon, S. Futures in substance abuse damage control: development of personal recovery alternatives through guided story telling. *Futurics: A Quarterly Journal of Futures Research* 17(1–2), Winter–Spring 1993.

Contributor(s): Sharon Aadalen, RN, PhD, consortium director; Stephen Gordon, RN, EdD, director; Patricia Cretilli, RN, PhD, associate professor; Mary Huntley, RN, PhD, acting associate dean

Contributor affiliation(s): Health Bond Consortium, south central Minnesota; Waseca Area Memorial Hospital Family Focus Treatment Center, Waseca, MN; and school of nursing, Mankato State University, Mankato, MN

Models Driving Change at Hartford Hospital

Name of model: Strategic Management

Name of key author(s)/thinker(s): K. Hatten and M. Hatten

Key features of model/theory/set of ideas and how they were used: Hatten and Hatten specify several principles key to strategic management success, which they define as the "process by which an organization formulates objectives and is managed to achieve them" (Hatten and Hatten, p. 1). (See figure A-4.) They believe that the key driving component of these principles is consistency — consistency with internal and external realities; with operational systems and other institutional strategies, including long-range planning; with the ability to take and recoup from risks; with the ability to implement planned change effectively; and with resources available both now and in the future.

Key publications/references:

Hatten, K., and Hatten, M. *Strategic Management: Analysis and Action.* Englewood Cliffs, NJ: Prentice-Hall, 1987.

Contributor(s): Cheryl B. Stetler, project director

Contributor affiliation(s): Hartford Hospital, Hartford, CT

Figure A-4. Hatten and Hatten's Key Principles of Strategic Management Success

1. The strategy must fit the environment, including the core values of the organization and its players. For example, at Hartford Hospital, collaborative practice is a core value and any innovation must take it into account.

2. Various components of the strategies must fit, one to another and with the whole. For nursing, this in particular speaks to the issues of decentralization within the department and to the need for interactive planning with key administrative and medical leaders. For example, the work of nursing cannot be examined or changed in isolation.

3. To be effective, strategies must focus rather than disperse resources. In this day of lean and mean organizations, and thus staff, the time of each department member must be well used.

4. To be effective, strategies should focus on departmental/organizational strengths versus the weakness of competitors. In today's competitive market for scarce health care dollars and scarce health care personnel, this business principle has direct applicability.

5. "Strategy is the art of the possible. Do what is feasible!" In other words, do only what your resources will allow. This suggests what Stevens (1985) describes as a resource rather than goal-driven model where you assess your resources and then determine the number and types of goals that you can logically take on.

6. To be effective, risks should not be taken lightly. They should be as thoroughly assessed as possible so that leaders know what they are, how to minimize them, and how to back out before irreparable damage is done. For example, expanding the scope of practice of a large number os nurses is a risk that should be thoroughly assessed and managed.

7. "A good strategy is controlled . . . surprises are failures of control." Detailed project planning, where accountability is well defined, and formative evaluation help to operationalize such control.

8. An effective strategy builds on successes, which implies and reenforces the value of ongoing evaluation, reward, and reenforcement.

9. "A sign of strategic success is support by the organization's stakeholders, particularly by the top and middle management." Such support is not only a positive indicator but a sine qua non of an effective strategy.

Source: Reprinted from *Nursing Economic$*, 1991, Volume 9, Number 2, p. 114. Reprinted with permission of the publisher, Janetti Publications, Inc., East Holly Avenue Box 56, Pitman, NJ 08071-0056; Phone (609) 256-2300; FAX (609) 589-7463.

Models Driving Change at MeritCare Hospital

Name of model: Kilmann's 5 Track Model for Organizational Change

Name of key author(s)/thinker(s): Ralph Kilmann

Affiliation(s) of key author(s)/thinker(s): Professor of organization and management, director of the Program in Corporate Culture, Joseph M. Katz Graduate School of Business, University of Pittsburgh, and president of Organizational Design Consultants, Pittsburgh.

Key features of model/theory/set of ideas: Kilmann's model offers a comprehensive program not only for understanding the organization but also for managing it. It is based on two assumptions: (1) Organizations are holistic and multidimensional, and (2) any effort to improve the functioning of an organization that ignores the full context and interrelated dynamics of the whole organization will most likely fail.

The framework identifies the key organizational variables (or tracks) that need to be managed: the culture track, the management skills track, the team-building track, the strategy–structure track, and the reward system track. The first three tracks can improve the informal organization (how people behave toward one another on the job), whereas the last two tracks can improve the formal organization (including the documents, systems, technologies, and resources that guide what people are supposed to do). As an integrated whole, these five tracks can assist managers and staff in diagnosing problems in the organization and managing planned change.

The *culture track* enhances trust, communication, information sharing, and the willingness to change among members — conditions that must exist before any other improvement effort can succeed. The *management skills track* provides all management personnel with new ways of coping with complex problems and hidden assumptions. The *team-building track* infuses the new culture and updated management skills into each work unit, thereby instilling cooperation organizationwide so that complex problems can be addressed with all the expertise and information available. The *strategy–structure track* develops either a completely new or revised plan for the firm and then aligns divisions, departments, work groups, jobs, and all resources with the new strategic direction. Finally, the *reward system track* clearly communicates to employees what performance and behaviors are rewarded by providing an instrument to measure performance and by ensuring that rewards are distributed based on performance.

In order for the five tracks to provide their potential benefits, they must be preceded by obtaining top management's support and an accurate understanding of the organization's problems and opportunities. A completely integrated program assesses the barriers to success and then provides the resources and ongoing activities required to manage systemwide change.

Definitions of concepts that had to be learned:

- *Adaptive culture:* A culture evident when members actively support one another's efforts to identify all the problems and implement workable solutions. There is a feeling of confidence. Members believe, without a doubt, that they can manage whatever new problems and opportunities come their way. There is a widespread enthusiasm, a spirit of doing whatever it takes to achieve organizational success. Members are receptive to change.
- *Assumptions:* Beliefs whose truth has been taken for granted but may turn out to be false under close scrutiny.
- *Culture:* Shared values, beliefs, expectations, and norms. Culture is the invisible force behind the tangibles and observables in an organization; a social energy that moves people to action.
- *Culture gap:* The difference between the desired norms and the actual norms can be dramatic, and is termed a *culture gap*. The Kilmann-Saxton Culture-Gap Survey (1983) is a measurement tool that can be used to detect the gap between what the current

187

culture is and what it should be. It contrasts current and desired norms in the following four dimensions of a work group's culture: (1) task support norms having to do with information sharing, helping other groups, and concern with efficiency; (2) task innovation norms for being creative, applying different approaches, and doing new things; (3) social relationship norms for socializing with one's work group and mixing friendships with business; and (4) personal freedom norms for self-expression, exercising discretion, and pleasing oneself.

- *Myers-Briggs Type Indicator:* An assessment tool for personality preferences and blind spots.
- *Norms:* The "unwritten rules of the game" that guide behaviors on the work site. When an organization's culture is dysfunctional, people may list norms such as these:
  - Look busy even when you're not.
  - Don't be the first to disagree.
  - Don't step on the toes of senior management.
  - When people suggest new ways, say, "We tried that ten years ago, and it didn't work then."
  - Blame the administrative team for all that is wrong in the organization.
  - Ask only questions to which you have answers.
  - Never question the status quo.
  - Don't congratulate your colleagues when they make improvements in their systems.
- *Reward system:* A system that deals with all documented methods to attract and retain employees, especially those used to motivate high levels of performance. The essential diagnostic issue is whether all these documented systems are barriers (or channels) to success.
- *Strategy:* Referring to all the documents that signify direction: statements of vision, mission, purpose, goals and objectives.
- *Structure:* Referring to the way resources are organized into action: organization charts, policy statements, job descriptions, formal rules and regulation, and work procedures.

How the model/theory/set of ideas was used: The theoretical framework used to transform MeritCare Hospital's unadaptive, bureaucratic, traditional culture into an adaptive, customer-centered and flexible culture arrived with Ralph Kilmann, who presented his transformational change model to MeritCare at the invitation of the leadership team. The model is designed to integrate and orchestrate long-term, corporatewide change.

Five distinct and consecutive processes led our organization toward our ongoing goal of becoming a customer-centered, innovative, effective, and flexible organization. The processes are:

1. *Culture track:* Examine the culture of each work group through the use of the Kilmann Culture Gap Instrument described earlier. Each work group was offered the opportunity, knowledge, and methods to change the norms of their culture to promote a flexible, adaptable, and innovative work environment.
2. *Management skills track:* As the environment was transformed from a traditional, bureaucratic, hierarchical style of management toward a participatory style, both front-line staff and executive management were offered opportunities to improve their interpersonal, communication, change management, and leadership skills.
3. *Team-building track:* In this track, staff and managers shared ideas and knowledge about the work environment and systems that may be inhibiting quality teamwork. Together, they examined their teams and planned to improve the ways in which they work together to serve their customers.
4. *Strategy-structure track:* Initially, this track involved management personnel, vice-presidents, and the CEO in analyzing the structure of the organization in order to assess and (ideally) eliminate barriers interfering with an efficient, customer-centered workplace. This work is ongoing and has become an important effort for leadership in conjunction with their respective work groups, to continue the restructuring process to improve job satisfaction, efficiency, and customer service.

5. *Reward system track:* To analyze the effects of the current reward system, managers and many of the staff learned about entitlement programs and contrasted this knowledge with the realities of today's changing and competitive health care environment. An outcome of this track was the design of a performance appraisal system that incorporates the organization's corporate values to measure and reward performance. A team recognition program was initiated, along with many efforts throughout the organization to spotlight and then recognize the excellent work of services, teams, and individuals.

Key publications/references:

Kilmann, R. H. *Making Organizations Competitive.* San Francisco: Jossey-Bass, 1991.

Kilmann, R. H. *Managing Beyond the Quick Fix.* San Francisco: Jossey-Bass, 1989.

Kilmann, R. H. Managing holistic improvement. *Clinical Laboratory Management Review* 7(5):395–97, 400–403, 406, Sept.–Oct. 1993.

Kilmann, R. H. *Workbook for Implementing the Five Tracks.* Vols. 1 and 2. Tuxedo, NY: XICOM, Sterling Forest, 1991.

Contributor(s): Ruth Hanson, MS, RN, project director; Betty Sayers, MS, group facilitator

Contributor affiliation(s): MeritCare Hospital, Fargo, ND

Name of model: Leading for the Situation

Name of key author(s)/thinker(s): Kenneth Blanchard, PhD

Affiliation(s) of key author(s)/thinker(s): Blanchard Training and Development, Inc., Escondido, CA

Key features of model/theory/set of ideas: The goal of a situational leader is to meet people where they are and to give them the direction and support they need, when they need it. An effective situational leader learns to use different leadership styles in response to people's needs for varying degrees of direction and support.

There are four different leadership styles: directing, coaching, supporting, and delegating. These may vary in three ways: (1) the amount of direction that leader provides, (2) the amount of support the leader provides, and (3) the amount of follower involvement in decision making.

When managers try to influence the behavior of others, they engage in two patterns of behavior: directive and supportive. *Directive behavior* is the extent to which a leader tells an associate what to do, how to do it, and when to do it, and then closely supervises performance. The three key characteristics of directive behavior are structure, control, and supervise. *Supportive behavior* is defined as the extent to which the leader lets the associate take responsibility for directing his or her own work. The three key characteristics of supportive behavior are praise, listen, and facilitate.

With a directing leadership style, the leader is in charge. With a coaching leadership style, the follower is more involved in the decision making. However, when push comes to shove, the leader decides.

With a supporting leadership style, the follower's role is to decide how the task should be accomplished. The leader's role is to listen and provide assurance, support, resources, and ideas, if needed. When a delegation leadership style is used, the follower decides how, when, where, and with whom the goal is to be accomplished.

Pertinent to note is that leaders can get results in any style. Therefore, there is no "one best" leadership style. As a situational leader, it is important to use "different strokes for different folks." Flexibility is important because no two people come to a task with identical skills, knowledge, confidence, or motivation. To effectively lead these people at different levels of development, leadership style must be varied to fit the needs of the situation.

Definition(s) of concepts that had to be learned:

- *Coaching style:* A combination of high-directive and high-supportive behavior. The leader explains directions, solicits ideas, praises approximately right behavior, but continues to direct task work until completed.
- *Delegating style:* A combination of low-directive and low-supportive behavior. The leader turns over responsibility for task/goal accomplishment to the follower. The follower then decides how, when, where, and with whom to complete the tasks at hand.
- *Directing style:* A combination of high-directive and low-supportive behavior. The leader provides specific instruction about roles and goals, then closely supervises the associate's performance.
- *Supporting style:* A combination of high-supportive and low-directive behavior. The leader and associate make decisions together. The role of the leader is to facilitate, listen, draw potential out from the associate, encourage, and support.

How the model/theory/set of ideas was used: With the framework of Ken Blanchard's situational leadership II model, a four-part series (14 hours) was designed. Six of the leadership trainers were identified as the situational leadership trainers.

Features of the course design included:

- Specific learning objectives were identified for each session.
- Exercises were designed so that participants could apply content before returning to the workplace.
- Evaluation tools were used to gain feedback from participants.
- Blanchard's leader behavior analysis II self-assessment was used along with the development task analysis II.
- Blanchard's situational leadership II videotape program was integrated into course work.

Key publications/references:

Blanchard, K., Zigarmi, P., and Zigarmi, D. *Situational Leadership II.* (Videotape) Escondido, CA: Blanchard Training and Development, 1988.

Contributor(s): Kay Modin, RN, BSN, MSEd, educator

Contributor affiliation(s): MeritCare Hospital, Fargo, ND

Name of model: The Five Leadership Practices of Exemplary Leaders

Name of key author(s)/thinker(s): James M. Kouzes and Barry Z. Posner

Affiliation(s) of key author(s)/thinker(s): James Kouzes, president, Tom Peters Group Learning Systems, Inc. (Leadership Challenge Workshop), in Palo Alto, CA; and Barry Posner, professor of management and director of graduate education and customer service, Leavey School of Business and Administration, Santa Clara University, Santa Clara, CA.

Key features of model/theory/set of ideas: Posner and Kouzes's research on the everyday actions and behaviors of exemplary leaders at all levels in a variety of settings has resulted in development of the five leadership practices of exemplary leaders. Their model includes:

1. *Challenging the process:* Leaders seek and accept challenging opportunities to test their abilities and look for innovative ways to improve their organizations. They motivate others to exceed their limits.
2. *Inspiring a shared vision:* Leaders look to the future with a sense of what is uniquely possible and passionately believe that people working together can make a difference. A leader must enlist others in a common vision by appealing to their values, interests, hope, and dreams, so that others clearly understand and accept the vision as their own.
3. *Enabling others to act:* Leaders know they cannot do the job alone. To accomplish extraordinary things in an organization, people must work in partnerships. Leaders create an atmosphere of mutual trust and respect. Getting people to work together begins with creating cooperative goals and sustaining trusting relationships. Leaders understand that by trusting others, they are rewarded with trustworthiness on the part of others. They make sure that when they win, everyone wins.
4. *Modeling the way:* Leaders have a philosophy—a set of high standards by which the organization is measured and a set of values about how employees, colleagues, and customers should be treated. Leaders build their credibility by maintaining consistency between their words and deeds.
5. *Encouraging the heart:* Getting extraordinary things done in organizations is hard work. Leaders encourage the heart by visibly recognizing people's contributions to the common vision. They express pride in the accomplishments of their teams. Leaders have high expectations of both themselves and their constituents.

Kouzes and Posner's leadership practices inventory (LPI) provides leaders with insightful information on their effectiveness as leaders. Individuals complete one assessment on themselves and also invite people with whom they work to complete an observer form. As a result of the data gathered, individuals can see how their leadership practices compare with other managers in the research data base. The design of the LPI was based on lengthy and repeated feedback from managers and on statistical analyses of various sets of behavior-based statements. Each statement is rated on a five-point Likert scale. Ongoing reliability and validity studies of the psychometric properties of the LPI now have been conducted with more than 35,000 managers and their associates.

Posner and Kouzes also have done extensive research on credibility. Recently, they published their second book *Credibility: How Leaders Gain and Lose It, and Why People Demand It.* Their videotape *The Credibility Factor: What Followers Expect from Leaders* identifies characteristics to be found in every effective leader: honesty, competence, inspiration, and vision.

How the model/theory/set of ideas was used: We have used Kouzes and Posner's work in both our interpersonal communication (IPC) class and Leadership MeritCare Style curriculum. Their research has assisted us in changing our leadership paradigm.

Their videotape has become a component of the trust and credibility course in the IPC curriculum. It focuses on what followers expect from their leaders, and highlights six men and women in successful organizations. Additionally, the Leadership MeritCare Style—Enhancing Leadership Practices curriculum has focused on their five leadership practices.

Key publications/references:

Kouzes, J. M., and Posner, B. Z. *The Credibility Factor: What Followers Expect from Leaders.* (Videotape) Carlsbad, CA: CRM Films, 1990.

Kouzes, J. M., and Posner, B. Z. *The Leadership Challenge: How to Get Extraordinary Things Done in Organizations.* San Francisco: Jossey-Bass, 1987.

Kouzes, J. M., and Posner, B. Z. *Leadership Practices Inventory LPI.* San Diego, CA: Pfeiffer & Company, 1993.

Contributor(s): Penny Dale, MEd, educator

Contributor affiliation(s): MeritCare Hospital, Fargo, ND

Models Driving Change at Vanderbilt University Hospital and Vanderbilt Clinic

Name of model: Interactive Planning

Name of key author(s)/thinker(s): Russell L. Ackoff

Affiliation(s) of key author(s)/thinker(s): Chairman of the Board, INTERACT, Inc., Philadelphia

Key features of model/theory/set of ideas:

- An organizational structure to support interactive planning—the board system.
- Creation of a desirable future. For us, this meant that we had to ask the question, If Vanderbilt Hospital and Vanderbilt Clinic no longer existed, what would we create instead? This helped us get beyond "reactive" thinking.
- Define the constraints of the idealized system up front.
- No one can effectively plan for anyone else.

Definition(s) of concepts that had to be learned:

- Desirable or idealized future as what we would create if Vanderbilt University Hospital and Vanderbilt Clinic no longer existed.
- Organizational democracy—a structure of unit boards on all inpatient and selected outpatient units.
- Shared accountability for decisions and agreements.

How the model/theory/set of ideas was used: We used Ackoff's board concept to structure unit-based, interdisciplinary planning committees on each of our inpatient units and on selected outpatient units. (See figure A-5.)

At Vanderbilt University Hospital and Vanderbilt Clinic, the term *shared governance* means that decision making about patient care and the work environment is done jointly by staff and leadership. This process is centered around unit-based groups, or boards. The boards are open to all who provide clinical or support service to that particular unit's patients. The board brings together the clinical staff of patient care services and other departments, management, and administrators to identify problems and plan for improvements.

The unit boards enable us to directly and creatively improve our patients' experience and care, as well as our work environment. They provide:

- Regular and continuous forums for staff to raise issues about quality of care and service
- "Faster" decision making by those who will "live with the changes" versus by centralized committees or administration
- A method by which staff and leadership can jointly identify problems and solutions, and can determine how to measure their success
- More frequent, regular open communication between staff and leadership
- More open communication between departments about patient care

Each unit board includes three levels of the organization—staff, management, and administration. Each clinical nursing service also has a board.

Figure A-5.   Interactive Planning Model at Vanderbilt University Hospital and Vanderbilt Clinic

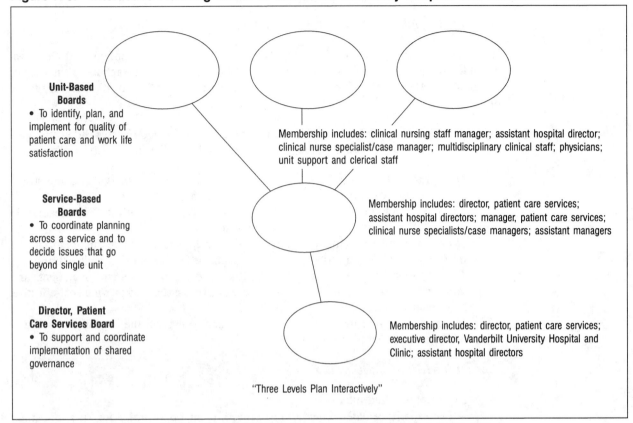

Unit-Based Boards
• To identify, plan, and implement for quality of patient care and work life satisfaction

Membership includes: clinical nursing staff manager; assistant hospital director; clinical nurse specialist/case manager; multidisciplinary clinical staff; physicians; unit support and clerical staff

Service-Based Boards
• To coordinate planning across a service and to decide issues that go beyond single unit

Membership includes: director, patient care services; assistant hospital directors; manager, patient care services; clinical nurse specialists/case managers; assistant managers

Director, Patient Care Services Board
• To support and coordinate implementation of shared governance

Membership includes: director, patient care services; executive director, Vanderbilt University Hospital and Clinic; assistant hospital directors

"Three Levels Plan Interactively"

Source: The Center for Patient Care Innovation, Vanderbilt University Hospital and Vanderbilt Clinic, Nashville, TN, 1994.

This structure was adapted from Ackoff's circular organizational model. The three levels of boards ensure interaction and coordination between and across levels of the organization. This creates the foundation to support unit-based planning and decision making.

The *unit board* is a regular, open meeting with no elected membership. "Members" are all the health care professionals and support staff who provide care and service to the unit. Most boards are chaired by a staff member. Currently, Vanderbilt has 58 unit boards. It is the interdisciplinary and interdepartmental participation that contributes to the most effective patient care outcomes in these boards. Each board meets at least monthly. At the meeting, the group discusses issues and solutions they have identified as priorities. The board does not base its decisions on a majority vote; the goal is to gain agreement on a proposed change that everyone on that unit can support and implement. The unit board works for win-win decisions through building consensus.

Key publications/references:

Minnen, T. G., Berger, E., Ames, A., Dubree, M., Baker, W. L., and Spinella, J. Sustaining work redesign innovations through shared governance. *The Journal of Nursing Administration* 23(7/8):25–40, July–Aug. 1993.

Contributor(s): Wendy Baker, RN, MS, project director; Karen Turner, EdD, training specialist; Terry Minnen, MEd, shared governance liaison

Contributor affiliation(s): Center for Patient Care Innovation, Vanderbilt University Hospital and Vanderbilt Clinic, Nashville, TN

Name of model: The Learning Organization

Name of key author(s)/thinker(s): Peter M. Senge

Affiliation(s) of key author(s)/thinker(s): Director of the Systems Thinking and Organizational Learning Program at the Sloan School of Management at Massachusetts Institute of Technology (MIT), Cambridge, MA, and a founding partner of Innovation Associates in Framingham, MA.

Key features of model/theory/set of ideas: Our redesign work encompasses the values, core behaviors, and performance expectations associated with the following leadership disciplines:

- *Organizational systems development:* Designing teams, budgets, policies, and strategies that reflect the mission and purpose of the organization
- *Facilitation:* Building shared vision by planning interactively with staff and leadership of patient care services and other hospital departments
- *Team learning:* Developing team and individual members to achieve the organization's mission and purpose (patient-focused care, cost-effectiveness, job satisfaction)
- *Patient focus:* Demonstrating in both attitude and action a concern for patients and families by developing, implementing, and evaluating systems to provide cost-effective, high-quality patient care
- *Personal learning:* Engaging in lifelong learning to expand the capacity of self and others to create and sustain learning

How the model/theory/set of ideas was used:

- Experienced-based interviewing:
  - The experience-based interviewing process is an opportunity for staff and their manager(s) to collaboratively define job competencies required for the job, as well as qualities valued in a successful coworker. These competencies and qualities are then translated into a set of open-ended interview questions used to objectively compare the experience of all candidates.
  - During the experience-based interview, the candidate provides examples from previous work and/or life experience that demonstrates how to use these competencies and qualities in the care of patients, working on a collaborative team, and so on. The unit staff thus gathers a more complete picture of past performance across critical job-related situations. Further, the candidate and the unit's team have the opportunity to create a common understanding of performance expectations on the unit.
- Mission-based job descriptions and evaluation:
  - New roles and changing leadership roles have prompted both managers of patient care services and central department heads to collaboratively redefine their accountability (shared and individual) and leadership priorities. As they joined together to write a new job description for the department heads, a shared understanding developed that is expected to support their working together in new ways.
  - It is critical that we recognize and reward the leadership qualities that support our mission and achieve our objectives for quality, service, and lower costs. Managers and their directors are using a performance review process built on their accountability to the hospital's mission which includes a customized development plan.

Key publications/references:

Senge, P. M. *The Fifth Discipline: The Art and Practice of the Learning Organization.* New York City: Doubleday/Currency, 1990.

Contributor(s): Wendy Baker, RN, MS, project director, director; Karen Turner, EdD, training specialist; Terry Minnen, MEd, shared governance liaison

Contributor affiliation(s): Center for Patient Care Innovation, Vanderbilt University Hospital and Vanderbilt Clinic, Nashville, TN

Name of model: Collaborative Organization Design (COD)

Name of key author(s)/thinker(s): Mary V. Gelinas, EdD, and Roger G. James, EdD

Affiliation(s) of key author(s)/thinker(s): Gelinas and James, Inc., Oakland, CA (a consulting firm specializing in helping organizations survive, thrive, and flourish through the alignment of people, structure, and technology in support of a strategic vision)

Key features of model/theory/set of ideas:

- The intent of COD is to inspire and enable members of organizations to rebuild their organizations in ways that respond to challenges and opportunities in the environment, to customer needs, and to their own aspirations; and to do so in ways that are understood and supported by those expected to do the rebuilding.
- Integrates the best of systems theory, organization and work design, visioning technology, sociotechnical systems perspectives, collaborative problem solving, quality programs, and organizational models.
- It is used when an organization's members want to re-create their organization, not just fix it.
- Requires that the following conditions and agreements be in place:
  - Top managers understand and are committed to the process.
  - Boundaries and constraints are crystal clear.
  - The basic organizational unit that is the focus of the design efforts is identified.
  - Mission and vision for parent organization are in place.
  - Top managers agree on the overall scope and purpose of the project, definition of roles and responsibilities, and resources to be committed to the effort.

Definition(s) of concepts that had to be learned:

- *Core goals and values:* The broad notions of future direction; the ways in which the organization wants to distinguish itself. They also represent what the organization stands for.
- *Culture:* Includes the leadership style and behavioral norms required for the organization to achieve its mission and vision.
- *Deliverables:* That which is provided to customers.
- *Design:* A comprehensive term that includes all aspects of an organization including work processes, deliverables, inputs, and feedback mechanisms. It also includes mission and vision of the organization, core goals and values, strategy, structure, systems, people, skills, leadership style, and culture.
- *Feedback mechanisms:* The vehicles through which the organization finds out whether it is meeting customer needs and requirements.
- *Inputs:* The materials, information, or services needed to produce the deliverables.
- *People and skills:* Includes the types of professions and skills of the people in the organizations and those needed to do the work. It also includes the need, potential, and resources/methodologies for development of skills and capabilities.
- *Strategy:* The organization's basic approach to achieving its mission.
- *Structure:* This is not just the boxes and lines on an organization chart. It includes definition of organization units, levels and spans of supervision, job design, delegation of authority, and the actual physical layout of the work areas.
- *Systems:* The procedures, formal and informal, that make the organization run, including planning and goals setting, monitoring, communications, resource allocation, organizational learning, and renewal and human resources systems (compensation, evaluation, promotion, and so on).

- *Work processes:* The ways in which critical decisions are made and products or services produced.

How the model/theory/set of ideas was used:

- Top management created a design team consisting of 10 members representing our patient care delivery system. Within a seven-month time frame, the team is expected to:
  - Develop efficient patient-focused systems
  - Ensure a stronger patient and customer focus
  - Obtain ownership and commitment to vision
  - Significantly improve competitive position by lower cost to purchaser and improved quality
  - Increase commitment to staff development
  - Decrease bureaucracy
- The design team worked through the COD process:
  - *Education and planning:* The team learns the overall purpose of the change effort, their job, and constraints. They find out what is involved and are shown how to plan their work, including identifying key stakeholders and informing them how they will be involved throughout the process.
  - *Definition and analysis:* The team defines and analyzes the organization, including how to assess the challenges and opportunities in the business environment, determining customer needs and requirements and examining work processes, inputs, customer feedback mechanisms, and human aspects of their work.
  - *Mission and vision phase:* The team agrees on the organization's business (mission) and what they are attempting to create (vision). This phase builds on organizational values and aspirations and on customers' needs and requirements.
  - *Design phase:* The team designs or redesigns the organization based on the mission and vision and on the findings from definition and analysis.
  - *Implementation planning phase:* The team determines what needs to happen to move them from present to future, including identifying specific steps, responsibilities, and resources needed to implement the design, *and* anticipates stumbling blocks.

Key publications/references:

Gelinas, M. V., and James, R. G. Creating profound change through collaborative organization design. *Vision/Action,* Sept. 1992, pp. 1–8.

Contributor(s): Wendy Baker, RN, MS, project director, director

Contributor affiliation(s): Center for Patient Care Innovation, Vanderbilt University Hospital and Clinic, Nashville, TN

Models Driving Change at Harbor-UCLA Medical Center

Name of model: Principle-Centered Leadership: Empowerment

Name of key author(s)/thinker(s): Stephen R. Covey, founder and chairman

Affiliation(s) of key author(s)/thinker(s): Covey Leadership Center, Provo, UT

Key features of model/theory/set of ideas: There are six conditions of empowerment, as shown in figure A-6:

1. *Character:* What a person is. Integrity, maturity, and an abundance mentality are essential for empowerment of others.

Figure A-6.   Six Conditions of Empowerment

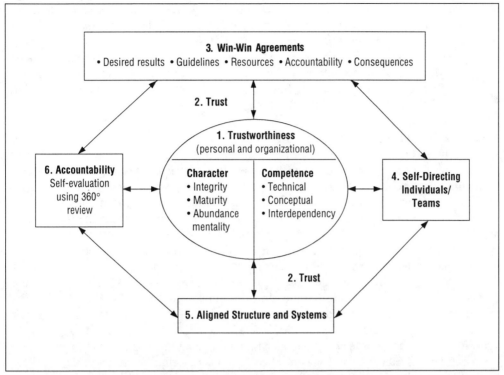

Source: S. R. Covey, A. R. Merrill, and R. R. Merrill. *First Things First.* New York City: Simon & Schuster, 1994. © 1994 Covey Leadership Center, Provo, UT.

2. *Skill:* Human competencies that are preconditions — communication, planning/organization, and synergistic problem solving.

3. *Win-win agreement:* Social contract that is mutually beneficial.

4. *Self-supervision:* A practical process of planning, executing, and controlling one's own performance within the boundaries of a win-win agreement.

5. *Helpful systems and structures:* In organizations we relate with many people in interdependent ways, and interaction requires some kind of structure and certain kinds of systems.

6. *Accountability:* People evaluate themselves against specified criteria and do whatever is necessary to accomplish the desired results within the guidelines.

Definition(s) of concepts that had to be learned:

- *Empowerment:* Creating conditions such that individuals and groups have the resources and opportunities they need to succeed at accomplishing the goals of the organization without compromising themselves. Win-win agreements are the cornerstone of empowerment.

- *Harmony:* A condition where group members agree that diverse options are possible without splintering the group's common purpose. The goal is to balance the needs of all stakeholders while experiencing a sense of unity and connection.

- *Win-win agreement:* A contract or solution(s) that favors all parties who then can commit to the decision and action plan. Rather than insisting on consensus, the leader searches for harmony.

- *Leaders:* The role of the leader is to engage the team in their vision and to facilitate their work. Leaders:
  - *Specify desired results:* Identify what is to be done, set goals and objectives, project time lines, and leave methods open.

— *Set some guidelines:* Parameters such as principles and policies that lay out any boundaries, restrictions, or style preferences related to accomplishing results.

— *Identify available resources:* Know human, financial, technical, and/or organizational support available for accomplishing results.

— *Define accountability:* Set out the standards by which performance will be judged, indicate time of evaluation and methods for measuring and monitoring progress.

— *Determine the consequences:* Stipulate what will happen as a result of evaluation, make clear the reason for undertaking the assignment.

How the model/theory/set of ideas was used: Transformational leadership is a major construct in the theoretical framework for the Community of Patient Care Leaders at Harbor-UCLA. Transformational leaders seek to empower others to become leaders themselves. Many of the strategic directions call for empowering individuals or groups. The empowerment aspect of Covey's leadership model provides practical assistance in coming to a common understanding of what we expect to see. The expectation is set that empowerment serves as a guideline. Our experience has been that there is increased willingness to empower others. However, most executives and managers have had little experience in empowering others. In fact, they may not have extensive experience in true empowerment for themselves.

Two areas seem to require the most attention. One is *guidelines*. We have learned that we need to articulate guidelines that are too often simply implicit. Often this requires that the leader/manager be clear about his or her own values and style preferences. *Being clear about consequences* seems to be the area where leaders are most shy and/or negligent. In many instances, leaders have not given much thought to consequences. Not surprisingly, they emerge in an unpredictable and uncontrolled fashion. Ignoring or underplaying these two areas can have a drastic impact on fledgling empowerment programs. When employees present their finished product, it is too late to say that you were looking for something else.

Examples of empowerment structures at Harbor-UCLA include an employee recognition program that rewards teams as well as individuals (Patient Care Leader(s) of the Month), a nurse recognition committee that takes initiative for programming and recognition, the four strategic direction councils, and focus groups for patients, staff, and volunteers.

Key publications/references:

Covey, S. R. *Principle-Centered Leadership.* New York City: Summit Books, 1991.

Contributor(s): Maryalice Jordan-Marsh, RN, PhD, director, nursing research, co-project director; Susan Goldsmith, MS, project coordinator, community of patient care leaders; Paula Siler, RN, MS, director, professional practice affairs — nursing

Contributor affiliation(s): Harbor-UCLA Medical Center, Torrance, CA

Name of model: Harmony Principle

Name of key author(s)/thinker(s): David Boje, professor

Affiliation(s) of key author(s)/thinker(s): School of Business Administration, Loyola Marymount University, Los Angeles, CA

Key features of model/theory/set of ideas: Harmony is a concept often used to describe how elements in nature coexist or to capture the ideal relationship between human beings and nature. The concept of harmony has similar value in understanding ideal relationships in organizations. Organizations can build harmony by paying attention to four elements of work, including:

1. *Plan for rhythm that gives pace to the work:* Work and patient care are designed to provide clear cycles with intervals for rest or transition. Consistency and predictability, where possible, provide comfort and energy to cope with the stress of unavoidable crises and interruptions. Rituals are established that serve as transitions between cycles and that reflect group values.
2. *Building in contrast:* Systems, structures, jobs—all elements of the organization design—demonstrate a value for differences by providing for comparisons and highlighting contrasting diversity. The organization promotes variety in unity. A community identity leaves room for diversity in style and appearance; subgroup identities are encouraged and supported. The goal is to maximize synergy and minimize monotony.
3. *Design changes with emphasis on the organizational vision:* Stakeholders are clear about the organization's niche in the world. Vision and values drive decisions. This aspect of harmony recognizes that each part of an organization is a reflection or microcosm of the whole.
4. *Work to achieve balance:* Care is given that people, systems, and structures are not overwhelmed by changing needs. Attention is given to the fit of environment, people, and organizational goals. There is flexibility with checks and balances.

Definition(s) of concepts that had to be learned:

- *Harmony:* A fitting, orderly, and pleasant joining of diversities.

Creating harmony requires attention to social psychological and physical environments. Designing organizational changes that result in a good fit between people and environment has been expressed as this formula:

$$Rhythm + contrast\ with\ emphasis\ on\ balance = harmony.$$

How the model/theory/set of ideas was used: Harmony is one of the six intertwined components of our conceptual framework. Application of this formula is evolving at Harbor-UCLA Medical Center and is reflected in new designs for architecture that give people a natural space with water and greenery, art on the walls, and harmonious but lively colors. The harmony formula also was applied to balancing intellectual presentations of the broad-scale change project with approaches that appealed to other senses and skills. A We Care Week was planned to spread the major concepts of community by involving stakeholders in creating a quilt; a community cookbook; showcasing special projects and groups to both patients and staff that drew on internal and external stakeholders; a customer service day with a speaker from the Ritz Carlton Hotel; innovative staff recognition; and finally a picnic. Another application of the harmony formula is seen in meetings where harmony is offered as a decision-making option. Majority votes and consensus usually mean the group is forced to select one option from among others that are rejected. A harmony decision recognizes that parallel options might work equally well and allows the group to select several choices. The next phase of application will be to work redesign.

Key publications/references:

Boje, D. M. The classical principles of organization design. Unpublished paper, Loyola Marymount University, College of Business Administration, Los Angeles, 1991.

Doczi, G. *The Power of Limits: Proportional Harmonies in Nature, Art, and Architecture.* Boston: Shambala, 1985.

Moore, N., and Komras, H. *Patient-Focused Healing: Integrating Caring and Curing in Health Care.* San Francisco: Jossey-Bass, 1993.

Contributor(s): Tecla Mickoseff, MBA, hospital administrator; Maryalice Jordan-Marsh, RN, PhD, director, nursing research, co-project director

Contributor affiliation(s): Harbor-UCLA Medical Center, Torrance, CA

Models Driving Change at University Hospital/University of Utah HSC

Name of model: Stages of School Improvement

Name of key author(s)/thinker(s): Matthew B. Miles, senior research associate

Affiliation(s) of key author(s)/thinker(s): Center for Policy Research, New York City

Key features of model/theory/set of ideas: Organizational change requires a dynamic and evolutionary process. Based on a series of studies of efforts to improve public schools, Miles and colleagues developed a model to guide the change process. Successful implementation of major innovations in the school system included three major phases: (1) initiation/mobilization—launching the effort; (2) implementation—testing and improving the design; and (3) institutionalization—imbedding the change.

This model was adapted to include the evaluation component of organizational change. (See figure A-7.) A dynamic and evolutionary model results as a prototype that is implemented in one or two areas, evaluated, revised, and tried again. These feedback loops, based on ongoing evaluation, provide opportunities to learn from the experience of each prototype and improve the design through an incremental change process. Evaluation of both process and outcomes is a critical and interactive component of the entire model.

Definition(s) of concepts that had to be learned:

Each of the phases of the process are marked by key activities:

- *Phase 1: Initiation/mobilization:* Primarily involves launching the program. Key activities include deciding to start, beginning the process, assessing needs, and developing commitment.
- *Phase 2: Implementation:* Focuses on testing and improving the design. Key activities of implementing change include setting goals, as well as designing and carrying out action plans.
- *Phase 3: Institutionalization:* The goal is to imbed the change. Activities focus on evaluating the plans, building processes to support the change, and making needed organizational change.

Figure A-7. The Evolutionary Process for Organizational Change

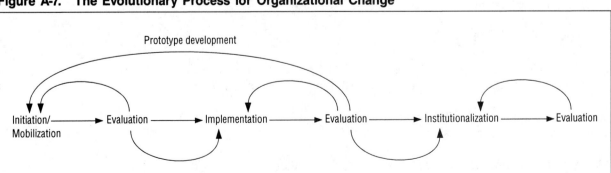

How the model/theory/set of ideas was used: University of Utah Hospital adapted this school-based model to health care. In planning for program implementation, core and evaluation activities were identified for each phase. These activities guided project work.

Phase 1: Initiation/mobilization—launching the program

- Core activities
  - Empower a design team of key stakeholders to develop the program.
  - Build commitment and a shared vision.
  - Obtain resources to support and facilitate change.
  - Prepare for implementation (structure, education, policies and procedures, communication patterns, job descriptions, and so on).
- Evaluation tasks
  - Establish quality baseline data and feedback mechanisms to share results.
  - Evaluate the process of initiation/mobilization.

Phase 2: Implementation—testing and improving the design

- Core activities
  - Carry out plans and improve the design of a series of evolving prototypes.
  - Proactively sense and solve problems.
  - Develop ongoing system support (information management, accounting, personnel policies, and so on).
- Evaluation tasks
  - Evaluate the process and outcomes of each program (prototype) and feedback results.
  - Evaluate the implementation process.
  - Evaluate final outcomes.

Phase 3: Institutionalization—imbedding the change

- Core activities
  - Extend changes throughout the institution.
  - Provide continuing resources (funding, staff, internal experts, and so on).
- Evaluation tasks
  - Establish an ongoing evaluation mechanism.
  - Evaluate the process of institutionalization.

Key publications/references:

Miles, M. B. 40 years of change in schools: some personal reflections. *Education Administration Quarterly* 29(2):213–48, 1993.

Contributor(s): Susan L. Beck, PhD, RN, project director

Contributor affiliation(s): University of Utah Hospital, Salt Lake City, UT

Name of model: Force-Field Analysis

Name of key author(s)/thinker(s): Kurt Lewin

Key features of model/theory/set of ideas: Lewin hypothesizes that the present situation in any social system (including hospitals and hospital units) is the result of dynamic forces that maintain the system and generally keep it from changing. For example, the roles of health care providers on an interdisciplinary team, once established, are not likely to change because the forces in the situation (in this case, the habitual expectations of the other team members) maintain each individual in his or her role.

For change to occur, it becomes necessary for the forces favoring change (called *helping* or *driving* forces) to be stronger than the forces opposing change (called *hindering* or *opposing* forces). In Lewin's use of force-field analysis, he found that change is much more likely to occur if the key hindering forces are identified and removed, rather than trying to overcome the hindering forces by increasing the helping forces.

Definition(s) of concepts that had to be learned:

- *Helping forces:* Forces favoring change.
- *Hindering forces:* Forces opposing change.
- *Stakeholder:* Any person or group who will be affected by the change and has the power to either help bring the change about or hinder it.

How the model/theory/set of ideas was used: Early in the Program to Improve Patient Care, key stakeholders at every level of the organization were interviewed to find out what the key helping and hindering forces were. These data were then used to build a change process that targeted the key hindering forces for action while supporting and enhancing the key helping forces. For example, the perception that the Program to Improve Patient Care was a nursing program rather than a hospital program was viewed as a key hindering force to its success. Thus, efforts were undertaken to change this perception. Also, on the helping side, the communication network that had been established by the program staff was identified as a key helping force. Thus, efforts were undertaken to maintain and enhance this helping force.

Key publications/references:

Lewin, K. *Field Theory in Social Science.* New York City: Harper and Row, 1951.

Contributor(s): A. E. Rothermich, PhD, organizational consultant

Contributor affiliation(s): University of Utah Hospital, Salt Lake City, UT

Models Driving Change at University Hospital/Penn State University

Name of model: Interactive Planning/Idealized Design

Name of key author(s)/thinker(s): Russell L. Ackoff

Affiliation(s) of key author(s)/thinker(s): Chairman of the Board, INTERACT, Inc., Philadelphia

Key features of model/theory/set of ideas: The main principles associated with the model are:

- *Participation:* People get excited and are interested in the implementation of plans when they have been part of the planning process.
- *Continuity:* Planning is integrated into the ongoing work of the organization, rather than an exercise conducted every five years.
- *Coordination:* The importance of involving people from different departments who work at the same level.
- *Integration:* The benefits of having a group of people who work at different levels of the organization involved in the planning.

The last two principles provide optimal planning because multiple perspectives are brought to the process.

Interactive planning and idealized planning can be described as follows:

A. Interactive planning

1. All stakeholders are identified and brought into the planning process.
2. Stakeholders from all levels, internal as well as and external, participate (that is, interactive planning is neither top-down nor bottom-up).
3. A comparison of the mess formulation with the ideal situation. The mess formulation is the result of a three-step process:
   * *Systems analysis:* How the organization works, its current state
   * *Obstruction analysis:* The internal and external conditions, policies, and practices that obstruct organizational development
   * *Reference projection:* Scenario of what the organization would look like, years into the future, if no changes were made

B. Idealized planning

1. Starts from the assumption that existing systems were out-of-date the moment they were implemented.
2. Assumes that people are constrained by a problem-solving mode, and planners are encouraged to "blow up" the existing system and design a new one.
3. The ideal should have three properties:
   * That it be technologically feasible (that is, the technology must be available or "inventable")
   * That it be operationally viable
   * That the system invented be capable of rapid learning

The planning process proceeds to fill the gap between the mess and the ideal.

Definition(s) of concepts that had to be learned:

* *Stakeholders:* Anyone who has a vested interest in the organization or its mission, including consumers.
* *The mess formulation:* Includes (1) a systems analysis (how the organization works, its current state), (2) an obstructional analysis (barriers to development), and (3) reference projection (a scenario of what the organization would look like years into the future if no changes were made).

How the model/theory/set of ideas was used: In November 1988, the project director obtained support to use the interactive planning model. She interviewed stakeholders to learn their ideas about creating a better system of patient care, as well as their assessment of the current situation. With this input, she developed a proposal to use interactive planning with three pilot units. The improvement of patient care through interdepartmental coordination (especially nurse–physician) had been the initial intent of the director of nursing, who spearheaded the initiative.

The planning proposal was funded and a system for planning developed using Ackoff's principles of participation (Plan or be planned for), coordination, and integration. Four planning boards were designated. Each of the pilot units had a board; a fourth board was designed to coordinate the work of the pilot unit boards.

The project staff and the planners worked concurrently; the staff collected data for the mess formulation and the planners concentrated on creating the ideal system of patient care. The mess formulation described a system where staff were working very hard and were perceived as technically competent and caring. The degree of fragmentation was strong and communication was perceived as being very poor.

The planners decided to adopt Ackoff's model of the circular organization, which is a concrete embodiment of the principles of interactive planning. The "classic" version of the model, used in industry, calls for managers of each department developing planning boards that have members from at least three levels of the organization on each board.

Because the mess formulation so strongly suggested the need for integration at every level, we modified the model to create multidisciplinary, interdepartmental boards at several levels of the organization. Our boards have been formed around patient populations rather than managers' departments.

Key features include:

- Integrated approach, that is, not top-down or bottom-up, but activates people from all levels of an organization in the creation of a plan.
- Includes internal stakeholders (anyone who has a stake in the outcome or business of the organization) as well as those who are external to the organization, such as customers, regulators, or payers.
- Two scenarios are developed — one that represents the ideal vision of the planners and one that represents the state of the organization several years into the future, if no substantive changes are made.
- The ideal is created through the process of idealized design, a process that removes constraints and enhances creativity.
- The second scenario of no change is called the mess formulation, which is produced by comparing what is known about the organization (via a systems analysis) with what is known about external and environmental trends. A reference projection also can be made. This is a prediction of what the system would look like in several years if no changes were made.
- The gap between the ideal and the mess is the basis for development of a plan.
- The steps of interactive planning are only sequential in writing; in actuality, there is an interaction or synthesis of all the above components as the planners work toward articulation and implementation of the plan.

Contributor(s): Joan Lartin-Drake, PhD, RN, director

Contributor affiliation(s): Center for Nursing Research, University Hospital/Penn State University, Hershey, PA

Name of model: Sociotechnical Systems

Name of key author(s)/thinker(s): Eric Trist

Affiliation(s) of key author(s)/thinker(s): Cofounder, Tavistock Institute of Social Relations, and professor emeritus, The Wharton School, University of Pennsylvania, Philadelphia. Trist's work was greatly influenced by the work of Kurt Lewin and early systems theorists such as von Bertalanfy and Fred Emery.

Key features of model/theory/set of ideas: One of the key features of this approach is the appreciation of the interwoven nature of the personal interactions and the technical aspects of the workplace in the context of the workplace as an open system (Trist, 1989). Other features include the concept of the work system as "the basic unit rather than the single jobs into which it [is] compatible" (Trist, 1989). Related to this is an emphasis placed more on the work group than on the individual worker.

Internal regulation of the work group rather than regulation through external supervision is a fundamental aspect of the sociotechnical systems approach. The rediscovery of autonomous work methods among miners in Britain after the Second World War triggered a natural partnering between Lewin's concepts relative to democratic work processes and the sociotechnical approach.

The development of multiple skills in an individual, which Emery termed the "redundancy of function" (1967) is assumed to benefit not only the individual but also the work group. Inherent in this feature is a valuing of the discretionary aspect of work as well as the prescribed roles. Ideally, individual workers are viewed as complementary to the technical aspects of their jobs, rather than having to adapt to these aspects.

A systemic way of thinking about the way jobs are organized and defined is preferable to the assembly-line approach of reducing a job to a few tightly regulated pieces of a whole. As Trist has articulated, the ideal is to find "the best match between the requirements of the social and technical systems" (1989, p. 9). The sociotechnical systems model developed the concept of work redesign as a way to help systems use these and related principles.

How the model/theory/set of ideas was used:

- *Democratic processes and leadership style:* Ackoff has described the circular organization as one in which no one person has ultimate authority; there is a shared system of governance and a balance of power similar to that found in democratic governments. To the extent that we have been successful in setting up boards that use consensus and work with multiple levels of the institution, we are attempting to bring more democratic processes and leadership to the medical center.
- *Intrinsic job characteristics:* The results of Lewin's early research on intrinsic characteristics (1935) have been tested and extended. Many readers will recognize the seeds of the quality improvement movement in this research, his action research model, his emphasis on democratic processes, and the sociotechnical systems model's contribution on autonomous work groups and work redesign.

Key publications/references:

Emery, F. The second design principle. In: E. Trist and H. Murray, editors. *The Social Engagement of Social Science.* A Tavistock Anthology, Vol. 11. Philadelphia: University of Pennsylvania Press, 1993.

Lewin, K. A. *A Dynamic Theory of Personality.* New York City: McGraw Hill, 1935.

Trist, E. *The Evolution of Socio-Technical Systems.* Toronto, Ontario: Ministry of Labor, 1981.

Contributor(s): Joan Lartin-Drake, PhD, RN, director

Contributor affiliation(s): Center for Nursing Research, University Hospital/Penn State University, Hershey, PA

Name of model: Group Relations

Name of key author(s)/thinker(s): Eric Trist

Affiliation(s) of key author(s)/thinker(s): Cofounder, Tavistock Institute of Social Relations, and professor emeritus, The Wharton School, University of Pennsylvania, Philadelphia, PA.

Key features of model/theory/set of ideas: Perhaps the key feature of group relations is *system-level defenses.* This is the idea that existing structures and characteristics of an organization, while appearing irrational or outdated on the surface, actually serve a purpose, which is to protect the members of the system from experiencing anxiety around a particular issue (Menzies, 1975). An example is:

The fragmentation of care in a hospital (persons or departments assigned accountability for pieces of care) and the prevalence of transferring patients from one unit to another can hypothetically serve to protect system members from the intense anxiety associated with the responsibility and discomfort of caring for very sick people.

Groups either focus on their work, the task at hand, or engage in defensive behaviors that protect them from anxiety concerned with the task. These defensive behaviors are referred to as acting on basic assumptions related to feeling threatened and/or overwhelmed and helpless. The three basic assumptions are: fight/flight, retreat into dependency, and the hope that a savior or brilliant idea will rescue the groups from the task at hand.

We as an institution have not used this theory explicitly. The project director, who has studied and used this approach, and the external consultant, who is also familiar with the theory, have used it as a way to understand system issues such as the functioning of the boards or resistance to a previously agreed-upon plan.

How the model/theory/set of ideas was used:

1. *As process and strategic consultants to the boards:* As boards began their work of problem solving and redesign, this theory has been useful in helping them become focused on workable issues when they have gotten off their task and focused on other issues, such as scapegoating. The emergence of scapegoating processes, excessive dependency on leaders and facilitators, and the hope that a couple of the board members would magically save the board have all been seen as symptomatic of anxiety or threat related to the task.

    Sometimes it is because the task is unclear or has been defined too broadly; other times the sheer inexperience of board members relative to systemic problem solving has made it difficult for the boards to get going. Rarely are "process comments" used (such as "The group seems to be experiencing some concern about the scope of the task"). Instead, the observation is made and translated into a comment such as "Would it be helpful to clarify the scope of this issue?"

2. *System-level defenses:* Again, this concept to date has been one used among the project staff to understand processes such as resistance to a previously agreed-upon plan or the degree of attachment to what appears to be an outmoded approach to patient care. The construct is similar to the concept of individual defense mechanisms: The person is by definition unaware that he or she is using, say, avoidance or projection. To bring the observation that this may be so often is rightfully perceived as intrusive in the absence of an explicit invitation to discuss the situation.

    An example would be the difficulty some clinical staff seem to be having in changing their patient rounds behavior to include patients in information sharing and decision making. The current process is to use rounds for teaching purposes and sometimes collaboration of care. It is generally unusual to think of patients and their families as collaborators; generally, they play passive, childlike roles. Although, several years ago, many of the planners were delighted to consider another model, there has been little change in the way people think and behave with regard to bedside rounds.

    One way to think about this is to ask: "What about the new model is scary or threatening?" That is, what "defensive purpose" does attachment to the status quo fulfill? One hypothesis is that shifting to a more participative model threatens the existing social role and its protective distance from the patient. Another hypothesis is that staff lack role models and sanctions for the new model. A plan based on these hypotheses is to create and share models of patient collaboration with interested staff, possibly providing them with role-modeling opportunities from physicians and staff who do use a more collaborative approach.

Key publication/reference:

Menzies, I. A case study in the functioning of social systems as a defense against anxiety. In: A. Coleman and H. Bexton, editors. *Group Relations Reader.* Sausalito, CA: GREX, 1975.

Contributor(s): Joan Lartin-Drake, PhD, RN, director

Contributor affiliation(s): Center for Nursing Research, University Hospital/Penn State University, Hershey, PA

Models Driving Change at the Vermont Nursing Initiative

Name of the model: Continuous Quality Improvement

Name of key author(s)/thinker(s): W. Edwards Deming and Joseph Juran

Affiliation(s) of key author(s)/thinker(s): W. Edwards Deming, international consultant on quality; Joseph Juran, founder, Juran Institute in Wilton, CT; Medical Center Hospital of Vermont, Burlington, VT, training workshops on continuous quality improvement—tools and techniques; Harvard Community Health Plan Demonstration Project—The Quality Management Network, Cambridge, MA.

Key features of model/theory/set of ideas: Current social, financial, and political reality requires a transformation of health care delivery in the United States from its present organization to systems that better meet the health care needs of the future. Quality improvement techniques, first developed in American industry, now offer a method for this transformation.

Transformation requires a deep understanding of systems theory and attention to three major aspects of change:

1. Strategy (focus on customers)
2. Techniques (tools and methods)
3. Culture (leadership, learning, teams, reward, fear)

Definition(s) of concepts that had to be learned:

- *Customer:* Anyone who depends on you.
- *Mission statement:* A written description of a problem that clearly defines the required task or project. A well-constructed mission statement sets boundaries for a project, time lines, expected outcomes, and resources. It connects the work of the team with the organization's overall improvement efforts.
- *Process:* A collection of activities that take one or more kinds of input and results in an output that is of value to the customer.
- *Quality:* Meeting the needs, wants, and capabilities of the customer. It results in care that is efficient, effective, appropriate, and caring.
- *Scientific method:* A systematic way for individuals and teams to learn about processes. It requires that decisions be based on data, that root causes for problems be identified, and that a careful process of plan–do–check–act be used to achieve permanent solutions.
- *Teamwork:* Groups of people pooling their skills, talents, and knowledge who agree to learn together, provide mutual support to each other, and dedicate themselves to a specific common goal.
- *Variation:* The difference in the outcomes of a process due to random chance and special circumstances.

How the model/theory/set of ideas was used:

1. *Emphasis on strategy: Customer orientation:* The Vermont Nursing Initiative (VNI) sponsored hospital restructuring projects to improve the coordination of services to patients. VNI nurses wanted to provide patient-centered care. The concept of patient and family as customers helped to explain and focus restructuring projects.

Treating nurses as customers helped the VNI to identify ways in which the needs of hospital nurses could be better understood and met. All of the hospital restructuring projects hoped to create an environment where professional nursing practice could thrive and result in continuously improving patient care. Nurses, nursing departments, and their institutions were challenged by this theory to flex, stretch, and restructure their nursing care, health care paradigms.

Continuous quality improvement (CQI) theory suggests that suppliers or providers of care become knowledgeable about the needs and expectations of customers. The CQI model led VNI participants through the questioning process; for example, who are the internal and external customers of a nursing department? Can the VNI participants be better customers and suppliers for each other? How can these projects be extended to other health care settings, other groups in Vermont? How can we use limited resources in a rural area to meet the needs of customers?

In addition, the idea of hospital health care providers, especially nurses, having many internal and external customers provided a useful perspective. Being sensitive to the many customer–supplier relationships in delivery of health care (for example, physician–nurse, nurse–pharmacist, third-party payers–nursing documentation) makes better teams, better communication, and better care.

2. *Emphasis on technique:* VNI participants attended three-day training sessions sponsored by the Vermont Program for Quality in Health Care and/or the Medical Center Hospital of Vermont to learn about the philosophy of total quality management and the tools and techniques needed to bring about continuous and lasting improvement in health care delivery.

Key concepts (those listed above) from the science of industrial quality management, as espoused by Deming and Juran, were presented, discussed, and practiced in these three days of training. Application of these concepts to the health care industry was just beginning when VNI became operational. The timing was fortuitous. The concepts were ideal for those working to strengthen hospital nursing.

Participants learned to flowchart a process, brainstorm, and collect meaningful data. Tools to help teams make better decisions—Pareto charts, run charts, control charts, analysis of variation—became everyday conversation.

Quality Improvement theory provided structure and process skills that were so important to the changes that VNI envisioned. CQI emphasizes the steps for implementing a change, measurement or "checking" of progress, readjustments, refinement, learning from mistakes, standardization of the improvement, and planning for continued improvement.

3. *Emphasis on culture:* CQI theory insists that the culture of organizations must change to produce environments with less authoritarian control and more participation, decision making, and shared responsibility. Traditional management approaches are not conducive to an environment where individuals can reach their full potential and where the organization can learn quickly and respond quickly to changes in the external environment.

Key components required for the cultural change which the CQI model describes include the following:

- *Leadership:* VNI provided strong leadership, structure, staff, and support for change efforts. Resources became available through the grant to recognize the importance of hospital nursing and of quality health care. VNI encouraged experimentation to enhance the role of hospital nurses in decision making. VNI provided a clear mission statement, leaders dedicated to improvement and understanding the process, resources to sustain constancy of purpose, and shared goals and a common aim.

- *Learning:* VNI provided a network for education. The project sponsored accessible and affordable continuing education to nurses throughout the state. Consultants to projects were identified and made available—for example, consultants on change theory, competency, case management, evaluation, group dynamics, and so on. Frequent meetings provided an avenue for local experts to share their skills and a common forum where learning could be shared as the projects developed.

- *Building better meetings:* Good meeting skills are essential for good teamwork. VNI participants learned how to conduct meetings in an efficient, effective, democratic way and how to lead, facilitate, and be active meeting members. Active listening, civilized disagreement, consensus decisions, shared leadership, style diversity, and periodic self-assessment are some of the essential concepts of good teams and good meetings.

   CQI teaches that good meetings and good communication require high levels of assertiveness and high levels of cooperation. VNI projects provided opportunities for nurses to develop these skills. Many meetings took place between VNI participants from several health care facilities requiring sensitivity to different organizational cultures and approaches. Agendas, minutes, and good record keeping helped with communications and progress toward goals.

- *Working in teams:* Teamwork is the core concept of CQI. VNI stimulated a variety of teams throughout the state—interdisciplinary teams and interhospital teams—to work together sharing staff in rural areas, planning educational programs, and reframing delivery systems. CQI training sessions stressed the importance of teamwork and provoked thoughtful discussion about group dynamics and the use of teams to achieve improvement.

- *Reward:* Being process oriented requires that teams understand and use feedback about how they are doing. Negative feedback has a way of finding its way back to process owners. Positive feedback, or reward, seems to need special attention. CQI theory emphasizes the power of recognition and reward to help teams perform and maintain high levels of performance. The VNI, in itself, is a form of reward for, or recognition of, the important role that nurses play in high-quality health care. The presence of staff and resources to support individual efforts and encourage collaboration are a strong source of renewal and renewed energy to Vermont nurses.

   Special training, development of individuals, sharing, responsibility, praise, and interhospital collaboration are all sources of reward that professionals find empowering. Quality management theory espouses these concepts and the VNI strives to provide them.

- *Driving out fear:* One of the most useful and refreshing concepts of the CQI model is the value placed on mistakes. "Every error is an opportunity for improvement" or "You learn more from mistakes than from success" are two frequently repeated tenets of the continuous improvement consultants. Fear of failure, of not knowing, of giving up control, and of change itself handicap many individuals and teams, and prevent them from achieving real improvement. Risk taking and experimentation with new ideas can flourish only in an environment where fear is eliminated. Leaders of the VNI are risk takers themselves, support that behavior in others, and are assisted in their work by statewide efforts to change the culture of health care organizations.

Key publications/references:

Berwick, D. M. Continuous improvement as an ideal in health care. *New England Journal of Medicine,* Jan. 5, 1989, pp. 53–56.

National Demonstration Project. *Methods and Tools of Quality Improvement: Putting Theory into Action.* Brookline, MA: Harvard Community Health Plan, 1990.

Plsek, P. E., and Onnias, A. *Quality Improvement Tools.* Wilton, CT: Juran Institute, 1989.

Scholtes, P. R. *The Team Handbook: How to Use Teams to Improve Quality.* Madison, WI: Joiner Associates, 1989.

Walton, M. *The Deming Management Method.* New York City: Dodd, Mead and Company, 1986.

Contributor(s): Patricia F. Donehower, RN, MSN CPHQ, quality assurance department

Contributor affiliation(s): Medical Center Hospital of Vermont, Burlington, VT

Models Driving Change at Northeast Health Consortium

Name of model: Team Learning

Name of key author(s)/thinker(s): Peter R. Scholtes

Affiliation(s) of key author(s)/thinker(s): Joiner Associates describe in their *Team Handbook* the author Peter R. Scholtes as one of the few leading proponents of continuous improvement whose professional background is in organizational development. It is Scholtes's belief that we can create a competitive, humane economy through a transformation of the relationships, environment, and dynamics within and between individuals and groups in our organizations. The cornerstones of his work are training and consultation devoted to educating managers on the theory, skills, methods, and tools needed to guide the efforts of their employees.

Key features of model/theory/set of ideas: The *Team Handbook* is a how-to book. Very specifically, its purpose is to help project teams succeed in improving quality and productivity and in all their efforts to improve processes. Because these are the activities our project staff are directly responsible for, we found this text invaluable. This model allows project managers to learn what to look for as a project unfolds. Scholtes points out that there have been projects and project teams of one kind or another since the first prehistoric tribe. Together, teams are able to accomplish tasks that team members are unable to accomplish alone.

According to Scholtes, *The Team Handbook* approach to projects differs from more conventional approaches in three ways:

1. The focus is on the pursuit of quality as taught by Deming, founder of the new economic and industrial era.
2. The approach relies heavily on the understanding and application of data. These data-based methods, which we call the *scientific approach,* draw from the discipline of statistics and classical logic that characterize Deming's teachings.
3. Included in the approach are methods for the formation and maintenance of groups, the planning and managing of projects, and the design and conduct of meetings. These approaches have been learned from Malcolm Knowles and other contributors to the field of group and organization development.

How the model/theory/set of ideas was used: Scholtes believes that for a project team to succeed in its task, it needs much more than technical knowledge of the work area under investigation. Expertise in the subject at hand is indispensable. But participants in a successful project also must know how to work as a team, plan and conduct good meetings, manage logistics and details, gather useful data, analyze the data, communicate the results, and implement changes.

Key publications/references:

Scholtes, P. R., and others. *The Team Handbook: How to Use Teams to Improve Quality.* Madison, WI: Joiner Associates, 1988.

Contributor(s): Peter R. Scholtes, Brian L. Joiner, Bill Braswell, Lynda Finn, Heero Hacquebord, Kevin Little, Sue Reynard, Barbara Streibel, Lonnie Weiss

Contributor affiliation(s): Joiner Associates, Inc., Madison, WI, and the Northeast Health Consortium

Models Driving Change at Mercy Hospital and Medical Center

Name of model: Inquiry Mode of Learning

Name of key author(s)/thinker(s): Cyril O. Houle, PhD

Affiliation(s) of key author(s)/thinker(s): Former senior program consultant at the W. K. Kellogg Foundation, Battle Creek, MI, and professor emeritus of education, University of Chicago, Chicago, IL; now retired to Sarasota, FL.

Key features of model/theory/set of ideas: Dr. Houle describes three modes through which professional learning can occur. In addition to instruction and performance, he describes the inquiry mode of learning.

Learning that occurs through the process of discovery and creation of a new idea, technique, or strategy is the result of the inquiry mode. Usually, this mode of learning is the by-product of participation in meetings and task forces. A conscious and structured application of this mode of learning may be employed, however, to promote a shared learning environment.

Discussion groups, clinics, seminars, and guided experiences to facilitate the achievement of new ideas and approaches are methods of structuring learning via the inquiry mode. The outcome of the process (which differs from traditional learning modes) cannot be predicted in advance. In fact, the learning objectives often are not evident until the experience is completed or until after the created product of the experience has been proven to be successful.

Conscious utilization of processes that support the inquiry mode of learning require trust in the ability of the participants, and a leadership style that envelops and recognizes the talents and willingness of staff to make contributions to the organization.

Definition(s) of concepts that had to be learned:

- *Facilitation:* Guiding through a process, the outcome of which is the result of the group's work (and is not predetermined by the facilitator).
- *Inquiry mode:* The process of creating some new synthesis, idea, technique, policy, or strategy of action.
- *Overlapping modes of learning:* Interplay of the modes of instruction, performance, and inquiry which produce professional knowledge. Although these may be employed independently, frequently they overlap.

How the ideal/theory/set of ideas was used: More than a strategic approach, the inquiry model is an influence or phenomenon that is to be respected for its ability to promote involvement and sound decision making. Conscious application of leadership's knowledge of this influence results in an environment that encourages discovery, risk taking, coaching, and shared success. Participants within this environment feel valued for their ability to positively impact the mission of the organization.

At Mercy, we have had several innovative and successful outcomes as a result of focusing on process and recognizing the value of the inquiry mode of learning. These include the Mercy School Nurse Program, staff-developed pressure sore protocols, and many others. Our process, which we believe fosters learning through the inquiry mode, includes these steps:

1. Define and clearly articulate the issue to be addressed. (Realize that the issue may change when new information is created by the participants.)
2. Include representatives of each stakeholder group (can be volunteers) to ensure expertise.

3. Select the appropriate process to address the issue (that is, creative process, problem-solving model, and so on).
4. Apply facilitation principles to the process.
5. Debrief to clarify and reflect on what was learned during the process.
6. Implement and evaluate the accomplishment of the group. The creation of Mercy's patient-driven vision is a result of the confidence of leadership in staff ability and the influence of the inquiry mode of learning.

Key publications/references:

Houle, C. O. *Continuing Learning in the Professions,* 4th ed. San Francisco: Jossey-Bass, 1984.

Houle, C. O. *The Design of Education.* San Francisco: Jossey-Bass, 1972.

Houle, C. O. *The Inquiring Mind.* Madison, WI: University of Wisconsin Press, 1961.

Contributor(s): Fran La Monica, RN, MS, professional development and special projects coordinator

Contributor affiliation(s): Mercy Hospital and Medical Center, Chicago, IL

Models Driving Change at University Hospitals of Cleveland

Name of model: Rogers's Diffusion of Innovation Model

Name of key author(s)/thinker(s): Everett M. Rogers

Affiliation(s) of key author(s)/thinker(s): Professor and chairperson, Department of Communications/Journalism, University of New Mexico, Albuquerque

Key features of model/theory/set of ideas: One commonly noted phenomenon in teams working on innovation projects is that not all members of the group will be at the same stage in the process of change at any given time. Indeed, adoption of new ideas or implementation of new concepts seems to cascade or diffuse through a social system whether it is a small group or the larger organization. This can present a challenge to individuals charged with managing the complexities of organizational change.

Rogers's diffusion of innovation model can be used to explain the occurrence of this phenomenon. Furthermore, understanding of the model can be helpful in planning and implementing a desired change within a social system. Rogers's model suggests that individuals will fall into one of several distinct categories of behavior pattern responses when faced with change. The model's categories include innovators, early adopters, early majority, late majority, and laggard. Understanding the behavior pattern responses associated with each category can be useful in providing leverage for change and designing strategies to promote momentum of the change process.

Following are Rogers's categories of behavior pattern responses to change:

- *Innovators:* Venturesome
  - Have "cosmopolite" social relations
  - Obsessed with searching out new ideas
  - Control substantial financial resources/technical know-how
  - Nonconformist thinkers
  - Often controversial
  - Deal well with uncertainty
  - Import new ideas into a system

- *Early adopters:* Respected
  - Well integrated into their local social system
  - Sought out as opinion leaders
  - Excellent role models of change behavior
  - Held in esteem for their judicious use of new ideas
  - Able to interpret change for others in a way that eases conflict/stress
- *Early majority:* Deliberate
  - Willing followers in change
  - Seldom are leaders
  - Have longer innovation-decision periods
  - Interact frequently with peers
  - Provide organizational connectedness
- *Late majority:* Skeptical
  - Have relatively scarce resources
  - Cautious about utility and safety of adopting change
  - Will adopt only after seeing peers succeed with adopting the innovation
  - Adopt due to economic necessity or peer network pressure
  - Have greater difficulty in dealing with abstractions
- *Laggard:* Traditional
  - Generally older, less educated, lower socioeconomic level
  - Safety is central in making change
  - Have almost no opinion leadership
  - Social isolates; limit communication network to those like themselves; revere the past
  - May openly resist change and/or exhibit passive negative behaviors

How the model/theory/set of ideas was used: The Rogers's innovation diffusion model was used to leverage education efforts and promote momentum in a specific organizational change project. Because *innovators* are eager, almost obsessed, with any activity that surrounds new ideas and innovation, we found that they serviced well as energetic champions of a cause. They are comfortable with uncertainty and almost careless of risk. This sort of attitude was important to the early discussions and planning of education offerings intended to support our collaborative care project. Their involvement helped in the task of getting everyone absolutely clear on all aspects of this new idea—pros and cons. We enlisted them in searching the literature, benchmarking with other organizations, and many other activities that assisted in exploring and formulating a clearer vision of the project.

Once we were ready to implement the collaborative care curriculum and design education offerings, we enlisted the *early adopters* as faculty. We chose people held in high esteem as opinion leaders within the organization because they often served as excellent role models. Their input on structuring of education offerings was vital because of their understanding of colleagues' educational needs and attitudes toward changing the approach to patient care delivery. They helped in applying new ideas to specific unit situations and were a source of exemplars based on their successful experiences. They also helped to interpret new ideas in such a way that conflict and stress surrounding change are decreased and trust is increased.

As Rogers suggests, we designed a "kick-off" program that targeted the *early majority* as an audience. Although they can seldom be expected to be the up-front leaders in change, they are deliberate and willing followers. We found that the kind of programming they responded to best provided them with ample time to examine and decide about the new ideas. The programs also offered them ample time to formally and informally interact with the expert faculty and colleagues as they "tried on" and deliberated over using the collaborative care approach to patient care delivery. We charged them with "bringing it home" to their colleagues on the patient units. We invited them to "test-drive" and report back or seek advice from the expert faculty at scheduled intervals. They were provided with printed materials from the educational programs that could be used as a reference or a "blueprint" of the collaborative care adoption process.

Rogers also suggests that organizations schedule ongoing education programs of a smaller scale for the *late majority*. This group usually seeks out information about the innovation only after it becomes an imperative for continuing their work or practice. The time investment and the breadth and depth of content was less than for the early majority. The content was light on theory because they tend to focus on evidence that supports the practicality, utility, and safety of using the innovation. They wanted to know very simply: What is it? What does it look like? What do I have to do? What's in it for me? Program content was structured toward an elegant answer to each of these questions.

The *laggard* group prefers the status quo to risking what they have. They focus on the past, tradition, ritual behavior, and isolate themselves from any experiences or interaction that differs from these values. Laggards may openly resist innovation or avoid the traditional education programs designed for the other groups. However, neglecting to develop other types of approaches to this group in the overall strategies could bring change efforts to a crawl. We encouraged respected opinion leaders in various patient care decisions to do small local presentations or one-on-one interventions with those having difficulty with the transition.

The rate of adoption by any group is affected by several variables. Compatibility with values, beliefs, or needs; advantages of the innovation; and even the name of the innovation can be important. Laggards may respond more favorably to change that is perceived to respect traditional values, such as quality or customer focus. Rather than entertain their preoccupation with negatives and problems associated with the project, the focus of any approach should be solely on its advantages, such as simplifying work or decreasing discomfort of work. The name of the project and the vocabulary surrounding the whole project should be planned and tested with audience perceptions in mind; people respond to both the denotative and the connotative meanings of the written and spoken word.

Key publication/reference:

Rogers, E. M. *Diffusion of Innovation.* New York City: Macmillan, 1983.

Contributor(s): Kathleen Canda, RN, MSN, education coordinator

Contributor affiliation(s): Strengthening Hospital Nursing Program, University Hospitals of Cleveland, Cleveland, OH

Models Driving Change at Beth Israel Hospital

Name of model: Clinical Narratives to Improve Nursing Practice

Name of key author(s)/thinker(s): Patricia Benner, RN, PhD, professor of nursing, and Christine Tanner, RN, PhD, professor of nursing

Affiliation(s) of key author(s)/thinker(s): University of California, San Francisco, and Oregon Health Sciences University, Portland, OR

Key features of model/theory/set of ideas:

1. Nurses progress from novice to expert as they accrue experience in actual clinical situations.
2. Nursing narratives reveal expertise in nursing practice.

How the model/theory/set of ideas was used: In 1986, three years after implementing the Professional Nurse Advancement and Recognition Program at Beth Israel Hospital, Boston (Horvath, 1990), we found ourselves at an impasse. Clinical nurse III in this clinical promotion program was described as "excellent" practice with little definition of what that meant.

Further, we were unable to describe expert nursing practice. Focus groups with advanced practice nurses were of little help because we did not have a conceptual framework with which to guide the developmental process for the program. Fortunately, we discovered the research of Patricia Benner (1984) and her colleagues (Benner and Tanner, 1987; Benner, Tanner, and Chesla, 1992; Tanner, Benner, Chesla, and Gordon, 1993) who applied the Dreyfus Model of Skill Acquisition (Dreyfus and Dreyfus, 1986) to nursing. The following describes lessons we learned at Beth Israel Hospital when we used this model to improve the Professional Nurse Advancement and Recognition Program.

The effectiveness of the Dreyfus model for nursing was tested through clinical research on actual patient care situations. Other models of clinical judgment were based on research using simulations of practice that may not capture the complexity of the real clinical world (Tanner, 1989). The Dreyfus model is a five-stage process of skill acquisition through which practitioners progress as they accrue experience with actual practice situations. With experience, the practitioner moves from abstract, analytic, rule-based decision making to wholistic, intuitive, deeply engaged clinical judgment. The following brief descriptions of each level is excerpted from Benner and Tanner (1987, pp. 23–31).

- *Level I: Novice:* For the most part, novices are nursing students. Because they have no experience with the situations in which they are expected to perform, novices must depend on rules to guide their actions. Following rules, however, has limits. No rule can tell the novice which tasks are most relevant in real situations nor when to make exceptions.
- *Level II: Advanced Beginner:* The beginner is a new graduate or someone with less than two years' experience. She or he has coped with enough real situations to note (or to have them pointed out by a mentor) the recurrent meaningful aspects of situations. A beginner needs help setting priorities because she or he operates on general guidelines and is only beginning to perceive recurrent meaningful patterns and therefore cannot reliably sort out what is most important in complex situations.
- *Level III: Competent:* Typically, the competent nurse has been in practice two to three years. This nurse can rely on long-range goals and plans to determine which aspects of a situation are important and which can be ignored. The competent nurse lacks the speed and flexibility of the nurse who has reached the proficient level, but competence is characterized by a feeling of mastery and the ability to cope with and manage many contingencies of clinical nursing.
- *Level IV: Proficient:* Usually achieved with 3–5 years of nursing experience with similar patient populations. With wholistic understanding, decision making is less labored because the nurse has a perspective on which of the many attributes and aspects present are the important ones. The proficient performer considers fewer options and hones in on an accurate region of the problem. The proficient nurse has expert, intuitive perceptual abilities, but may resort to logical analysis for a plan of action.
- *Level V: Expert:* Usually achieved with 5–7 or more years of experience with the same or similar patient populations. The nurse who no longer relies on an analytical principle (rule, guideline, maxim) to connect an understanding of the situation to an appropriate action. The expert nurse, with an enormous background of experience, has an intuitive grasp of the situation and zeros in on the accurate region of the problem without wasteful consideration of a large range of unfruitful possibilities.

To implement the model, a core group of three or four people must make a commitment to learn the narrative methodology that forms the foundation for both the model and the developmental process that it supports. Clinical narratives or stories about patient care reveal nurses' knowledge and concerns and the difference they make in patient outcomes (Benner and Benner, 1991). When nurses tell patient stories, they get situated in the context of what happened, noticing aspects and qualitative distinctions that are hallmarks of expert practice. Key references for learning the model and its implementation are included below. In addition, formal consultation by Dr. Benner and/or the video *From Beginner to Expert: Clinical Knowledge in Critical Care Nursing* produced by the Helene Fuld Trust also are helpful. The video and the teaching guides that accompany it are integral components of the Clinical Entry Nurse Residency Program introduced at Beth Israel Hospital. This is a two-year planned work experience that brings new graduates from beginner to competent levels of practice. In addition, clinical narratives now provide the structure for nursing rounds on many units, and are used by many nurse managers to make the performance review process more meaningful.

Finally, broader organizational constraints on expert practice are often revealed in clinical narratives (Benner and Benner, 1991). For example, in a narrative about a patient undergoing coronary angioplasty, an expert nurse knew the patient and her illness trajectory in such a way that she was able to reverse a decision to transfer the patient to the ICU, a terrifying prospect for the patient who had developed trust and confidence with the staff on the floor. Additionally, the narrative revealed outdated procedures that impeded patient care and interdisciplinary collaboration. While the house staff reviewed results of a coronary angioplasty in a conference room in another part of the hospital, the primary nurse had consulted the attending physician and begun pharmacologic interventions to alleviate the patient's distress. With some additional history of baseline function from the patient, the nurse had a more immediate picture of the patient's status than the house staff team who had initiated the transfer. Though a good outcome was achieved because of the nurse's confidence and excellent relationships with the attending physician and house staff, the nurse had to expend a tremendous amount of energy to reverse a decision that was not in the patient's best interest. The unfortunate fragmentation revealed by this narrative demonstrated for us the need for improvement in continuity collaboration — key components of integrated clinical practice.

Admittedly, we have not pursued this potential use of clinical narratives to a great extent, but with the pressures of health care financing reform and the need for institutions to restructure, clinical narratives may provide an invaluable source of information about outdated systems.

Key publications/references:

Benner, P. A dialogue with excellence. *American Journal of Nursing,* Sept. 1987, pp. 1,170–72.

Benner, P. *From Novice to Expert: Excellence and Power in Clinical Nursing Practice.* Menlo Park, CA: Addison Wesley, 1984.

Benner, P. Uncovering the knowledge embedded in clinical practice. *Image: The Journal of Nursing Scholarship* 15(2):36–41, 1983.

Benner, P., and Benner, R. Stories from the front lines. *Healthcare Forum Journal,* July–Aug. 1991, pp. 69–74.

Benner, P., and Tanner, C. Clinical judgment: how expert nurses use intuition. *American Journal of Nursing* 87(1):23–31, 1987.

Benner, P., Tanner, C., and Chesla, C. From beginner to expert: gaining a differentiated clinical world in critical care nursing. *Advances in Nursing Science* 14(3):12–28, 1992.

Benner, P., and Wrubel, J. Skilled clinical knowledge: the value of perceptual awareness. *Nurse Educator* 7(3):11–17, 1982.

Dreyfus, H. L., and Dreyfus, S. E. *Mind over Machine: The Power of Human Intuition and Expertise in the Era of the Computer.* New York City: Macmillan Free Press, 1986.

Horvath, K. J. Issues in the development, implementation, and evaluation of a professional nurse advancement and recognition program. In: J. C. Clifford and K. J. Horvath, editors. *Advancing Professional Nursing Practice: Innovations at Boston's Beth Israel Hospital.* New York City: Springer Publishing Co., 1990.

Tanner, C. A. Use of research in clinical judgment. In: C. Lindemann and C. A. Tanner, editors. *Using Nursing Research.* New York City: National League for Nursing, 1989.

Tanner, C. A., Benner, P., Chesla, C., and Gordon, D. The phenomenology of knowing the patient. *Image* 25(4):273–80, 1993.

Tofias, L. Expert practice: trading examples over pizza. *American Journal of Nursing,* Sept. 1989, pp. 1,193–94.

Contributor: Kathy Horvath, RN, MS, director

Contributor affiliation(s): The Center for Advancement of Nursing Practice, Beth Israel Hospital, Boston, MA

Models Driving Change at Abbott Northwestern Hospital

Name of model: Reengineering

Name of key author(s)/thinker(s): Michael Hammer

Affiliation(s) of key author(s)/thinker(s): Managing director, Center for Reengineering Leadership, Cambridge, MA, and president, Hammer and Company, Cambridge, MA

Key features of model/theory/set of ideas: Reengineering is defined as the fundamental rethinking and radical redesign of an entire business system, including business processes, job definitions, organizational structures, management and control systems, beliefs, and behaviors to achieve dramatic improvements in critical measures of performance (cost, quality, capital, service, and speed). Reengineering is starting from scratch, rejecting conventional wisdom, "thinking out of the box." It is the reversal of the Industrial Revolution, a transition to process management, and an umbrella for diverse change programs. Reengineering means industrial-strength change. It is a cross-functional effort. It is a major undertaking that will be resisted; it must be driven top-down.

There is a difference between innovation/reengineering and improvement. *Improvement* is incremental improvement of a process based on the assumption that what we have is okay, thereby fixing something that already exists. On the other hand, *innovation* represents a big leap, creating something that perhaps does not exist or needs to be a radical change from the current process.

Definition(s) of concepts that had to be learned: Central to the notion of reengineering is the idea that if the vision is not supported by staff or if it is incongruent with their beliefs, there will not be any real change in behaviors or any incentive to move in the direction of the vision.

The business processes in health care have been very hard to identify because they have been buried for years under increasing complexity and Band-Aid® repairs. Isolating and identifying them is key to redesigning the organization.

We also learned that creating new roles to support the redesign process is more difficult in a union environment and presents different challenges. We are a very traditional organization, with a specific job description for every job and approximately 600 job categories. It is hard for many of us to think about different roles within a job category, depending on where the employee works, as the job structure is complex.

We learned that there will be resistance to change; the response, when you encounter it, is to just push through it. The strength of the design itself will not carry it through to fruition. The moment a design is created, there will be someone there to change it. Team members have to be prepared to deal with people altering the design. Knowing how far you can go and what you are trying to accomplish at the start is very helpful. Be creative; you can get regular employees to think differently. You need to design a process, to map it out, instead of just throwing things together. We would encourage that reengineering be a sincere, thoughtful decision; it's hard work and it's not for the faint of heart.

Key publications/references:

Hammer, M., and Champy, J. *Reengineering the Corporation: A Manifesto for Business Revolution.* New York City: HarperBusiness (a division of HarperCollins), 1993.

Contributor(s): Ginger Malone, RN, MSN, director, innovation and consultation

Contributor affiliation(s): Abbott Northwestern Hospital, Minneapolis

Name of model: Interactive Planning

Name of key author(s)/thinker(s): Russell Ackoff

Affiliation(s) of key author(s)/thinker(s): Author of numerous articles on interactive planning and idealized design related to organizational restructuring.

Key features of model/theory/set of ideas: The design recognizes the unique contributions of multiple disciplines to a planning process. Ackoff's focus on idealized design includes creation of a feasible design for a desirable future. His work also stresses the involvement of stakeholders in the creation of the vision.

How the model/theory/set of ideas was used: The two concepts Abbott Northwestern used were idealized design/creating a vision for the future and interactive communication, particularly during the planning year activities for the Robert Wood Johnson Foundations/Pew Charitable Trusts grant for Strengthening Hospital Nursing. His work helped us focus on the use of multidisciplinary, multilevel teams, and his theories supported the participative decision-making goals of the nursing department's collaborative governance structure. His influence continued as we created the "ideal patient experience" and the "ideal work experience" through a visioning process.

Key publication/reference:

Ackoff, R. The circular organization: an update. *Academy of Management Executives* 3(1):11–16, Feb. 1989.

Contributor(s): Ruth Hanson, MS, RN, project director

Contributor affiliation(s): MeritCare Hospital, Fargo, ND

Models Driving Change at Providence Portland Medical Center

Name of model: Finding Your 15%

Name of key author(s)/thinker(s): Gareth Morgan, distinguished research professor

Affiliation(s) of key author(s)/thinker(s): York University, Toronto, Ontario

Key features of model/theory/set of ideas: According to Morgan, major change is created through small but significant initiatives. Therefore, organizations should focus on finding the 15 percent leverage point/situation that staff have control over in any change situation.

How the model/theory/set of ideas was used: The planning component of care delivery redesign absorbs much time and effort. In completing this phase of redesign, those involved invest in the plans produced and often make assumptions that the plan will be implemented in its totality in a short period of time. Morgan's concept of "finding your 15%" was used to help nursing units translate their planning work relating to redesign of their unit model of care delivery into an implementation plan.

According to Morgan, each of us has control over 15 percent of our work environment. To increase the potential success and effectiveness of implementation, it is necessary to identify a situation that can serve as a leverage point and bring quick, visible success for all involved. The concept of "finding your 15%" helped redesign participants to learn to: (1) be more realistic about unfolding the implementation of their redesigned care delivery, (2) think strategically in implementing change, and (3) look for successful experiences as a way of engaging support for their efforts. Morgan's focus on small but significant opportunities alleviates pressure of an "all or nothing" approach to implementing a change and reorients participants to learn with and from each other and make redesign plans operational.

Key publications/references:

Morgan, G. *Finding your 15%.* (Videotape) Toronto, Ontario: Imaginization Learning Systems, 1994.

Contributor(s): Marie Driever, PhD, RN, project director

Contributor affiliation(s): Providence Portland Medical Center, Portland, OR

Appendix B

Approaches, Methods, and Tools That Work

Throughout this book, we have presented examples from our organizations of how we fit the content to be learned with the learner characteristics, teaching approach, and teaching method to create compelling learning experiences. In this appendix, we offer more detailed information on the approaches, methods, and tools that have worked particularly well for us in our journey toward becoming learning organizations. For each approach, method, or tool, there is a summary that includes some or all of the following:

Name of approach/method/tool: This is usually the name by which the approach, method, or tool is known in the organization. It also is the name by which it can be found in the map in table B-1.

Learning objectives: This is usually a general discussion of what the organization was trying to accomplish with the learning experience. Some organizations have included behavioral objectives for learners, others give competency-based outcomes for learning experiences.

Target audience: It is important to know for whom the learning experience worked well. This section contains information about who was in the session, or who was in the group with which a tool was used.

Key features of the approach/method/tool: In this section, the organization presents what it considered to be the key things about the approach, method, or tool that would be of interest to those who might like to replicate it. Examples might be background information on changes that set up the need for the learning experiences, how the content for the experience was developed, how consensus was developed for offering the experience, the roles of various participants in the experience, explanations of new roles of teams and groups for which the experience was successful, and a general description of the components of the approach, method, or tool.

How the approach/method/tool was used: This section includes details on how the approach, method, or tool was used, including physical setting, curriculum description, descriptions of how exercises were done, and equipment and materials that might be needed.

Outcomes (including measurable outcomes where available): Descriptions of and data on outcomes of the learning experience are included in this section.

Information on availability (copyright, price, included in other publications, and so on): Many of the approaches, methods, and tools that are discussed are available from the organization

Table B-1. Guided Tour of Appendix B

Organization	Page No.
Abbott Northwestern Hospital Manual for Quality Improvement Techniques Personal Mastery Retreat Learning Styles/Myers-Briggs Baseline Measures of Organizational Change Leadership Development Courses I, II, III	223
Beth Israel Hospital Competency-Based Orientation The use of histograms as a tool for process redesign The use of case presentations as a team-building tool Leadership Training Program	226
Harbor-UCLA Medical Center Neutral Third-Party Facilitation Transition Management Structure Strategic Management Tool Kit	234
Health Bond Together Everyone Achieves More: Health Bond's T.E.A.M.	238
Mercy Hospital and Medical Center Clinical Partner Orientation Utilizing Critical Thinking in Problem Solving	240
MeritCare Hospital Caring Touch Series Opportunities for Team Building Case Management Curriculum	242
Northeast Health Consortium Interaction Management®: Techniques for an Empowered Workforce℠	247
St. Luke's Regional Medical Center Development of a Common Language Based on Quality Improvement Training	248
Tallahassee Memorial Regional Medical Center The Who's Working on What (WWOW) Database Start-up Educational Sequence Keeping-on Educational Sequence The Red Bead Game Staff Work Redesign Survey Mental Models	253
University of Utah Hospital Syllabus for Multidisciplinary Apprentice Program (MAP) Training Goals and Roles Retreat	269
Vanderbilt University Hospital and Vanderbilt Clinic Transition Teams Shared Governance	273
Vermont Nursing Initiative Vermont Interact TV Summer Symposium	274

or some other source. This section includes guides on how to get more information or how to actually get the material.

Contributor(s): Name and position of the person(s) writing the description.

Contributor affiliation(s): Organization of the person(s) writing the description.

Approaches, Methods, and Tools That Work at Abbott Northwestern Hospital

Name of approach/method/tool: Manual for Quality Improvement Techniques

Learning objectives: Abbott Northwestern's quality improvement program is called Team Quality Improvement: Tools and Methods, which includes development of a curriculum for team members and leaders. Its objective is to familiarize them with a number of problem-solving techniques and tools and to make them aware of when/how they should be applied. It also provides them with an overall road map of the process they will be using to make improvements in their area of focus.

Target audience: Team member training is a two-day program targeted for any employee, supervisor, or manager who will be part of a quality improvement effort. We have identified 5 phases and 10 steps in the team quality improvement process.

How the approach/method/tool was used: The first phase is called *charting the focus.* This phase involves two steps: selecting the problem theme, and defining and organizing the project. This is really the phase during which people begin to think about what really is the problem and how they will know when it is solved. All team members learn how to create a team charter which will guide their efforts. The second phase focuses on *investigating the facts,* and there are two steps involved: They form theories of causes of their problem and collect relevant data to test the theories. A couple of tools have been particularly useful for team members to learn: flowcharts of the processes and cause-and-effect diagrams. The third phase is called *discovering the cause,* and there are two steps involved: analyzing the data that was collected during the previous phase and identifying root causes. Pareto analysis is a tool that is very useful in helping teams get to root causes. The fourth phase is called *creating the breakthrough.* This phase involves developing and evaluating alternative solutions, then selecting the solution and designing the implementation. This is the phase in which people get to be the most creative. The fifth and final stage, called *proving the quality,* involves implementing solutions and measuring improvements and monitoring and maintaining improvements. One of the major tools used in this phase is control charts. About 16 different tools are taught throughout the course of this program. Participants have an opportunity to use the tools in a case study situation prior to the program's conclusion.

For the folks who are designated team leaders, there is an additional three-day program. The first day is spent in understanding the dynamics of group formation and actually leading or facilitating a problem-solving process with unique and diverse team members. The second and third days are spent in more intense case studies applying the various tools and methods that were learned in the team members training program.

We have put together a comprehensive *Team Quality Improvement Manual* that serves as a resource for those who have completed the training and which people have found to be extremely valuable.

Outcomes: We have done some experimenting to try to analyze outcomes of the training. We have found that team members and leaders who have completed training are able to complete projects much more quickly and become less frustrated than those who have not completed training. We also have found that people who have the knowledge of the improvement tools have been better able to engage in the innovation projects.

Contributor(s): Debra Waggoner, MA, MBA, director, consulting and development

Contributor affiliation(s): Abbott Northwestern Hospital, Minneapolis, MN

Name of approach/method/tool: Personal Mastery Retreat

Target audience: Finding time to think and talk about personal and professional goals is a rarity in nursing. Four times a year, groups of 50 nurses gather for three days for individual reflection, small group work, and sharing with colleagues.

Learning objectives: This three-day retreat, which is part of the Professional Development Curriculum for the nursing department, focuses on nurses as people, colleagues, and integrators of patient care. For those staff members who attend, the time for reflection that the retreat offers is a chance to focus on their strengths, practice, and contributions to patient care.

The retreat provides the time and environment for individual nurses to come together to reflect on the art of nursing. Participants experience caring, healing of self and others, strengthening relationships, learning as a lifelong endeavor, and the joy and value of humor and lightheartedness in the work setting. Participants define strategies to move their personal vision into practice.

How the approach/method/tool was used: During the first day of the retreat, participants focus on understanding themselves by identifying their personal visions, values, and uniqueness; finding a healthy balance of mind, body, and spirit; and discussing how these factors influence their work and others. On the second day, understanding others and the nursing profession is the topic, with participants exploring caring and curing behaviors from a nursing and patient perspective. On the final day of the retreat, nurses concentrate on understanding the shared vision of the department, comparing their vision of professional practice to the shared vision of nursing practice at Abbott Northwestern. Since the program was first offered in 1992, more than 650 nurses have attended.

Contributor(s): Mary Koloroutis, MS, RN, director, and Mae McWeeny, MA, RN, learning specialist

Contributor affiliation(s): Center for Professional and Clinical Development, Abbott Northwestern Hospital, Minneapolis, MN

Name of approach/method/tool: Learning Styles/Myers-Briggs

How the approach, method, or tool was used: When the Sister Kenny Institute innovation design team first formed, we took them on a retreat for two days to focus on team development. We had all participants complete the Myers-Briggs Type Indicator (MBTI) and the Learning Styles Inventory (LSI). These two instruments served as a springboard to dialogue about the strengths and weaknesses of the team, and what it was they wanted to be in the future and what each team member brought to the process. As new, spin-off teams have been formed at Sister Kenny, we also have used the LSI and MBTI as a way of helping folks understand themselves and appreciate differences in others.

Throughout the team quality improvement and innovation efforts, we have found that the MBTI is a way for people to begin sharing a common language and begin talking about similarities and differences.

Contributor(s): Debra Waggoner, MA, MBA, director, consulting and development

Contributor affiliation(s): Abbott Northwestern Hospital, Minneapolis, MN

Name of approach/method/tool: The Establishment of Baseline Measures of Organizational Change

How the approach, method, or tool was used: Once we received the Robert Wood Johnson Foundation/Pew Charitable Trusts Grant, one of the things that we wanted to do was establish baseline measures. In particular, we wanted to get at how ready, willing, and able the members of our Innovation teams were to embark on the change process and the redesigning of their work. We developed, in house, a survey called Ready, Willing and Able and from it, were able to compile some descriptive data about the teams' level of preparedness. We were unable to establish the reliability and validity of the instrument, however. Since there are so many other instruments that are reliable and valid, we would suggest to anyone interested in gauging readiness for organizational change they take advantage of them. We have not readministered our own since then.

The William Bridges Instrument, or the Organizational Character Index, is like a Myers-Briggs for the whole organization that we used to compare our organization to others in HealthSpan. It was administered once, during the summer of 1993, to examine Abbott Northwestern's culture. The results were useful in terms of our recent merger with other metropolitan hospitals into a new health care system. We discovered that, at Abbott Northwestern where we're involved in visioning processes, we have a strong N (intuitive) preference as well as a strong F (feeling) preference which is consistent with our innovation processes.

Outcomes: The Organizational Effectiveness Survey has been administered bi-yearly since 1985. The survey monitors employees' perceptions of how well the organization is doing related to a number of different issues such as customer service, job barriers, innovation, employee commitment/involvement, and organizational values. We have been able to use the results of this survey to track innovation teams over time. In addition, we used a 1,000-employee sample to look at power and locus of control.

Using the nursing department as a barometer for the organization, a survey was administered to a random sample of 300 RNs in 1993. This survey used an instrument from the literature with a known reliability and validity. The constructs measured included: organizational commitment, power/autonomy, locus of control and practice environment/climate. We plan to track these baseline measures over time to assess the changing profile of the nursing staff as it matures with the organization.

Contributor(s): Ginger Malone, RN, MSN

Contributor(s) affiliation(s): Abbott Northwestern Hospital, Minneapolis, MN

Name of approach/method/tool: Leadership Development Courses I, II, III

Learning objectives: In 1986, consulting and development staff members determined that it would be important to develop leadership skills particularly among the hospital's middle management groups as well as other key employee leaders in the organization. Since that time, we have developed three leadership courses called leadership development I, II, and III.

How the approach/method/tool was used: Leadership development I (LPDI) is an intense week-long program. The goals of the program are to understand personal strengths and weaknesses, discover how others see your leadership behavior, use influence to create a climate that fosters commitment and respect, to become more aware of your impact on others and to become more influential in group meetings, articulate a vision and develop a plan to communicate to others, improve skills in giving feedback, clearly define personal and career goals for self-development.

Prior to coming to the program, participants complete a series of surveys/instruments such as the Strong/Campbell Inventory, Firo-B, Myers-Briggs Type Indicator, and the Leadership Development Survey. Through the course of a week, people get feedback on the various instruments that they completed, and they receive feedback from other participants in the class, as well as faculty members, based on their interactions during three leaderless group discussions. They also are videotaped and have a chance to give themselves feedback on their behaviors. The key content pieces of the week, in addition to the gaining of self-knowledge, are the differences between leadership and management, visioning and being able to articulate a vision, what it is or is not.

Leadership development II (LPDII) is a week-long program that is a natural continuation of LPDI. Participants complete additional feedback instruments prior to the start of the program. One of the instruments is called Sima, which looks at participants' motivated abilities. The second comprehensive instrument is called Benchmarks, a survey developed by the Center for Creative Leadership, which involves 360-degree feedback. In addition, the week's content focuses on principled negotiation, conflict management, and change and how to manage a change project. Once again, each participant is asked to identify a personal/professional development plan as a result of his or her learning from the week.

During the past year, we have offered a four-day leadership development III (LPDIII) program. This program focuses on human dynamics, which is based on the work of Sandra Seagal and looks at human beings as systems. This has been a nice complement to previous leadership development programs and provides more depth of self-knowledge, as well as focuses on how we communicate with people who are different from ourselves and how we can share meaningful dialogue despite our differences.

These programs have been invaluable in developing leadership skills over the past seven years.

Contributor(s): Debra Waggoner, MA, MBA, director, consulting and development

Contributor affiliation(s): Abbott Northwestern Hospital, Minneapolis, MN

Approaches, Methods, and Tools That Work at Beth Israel Hospital

Name of approach/method/tool: Competency-Based Orientation

Learning objectives: Beth Israel Hospital, in Boston, is a values-driven organization. The nursing service works hard to instill values in its nurses that are consistent with the institutional values that lead to high-quality patient-centered care. There are forums for formal discussion on values and ethics, as well as an emphasis on supporting informal discussion of this nature. In an effort to create support services that are patient centered, an interdisciplinary team, including representatives from nursing, human resources, environmental services, transportation services, nutrition services, and administration, designed the role of the support assistant. Nurses on the team felt strongly that a well-designed orientation program that exemplified values around patient needs would be vital to the success of a role in which support services staff, who previously had little patient contact, would be constantly interacting with patients.

Key features of the approach/method/tool: Much of the effort to restructure patient care in this time of "cost crisis" has focused on redesigning work to incorporate several skills into one role. At Beth Israel Hospital we created a new role that combines the tasks of environmental services, transportation services, and some aspects of nutrition services. The people in the new role, called support assistants, are unit based instead of centrally based as they had been in their previous support service roles. The orientation program for the support assistant was one key to the success of the new role. Following is a description of the evolution of a competency-based orientation program for support assistants.

How the approach/method/tool was used: The demonstration unit for the support assistant role was a 44-bed general medical unit. Five out of the six people hired in the role were internal candidates from either environmental services, transportation services, or nutrition services. Orientation in the departments from which the support assistants came consisted of a one-day hospitalwide orientation (mandatory for all new employees) and two or three days of "shadowing" as fellow employees taught them how to do the tasks expected from a person in their role. The nurses involved in planning the support assistant role had a very different experience in their orientation, which included a six-week competency-based orientation program with a preceptor. The competency-based approach to orientation emphasizes achievement of performance objectives rather than acquisition of information, and suggests that orientation should encourage people to learn rather than simply to be taught.[1] In a competency-based orientation program, staff, not supervisors, do the teaching. This helps put people at ease and allows them to concentrate on learning rather than impressing their supervisor.

The team members developed a four-week competency-based orientation program. During orientation, support assistants learned how to clean their patient's rooms, transport their patients to and from procedures, and deliver and assist with meals. The support assistant had to perform each skill competently in order to complete the orientation program successfully. In addition to ensuring competency in performing tasks, it was important to ensure that support assistants began developing communication skills, listening skills, and the ability to work with a team. Through role modeling and review of patient scenarios with a nurse on the unit, the support assistants began to develop critical thinking skills. We hoped that, through the competency-based program, the support assistant would gain an understanding that learning about patients was an ongoing process and that development should continue beyond the formal orientation period.

A clinical nurse on the demonstration unit coordinated the orientation. We thought a nurse would be best for this role because of the importance of education on the values around patient needs. Some of the content the nurse addressed included understanding special needs of confused patients, patients at risk for aspiration, and the issue of confidentiality.

The nurse chosen to coordinate the orientation attended a program designed by the nursing service for preceptor development. During the day-long program, participants review teaching and learning principles, and time is devoted to the role playing of common situations that might occur. When it was time to start the orientation, the nurse coordinator was pulled from the staffing pattern for the four-week orientation period. Since the initial orientation, support assistants are responsible for the orientation of newly hired support assistants with continued involvement from nursing.

Outcomes: Competency-based orientation facilitated development of support assistants by setting out clear, concise expectations, demanding accountability, and providing a standardized experience for each person in the role. It also served as a tool to evaluate the work of each support assistant. The support assistants benefited from having a nurse involved in their orientation as it allowed them to model behaviors that are important when working with patients—such as listening, and exhibiting patience and compassion. There were benefits for nurses too. Because the nursing staff was familiar with and respectful of competency-based orientation, any concerns they had about the quality of work the support assistants would provide were lessened.

The reward for thoughtful planning for the education and development of support assistants was the successful transition of individuals from a centrally based support service position to a unit-based patient-focused role. Successful embodiment of the tasks and values associated with the role was perhaps best articulated by a support assistant who stated, "It's very satisfying to feel like I can make a difference in a patient's stay."

Reference:

1. Liston, E., Dick, K., and Greenspan, M. The evolution of nursing practice. In: J. Clifford and K. Horvath, editors. *Advancing Professional Nursing Practice: Innovations at Boston's Beth Israel Hospital.* New York City: Springer, 1990, pp. 64–65.

Contributor(s): Laura Duprat, RN, MS, MPH, project director, integrated clinical practice; Eileen Keefe, BSN, clinical nurse

Contributor affiliation(s): Beth Israel Hospital, Boston, MA

Name of approach/method/tool: The use of histograms as a tool for process redesign

Key features of the approach, method, or tool: The histogram is a useful tool in the diagnostic phase of a quality improvement project because it is simple to construct and easy to read. It helps the team establish a common understanding of the process, depicts how the process currently works, and reveals obvious breakdowns in the system. The visual impact of data, arranged and analyzed with a histogram, helps a team avoid the quick-fix solution based on a personal opinion or the experience of a few.

How the approach/method/tool was used: At Boston's Beth Israel Hospital, a team of nurses, pharmacists, and pharmacy technicians studied the process of ordering, preparing, and delivering IV medications. Nurses reported that IV medications frequently were missing when they were scheduled to be given to patients; pharmacists were frustrated by the rework of making another dose or recycling a medication that was prepared but never given. The goal was to reduce variation in the process as much as possible so that we could predict from hour to hour, shift to shift, and weekday to weekend when medications would be delivered and when to schedule the first dose.

In this project, we used the histogram to look at the pattern of variation in cycle time for new IV medication orders. The horizontal axis of the histogram is the time in minutes; the vertical axis measures the number of IV medications that fall into each time category. For example, when the time for posting the order until delivery to the unit is plotted on the histogram, the variation in cycle time is apparent. (See figure B-1.) Eighty IV medication doses, or 81 percent, were available in two hours. The remaining 19 doses, however, took between 121 minutes and 280 minutes to arrive. The time from posting the order until delivery of the order to the pharmacy shows similar variation. (See figure B-2.) Twenty-nine orders, or 62 percent, were delivered in one hour. Thirty-eight percent of the new orders were received in 61 minutes to 150 minutes. As we analyzed the data, the same IV doses with long cycle time for figure B-1 also had a prolonged figure B-2 cycle time. These data helped pinpoint the root causes of the delays in getting a new IV medication order to the pharmacy. There are variations in the amount of time a new order might wait to be picked up by the pharmacy technician after being placed in the basket by a nurse. (See figure B-3, p. 230.) Also, run times and pick-up routes were not standardized, which led to variation in the delivery time to the pharmacy. (See figure B-4, p. 230.)

Outcomes: Decisions about permanent solutions to a problem are much easier to agree on when they are based on data. The team recommended faxing all orders to the pharmacy as a way of improving cycle time from posting the order until delivery of the order to the pharmacy (figure B-2). The improvement in the process was dramatic. (See figure B-5, p. 231.) Forty-three new orders, or 91 percent, faxed to the pharmacy, arrived within 30 minutes!

Contributor(s): Nancy Miller, RN, MS, nurse specialist, quality assurance and special projects

Contributor affiliation(s): Beth Israel Hospital, Boston, MA

Figure B-1. Time from Posting until Delivery to Unit

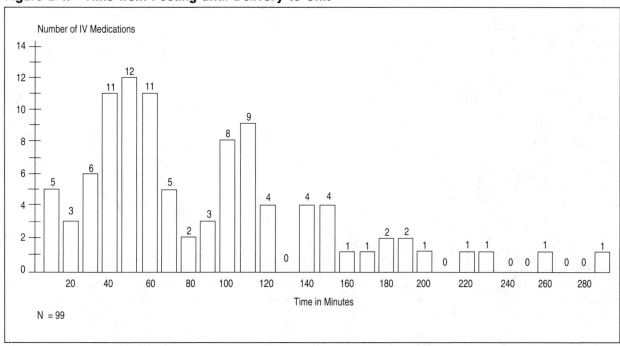

Figure B-2. Time from Posting until Delivery to Pharmacy

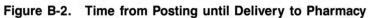
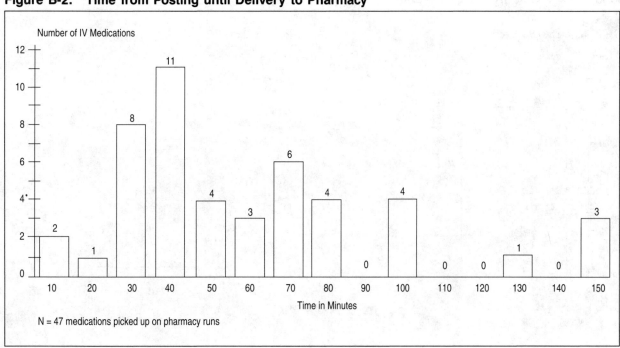

Figure B-3. Time in Basket until Pick Up on Run

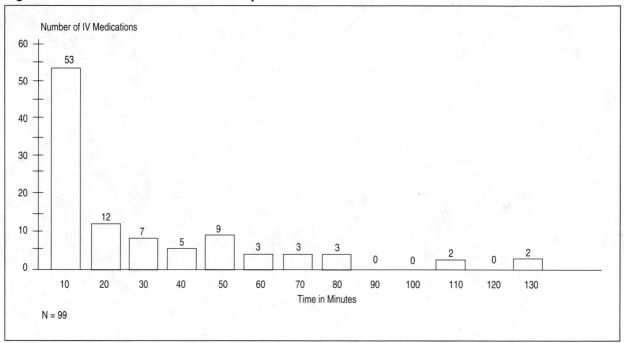

Figure B-4. Time from Pick Up until Delivery to Pharmacy

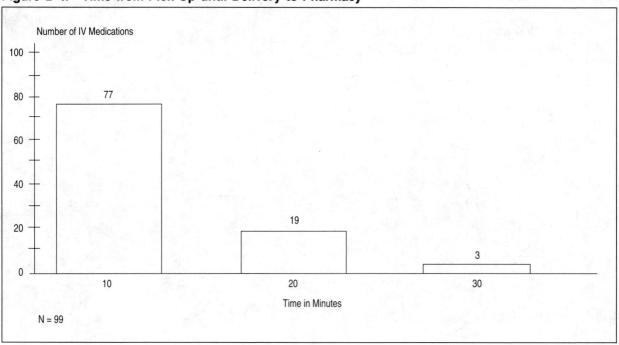

Figure B-5. Time from Faxing until Delivery to Pharmacy

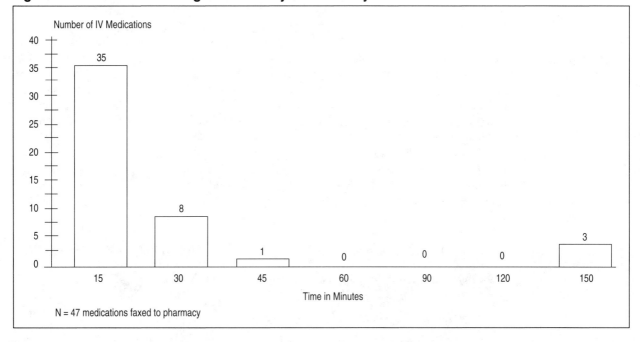

Name of approach/method/tool: The use of case presentations as a team-building tool

How the approach/method/tool was used: Although most health care providers would agree that enhancing the continuity of patient care is a good thing, they might be less likely to agree on just how to go about creating systems that support continuity. At Beth Israel Hospital, we found that providers need education regarding the roles of others who share responsibility in caring for patients to enhance their ability to work together to create systems that are better for patients. Without exposure to the roles of coproviders, people in different disciplines, and even those within the same discipline, may work in isolation, never getting a sense of the whole picture as only the patient sees it.

Patient care for people with HIV/AIDS is medically and socially very complex. Patients are cared for in a variety of settings by a variety of health professionals. Beth Israel Hospital is fortunate to have many providers with expertise in caring for this population of patients. For these reasons, we decided to work to improve the continuity of care for patients with HIV and their friends/families. We hypothesized that continuity of care would be further enhanced in a collaborative approach.

A committee of nurses, physicians, and social workers, all involved in caring for patients with HIV/AIDS, was given the charge to articulate the current and potential HIV populations at Beth Israel Hospital and develop programs that are responsive to their care needs. During the initial meetings of the group, there was a sense that each person in the room "owned" a portion of the care of "his or her" patients. We identified the obstacles to caring for patients with HIV in a brainstorming exercise. Some of the obstacles identified included: communication between all members of the team; difficulty in networking with providers in different roles; and conflict among caregivers, sometimes based on different information or "wishes" for the patient.

One of the members of the team, a psychiatrist, suggested that we needed "something" to help the individuals in the room gel as a team. He suggested that we start each meeting with a case presentation by one of the committee members. Patient confidentiality could, of course, be maintained. Case presentations would keep the focus on the patient, illustrate the complexity of each case, and help people understand the roles of individuals and disciplines involved in caring for people with HIV/AIDS.

The following month, one of the committee members presented a case about a 30-year-old woman with an extensive history of intravenous drug use who was currently being maintained on methadone. She had been admitted to the hospital on several occasions for HIV-related problems. During the discussion, it became apparent that several individuals in the room were involved in the care of this particular patient. People were able to add information to the case presentation that gave everyone better insight into the patient and her care needs. It was one of those "ah ha!" feelings for everyone in the room. Each of them had an important role to play in the care of this patient. By listening to the other providers talk about their involvement with the patient, members of the committee gained a basic understanding of each person's role and the value of that role.

As committee members continued to present cases each month, there was the sense that they had become a "team." Committee members are now working together to plan systems of care for patients. They are working together toward the same goals of excellent patient care, instead of working in isolation. One key to success, this group has found, was understanding each other's roles and in learning the intrinsic value of that work.

Contributor(s): Laura Duprat, RN, MS, MPH, project director, integrated clinical practice

Contributor affiliation(s): Beth Israel Hospital, Boston, MA

Name of approach/method/tool: Leadership Training Program

Learning objectives: We began our leadership training program by first recognizing an organizational need for training and then soliciting learner involvement in the design. When Beth Israel Hospital adopted the Scanlon Plan, senior leadership thought that the initial training and education would be sufficient to create a more participative environment in which all employees and managers would own the problems and successes of the organization. Despite the initial success of the plan, senior leadership and many managers perceived a need to:

- Increase work team leaders' (directors, managers, and supervisors) knowledge of how the hospital works: its goals and strategy, key challenges, customer needs, and the competitive environment
- Help managers foster a more participative, self-managing environment in which people at all levels of the organization would feel empowered to make suggestions and improvements
- Increase managerial competence by helping managers find ways to define what the right job is and to learn how to become more open-minded regarding employees' ideas on how to do the job

Target audience: Work team leaders, managers

Key features of the approach/method/tool: The hospital leadership team asked the training and organization development (OD) department to develop a training program and ongoing support for achieving the above objectives. Training and OD began to assess training and organization development support needs by shadowing and individually interviewing managers about their needs. They used this information to develop focus group questions which they posed to groups of directors, administrative managers, nurse managers, supervisors, and employees. The questions included:

- What behaviors do you or other managers/employees exhibit that help or hinder a participative environment?
- What does your manager do well? What does your manager need to improve?
- What skills do you need to create to maintain a participative environment?
- What could human resources (which includes training and OD) provide to help create a more participative environment?

When we asked more specifically what training was needed, the answers included:

- Listening skills
- Creativity and flexibility
- Conflict management
- Risk taking
- Prioritizing
- How to be more comfortable in a managerial/supervisory role
- How to turn complaints into positive ideas
- Cultural sensitivity and diversity

The participants also wanted more opportunity to establish relationships with other departments and hoped that the training program could do this.

How the approach/method/tool was used: The above questions created a fascinating dialogue among participants and helped us understand what a training program should include. Not surprisingly, most people could talk more about what others needed than what they themselves needed. Employees, supervisors, and managers in many areas felt that managers should get to know employees at a more personal level and that internal training within departments could be improved. They felt that collaboration with other departments of the hospital was weak and that interdepartmental cooperation could be strengthened by improving informal relationships. We also heard that, except at the most senior level, people wanted more input in decisions that would impact them.

The focus groups allowed us as course designers to begin to develop what we called the competencies for a participative environment. The seven competencies (highlighted below) were discussed and reviewed by the vice-presidents' work team:

- *Identity:* Communicates the importance of every employee's individual contribution toward achieving the vision and mission of the department and the hospital
- *Customer expectations:* Helps the work team to determine, meet, and exceed internal and external customer expectations
- *Facilitation skills:* Facilitates effective, participative work team meetings
- *Problem-solving skills:* Trains and uses a variety of problem-solving approaches including creative problem solving and quality improvement methodology
- *Employee development:* Develops employees' technical and interactive skills
- *Leadership development:* Continually develops and models leadership skills
- *Team building:* Fosters a collaborative work team environment

From the competencies, we began to develop a set of objectives for phase one of the training program, the Leadership Track. All work team leaders in the organization are required to complete the program. The objectives for the first phase of the program focused on some of the competencies: identity, facilitation skills, problem-solving skills, and team building. We viewed the "track" as one piece of a long-term effort devoted to organizational learning and competence.

Recognizing that we would need external help to shorten development time and provide us with an outsider's perspective, we began researching approximately 15 training and consulting firms. We spoke with about half in person and narrowed our final selection to three. Our goal was not to have a company design and deliver a program but, rather, to work with us as a team to jointly design a curriculum that would be embraced by the culture at Beth Israel. We decided from the start that the delivery of the actual training would be done by our own staff.

To test some of our assumptions about our managerial and supervisory staff, we invited each of the three finalist training and consulting companies to present a one and one-half hour snippet of their training design ideas and materials to about 15 Beth Israel work team leaders. We wanted to make sure that the company we chose to work with could design a program that met the needs of our customers. Fifteen work team leaders participated in the minisessions and gave us feedback about each. We found that one company was clearly unsuited to our culture, although one of our competitors thought highly of its work. The other two companies were rated very favorably, with a slight preference toward one. We heard everyone's comments and concerns and did our best to integrate them into our design.

Contributor(s): Daryl Juran, MPPM, internal quality improvement consultant

Contributor affiliation(s): Beth Israel Hospital, Boston, MA

Approaches, Methods, and Tools That Work at Harbor-UCLA Medical Center

Name of approach/method/tool: Neutral Third-Party Facilitation

Learning objectives:

- To conduct meetings that promote group decisions
- To manage diversity of opinion within groups

Target audience: Groups who hold meetings to accomplish work in contrast to meeting for information sharing.

Key features of the approach/method/tool: At Harbor-UCLA Medical Center (HUCLA), the third-party facilitation tool has been adapted from the model developed by Interaction Associates. Planning time for a meeting includes assigning roles, outcomes, methods to achieve outcomes, including decision mode and time allotted. This information is displayed on an easel with a paper-sized, visible agenda (format includes outcomes and a table of who, what, how, and time). Meetings begin with a call for ground rules to be determined by participants. Groups that meet regularly carry their ground rules over to the next meeting, revising as desired. Key roles include: leader (content expert/decision maker who participates as group member), facilitator (process expert who "chauffeurs" the meeting, usually on his or her feet in front of the group), recorder, timekeeper. Decision format is often part of the ground rules or is declared by the leader as needed during a meeting.

The decision model utilized has two aspects. The first is the extent of group involvement in the decision, as determined by the leader. The least involvement is labeled "decide and announce." The next levels are: leader obtains input from leader individually; leader obtains input from the group; group decides with input from the leader as member; group delegates the decision to a subgroup.

The second aspect relates to the style of obtaining the preference of the group. When it is determined that the decision is the responsibility of the group, three styles are frequently considered. These decision styles, as they have emerged at HUCLA, are: majority rules (the proportion of votes must be announced before the vote); consensus (proposals are reshaped until everyone can agree; one no is a veto); and harmony (diversity of opinion is allowed, more than one option is selected, or some members agree to go along with the majority on a trial basis).

A group memory is created by the recorder on easel sheets as the group shares ideas and develops plans. The recorder uses beveled markers and multiple colors, and prints up members words. The recorder does not paraphrase. The recorder does not seek clarification from the group. Instead, one gets signals and coaching on missing ideas or wording from the facilitator. This minimizes confusion and role blurring.

How the approach/method/tool was used: Neutral facilitation is used for all of the core meetings related to our restructuring efforts. This includes the oversight leadership team and the councils responsible for implementing our four strategic directions.

Outcomes: The technique has spread informally across the campus. A neutral facilitator is considered the ideal for groups tackling complex issues. Class enrollments continue to average 15 people per quarter. The technique has promoted key restructuring values in the focus on decision making by the group, clarity of expectations, and focusing on shared understanding.

Information on availability: Interaction Associates, 600 Townsend Street, Suite 8000, San Francisco, CA 91103 (Fax: 415/241-8010).

Contributor(s): Maryalice Jordan-Marsh, RN, PhD, director, nursing research; Susan Goldsmith, MS, project coordinator, community of patient care leaders

Contributor affiliation(s): Harbor-UCLA Medical Center, Los Angeles, CA

Name of approach/method/tool: Transition Management Structure

Learning objectives:

To develop a critical mass of stakeholders into a cadre of experts, advocates, ambassadors, and so on in order to diffuse Community of Patient Care Leader (CPCL) innovations into the culture of Harbor-UCLA.

Target audience: Executive medical center leadership, critical organizational gatekeepers, representatives of key stakeholder groups (administration, medicine, nursing, staff, patients).

Key features of the approach/method/tool: The transition management structure is a network of interrelated teams whose mission is to strategically manage the cultural change to a CPCL. The network is composed of three groups: an executive leadership team, four strategic direction councils, and myriad process action teams. The specialized mission of each group is as follows:

- The CPCL leadership team is composed of major hospital leadership figures (hospital administrator, medical director, director of nursing), three associate hospital administrators (finance, operations, and information systems), director of quality improvement, director of nursing research, director of nursing professional practice affairs, associate medical director, and president of the Professional Staff Association. The mission of this group is to provide guidance and oversight for strategic management of CPCL activities and direction with respect to vision and strategic direction. To ensure consistency of vision and mission with the medical center strategic focus, the players overlap with the hospital administrative council. The highly visible nature of this group affords many opportunities to demonstrate key aspects of the CPCL vision and values to other medical center personnel. This helps to infuse restructuring principles into the Los Angeles health care community.
- The strategic direction councils (SDCs) relate to the four CPCL strategic directions: (1) creation of a community initiative, (2) establishment of a leadership culture of continuous improvement, (3) development of a user-friendly environment that empowers stakeholders, and (4) development of systems to facilitate transitions. The mission of each SDC is to bring the four strategic directions to life through implementation of specific restructuring activities. Council members were deliberately selected based on their interest, skill, resources, or gatekeeper status in the area of a particular strategic direction. Each SDC is co-led by a nurse/physician or nurse administrator team. Coleaders were also thoughtfully chosen based on the fit of their interest, leadership history, and potential for investment of time and energy. Patient involvement is critical at this level to ensure consistency of restructuring efforts with customer needs. The

SDCs have a specialized role in the transition management mosaic. They provide a critical link between the architects of the CPCL vision and values (the CPCL leadership team) and those closest to the work, implementation teams. They are the means of bringing stakeholders from diverse background disciplines together around work within the restructuring process. Through involvement in the SDC, these stakeholders too become architects of the process.

- The process action teams (PATs) are small groups of stakeholders who work within a specific process or area that is related to the CPCL. The philosophy behind the PAT model is that people closest to the work have the most knowledge about the work process and are therefore the "experts." They are then given the opportunity to make continuous quality improvement redesign or reengineering within a given area (with the appropriate guidelines of a management or oversight group to ensure consistency with medical center mission and vision). The PAT model complements the SDC structure in that the SDC identifies an area requiring improvement and then invites the team of experts (the PAT) to implement the change.

How the approach/method/tool was used: The transition management structure was developed at Harbor-UCLA Medical Center at the onset of restructuring activities. It was developed in response to the following felt needs:

- Desire to create lasting and meaningful change through the involvement of a critical mass of stakeholders in the restructuring process. It was anticipated that promoting both vertical and horizontal involvement would avoid the limitations of a top-down approach to change.
- An imperative to align restructuring efforts with the overall vision and mission of the medical center as well as to communicate that vision and mission to all medical center stakeholders. It was anticipated that this would be accomplished through shared accountability for restructuring efforts with medical center leadership, middle management, staff, and patients.
- A desire to formally partner hospital administration and ancillary services, medical and nursing staff in every aspect of the restructuring process.
- A need to create a formalized, representative structure in which to test projected strategies and innovations. Under the philosophy that small teams can represent a microcosm of the organization, each group in the transition management structure has become an ideal arena in which to learn about the organizational culture and responses to change. The structure was deliberately designed recognizing that culture change would begin with internal shifts within the team. Peter Senge writes that "Organizations change when people change."[1] Each group in the transition management structure sees its own group as a laboratory in which to experience restructuring principles and concepts firsthand. Creating a positive experience of change for team members in turn facilitates change throughout the organization.

Outcomes: Outcomes of utilizing the transition management structure model as described above are as follows:

- Development of a cadre of committed, educated, and actively participating stakeholders who hold strategic leadership positions within the medical center
- Dissemination of restructuring ideals and concepts to representative stakeholder groups
- Implementation of restructuring activities and deliverables
- Development of leadership initiatives in all participating stakeholders
- Development of a model (and related tools) transferable to other organizations

Contributor(s): Susan Goldsmith, MS, project coordinator, community of patient care leaders; Peggy Nazarey, RN, MSN, director of nursing, project director; Paula Siler, RN, MS, director, professional practice affairs—nursing; Maryalice Jordan-Marsh, RN, PhD, director, nursing research; Elisa Sanchez, administrative assistant

Contributor affiliation(s): Harbor-UCLA Medical Center, Torrance, CA

Reference:

1. Senge, P. M. *The Fifth Discipline: The Art and Practice of the Learning Organization.* New York City: Doubleday/Currency, 1990.

Name of approach/method/tool: Strategic Management Tool Kit

Learning objectives:

- To empower individuals and groups with tools needed to effect cultural change to a "community of patient care leaders (CPCL)
- To create a climate in which stakeholders become actively involved in "building" and maintaining the upkeep of a new organizational culture
- To diffuse innovations to a wide range of stakeholders in a time-effective manner
- To catalogue customized, internally developed innovations in a format transferable to other change efforts

Target audience: All stakeholders involved in change management activities.

Key features of the approach/method/tool: The strategic management tool kit is a means of empowering stakeholders at all levels, with the resources to build a new organizational culture. It is structured in six primary sections:

1. *Strategic management:* These tools were designed to assist in the planning, implementation, evaluation, and integration of broad-scale organizational change projects. [Examples: Idea framework inventory, 7-S framework chart, time line development questions]
2. *Project management:* These tools were designed to assist in the planning, execution, and control of small, measurable projects. A project has a defined beginning and ending. [Examples: Project management overview, major elements of project management]
3. *Team development:* These tools were designed to provide resources for teams in their development. Most tools are sensitive to the stages of group development: forming, norming, storming, and performing. [Examples: Tool for organizing strategic direction (SDC) work, SDC meeting tracking tool, SDC developmental cycle]
4. *Group process:* These tools were designed as activities or interventions that teams can use to enhance their development. [Examples: Role clarification worksheet, Walk a Day in My Shoes, group culture exercise]
5. *Continuous quality improvement:* These tools were designed to assist in process improvement or redesign projects. A process is a series of smaller tasks that has a defined beginning and ending. [Examples: FOCUS PDCA questions, fishbone diagram, PAT application form]
6. *CPCL content exploration:* These tools were designed as activities to assist the CPCL SDCs explore their particular strategic direction. Although they are represented as content-specific, the activities can be applied to other topic areas. [Examples: Transition planning grid, ingredients of community exploration, leadership culture SDC objectives debate]

Each section contains a selection of tools, with explanation of purpose, use, source, related readings and topics, and target audience. Tools are primarily those that have been developed at Harbor-UCLA specifically for the transition to a CPCL. Some tools have been developed for other purposes and adapted for use within the CPCL (and are so noted). All tools are cross-referenced, in that they may appear in more than one section.

How the approach/method/tool was used: The strategic management tool kit was developed as a way to reach a large audience in a short amount of time, as well as a means of cataloguing internally developed innovations for diffusion throughout the organization. It has facilitated related spin-off activities, such as individualized tool kits, resource manuals, and team storyboards. Primary maintenance of the kit rests with the CPCL project staff as they currently provide the greatest degree of continuity for restructuring process activities. Future plans to integrate the tool kit concept are being developed by the Transition Systems SDC.

Outcomes: Outcomes of utilizing the strategic management tool kit are:

- Development of resources that all stakeholders can access and utilize to facilitate change in their workplace
- Employees who are empowered to develop and utilize innovative resources
- A model for thinking about resources as tools that are to be utilized according to the specialized nature of a certain task
- An historical account of innovations initiated by the CPCL restructuring process
- A vehicle for adapting new ideas into the culture and process of Harbor-UCLA
- Proven "tools," techniques, and strategies to assist in BSO
- Competence development for individuals undergoing transitions

Information on availability: All tools are copyrighted by Harbor-UCLA Medical Center, A Community of Patient Care Leaders, unless otherwise noted.

Contributor(s): Peggy Nazarey, RN, MSN, director of nursing, project director; Susan Goldsmith, MS, project coordinator, community of patient care leaders; Paula Siler, RN, MS, director, professional practice affairs—nursing; Elisa Sanchez, administrative assistant

Contributor affiliation(s): Harbor-UCLA Medical Center, Torrance, CA

Approaches, Methods, and Tools That Work at Health Bond

Name of approach/method/tool: Together Everyone Achieves More: Health Bond's T.E.A.M.

Learning objectives: One of Health Bond's five objectives is to promote cultural change among members of the health care team to facilitate continuous quality improvement. A consulting relationship with creative nursing management (discussed in appendix A) and its Leaders Empower Staff (LES) program, gave consortium hospital members and education partners access to experiential education related to communication, commitment to coworkers, leadership development, problem-solving techniques, continuous quality improvement, and decentralized decision making.

Target audience: A primary challenge was communicating principles of LES supportive of culture change to new employees and reinforcing them with existing employees on an ongoing basis at all three service settings. A strategy developed at Immanuel-St. Joseph's Hospital (ISJ) to communicate with over 800 employees was T.E.A.M. (Together Everyone Achieves More) Education Days.

How the approach/method/tool was used: Prior to the awarding of the Strengthening Hospital Nursing grant (1989), ISJ conducted annual day-long mandatory nursing education days planned by nurses, for nurses. They included information on new clinical equipment, procedures, and safety. Other employees were offered a half-day of training each year, with input from their staff and consisting of required topics. This was also the case at Waseca Area Memorial and Arlington Municipal Hospitals.

Between 1989 and 1990, the planning grant year for the Strengthening Hospital Nursing Program, a number of forces converged to create a new vision for those education days at ISJ. To accomplish real change in how patients were cared for, these leaders were convinced that nursing would be strengthened in an interdisciplinary, interactive planning/problem-solving environment.

The education coordinator at ISJ and key personnel recognized the opportunity to use the existing education days in a new way—to communicate the principles of LES to every employee and to reinforce them. A proposal was made to ISJ's administration in the fall of 1991 for an 8-hour education day for nurses and allied staff together. The morning session consisted of safety and other mandatory education information and the afternoon contained the basic elements of decentralization and responsibility, authority and accountability principles.

The 1992 education day was renamed T.E.A.M. Day. It was attended by 745 (of 825) personnel from ISJ. An advantage of this day was that it included, for the first time, an interdisciplinary planning team (administration, nursing, employee assistance, human resources, and so on).

In an effort to measure the effectiveness of the day, a survey with five sets of statements related to hospital culture was rated by the participants before and after attendance. March through December responses closer to 1 (on a 1–9 scale) indicated "greater agreement with the negative statements" and responses closer to 9 indicated "greater agreement with the positive statements." The statements were:

1. Department/staff don't even try to work together. Departments/staff work well together to provide quality care.
2. I think about quitting or working elsewhere frequently. I like working at ISJ.
3. There is a lot of bitching, backbiting, and bickering around here. People are able to be honest and open with each other.
4. It's embarrassing to tell people I work here. I am proud of the quality of service our organization provides.
5. I never know what's going on in my department or in this organization. I am able to keep as up-to-date as I want with information and communication in this organization.

A posttraining survey was administered to all February participants at the end of the day they participated. There were no preday to postday differences in their responses to the questions; however, that is to be expected given they had just heard this information and cultural attitude changes take time and reinforcement to take hold. Also, March to December participants were given a postday survey in December. A comparison of the findings in February and December is as follows:

Item	February	December
1. Staff working well together	6.4	6.0
2. Like working at ISJ	6.0	6.6*
3. Bitching, backbiting, etc.	4.7	4.6
4. Proud of quality of care	6.7	7.0*
5. Keeping informed	6.0	6.2

*Differences are statistically significant at the 90 percent (.10) level.

To continue this culture change, every employee needs regular reminders and opportunities to see that these are consistent principles and values of the organization and new employees need to be introduced to these concepts. Given that T.E.A.M. Days can devote only about four hours each session to cultural concepts, training is extended over several years. In 1992, the focus was on team building, decentralization, and levels of responsibility, authority, and accountability. In 1993, these themes were repeated with the addition of the role of CQI [continuous quality improvement]. In 1994, the focus was on professionalism and pride in our work. Problem-solving processes from LES and customer service focus from CQI will be integrated under the umbrella of Pro—T.E.A.M. (Professionals—Together Everyone Achieves More).

The shared vision that has evolved from the planning teams at Health Bond is to have our regional hospitals treat patients as fine hotels do, with a focus on making their experience as pleasant, smooth, and caring as possible; where the employees see the hospital as theirs; where their work is something they are proud to sign their name to; and where they are treated like, and expected to perform as, professionals.

Contributor(s): Mary Grams, RN, educational coordinator; Yvonne Karsten, MBA, research associate

Contributor affiliation(s): Health Bond, Immanuel-St. Joseph's Hospital, Mankato, MN

Approaches, Methods, and Tools That Work at Mercy Hospital and Medical Center

Name of approach/method/tool: Clinical Partner Orientation

Learning objectives:

- To appreciate the value of the role of a clinical partner in a patient-driven system
- To demonstrate infection control principles, safety, and accuracy in skills required within the clinical partner role
- To communicate appropriately and effectively with patients, families, and staff

Target audience: Selected paraprofessionals interested in working with an RN as a clinical partner in the delivery of efficient/effective patient-driven care.

Key features of the approach/method/tool: The orientation process is six weeks. The key features of the orientation include:

- Role of a clinical partner in a patient-driven system
- Personal care of the patient
- Patient safety
- Communication with the patients
- Communication with the registered nurse
- Infection control
- Vital signs
- Assisting with nutritional care
- Reinforcing occupational and physical therapies
- Phlebotomy
- EKG collection
- Nonmedicated respiratory therapies
- Maintaining a safe and pleasant environment

Technical, basic theory, and psychosocial aspects of care are emphasized. The patients' expectations and rights related to confidentiality, privacy, acceptance, and dignity are threaded throughout the orientation.

How the approach/method/tool was used: Adult learning methods are incorporated into the orientation process. Classroom and clinical settings are integrated to evaluate the effectiveness of the orientation. The orientation team is multidisciplinary. A phlebotomist, an EKG technician, a nutritionist, an occupational therapist, a physical therapist, and a respiratory therapist are involved in teaching the appropriate skills and expectations for safe and effective patient care. Clinical skill tracks and special classes give the clinical partner orientees the knowledge to perform the duties expected. Proper technique is demonstrated for all skills in a classroom setting. The clinical partner, in return, demonstrates each skill being validated by an expert from the field, both in lab and then in the clinical setting.

A clinical procedures lab is designed to teach personal patient care activities. Didactic teaching methods, discussion, and hands-on procedures are used throughout the orientation process.

Outcomes: Clinical partners are evaluated via written tests to validate their knowledge. A skills checklist is used on the units to validate the skills related to patient care and safety. The clinical partner is evaluated on the respiratory, phlebotomy, and EKG components by means of two validation tools and two successful supervised attempts at performing these activities in a clinical setting. A clinical instructor meets with the orientee, preceptor, and unit director weekly to identify problem areas and strengths, thus individualizing the orientation for each participant. Ongoing evaluation and re-in-servicing of patient care skills occurs based on deficits. An example of this was when the EKG department received many EKGs that had an artifact. Electrode misplacement was the issue. Housewide in-servicing and revalidation was conducted.

Contributor(s): Gail Dunleavy, RN, clinical instructor; and Char Bermele, RN, clinical instructor

Contributor affiliation(s): Mercy Hospital and Medical Center, Chicago, IL

Name of approach/method/tool: Utilizing Critical Thinking in Problem Solving

Learning objectives:

- To discuss the basic types of thinking and how they are integrated in a critical thinking model
- To describe components of critical thinking
- To apply a critical thinking process to issues encountered in a resource coordinator role
- Through peer/expert feedback, to evaluate the effectiveness of the solutions to the issues

Target audience: Professional staff within the Division of Patient Care Services whose responsibilities include resource coordinator (charge) on the PM, night, and weekend shifts.

Key features of the approach/method/tool: This learning experience is structured as an interactive method that enhances understanding and provides for application of critical thinking skills to real-life issues.

After a short briefing on the critical thinking process, participants seated in small groups apply the process to vignettes. The vignettes have been developed from situations identified in a log, kept by house supervisors.

Participant groups are integrated to include nurses and professionals from various patient care disciplines. Each small group is facilitated by a director who has had experience in a house supervisor role and/or who is a department head of a patient care department.

Small groups are given 45 minutes to an hour to apply the critical thinking process to as many vignettes as possible within the time frame. Each group shares two of its issues, solutions, and rationales with the large group. The groups are encouraged to present those solutions of which they are proud and/or those they would like to explore further with their colleagues (resources).

Participants are encouraged to ask questions, clarify, and challenge each other. Facilitators (experts) share solutions chosen in "real life," give the rationale and outcome.

How the approach/method/tool was used:

- Orientation of resource coordinators
- Group size 20–50 (small groups 5–8)
- One facilitator for each small group

Outcomes: Participant evaluations indicated:

- Greater knowledge of systems and resources
- Decreased anxiety related to expanded role
- Confirmation that they enjoyed this learning experience because it promoted thinking and networking with peers
- A recommendation that this format be used as a method of continuing education with situations they experience

Facilitators indicated that it:

- Served as a means of clarifying scope of responsibilities
- Was a good means of assessing strength and areas for further development among their staff related to decision making in the resource coordinator role

Contributor(s): Fran La Monica, RN, MS, professional development and special projects coordinator

Contributor affiliation(s): Mercy Hospital and Medical Center, Chicago, IL

Approaches, Methods, and Tools That Work at MeritCare Hospital

Name of approach/method/tool: Caring Touch Series

Learning objectives: In an attempt to improve patient care, the Holistic Care Design Team at MeritCare Hospital identified strategies that we would use to integrate holistic concepts into patient care. Several of the strategies we initiated were classes that were part of a series called "Caring Touch." Over a timespan of 1½ years, several courses were designed that would assist nurses and other interested caregivers and hospital associates to develop or improve their skills in the area of human touch. Courses that were developed for hospital associates were:

1. The use of touch in communication and healing
2. Therapeutic massage workshop
3. Back, neck, and shoulder massage
4. Introduction to acupressure
5. Therapeutic touch

The massage classes in this series will be the focus of this section. The primary objectives of both versions of massage classes were to teach associates, primarily direct care providers, basic massage techniques that could be used in their personal lives with family and friends and in their work with patients. Although nurses and other direct care providers were the target audience, any hospital employee that wanted to attend was able to.

How the approach/method/tool was used: The massage classes, a two-hour back, neck, and shoulder class and the six-hour workshop were taught by a licensed and certified massage therapist. The classes utilized a hands-on approach which made learning fun and participants both gave and received massages.

The classes were very well received by all participants. The major suggestion was that participants wanted and needed further practice and support. This request was addressed by scheduling various kinds of massage practice sessions. Initially, practice sessions for previous class participants were scheduled and hospital employees were invited to sign up to receive a mini-massage. This was very well received by employees; in fact there was a waiting list of staff that wanted to attend, but there were a limited number of "massagers," therefore we could accommodate only a limited number. The difficulty with this approach is that there needed to be a commitment on the part of those persons willing to give massages to actually show up when the time came, or there were more "clients" than we could accommodate. We then tried another variation—bringing a volunteer massage team to patient care units to offer massages to staff, patients or their family members. The volunteer team goes to patient care units one hour, about once a month. A general notice was placed in the hospital daily paper to let staff know it was happening, but not where. A flyer in the shape of a hand went to the unit a few days before the scheduled time alerting staff to this opportunity. The outside of the flyer said "Wait'll We Get Our Hands On You!" and the inside encouraged staff to take a healthy break and experience the benefits of massage. Also included was the date, time and location where the massage "team" would be giving massages. This was first initiated on December 24, 1992, on Christmas Eve day. Patient and family were astounded. Their comments ranged from "Now that's service," "I had no idea how relaxing a hand massage could be," and "This is the best Christmas present I could have received, my back has been so painful."

Engaging staff in learning and experiencing for themselves the healing benefits of touch has been a powerful and rewarding experience. The outcomes to date have not been adequately measured, but requests continue for further education and, as of the fall of 1993, massage classes are being offered as a community class.

Contributor(s): Nancy Ruud, MS, RN; Barb Edin, PT; Janet Dietz, RD; and Terry Miller, MS, RN

Contributor(s) affiliation(s): MeritCare Hospital, Fargo, ND

Name of approach/method/tool: Opportunities for Team Building

Learning objectives: The objectives are individualized to the team we are working with. The sessions usually focus on two to three aspects of team behavior such as communication, team type, decision making; so depending on the focus, the objectives may change. Following are examples of some objectives. Participants will:

- Have an opportunity to examine their own type and reaffirm a good fit for themselves
- Have an opportunity to explore their group's and team's types
- Have an opportunity to "look" through the "function lens" to understand communication/miscommunication, and increase cross-functional team effectiveness[1]

Target audience: The teams or work groups self-select to have this opportunity made available to them. Once all team members have received feedback on type preference, the leaders of the organization are given a similar opportunity. At present, our organization has four members who are qualified to administer and interpret MBTI [Myers-Briggs Type Indicator] results, which must be carried out face-to-face so to enable interaction. Individuals are given a choice to take the indicator. Results are the property of the individual and kept confidential; that is, one's boss is not automatically informed of the findings. As such, before participating in a team-building experience, all team members are given the opportunity to decide whether they wish to share the results during the exercise.

Key features of the approach/method/tool: There are three key features to this approach:

1. Consultation/analysis
2. Individualized approach
3. Flexibility

These will be described in the next section.

How the approach/method/tool was used:

- *Consultation/analysis:* The success of the team-building opportunity depends on the quality of time spent consulting with the interested group in the beginning. The facilitator sets up consultative visits with the leaders of the group to determine needs, see if this is the best approach to enhance team building, and define specifically what they would like to improve. Information is then gathered from each team member. (See figure B-6.) All of this is analyzed and a proposed session is negotiated with the leaders of the group.
- *Individualized approach:* From the written information, consultation visits, and looking at the mix of type preferences, an individualized approach to the team-building opportunity is developed. This is a key feature because it lends itself well to allowing a team to focus on one set of behaviors at a time. We may come back to the same team on a rotating basis and facilitate growth and development in a different area. It allows the teams to indicate what they want to work on, showing their readiness to modify or change certain behaviors.
- *Flexibility:* This is a key feature of the process and the facilitator because working with teams is a dynamic experience. The use of type often provide individuals a way to address frustrating behaviors they have never been able to address before. That may create a degree of unsteadiness within the group that the facilitator needs to be sensitive to. We have found it helpful to have two facilitators so that, as one is leading, the other can be observing the group interaction and add clarification of observations as needed.

Outcomes: The team-enhancing opportunity is evaluated using a written tool of five open-ended questions. (See figure B-7, p. 246.) These question were adapted from the work of Stephen Brookfield. As received at Staff Development '93 Mosby Resource Application, February 11, 1993, the answers are analyzed for trends and written follow-up is provided if necessary. Conversations with the leaders are conducted to bring closure to the experience.

Information on availability: The framework or conceptual model used for team-building experiences has been the Myers-Briggs Type Indicator (MBTI). Our primary resource has been *MBTI Team Building Program: Leader's Resource Guide,* by Sandra Krebs Hirsh. This guide uses a series of "lenses" to look through and examine team behavior and the team member's behavior.

Contributor(s): Roberta Young, BSN, RN, educator

Contributor affiliation(s): MeritCare Hospital, Fargo, ND

Reference:

1. Hirsh, S. K. *MBTI Team Building Program: Leader's Resource Guide.* Stanford, CA: Consulting Psychologists Press, 1992.

Figure B-6. Exploring Opportunities for Team Building

Sample consulting letter that outlines a process for the team-building experience.

Thank you for consulting us to be of support to your team. Following is the step-by-step process of having an "enhancing team effectiveness session." We want this to be a positive experience for all involved, so please do not hesitate to call for clarification.

Step one: All team members need basic information about their "type."

The enhancing team effectiveness experience is built on foundation information on type covered in "appreciating gifts and differences." Enclosed is a flyer advertising the next "appreciating gifts and differences" session, for you to share with team members who did not have the opportunity to attend, whether at a retreat or in education services.

Step two: Negotiate logistical details.

The first available time we can work with you is during the month of _____ . Any time after that is negotiable.

We will contact you for an interview (either in person or over the phone) in order to plan the event and gather information about your team.

Set the date, time, place, and duration of the event. We find that a minimum of 1½–2 hours is needed for the group to process the exercises.

Step three: Gather information and negotiate on content.

Following are questions that you will need to think about so we can individualize the session for your team. Besides wording out logistical details, we will discuss the following in the presession interview.
- What would you like to accomplish with the experience?
- What areas would you like to focus on (for example, communication, culture issues, leadership issues, and team decision making)?
- Which presession survey questions do you think would give us the best knowledge about your team (see below)?
- What and how would you choose to communicate these sessions with your team?

Step four: Gather information from yourself, your advisors, or whoever you choose to include in the presession interview(s).

Step five: Analyze data and plan content.

After our interview, we will provide the survey for you to distribute to your team. The survey will include instructions to send the surveys back to your designated correspondents. We will ask them to share their type with us on the survey. Their type and all information will be held confidential. It will be used to analyze a team type and plan a team enhancement session.

Step six: The enhancing team effectiveness session(s).

Step seven: Evaluation.

The team will evaluate the session, compile feedback, and share that feedback with you. Any items or concepts that remain unclear will be clarified in a written format and sent to your team.

We are looking forward to working with you and your team. With our resources and commitment to working together, we look forward to a positive outcome.

Questions for selection during step three:

Team questions
- What works well on this team?
- What does not work well on this team?
- What methods does this team use to solve problems?
- What is the toughest issue facing the team?
- How does communication take place on this team?
- Are there causes or factors outside of this team that moderate its effectiveness?
- What three things would you change to make this team more effective?
- How does this team handle change?
- What goals and aspirations do you have for this team?
- What barriers do you perceive to achieving your team's goals?
- What steps would you be willing to take to remove those barriers?
- When you think about the climate, communication, leadership, interpersonal relationships, and organizational issues affecting this team, which do you feel is most important to address in the team building session, and why?
- What do you think causes the problems that exist on this team?
- What keeps the team from being as effective as it could be?
- What else do I need to know to make the team building session successful?
- What questions should I have asked that I didn't? (Use this question at the end of the interview, if there is time.)

MBTI Questions
- Have you ever taken the MBTI?
- If so: What do you remember about the MBTI? Do you have any concerns or issues about using the MBTI in this team building session? Do you have any other comments about the MBTI?

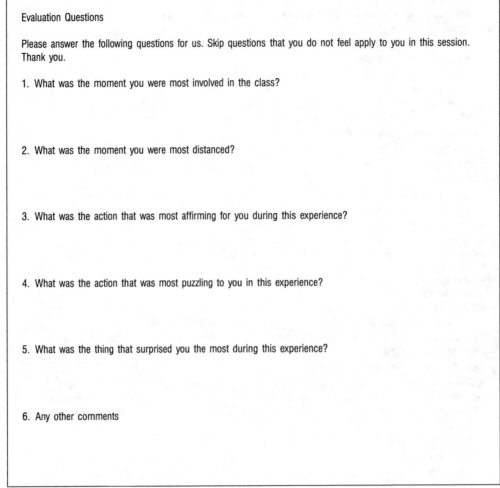

Figure B-7. Opportunities for Team Building Sample Evaluation Questions

Evaluation Questions

Please answer the following questions for us. Skip questions that you do not feel apply to you in this session. Thank you.

1. What was the moment you were most involved in the class?

2. What was the moment you were most distanced?

3. What was the action that was most affirming for you during this experience?

4. What was the action that was most puzzling to you in this experience?

5. What was the thing that surprised you the most during this experience?

6. Any other comments

Source: Adapted from Steven Brookfield, Ph.D., MBA, University of St. Thomas, St. Paul, MN.

Name of approach/method/tool: Case Management Curriculum

Learning objectives: The participants will learn to synthesize, sequence, and articulate in writing, diagnostic, and therapeutic measures necessary in the care of specified patient populations to achieve stated desired outcomes.

Target audience: Clinicians, financial analysts, and quality management staff

Key features of the approach/method/tool: To support the learning process of developing clinical pathways, several building blocks have been constructed. These foundation pieces include preassignments to be completed prior to the first group meeting, a detailed how-to guidelines manual, and a four-hour kick-off retreat which is designed to teach core values, principles, and begin the interactive, interdisciplinary pathway building process. Examples of the preassignments include viewing Joel Barker's video *The Business of Paradigms* (if they have not already seen the tape), conducting a retrospective audit of 5 to 10 charts of patients who had been hospitalized with the diagnosis for which the pathway is to be built, and comparing the course of treatment among patients, paying particular attention to variations.

The retreat day begins with warm-up activities to acquaint group members with one another, and an overview of the core values, goals, and case management model that have been developed specific to MeritCare. Key resource people from financial services, quality management, and planning and research explain how they support each team in evaluation efforts to measure the effectiveness of initiating development of the interdisciplinary pathway. Depending on the size of experience of the team and the complexity of the diagnosis, the building process any require two to six months to complete.

Pathway development has been a continuous learning process, with additional tools being created as the need has been identified. Examples of recent additions include an institutional directory that identifies which department and contact person(s) provides what types of data/information to evaluate the potential and actual impact of clinical pathways, and a standardized data matrix indicating the minimum data set required for ongoing assessment of pathway effectiveness. In the future, all policy/procedure and guidelines references pertaining to clinical pathways will be available on-line through our computer automation tool, Smartext, which is a Lotus hyper-text-on-line product that we have adapted for our use. This will improve access, minimize time needed to update and revise, and reduce storage needs for manuals.

In summary, we have attempted to support and sustain learning at three levels: individual, team, and organizational. The preretreat assignments and the how-to guidelines support individual learning, whereas the retreat day and all ongoing interdisciplinary planning meetings provide opportunities for team learning. Through standardizing the data set, identifying clearly the data resources, and building the reference documents into our on-line Smartext system, we have also attempted to design institutional resources that are independent of individuals who may come and go from our organization.

Outcomes: Have our pathways made a difference? We offer the following outcomes: In one fiscal year, we managed 1,241 patients on 10 different pathways and reduced direct costs by $1.9 million, decreased inpatient days by 2,500, and maintained or imported the clinical quality and level of patient satisfaction for the populations managed. The above calculations were based on comparing the average length of stay and costs for fiscal year 1993–94, with average baseline length of stay and unadjusted baseline costs for the same population prepathway management.

Contributor: Ruth B. Hanson, MS, RN, project coordinator

Contributor affiliation(s): MeritCare Hospital, Fargo, ND

Approaches, Methods, and Tools That Work at Northeast Health Consortium

Name of approach/method/tool: Interaction Management®: Techniques for an Empowered Workforce^{sm}

Target audience: The learning audience is a mixed group of employees from across the organization. It includes all full-time/part-time employees across the consortium, an initial learning group at Penobscot Bay Medical Center, and employees of the Knox Center (a long-term care facility).

Key features of the approach/method/tool: Interaction management® is a very structured curriculum. Educators are trained by DDI [Development Dimensions International] in a consolidated and intense training session. Three individuals in our organization have received this training. The setting is classroom based. DDI provides multimedia resource tools including literature and videotapes.

The learning approach incorporates learning principles of the adult learner including participation, ownership, motivation, expectations, practice, reinforcement, and feedback. There was a preestablished consensus by department managers to support this effort and to facilitate staff's participation in the session(s) for which they are scheduled. Groups of 30 employees are invited several weeks in advance to participate in a two-day, eight-hour each, workshop.

How the approach/method/tool was used: The program is divided into modules. Each module contains a presentation portion, a review and discussion portion, a reinforcement portion, a practice portion, and re-review. The conceptual framework for this technique is shown in figure B-8.

Outcomes: We have just implemented these particular modules, so it is premature to discuss outcomes. However, the acute care facility has used the DDI interaction management modules in the past with great satisfaction and success. We believe this program can assist all employees in developing the skills required to function effectively and successfully in the new system that we will come to know as our "community health care system."

Information on availability: Development Dimensions International, 1225 Washington Pike, Bridgeville, PA

Contributor(s): Paula Delahanty, RN, project director

Contributor affiliation(s): Penobscot Bay Medical Center, Rockland, ME

Approaches, Methods, and Tools That Work at St. Luke's Regional Medical Center

Name of approach/method/tool: Development of a Common Language Based on Quality Improvement Training

Learning objectives: Upon completion of the quality improvement training, a common language and philosophy affecting quality improvement principles and tools will be exhibited by team leaders when working with supervisors, coworkers, and subordinates.

Target audience: Supervisors, managers, directors, team leaders, quality advisors/executive staff

Key features of the approach/method/tool: Developed using St. Luke's model of quality improvement which focuses on integrating interactive planning and quality improvement strategies into St. Luke's organizational structure.

How the approach/method/tool was used: Materials were presented in a workshop format where the degree and amount of information delivered was constantly changing based on the level of the audience, the objectives identified, and the outcomes sought.

Outcomes: At the completion of the workshop:

- Quality improvement training participants will be able to work with one internal customer to identify their requirements and how to meet them.
- Quality improvement training participants will analyze a business decision in light of its impact on the four components of: (1) quality, (2) customer and employee satisfaction, (3) process/system improvement, and (4) financial impact.
- As group members, quality improvement training participants will work on an identified problem/opportunity demonstrating:
  - A systematic approach including problem/opportunity identification, process analysis, solution generation, implementation, and monitoring;
  - The use of the seven quality management tools
  - The key points of data collection by utilizing a work sheet to collect data concurrently and identifying a method appropriate for the use of graphs with staff. The evaluation sheet used to assess the progress of workshop participants is found in figure B-9 (pp. 250–52).

Figure B-8. Conceptual Framework for Training in Interaction Management®: Skills for a High-Involvement Workforce℠

Service Plus®

Beyond Customer Expectations
The service challenge
Keys to success
Steps to service
Everyday service excellence
Extraordinary service opportunities

Supporting Service Excellence®

Service leadership
Service initiatives

InterAction®

Building trust
Communicating with others
Influencing others
Supporting others
Training others
Handling conflict

Techniques for an Empowered Workforce®

Making the difference
Personal empowerment
The empowering leader℠

Team Action℠

Working in teams
Valuing differences
Participating in meetings
Leading effective meetings
Rescuing difficult meetings
Reaching agreement in teams
Self-directed teams

Team Start-up Kit
Team Development Kit

Taking Action®

Partnerships for improvement℠
Assessing improvement opportunities
Determining causes
Targeting improvement ideas
Implementing ongoing improvement

Taking Action Handbook

Interaction Management®

The Challenge of Leadership
Coaching for success
Reinforcing effective performance
Initiative: creating the environment
Encouraging initiative
Developing collaborative relationships
Delegating for results
Training job skills

Improving employee performance
Improving work habits
Utilizing effective follow-up action
Utilizing effective disciplinary/corrective action
Maintaining improved performance

Identifying performance expectations
Discussing performance expectations
Performance tracking and feedback
Conducting performance reviews

Your role in handling conflict
Resolving conflict
Overcoming resistance to change
Handling complaints

Strategies for High-Involvement Leadership℠

Leadership: facilitating change
Coaching: developing high performance
Trust: strengthening the foundation
Partnerships: creating synergy
Teams: reaching new heights
Key principles for high involvement

Empowerment Mirror℠
Empowering Leader Assessment System℠

Foundation skills
Expanding leadership skills: IM applications
Management support: coaching
Management support: reinforcing

Figure B-9. Quality Improvement Team Worksheet

St. Luke's Regional Medical Center
Boise, Idaho

Quality Improvement Team Worksheet

Team Name: _____

Date Formed: _____

Contracted

Team Leader: _____ _____

Quality Advisor: _____ _____

Process Manager: _____ _____

Proposed problem/opportunity statement: (concise, current, measurable, no solutions, agreed upon)

_____

_____

_____

_____

_____

Team Members

Name/title	Department	Name/title	Department
_____	_____	_____	_____
_____	_____	_____	_____
_____	_____	_____	_____
_____	_____	_____	_____
_____	_____	_____	_____
_____	_____	_____	_____
_____	_____	_____	_____
_____	_____	_____	_____

What was done to confirm problem/opportunity?

　　Primary Tools: Data collection _____ Brainstorming _____

　　　　　　　　　Pareto chart _____

Data Type: Attribute (discreet, counted, yes/no) _____

　　　　　Variable (continuous, measurable) _____

Collected by: _____

Time period: from: _____ to: _____

Figure B-9. (Continued)

Presentation form: Line graph _____ Pie chart _____

Bar graph _____ Pareto chart _____

Control chart: P _____ NP _____ (attribute data)

X _____ X-bar with R _____ (variable)

Stratified by: _____
(Attach copy of data)

Group norms: _____
(VII-4)

_____

_____

_____

_____

_____

Problem/opportunity statement (first revision):
(current, concise, measurable, without solutions, agreed upon)

_____

_____

_____

_____

_____

Analysis of the current process:

Data collection _____ Brainstorming _____ Flowchart _____

Cause/effect _____ Histogram _____ Scatter diagram _____

Data type: Attribute (discreet, counted, yes/no) _____

Variable (continuous, measurable) _____

Collected by: _____

Time period: from: _____ to: _____

Presentation form: Line graph _____ Pie chart _____

Bar graph _____ Pareto chart _____

Control chart: P _____ NP _____ (attribute data)

X _____ X-bar with R _____ (variable)

Stratified by: _____

Problem statement (second revision): _____

_____

_____

_____

(Continued on next page)

Figure B-9. (Continued)

Root cause(s): _____
(brainstorming, fishbone)

_____

_____

_____

_____

_____

_____

_____

Proposed solution: _____
(brainstorming, flowchart, graphs, control charts, scatter diagram)

_____

_____

_____

_____

Key quality indicators: _____

_____

_____

_____

_____

Solution implemented: _____
(flowchart)

_____

_____

_____

Results monitoring: _____
(data collection, graphs, stratification, Pareto, control charts, histogram)

_____

_____

_____

_____

Cost of solution: _____

_____

- To follow up, quality improvement training participants will be administered a questionnaire, shown in figure B-10, which measures the degree to which a common language relating to quality improvement principles and tools has been embedded in the day-to-day work of the participants. The results of the survey are shown in figure B-11.

Contributor(s): Jeanette Ullery, project director, director of education; Betty VanGheluwe, quality management coordinator

Contributor affiliation(s): St. Luke's Regional Medical Center, Boise, ID

Approaches, Methods, and Tools That Work at Tallahassee Memorial Regional Medical Center

Name of approach/method/tool: The Who's Working on What (WWOW) Database

Learning objectives: The purpose of the WWOW database is to provide a mechanism for teams to "link up" their improvement efforts and learn from one another's efforts. Teams have the ability to search for others who are working on the same or similar issues or for work on which they can build. In addition, by providing a means of identifying improvement efforts by organizational priority, senior management can identify potential learning

Figure B-10. Quality Improvement Training Survey on the Use of Common Language

Training date: _____

This survey is developed to measure the Quality Advisor and Quality Improvement Team Leader Training outcome measurement of "participants will use a common language related to quality improvement principles and tools." Please check the phrase below each statement that comes closest to your actions since attending the quality improvement training. Thank you for your time in completing the following five questions.

Since participating in quality advisor training 4–6 weeks ago:

1. I encourage the use of stakeholder involvement in the hospital's efforts to improve quality.

    _____ Majority of the time _____ Half of the time _____ Not very often

2. I encourage quality improvement efforts to remain customer focused.

    _____ Majority of the time _____ Half of the time _____ Not very often

3. To assist with solution development, I request or gather data relevant to problem/opportunity identification and process analysis.

    _____ Majority of the time _____ Half of the time _____ Not very often

4. When involved in decision making, I take into account the impact it will have on the four components of quality: employee satisfaction, customer satisfaction, process/system improvement, and financial impact.

    _____ Majority of the time _____ Half of the time _____ Not very often

5. My interaction with staff model that problems are primarily rooted in process/systems rather than people.

    _____ Majority of the time _____ Half of the time _____ Not very often

Comments: _____

_____

_____

Figure B-11.   Quality Improvement Training Objective: Participants Will Use Common Language and Tools

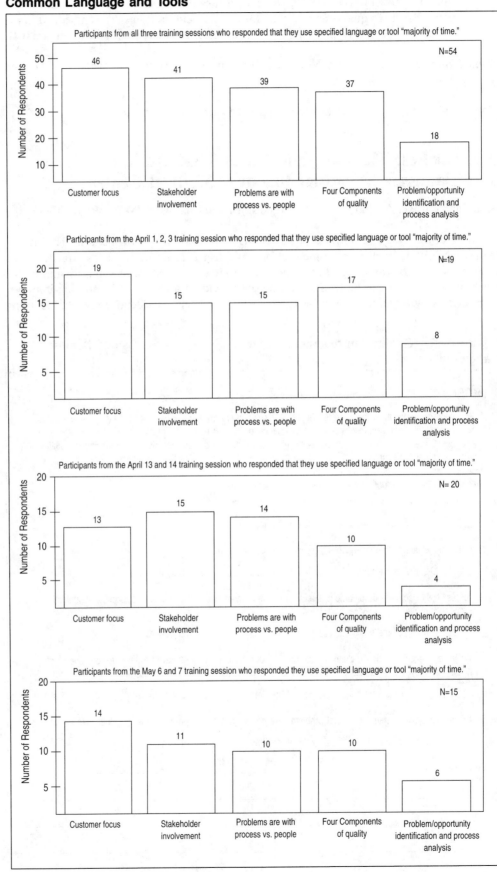

opportunities that may need to be addressed in order to move the organization in the desired direction. Lastly, the WWOW database provides IQM [interactive quality management] and senior management a way to examine work that is moving the organization in the desired direction and provide managers with the ability to monitor the work of several units to ensure accountability.

Target audience: Work groups and cross-functional/interdisciplinary teams, senior staff, department heads, managers.

Key features of the approach/method/tool: Several key features of the WWOW database are that it demonstrates compliance with JCAHO [Joint Commission on Accreditation of Healthcare Organizations] standards for improving organizational performance; provides a mechanism for teams to link up their improvement efforts; reduces duplication of effort and allows teams to learn from each other; provides senior management with the ability to examine work that is moving the organization in the desired direction; and provides managers with the ability to monitor work of several units to ensure accountability.

How the approach/method/tool was used: Information is submitted quarterly by each team/department by means of a quarterly report and WWOW coding sheet. (See figure B-12, p. 256.) Each improvement opportunity is categorized according to key processes, important functions, performance measures, organizational priorities, performance dimensions, quality tools utilized, and so on, and entered into a relational database that allows for easy access and reporting. (See figure B-13, p. 257.) Senior management receives reports quarterly and teams/departments can receive ad hoc reports on demand. Recently, the WWOW database was incorporated as part of the "idea bank." The idea bank was started in an attempt to get employees involved in certain price competition efforts being launched within the medical center. Cost savings ideas are checked in the WWOW database to determine if anyone in the medical center (for example, planning board, interdisciplinary team, cross-functional team or department) is currently working on or has worked on a similar issue in the past. If so, a "link-up alert" is submitted to the appropriate party for consideration and resolution of the idea. This helps ensure that duplication of effort is kept to a minimum.

Information on availability: Contact Gina Kuperberg in the project office (904/681-5328) at Tallahassee Memorial Regional Medical Center, Tallahassee, FL, for additional information.

Contributor(s): Gina Kuperberg, project analyst/measurement

Contributor affiliation(s): Tallahassee Memorial Regional Medical Center, Tallahassee, FL

Name of approach/method/tool: Start-up Educational Sequence (See table B-2.)

Learning objectives:

- Teams will be able to identify their unique role in patient/family care.
- Teams will be able to describe the interaction of the functions within their department, within the medical center, and outside the medical center.
- Teams will be able to describe their department's current level of performance and their contribution toward organizational performance.
- Teams will be able to involve all members of their staff using the concept of the circular organization, and the planning board process and structure.
- Teams will be able to utilize the steps of unit-based work redesign within their work areas.
- Teams will be able to explain the major concepts.

Figure B-12. WWOW Database Coding Sheet

Topic:

Service/dept./team:
Starting date:
Reporting period:
Status: active/inactive/complete/
change/transferred to team

Type: (Check all that apply)

1. Routine quality control ☐
2. Routine quality assurance ☐
3. Improvement opportunity ☐
4. Other ☐

Process topic: (Check all that apply)

High volume ☐
High risk ☐
Problem prone ☐
Regulatory requirement ☐

Performance dimensions:
(Check all that apply)

Efficacy ☐
Appropriateness ☐
Availability ☐
Timeliness ☐
Effectiveness ☐
Continuity ☐
Safety ☐
Efficiency ☐
Respect and caring ☐

Approach: (Check all that apply)

Interdisciplinary ☐
Interdepartmental ☐
Intradepartmental ☐
Committee name:
Contact name:
Extension:

Performance measures:
(Check all that apply)

Patient outcome ☐
Service excellence ☐
Job satisfaction ☐
Cost ☐
Productivity ☐

Important functions (Check all that apply)

I. Care of the patient

1. Assessment of patients ☐
2. Treatments of patients ☐
3. Operative/other procedures ☐
4. Education of patient/family ☐
5. Entry to setting or service ☐
6. Nutritional care ☐
7. Coordination of care ☐
8. Rights of patient ☐

II. Organizational functions

1. Leadership ☐
2. Management of information ☐
3. Improving organizational
   performance ☐
4. Management of human
   resources ☐
5. Management of the
   environment of care ☐
6. Surveillance, prevention,
   and control of infection ☐

Quality tools: (Check all that apply)

Control charts ☐
Flow charts ☐
Pareto charts ☐
Cause & effect diagram ☐
Statistical technique
(e.g. mean, mode, SD) ☐
Surveys ☐
Other ☐
Data available? ☐

Results:

Organizational Priorities (Check all that apply)

1. Effective and efficient use of resources ☐
2. Improve patient outcomes ☐
3. Meet customer expectations ☐
4. Develop a system to deliver a seamless
   continuum of patient/family care ☐

IOP success story:
(Check all that apply)

Note: Applicable only if process/topic
submitted to IQM Steering Committee
for consideration

Submitted to IQM: ☐ Date:

Selected by IQM: ☐ Date:

Source: Tallahassee Memorial Regional Medical Center, Tallahassee, FL.

Figure B-13. WWOW Database Report

Units/Departments Working on "Pain"	
Unit/Department/Team	**Description of Improvement Opportunity**
Cardiac pain management committee	Improving patient satisfaction with cardiac pain management
Endoscopy	Improving patient satisfaction by managing pain during endo procedures
Family care unit	Improving patient satisfaction re: effectiveness of postpartal pain
Labor and delivery	Monitoring epidural pain management
Neuro intensive care unit	Monitoring of pain management
Pediatric pain management committee	Improving service excellence of the pediatric pain management process
Pediatric special care unit	Improving pediatric pain management
Postanesthesia care unit	Monitoring appropriateness of interventions for pain management
Surgical nursing unit/3A	Improving patient satisfaction with management of pain

Source: Tallahassee Memorial Regional Medical Center, Tallahassee, FL.

Target audience: Start-up team members including the coordinator, the manager, the analyst, and facilitators-in-training attend the weekly educational session; and using the cascading model of learning, train the other staff members on the unit/department. All TMRMC employees are exposed to the material presented in the educational sequence via the cascading model of learning.

Key features of the approach/method/tool:

The seven steps of the TMRMC unit-based work redesign model are:

1. Idealized design
2. Formulation of the MESS (systems analysis; obstruction analysis; reference projection)
3. Gap analysis
4. Hit list
5. Means
6. Resources
7. Implementation

The major concepts include:

- Systems thinking
- Interdependency
- Continuous learning
- Employee empowerment (planning boards)
- Personal mastery/responsibility
- Continuous data-driven improvement

How the approach/method/tool was used: Cascading model of learning (See figure 4-10, p. 75)

Outcomes:

- All 74 teams at the medical center have completed the start-up educational sequence.
- Cognitive and behavior learning as a result of the educational sequence are evaluated by group exercises and back-on-the-unit projects. To meet the criteria for graduation (completion of start-up), each team completes and submits 12 assignments to the project office.
- The completion and submission of the interactive quality management quarterly report.

Table B-2. The Start-Up Educational Sequence at TMRMC

Date/Time/Location	Topic	Speaker/Presenter	Notes/Things to Do
January 4, 1995 8:00 a.m.–12:00 noon Auditorium Week 1	• General introduction • Walking the talk • "Big picture" presentation Brunch • Start-up teams • Planning boards • Cascading model of learning • Videotape *Paradigm Pioneers* by Joel Barker	Vivian Booth Duncan Moore Bill Giudice Vivian Booth Vivian Booth Vivian Booth Suzi Fite	Review content of your notebook. Videotape available to be used in your planning boards.
January 11, 1995 10:00 a.m.–12:00 noon Auditorium Week 2	• Comment forms, tracking hours, and resources • Systems thinking • Team meeting skills	DeeDee Lumpkin Winnie Schmeling Vivian Booth	
January 18, 1995 10:00 a.m.–12:00 noon Auditorium Week 3	• Focus on getting what you want • Patient family care focus (idealized design) • Systems modeling	Winnie Schmeling Winnie Schmeling Vivian Booth	Forward systems models to the project office by 3/1/95.
January 25, 1995 10:00 a.m.–12:00 noon Auditorium Week 4	• Videotape *Management Styles* by Russell Ackoff	Vivian Booth	Videotape available.
February 1, 1995 10:00 a.m.–12:00 noon Auditorium Week 5	• Videotape *The Power of Vision* by Joel Barker • Interactive model	Irma Daleen	Videotape available.
February 8, 1995 10:00 a.m.–12:00 noon Auditorium Week 6	• Videotape *Bell Labs Project* by Russell Ackoff • Ideal care using nominal group technique	Richard Zyski Keith Ivey	Videotape available. Forward idealized design to the project office by 3/15/95.
February 15, 1995 10:00 a.m.–12:00 noon Auditorium Week 7	• Overview of performance measurement • IQM quarterly report format and WWOW database	Mary Bland Kathy Holder/ Gina Kuperberg	
February 22, 1995 10:00 a.m.–12:00 noon Auditorium Week 8	• Formulation of the MESS (systems analysis) • Formulation of the MESS (reference projection)	Vivian Booth Ann Kaplan	Forward formulation of the MESS to the project office by 3/29/95.
March 1, 1995 10:00 a.m.–12:00 noon Auditorium Week 9	• Team presentations: Systems models • Formulation of the MESS obstruction analysis (work redesign survey)	Linda Harris	Assignment due. Forward surveys to the project office by 3/29/95.
March 8, 1995 10:00 a.m.–12:00 noon Auditorium Week 10	• Understanding reengineering		Videotape available.
March 15, 1995 10:00 a.m.–12:00 noon Auditorium Week 11	• Process flow analysis presentation	Nan Cuchens/ Mike Stallard	Forward process flowchart to the project office by 4/12/95.

Table B-2.   (Continued)

Date/Time/Location	Topic	Speaker/Presenter	Notes/Things to Do
March 22, 1995 10:00 a.m.–12:00 noon Auditorium Week 12	Quality tool kit	Gary Heald	
March 29, 1995 10:00 a.m.–12:00 noon Auditorium Week 13	• Planning for data collection videotape • Team presentation: Formulation of the MESS • Team presentation: Idealized design	Elise Brown	Videotape available. Forward data collection plan to the project office by 5/3/95. Assignment due.
April 5, 1995 10:00 a.m.–12:00 noon Auditorium Week 14	• Data collection methods videotape • Mental models	Vivian Booth Vivian Booth	Videotape available. Forward data collection methods to the project office by 5/3/95. Forward mental models to the project office by 5/10/95.
April 12, 1995 10:00 a.m.–12:00 noon Auditorium Week 15	• Pareto analysis • Team presentation: Process flowcharting	Rich Echols	Forward Pareto analysis to the project office by 5/3/95. Assignment due.
April 19, 1995 10:00 a.m.–12:00 noon Auditorium Week 16	• Quality or Else: A Global Marketplace videotape • Gap analysis and hit list presentation	DeeDee Lumpkin/ Gina Kuperberg Mike Russell	Videotape available. Forward gap analysis and hit list to the project office by 5/17/95.
April 26, 1995 10:00 a.m.–12:00 noon Auditorium Week 17	• Videotape *Growth vs. Development* by Russell Ackoff • Means and resource analysis presentation	Vivian Booth Sharon Owens	Videotape available. Forward means, resource analysis, and implementation plan to the project office by 5/31/95.
May 3, 1995 10:00 a.m.–12:00 noon Auditorium Week 18	• Implementation planning • Succeeding at reeginineering videotape	Vivian Booth Vivian Booth	Forward means, resource analysis, and implementation plan to the project office by 5/31/95.
May 10, 1995 10:00 a.m.–12:00 noon Auditorium Week 19	• Celebrating differences presentation	Fred Seamon	
May 17, 1995 10:00 a.m.–12:00 noon Auditorium Week 20	• Interdependency • Team presentations: Gap analysis and hit list	Vivian Booth	Assignment due.
May 24, 1995 10:00 a.m.–12:00 noon Auditorium Week 21	• Managing conflict presentation	Keith Ivey	
May 31, 1995 10:00 a.m.–12:00 noon Auditorium Week 22	• Team presentations: Data collection plan, methods and Pareto analysis • Team presentations: Means, resources, and implementation plan		Assignment due. Assignment due.
June 7, 1995 10:00 a.m.–12:00 noon Auditorium Week 23	• Graduation ceremony • Variation videotape	Vivian Booth Vivian Booth	Videotape available.

(Continued on next page)

Table B-2. (Continued)

Date/Time/Location	Topic	Speaker/Presenter	Notes/Things to Do
June 14, 1995 10:00 a.m.–12:00 noon Auditorium Week 24	• Team presentation: videotaping sessions	Dennis Watson	
June 21, 1995 10:00 a.m.–12:00 noon Auditorium Week 25	• Poster construction: Bill's Art City	Patty Backis	
June 28, 1995 10:00 a.m.–12:00 noon Auditorium Week 26	• Graduation ceremony • Poster presentation July 26, 1995, 10:00 a.m.–2:00 p.m. in the auditorium		

Information on availability: Tallahassee Memorial Regional Medical Center holds the copyright for the unit-based work redesign model.

Contributor(s): Vivian D. Booth, RN, project analyst, work redesign

Contributor affiliation(s): Tallahassee Memorial Regional Medical Center, Tallahassee, FL

Name of approach/method/tool: Keeping-on Educational Sequence (See table B-3.)

Learning objectives:

- Team meeting skills
  - You will be able to describe the importance of using a defined meeting process that includes steps and roles.
  - You will be able to use the seven-step meeting process.
  - You will be able to use special meeting roles to improve meeting effectiveness.
- Idea-generating tools
  - You will be able to use brainstorming to generate a long list of ideas.
  - You will be able to use nominal group technique to generate a long list of ideas.
- Consensus decision-making tools
  - You will be able to use multiple voting to reduce a long list of ideas.
  - You will be able to use rank ordering with a list of 10 or fewer ideas to get a visual display of the degree of agreement among team members.
  - You will be able to use structured discussion to lead a group to a consensus decision.
- The cause-and-effect diagram: Understanding the whys
  - You will be able to use the elements of a cause-and-effect diagram.
  - You will be able to use seven steps in developing a cause-and-effect diagram.
  - You will be able to describe how diagraming helps a team understand the causes which contribute to an effect.
- The flowchart: Picture of a process
  - You will be able to use standard flow symbols.
  - You will be able to use six steps to create a flowchart.
  - You will be able to describe three approaches to developing a flowchart.
  - You will be able to explain how flowcharting helps a team understand a process.
- Planning for data collection
  - You will be able to describe the eight questions to consider in developing a data collection plan.
  - You will be able to use the questions to develop a data collection plan.

Table B-3.   Keeping-On Educational Sequence at TMRMC

January 1995–June 1995			
Thursdays		**Fridays**	
Week 1—Jan. 12, 1995 (10:00 a.m.–12:00 noon) in auditorium	• Tools of Continual Improvement: Team Meeting Skills Christie Sloan	Week 1—Feb. 3, 1995 (8:30 a.m.–10:30 a.m.) in the Heart Institute classroom	Survey design part 1 Gary Heald
Week 2—Jan. 26, 1995 (10:00 a.m.–12:00 noon) in auditorium	• Tools of Continual Improvement: Idea Generation Keith Ivey	Week 2—Feb. 10, 1995 (8:30 a.m.–10:30 a.m.) in the Heart Institute classroom	Survey design part 2 Gary Heald
Week 3—Feb. 9, 1995 (10:00 a.m.–12:00 noon) in auditorium	• Tools of Continual Improvement: Consensus Decision Making Karen Pietrodangelo	Week 3—Feb. 17, 1995 (8:30 a.m.–10:30 a.m.) in the Heart Institute classroom	Survey design part 3 Gary Heald
Week 4—Feb. 23, 1995 (10:00 a.m.–12:00 noon) in auditorium	• Tools of Continual Improvement: Process Flowcharting Nan Cuchens and Mike Stallard	Week 4—Feb. 24, 1995 (8:30 a.m.–10:30 a.m.) in the Heart Institute classroom	Survey design, help session
Week 5—Mar. 9, 1995 (10:00 a.m.–12:00 noon) in auditorium	• Tools of Continual Improvement: Cause-and-Effect Diagram Judy Greenwald	Week 5—Mar. 3, 1995 (8:30 a.m.–10:30 a.m.) in the Heart Institute classroom	Statistics part 1 Gary Heald
Week 6—Mar. 23, 1995 (10:00 a.m.–12:00 noon) in auditorium	• WWOW Database Reports Linking Up the Efforts Gina Kuperberg and Mary Bland	Week 6—Mar. 10, 1995 (8:30 a.m.–10:30 a.m.) in the Heart Institute classroom	Statistics part 2 Gary Heald
Week 7—Apr. 13, 1995 (10:00 a.m.–12:00 noon) in auditorium	• Tools of Continual Improvement: Planning for Data Collecting Julie Burnett	Week 7—March 17, 1995 (8:30 a.m.–10:30 a.m.) in the Heart Institute classroom	Statistics part 3 Gary Heald
Week 8—Apr. 27, 1995 (10:00 a.m.–12:00 noon) in auditorium	• Tools of Continuous Improvement: Data Collection Methods Elise Brown	Week 8—Mar. 24, 1995 (8:30 a.m.–10:30 a.m.) in the Heart Institute classroom	Statistics part 4 Gary Heald
Week 9—May 11, 1995 (10:00 a.m.–12:00 noon) in auditorium	• Understanding Reengineering Vivian Booth	Week 9—Mar. 31, 1995 (8:30 a.m.–10:30 a.m.) in the Heart Institute classroom	Statistics part 5 Gary Heald
Week 10—May 25, 1995 (10:00 a.m.–12:00 noon) in auditorium	• Tools of Continuous Improvement: Pareto Analysis Kathy Holder	Week 10—Apr. 7, 1995 (8:30 a.m.–10:30 a.m.) in the Heart Institute classroom	Statistics part 6 Gary Heald
Week 11—June 8, 1995 (10:00 a.m.–12:00 noon) in auditorium	• Six Colored Hats; More Tools of Creativity Vivian Booth	Week 11—Apr. 14, 1995 (8:30 a.m.–10:30 a.m.) in the Heart Institute classroom	Statistics part 7 Gary Heald
Week 12—June 22, 1995 (10:00 a.m.–12:00 noon) in auditorium	• First Things First by Stephen Covey and Vivian Booth		

Poster presentation—July 26, 1995
in auditorium: 10:00 a.m.–2:00 p.m.

- Data collection methods
  - You will be able to describe the three components of an operational definition.
  - You will be able to determine if the measure is count data or measurement data, and describe the significance of these data types when determining the measure.
  - You will be able to describe how stratification is used in data collection.
  - You will be able to describe how block and systematic sampling are used in data collection, and the steps for each.
- Pareto analysis
  - You will be able to describe the Pareto principle.
  - You will be able to list and describe the five steps of Pareto analysis.
  - You will be able to construct and interpret a Pareto diagram.
  - You will be able to describe how the Pareto analysis process can aid process improvement efforts.
- Statistics
  - You will be able to define *measurement.*
  - You will be able to describe descriptive measures and calculations.
  - You will be able to report descriptive measures in tables and in graphics.
  - You will be able to use, calculate, and interpret tests of significance (types of errors in samples, measures of association, and measures of difference/change).

Target audience:

- Teams that have completed the start-up educational sequence and anyone else who is interested in the topics presented.
- All TMRMC employees are exposed to the material presented in the educational sequence via the cascading model of learning.

Key features of the approach/method/tool:

- Tools for continuous improvement
  - Team meeting skills
  - Idea generating
  - Consensus decision making
  - The cause-and-effect diagram
  - Process flowcharting
  - Planning for data collection
  - Data collection methods
  - Pareto analysis
- Basic statistics
- Survey design
- Tools of creativity

How the approach, method, or tool was used: Cascading model of learning (See figure 4-10, p. 75.)

Outcomes:

- Cognitive and behavior learning as a result of the education sequence are evaluated by group exercises and back-on-the-unit projects. The back-on-the-unit assignments are submitted to the project office for detailed feedback.
- Improved accuracy in the completion and submission of the interactive quality management quarterly report.

Information on availability: Tallahassee Memorial Regional Medical Center holds the copyright for the tools for continuous improvement.

Contributor: Vivian D. Booth, RN, project analyst, work redesign

Contributor affiliation(s): Tallahassee Memorial Regional Medical Center, Tallahassee, FL

Name of approach/method/tool: The Red Bead Game

Note: This experiment was created by W. Edwards Deming and used in his Four-Day Seminars.

Learning objectives: The learning objectives can be summarized as follows:

- Variation is part of every process.
- Planning requires prediction of how things and people will perform. Tests and experiments of past performance can be useful, but not definitive.
- Workers function within a system that—try as they might—is beyond their control. It is the system, not their individual skills, that determines how they perform.
- Only management can change the system.
- Some workers will always be above average, some below.
- Statistics can be used to look for problems areas.

Target audience: This game is primarily geared toward organizational change courses, and so its audience varies from executive teams to managers at all levels, to line workers.

Key features of the approach/method/tool: The key features of the game are:

- Humorous, but a very potent learning tool
- Provides hands-on learning of complex phenomena
- Easy to digest

How the approach/method/tool was used: The tools necessary for this experiment are a plastic box with white and red beads, a paddle with 50 holes in it, and the ability to easily scoop up beads out of the plastic box. In this experiment, red beads represent defective items and white beads represent good items. The process begins with the leader playing the role of the "boss." He or she hires five people to work at the White Bead Company, Inc. One additional person is hired to be the inspector. He or she explains that the purpose of the company is to produce white beads. The process of making white beads is standardized and must be adhered to without alteration. (Ham it up. It will be the role of the inspector to monitor the workers' productivity. Overexaggerate whenever possible.)

The boss explains to the workers that they must first pick up the box, shake it to the left once, right once, left once again, and then right twice each time prior to inserting the paddle into the box (without alteration). The worker must insert the paddle into the box at a 45 degree angle and remove the paddle from the box so that 50 beads are remaining on the paddle. The inspector counts the number of red beads, writes that number on a check-sheet, and plots the number on a line graph as well. This process is repeated until all five employees have had their turn, representing one day's work. This process is repeated for "five days." When completed, you should have 20 observations on the graph and checksheet. What will be noticed on the chart is that variation will run rampant. During the process of the five-day observations, the leader should harangue each employee as the number of red beads increases and decreases. Again, overexaggerate whenever possible and make it extremely funny. After all, it is a stupid experiment but one they will not forget. The messages this experiment sends are listed above under learning objectives. Oh! Don't forget to fire all of your employees at the end of the session and thank them for making you go out of business!

Note: If time permits, this example can be taken further in the sense that you can talk about a system that is in control versus out of control and wherein lies the responsibility for changing the system, with the workers or management. More specifically, statistics can be used to uncover areas in need of improvement. To illustrate the concepts, it is necessary to go through the calculations of control limits and explain their purpose with data that the group just generated. This game yields some very powerful insights into the nature of variation and, if time permits, should lead a discussion about the implications of statistics-based tools for work redesign.

Contributor(s): R. Darrell Lee, MS, former project analyst, measurement

Contributor affiliation(s): Tallahassee Memorial Regional Medical Center, Tallahassee, FL

Name of approach/method/tool: Staff Work Redesign Survey

Learning objectives:

1. You will be able to identify the role of team members in the survey process.
2. You will be able to review the purpose of the survey tool.
3. You will be able to provide instructions on administering the survey tool.
4. You will be able to describe the types of reports you can expect to get.
5. You will be able to interpret the survey results.
6. You will be able to list what the survey results can be used for.
7. You will be able to list what the survey results should not be used for.
8. You will be able to identify available resource persons.
9. You will be able to complete the staff work redesign survey.

Target audience:

- All TMRMC employees are exposed to the material presented in the educational sequence via the cascading model of learning.
- All teams concerned with identifying obstructions to excellent patient and family care.
- Any team working to improve their interpersonal, interdepartmental, and intradepartmental relations and/or work environments.

Key features of approach/method/tool: A clear, concise analysis, three-page survey tool. (See figure B-14.)

How the approach/method/tool was used: Cascading Model of Learning

```
Learn———Do———Teach————Mentor
          |              |
        Learn———Do———Teach————Mentor
```

Outcomes: Teams are able to statistically quantify the top five barriers to effective interdepartmental relationships. Once the current level of performance is identified, teams can continuously improve their performance. Team members can use the data to compare themselves against other work units, and also against themselves over time.

Contributor(s): Vivian D. Booth, RN, project analyst, work redesign

Contributor(s) affiliation(s): Tallahassee Memorial Regional Medical Center, Tallahassee, FL

Figure B-14.   Work Redesign Survey

The following questions concern your awareness and evaluation of "The Program to Improve Patient Care" at TMRMC.

Please answer each item for each question, checking the response that best represents your ideas and opinions. If you are unsure of your answer or neutral, check the middle space. All answers will be completely confidential.

1. In general, how familiar are you with "The Program to Improve Patient Care"?

	(example)	1	2	3	4	5	6	7	
Not familiar		—	—	—	—	—	—	—	Familiar

2. Based on what you know or have read, how would you describe the following features of the program?

  a. The "Unit-Based Interactive Redesign Process"

Not important	—	—	—	—	—	—	—	Important
Not clearly understood	—	—	—	—	—	—	—	Clearly understood
Not regularly emphasized	—	—	—	—	—	—	—	Regularly emphasized
Not effective	—	—	—	—	—	—	—	Effective

  b. Employee participation in work redesign

Not important	—	—	—	—	—	—	—	Important
Not clearly understood	—	—	—	—	—	—	—	Clearly understood
Not regularly emphasized	—	—	—	—	—	—	—	Regularly emphasized
Not effective	—	—	—	—	—	—	—	Effective

  c. Data-driven decision making

Not important	—	—	—	—	—	—	—	Important
Not clearly understood	—	—	—	—	—	—	—	Clearly understood
Not regularly emphasized	—	—	—	—	—	—	—	Regularly emphasized
Not effective	—	—	—	—	—	—	—	Effective

  d. The goal of high-quality customer service

Not important	—	—	—	—	—	—	—	Important
Not clearly understood	—	—	—	—	—	—	—	Clearly understood
Not regularly emphasized	—	—	—	—	—	—	—	Regularly emphasized
Not effective	—	—	—	—	—	—	—	Effective

(Continued on next page)

Figure B-14. (Continued)

3. Please answer this question by:

    a. Checking ( ) which, if any, of the following problems you regularly have in doing your job at TMRMC.

    b. Ranking the top five (5) problems that you have in doing your job. Place a "1" by the box next to the most serious problem, a "2" by the second most serious problem, a "3" by the third most serious problem, etc.

Problems within and between Work Unit(s)   **Checks**   **Top Five**

A.   Other people in my unit(s), whom I depend on, do not do their work quickly.
B.   Other people in my unit(s), whom I depend on, do not do their work correctly.
C.   Other people in my unit(s), whom I depend on, do not keep me informed.

D.   People in other unit(s), whom I depend on, do not do their work quickly
E.   People in other unit(s), whom I depend on, do not do their work correctly.
F.   People in other unit(s), whom I depend on, do not keep me informed.
G.   People in other unit(s), whom I depend on, are hard to reach.

H.   I regularly do work that should be done by another licensed person.
I.   I regularly do work that should be done by another nonlicensed person.
J.   I regularly do work that should be done by another person who is not in my unit.

K.   I am not allowed to do certain tasks that should be combined with my work.
L.   I am assigned certain tasks together that should be done separately.

M.   I cannot do my assigned tasks effectively (the way they should be done).
N.   I cannot do my assigned tasks efficiently (saving time/minimizing expenses).

O.   Some of my assigned paper work unnecessarily duplicates other paper work.
P.   Some of my assigned tasks unnecessarily duplicates work done by other people.
Q.   Some of my assigned tasks requires too many unnecessary trips outside of my unit.
R.   Some of my assigned tasks are unnecessary and should be eliminated.

S.   I am responsible for other peoples' work over whom I do not have adequate control.
T.   I am responsible for other people, but I do not have adequate time to review their work.
U.   I have too many people who report to me.

V.   My supervisor does not give me clear assignments.
W.   My supervisor does not adequately coordinate assignments among various employees.
X.   My supervisor does not adequately review my work.
Y.   My supervisor does not give me adequate feedback on the quality of my work.

Z.   I do not have enough equipment to do my job well.
AA.   I do not have enough equipment that works to do my job well.
AB.   I do not have enough new/updated equipment so that I can do my job well.
AC.   I do not have enough supplies to do my job well.
AD.   I do not have enough space to do my job well.
AE.   I do not have enough time to do my job well.
AF.   I do not have enough information to do my job well.
AG.   I do not have enough time to communicate with my supervisor.
AH.   I do not have enough time to communicate with my fellow workers.
AI.   I do not have enough time to communicate with patients.
AJ.   I do not receive enough in-service training to do my current job well.
AK.   I do not receive enough in-service training to allow me to advance.

AL.   I have to report to too many people.
AM.   I have too many people who give me orders/assignments.
AN.   I do not receive adequate feedback to help me improve my work.

AO.   We do not have enough professional staff in my unit.
AP.   We do not have enough support staff in my unit.
AQ.   The staff work schedules in my unit are not assigned fairly.
AR.   The "on-call" schedules in my unit are not assigned fairly.

Figure B-14.   (Continued)

4. Which days, if any, are busier than usual on your unit?

   (Please check all that apply)

   ☐ Sunday   ☐ Thursday

   ☐ Monday   ☐ Friday

   ☐ Tuesday   ☐ Saturday

   ☐ Wednesday

5. Which shift(s), if any, are busier than usual on your unit?

   (Please check all that apply)

   ☐ Days

   ☐ Evenings

   ☐ Nights

6. What is the unit where you typically work?

1. CPCU	20. Neurology	39. Pediatric specialty care	58. Inpatient dialysis
2. Family care unit	21. Outpatient	40. Pharmacy	59. Antenatal care unit
3. Oncology	22. Pediatrics	41. Information center	60. Adult special care unit
4. Orthopedics	23. Rehabilitation	42. PACU	61. Computer operations
5. CCU	24. Quality assessment	43. Ambulance/life flight	62. "Clinical services team"
6. DCI	25. Materials management	44. Cafeteria services	63. Laboratory
7. ED	26. NICU	45. Social ser. and util. mgt.	64. Nutritional support
8. GYN/URO	27. OR	46. Staff development	65. Women's resource center
9. Pulmonary	28. Public relations	47. Heart institute	66. CME department
10. CVSICU	29. Psych center	48. Anesthesia	67. Medical records
11. NBICU	30. Radiation therapy	49. Child care center	68. Plant engineering/safety
12. Extended care	31. Finance/accounting	50. Compensation	69. Infection control
13. Surgery	32. Education	51. Diabetes center outpt.	70. Employee health
14. Respiratory care	33. Home health care	52. Endoscopy	71. Laundry
15. Dietary	34. Labor and delivery	53. Family practice res. prog.	72. Security, POB, parking and
16. Admit/Reg	35. Long term care	54. Intermediate care unit	grounds
17. Employee relations	36. Adult intermediate care	55. IVT	73. Senior adult unit
18. Environmental services	37. MSICU	56. Neuroscience center	74. Radiology
19. MIS-S/P	38. Patient accounts	57. Volunteer services	75. Other

7. What is your title/position?

   (Please check only one)

   1. RN   4. Specialty tech   7. Representative

   2. LPN   5. Unit secretary/assistant   8. Supervisor/manager/coordinator

   3. Nurse tech   6. Specialist   9. Analyst

                                                            10. Other (please specify) _____

8. Which shift(s) do you typically work?

   (Please check only one)

   ☐ Days   ☐ Baylor days

   ☐ Evenings   ☐ Baylor nights

   ☐ Nights

9. In a typical week, how many hours do you work?   _____ Hours

10. How long have you worked at TMRMC?   _____ Years   _____ Months (if less than 1 year)

11. How long have you worked in your current unit?   _____ Years   _____ Months

12. How long have you worked in your current position on this unit?   _____ Years   _____ Months

13. How long have you held your current title?   _____ Years   _____ Months

Source: Tallahassee Memorial Regional Center, Tallahassee, FL.

Name of approach/method/tool: Mental Models

Learning objectives:

- Teams will be able to discuss the concepts of mental models.
- Teams will be able to describe the difference between traditional and learning organizations.
- Teams will be able to list the five disciplines of the learning organization.
- Teams will be able to identify the four skills needed to manage mental models.
- Teams will be able to quantify the levels of dialogue, trust, and willingness to be open and honest and the degree of risk associated with being open and honest.
- Teams will be able to generate a list of ways to get the dialogue going on their unit/department.

Target audience:

- All TMRMC employees exposed to the material presented in the educational sequence via the cascading model of learning.
- All teams concerned with becoming "learning teams" by increasing their dialogue.
- Any team working to improve their interpersonal/interdepartmental relations and or work environments.

Key features of approach/method/tool: Many of the best ideas never get put into practice. Usually, this failure stems not from weak intentions, wavering will, or even nonsystemic understanding, but from mental models. New ideas fail because they conflict with deeply held internal images of how the world works, images that limit us to familiar ways of thinking and acting.

Mental models are active—they shape how we act. Although people do not always behave congruently with their espoused theories (what they say), they do behave congruently with their theories-in-use (their mental models).

The problem with mental models arises when they are tacit—when they exist below the level of awareness. We trap ourselves in defensive routines that insulate our mental models from examination—we develop "skilled incompetence"—becoming highly skilled at protecting ourselves from pain and threat posed by learning situations—but consequently failing to learn how to produce the results we really want.

Traditional organizations focus on managing, organizing, and controlling. Learning organizations focus on visions, values, and mental models. Core values of learning organizations are *merit* (doing what is right) and *openness* (telling the truth).

Skills needed to manage mental models:

1. Recognizing leaps of abstraction (jumping from observation to generalization)
2. Exposing the "left-hand column" (saying what we usually do not say)
3. Balancing advocacy and inquiry (skills for honest investigation)
4. Facing up to the distinction between espoused theories and theories-in-use.

Most of us can deal with differences so long as the learning process is open, and people act with integrity.

Systems thinkers shift from mental models dominated by events to mental models that recognize longer term patterns of change and the underlying structures producing those patterns.

The major concepts of building a learning organization are:

1. Systems thinking
2. Personal mastery
3. Mental models
4. Shared vision
5. Team learning

How the approach/method/tool was used: Cascading Model of Learning

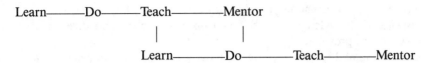

Outcomes:

- Teams are able to quantify unit/department level of dialogue and trust; the willingness to be open and honest; and the degree of risk (for themselves and others) for being open and honest.
- Cognitive and behavior learning as a result of the educational material is evaluated by the surveys completed during the group exercises. Analyses of the survey results are provided by the project office.
- The completion and submission of the Interactive Quality Management Quarterly Report.

Information available:

- Building the learning organization
- Mental models
- Advocacy matrix
- Mental models exercise (see figure B-15)

Contributor(s): Vivian D. Booth, RN, project analyst, work redesign

Contributor(s) affiliation(s): Tallahassee Memorial Regional Medical Center, Tallahassee, FL

Approaches, Methods, and Tools That Work at University of Utah Hospital

Name of approach/method/tool: Syllabus for the Multidisciplinary Apprentice Program (MAP) Training

Learning objectives: At the completion of the course, students will:

- Familiarize themselves with the employee benefits and responsibilities as a University Hospital employee
- Know the physical layout of the hospital as well as location of the policies and procedures manual
- Understand how health care institutions are organized
- Differentiate the ways in which health care is delivered, including nursing care delivery
- Understand and demonstrate correct use of communication
- Establish good rapport with patients, visitors, and other members of the health care team
- Know and practice principles of infection control
- Demonstrate the ability to function as a health unit coordinator
- Stock and order equipment and supplies
- Practice assertive communication and behavior
- Develop an awareness and knowledge of health career opportunities
- Demonstrate the ability to transport patients, equipment, and supplies from one department to another
- Demonstrate knowledge and skills in effective communication to patients and staff
- Demonstrate knowledge and understanding of basic human needs

- Demonstrate skills in providing direct patient care such as meeting patients' personal care needs
- Demonstrate skills in assisting patients with activities of daily living
- Demonstrate the knowledge and ability to observe, report, and document patient responses to care provided
- Demonstrate the ability to work effectively as a member of the health care team

Target audience: Students accepted into the multidisciplinary apprentice program are adult learners with a minimum of a high school education. Ages range from 18 to 55. The course is made up of students who are interested in a health care career. Students are very diverse and represent multiple target groups including youth, minorities, older workers, dislocated workers, and displaced homemakers.

Key features of the approach/method/tool: Time allotment: 100 hours of theory, skills laboratory, and supervised clinical practice.

Figure B-15. Mental Models Exercise

Working individually and silently, answer the following questions as honestly as you can:

1. On a 1 to 10 scale (with 1 being awful and 10 being fantastic), how would you rate:

   The dialogue you have now on your unit? _____

   The level of trust among the workers on your unit? _____

2. On a 1 to 10 scale (with one being not at all willing, and 10 being very willing), how would you rate:

   The willingness of the workers on your unit to be open and honest? _____

3. On a 1 to 10 scale (with one being no risk and 10 being great risk), how would you rate:

   The degree of risk to you of being open and honest? _____

   The degree of risk to other workers on your unit of being open and honest? _____

4. How will you get the dialogue going in your unit?

5. What are the biggest obstacles? How will you deal with them?

6. What are the risks—really? Can they be overcome?

7. What are you willing to do?

Source: Tallahassee Memorial Regional Medical Center, Tallahassee, FL.

Course description: This course is designed for individuals who are accepted as apprentices in the multidisciplinary apprentice program (MAP) at University Hospital. This course is appropriate for people seeking an entry-level position in the health care setting, with limited or no experience. One goal of the apprenticeship is to help them decide whether health care is the field they would like to pursue; and if so, to develop an interest in a specific career.

The course includes the initial hospital orientation offered to all employees of University Hospital. This orientation covers some of the basic information each employee should know about University Hospital, such as physical layout; how to find the policies and procedures manual; and safety practices including infection control, fire safety, handling of hazardous material, and basic cardiac life support. The orientation discusses all the benefits that are available for University Hospital employees.

A general overview includes an explanation of the multidisciplinary apprentice program: policies and procedures, responsibilities, and expectations. Students review how to study, take notes, take a test. Assertiveness training and customer service are also a part of this course.

Students learn the varied ways in which health care institutions are organized and how health care is delivered in these settings. They learn principles of good communication including: how to answer the unit telephone and patient's call light, and establishing rapport with patients, visitors, and other members of the health care team. Students rotate through the different departments to observe how they operate. These departments include radiology, physical therapy, pharmacy, and respiratory therapy.

Students learn the duties of a unit secretary as well as transporting patients, supplies, and equipment from one unit to another. Ensuring safety in the unit as well as when transporting patients is included.

Finally, students learn concepts and skills to guide direct patient care. Content includes basic human needs; observing and reporting patient data; performance of personal care and activities of daily living; monitoring of vital signs and intake and output; collecting specimens; and other specific applications included in the certified nursing assistant curriculum of the state of Utah.

Methods of Instruction:

- Lecture
- Skills laboratory—demonstration and skills practice sessions
- Video/filmstrips
- Supervised clinical practicum
- Structured individual learning experiences
- Sharing experiences in the clinical area and debriefing before each class
- Journaling

Recommended Textbooks:

Lindberg, J., Hunter, M., and Kruszewski, A. *Skills Manual for Introduction to Person-Centered Nursing.* Philadelphia: J. B. Lippincott, 1983.

Schniedman, R. B., Lambert, S. S., and Wander, B. R. *Being a Nursing Assistant.* Upper Saddle River, NJ: Regents/Prentice Hall, 1991.

How the approach/method/tool was used: This syllabus provides the foundation for the training component of the MAP. A more detailed curriculum includes specific objectives for each unit; projected hours of classroom, laboratory, and clinical time; reading assignments; and specific learning experiences.

Outcomes: Three classes of apprentices composed of 25 students have successfully completed the course. Of these, 24 have successfully passed the state knowledge and skills examination for certified nursing assistants. During the first two years of program implementation, 7 students have left the program and 22 continue to work as assistive workers within the hospital setting.

Information on availability: The curriculum, job descriptions, and policies are available from the University Hospital Program to Improve Patient Care, Box 45, 25 South Medical Drive, Salt Lake City, Utah 84112 (801/581-5606). A *Resource Guide for Nursing Assistant Training* is available from the Utah Registry of Health Occupations, 550 East 300 South, Kaysville, Utah 84037 (800/872-0343).

Contributor(s): Miriam O. Young, former MAP facilitator/educator; Kay Hart, former MAP facilitator/educator; Susan L. Beck, project director

Contributor affiliation(s): University of Utah Hospital, Salt Lake City, UT

Name of approach/model/tool: Goals and Roles Retreats

Learning objectives: The success of University of Utah's service teams with appropriate resources (STARs) depends on the convergence of individuals who had previously functioned in segregated worlds. One of the initial methods used to unite the team in a common vision and approach was a goals and roles retreat. The objectives of the retreat were to:

- Provide an opportunity for STAR members to become acquainted
- Establish a common vision of the STAR concept
- Identify what will constitute success for the STAR and what individual member contributions are necessary for success
- Identify roles of individual members with regard to patient care and the STAR
- Begin to establish the norms of the STAR
- Establish the communication methods for the STAR

Target audience: Each of the four initial demonstration STARs consisted of 35–45 clinical professionals. Although members of the newly formed, interdisciplinary teams had been caring for the same group of patients, many had never met in person.

Key features of the approach/model/tool: Throughout the day-long retreat, multiple approaches were used to help members clarify and make meaningful "the vision" — a consistent team of care providers collaborating across the continuum:

1. Information was provided on the conceptual history as well as the purpose, characteristics, and objectives of STARs. An organizational change consultant discussed with the group the concept of interdependence and essential characteristics of a successful team.
2. Results were shared from previously held stakeholder interviews to initiate discussion on predicted outcomes of success and perceived helping and hindering forces.
3. In a group activity, each team was asked to describe what would constitute success. What will be in place when you achieve your objectives? When and how will you know you are there? By building on the stakeholder information provided, the groups agreed on specific outcomes that would define their success.
4. Through individual work, team members identified their role in the care of the patient, their role as a team member, what they need from the team, and one norm they would like to see established in the STAR. Each member shared his or her views with the group.

Outcomes: A self-administered evaluation of the retreat was conducted at the end of the day. Results showed that participants felt the objectives had been met, especially the objectives to establish a common vision and become more acquainted. Even so, members desired more "get-acquainted time." Some commented they feared the norms were "idealistic." Others conveyed the interactive, group activities were most effective ("got at the nuts and bolts") and they would have liked less presentation time. Some suggested a half-day rather than a full-day retreat. Members described new linkages to other team members and resources.

Participants realized the effects of the organization's functional structure as they struggled to articulate their role on the team. This struggle helped to break through the perception that "we're already doing this" and persuaded the group that team development was an important area for them to tackle. Gaps and potential areas of overlap in care and roles were identified, and action plans were set and implemented following the retreat.

Successful outcomes were evident in the behavior and comments made by STAR members after the retreats. One norm established by the group was termed *glitch patrol:* Everyone on the team is responsible for identifying potential or actual glitches in the system and for pulling together the STAR for discussion and problem solving. This norm was used by STAR members following the retreat as a way to turn "role bumps" into opportunities for better clarity and use of resources in providing patient care, rather than becoming conflicts between team members. New relationships were developed in the weeks following the retreats. As one physician in attendance stated, "I'm working with people now whom I previously had communicated with only through the chart!"

The information gleaned from the retreat evaluation was utilized by the project staff to plan the STAR retreats for the following year. Half-day retreats with aggressive agendas were scheduled. The focus and objectives of the second round of retreats shifted from conceptual understanding to accomplishing work to further transform the vision to reality (the nuts and bolts). The amount of individual and small group work was increased. When information was presented, it was presented by STAR members themselves. Informal interaction time and fun exercises were scheduled to allow for relationship building.

The goals and roles retreat helped STAR members to value and see the goals for which they were striving. The activities worked to reveal the fragmented, departmental nature of their current reality. The day provided an opportunity for team members to say to each other, "Lets not let this fizzle out. Take this seriously and stay committed." Members gained a broadened appreciation of the complexity involved in the many phases of care of their patient population. They acknowledged the tremendous potential in collaborating as an interdepartmental, interdisciplinary team to achieve the highest-quality care for these complicated groups of patients.

Contributors to the retreats: Susan Beck, project director, University Hospital's Program to Improve Patient Care, University of Utah Hospital; Cheryl Kinnear, program manager, University Hospital's Program to Improve Patient Care, University of Utah Hospital; A. E. Rothermich, organizational change consultant, University of Utah.

Contributor(s): Cheryl Kinnear, RN, BSN, program manager, University Hospital's Program to Improve Patient Care

Contributor affiliation(s): University Hospital, University of Utah, Salt Lake City, UT

Approaches, Methods, and Tools That Work at Vanderbilt University Hospital and Vanderbilt Clinic

Name of approach/method/tool: Transition Teams

Target audience: We developed unit-based transition teams to help support implementation of new care delivery models on inpatient units.

Key features of the approach/method/tool: Specifically, the purpose of the transition team (as described in their charter) is to develop, plan, and implement with other members of the unit activities that will achieve the desired outcomes for your patient-focused care team during its transition:

- Integration of the new roles on the unit
- Understanding of everyone's role in relationship to all other roles on the unit
- Understanding of the patient care model and how this new configuration relates to the mission of the hospital
- A spirit of patient-focused teamwork on the unit
- A process for identifying emerging issues that seem ripe for applied team-building skills

How the approach/method/tool was used: The transition team participated in a one-day training session that prepared them for their nine-month commitment. The training helped the team learn skills in assertive communication, team development, and how to be supportive of others during change. They planned strategies to involve every member of the unit to become responsible for being cost-effective, maintaining excellent quality and service, and increasing commitment and satisfaction during this transition.

The team charter further outlined the roles and responsibilities of each person on the team, the role of the sponsor (assistant hospital director), the ground rules, and the decision-making process. The charter also specified the criteria for selection and individual criteria for volunteering for the transition team.

Contributor(s): Karen L. Turner, EdD, training specialist

Contributor affiliation(s): Vanderbilt University Hospital and Vanderbilt Clinic, Nashville, TN

Name of approach/method/tool: Shared Governance

Learning objectives: Learning how to participate in unit boards (discussed in appendix A) is an ongoing, two-pronged effort. This effort is focused on cultivating a common understanding of shared governance and developing the "meeting skills" of staff, leadership, and the board chairpersons.

How the approach/method/tool was used: Many individual unit boards discuss the concepts and boundaries of shared governance annually as they set goals for the board or rotate board leadership. Monthly housewide forums encourage unit board leadership to provide "real" examples of the basic concepts of shared governance at Vanderbilt. These "basics" include interactive planning, consensus decision making, and quality improvement. As boards are continually challenged to be more multidisciplinary, more patient focused, and more innovative, reinforcing a shared understanding of shared governance continues as important learning.

Training staff and managers to enhance their skills of planning, leading, and facilitating meetings is critical to the success of the boards. Annual workshops for those chairing boards and other unit-based committees are held to continually upgrade these skills. We also introduce board leaders and managers to using data more effectively for problem solving and some simple quality tools. These workshops are valued for their content, as well as for the collaboration that results when manager–staff "teams" attend the workshops together and apply the skills jointly to their specific board needs.

Contributor(s): Terry G. Minnen, MEd, shared governance liaison

Contributor affiliation(s): Center for Patient Care Innovation, Vanderbilt University Hospital and Vanderbilt Clinic, Nashville, TN

Approaches, Methods, and Tools That Work at Vermont Nursing Initiative

Name of approach/method/tool: Vermont Interact TV

Learning objectives:

To enhance the accessibility, availability, and affordability of educational programs for nurses working in rural areas

Key features of the approach/method/tool: The VICE (Vermont In-service and Continuing Education) group, together with the working committee for the Network for Education, identified two general areas of content to address in these interactive TV courses. The first was coronary care and the second was adult health. A third program in leadership development combined two sessions on Interact TV with an all-day workshop which was carried out at a central location.

The two clinical interact programs consisted of a series of six-, three-, and four-hour classes.

How the approach/method/tool was used: The content was divided into blocks of about 90 minutes each. Instructors from the various 15 participating hospitals in the state selected a topic of interest and prepared the information for presentation over Interact.

During the summer, a faculty member from the UVM school of nursing worked with VICE to develop a workbook with objectives and content to support the planned topics. Each individual participating in the learning program received an instructional workbook. Participants from each hospital attended the program at their nearest Interact site. Each hospital paid a flat fee for their staff to attend the series of six sessions, which were offered weekly for four hours during the fall. A permanent tape was made for each of the programs, which was then made available to the in-service education department of each of the hospitals. Many hospitals have subsequently used these tapes for orientation and update purposes. Participation in these educational courses included representation from virtually every hospital in both cases.

One problem encountered using this format was the scheduling of Interact time at times convenient to hospital staff nurses. Availability of Interact time has become quite competitive as more agencies successfully use this medium.

Contributor(s): Jane Hayward, RN, MSN, cochair, Network for Education

Contributor affiliation(s): Vermont Nursing Initiative, Montpelier, VT

Name of approach/method/tool: Summer Symposium

Key features of the approach/method/tool: The summer symposium is another important educational component of the Network for Education. It was started in the first year of the grant and has become a very popular annual educational event. This is a two-day workshop that has been held for project leaders and staff from each hospital. The symposium encourages networking and sharing among various staff and their projects through formal and informal methods. An expert consultant provides a keynote speech on a topic or issue that is common to all the participants. The workshop provides a retreat-type atmosphere for staff and leadership to immerse themselves in the creative challenge of furthering the work of their projects and staff development programs. The symposium offers the opportunity to learn from expert consultants as well as from each other during the two days of presentations, workshops, and camaraderie.

How the approach/method/tool was used: During the 1991 summer symposium, our keynote speaker discussed the issue of restructuring nursing services, which had implications for all hospitals in Vermont.

In 1992, our expert consultant addressed the area of work redesign. Our theme for the symposium that year was The Spiraling Journey—Maintaining the Momentum.

Our symposium in the summer of 1993 featured Marjorie Beyers. Her topic, Managing Choices in Changing Times, introduced two days of exciting presentations that featured staff from each of our hospitals who served as experts. These shared learning experiences laid the groundwork for the nurse-to-nurse consultation which has subsequently ensued between hospitals.

There have been a series of other workshops and educational experiences that have been developed in response to needs identified by various hospitals or groups of hospitals. In these instances, the network has helped to provide consultants and plan workshops to help meet these needs. These topics have included case management workshops with Cathy Bowers, a publishing workshop presented by Suzanne Hall Johnson, and a two-day workshop on the competency-based educational model using consultant Grif Alspach. These workshops have been developed in response to very specific staff needs.

Contributor(s): Jane Hayward, RN, MSN, cochair, Network for Education

Contributor affiliation(s): Vermont Nursing Initiative, Montpelier, VT

Appendix C

Bibliography

Ackoff, R. L. *Ackoff's Fables: Irreverent Reflections on Business and Bureaucracy.* New York City: John Wiley & Sons, 1991.

Ackoff, R. L. *Creating the Corporate Future.* New York City: John Wiley and Sons, 1981.

Ackoff, R. L. *The Democratic Corporation: A Radical Prescription for Recreating Corporate America and Rediscovering Success.* New York City: Oxford University Press, 1994.

Ackoff, R. L. *Management in Small Doses.* New York City: John Wiley & Sons, 1986.

Ackoff, R. L., Finnel, E. V., and Gharajedaghi, J. *A Guide to Controlling Your Corporation's Future.* New York City: John Wiley and Sons, 1984.

Aiken, L., and Fagin, C. *Charting Nursing's Agenda for the 1990s.* Philadelphia: J. P. Lippincott Co., 1992.

American Association of Colleges of Nursing. *Essentials of College and University Education for Professional Nursing.* Washington, DC: AACN, 1986.

American Organization of Nurse Executives. *Nursing Leadership: Preparing for the 21st Century.* Chicago: American Hospital Publishing, 1993.

Argyris, C. *Overcoming Organizational Defenses: Facilitating Organizational Learning.* Boston: Allyn and Bacon, 1990.

Aubrey, R., and Cohen, P. M. *Working Wisdom: Timeless Skills and Vanguard Strategies for Learning Organizations.* San Francisco: Jossey-Bass, 1995.

Barker, J. A. *Future Edge: Discovering the New Paradigms of Success.* New York City: William Morrow and Company, 1992.

Becker-Reems, E. D. *Self-Managed Work Teams in Health Care Organizations.* Chicago: American Hospital Publishing, 1994.

Benner, P. *From Novice to Expert.* Reading, MA: Addison-Wesley Longman Publishing, 1984.

Bennis, W. *An Invented Life: Reflections on Leadership and Change.* Reading, MA: Addison-Wesley Longman Publishing, 1993.

Berwick, D. M., Godfrey, A. B., and Roessner, J. *Curing Health Care: New Strategies for Quality Improvement.* San Francisco: Jossey-Bass, 1990.

Bevis, E. O., and Watson, J. *Toward a Caring Curriculum: A New Pedagogy for Nursing.* New York City: National League for Nursing, 1989.

Blanchard, K., Zigarmi, P., and Zigarmi, D. *Situational Leadership II.* Escondido, CA: Blanchard Training and Development, 1988.

Bridging the Leadership Gap in Healthcare. Executive Summary of a National Study Conducted by the Leadership Center of the Healthcare Forum. San Francisco: The Healthcare Forum, 1992.

Calvert, G. *Highwire Management: Risk-Taking Tactics for Leaders, Innovators, and Trailblazers.* San Francisco: Jossey-Bass, 1993.

Carroll, P. *Big Blues: The Unmaking of IBM.* New York City: Crown, 1993.

Champy, J. *Reengineering Management: The Mandate for New Leadership.* New York City: HarperCollins, 1995.

Charns, M. P., and Smith Tewksbury, L. J. *Collaborative Management in Health Care: Implementing the Integrative Organization.* San Francisco: Jossey-Bass, 1993.

Chin, R. The utility of system models and developmental models for practitioners. In: W. G. Bennis, K. D. Benne, and R. Chin, editors. *The Planning of Change.* 2nd ed. New York City: Holt, Rinehart and Winston, 1968.

Clifford, J., and Horvath, K., eds. *Advancing Professional Nursing Practice: Innovations at Boston's Beth Israel Hospital.* New York City: Springer, 1990.

Cohen, E. L., and Cesta, T. G. *Nursing Case Management: From Concept to Evaluation.* St. Louis: Mosby, 1993.

Covey, S. R. *First Things First: To Live, to Love, to Learn, to Leave a Legacy.* New York City: Simon & Schuster, 1994.

Covey, S. R. *Principle-Centered Leadership.* New York City: Simon & Schuster, 1992.

Covey, S. R. *The Seven Habits of Highly Effective People: Powerful Lessons in Personal Change.* New York City: Simon & Schuster, 1990.

Cross, K. P. *Adults as Learners: Increasing Participation and Facilitating Learning.* San Francisco: Jossey-Bass, 1981.

Cummings, T. G., and Worley, C. G. *Organization Development and Change.* 5th ed. St. Paul: West Publishing Co., 1993.

de Bono, E. *Lateral Thinking: Creativity Step by Step.* New York City: Harper and Row, 1970.

Delbecq, A. L., Van de Ven, A. H., and Gustafson, D. H. *Group Techniques and Program Planning: A Guide to Nominal Group Technique and Delphi Process.* Glenview, IL: Scott Foresman, 1975.

Deming, W. E. *Out of the Crisis.* Boston: MIT Center for Advanced Engineering Study, 1986.

De Pree, M. *Leadership is an Art.* New York City: Currency/Doubleday, 1989.

De Pree, M. *Leadership Jazz.* New York City: Currency/Doubleday, 1992.

Drucker, P. F. *The Five Most Important Questions You Will Ever Ask about Your Nonprofit Organization.* San Francisco: Jossey-Bass, 1993.

Drucker, P. F. *Managing for the Future: The 1990s and Beyond.* New York City: Truman Tally Books/Dutton, 1992.

Drucker, P. F. *Post Capitalist Society.* New York City: HarperCollins, 1993.

Ferguson, M. *The Aquarian Conspiracy: Personal and Social Transformation in Our Time.* New York City: St. Martin Press, 1980.

Flarey, D. L. *Redesigning Nursing Care Delivery.* Philadelphia: J. B. Lippincott Co., 1994.

Gerth, H. H., and Wright-Mills, C. P., eds. *From Max Weber: Essays in Sociology.* New York City: Oxford University Press, 1946.

Gibson, J. L., Ivancevich, J. M., and Donnelly, Jr., J. H. *Organizations, Behavior, Structure, Process.* 8th ed. Burr Ridge, IL: Richard D. Irwin, Inc., 1994.

Gilley, J. W., and Coffern, A. J. *Consulting for HRD Professionals: Tools, Techniques, and Strategies for Improving Organizational Effectiveness.* Burr Ridge, IL: Irwin Professional Publishing, 1994.

Graham, R. J. *Project Management As If People Mattered.* Bala Cynwyd, PA: Primavera Press, 1989.

Gregorc, A. F. *An Adult's Guide to Style.* Columbia, CT: Gregorc Associates, 1982.

Hammer, M., and Champy, J. *Reengineering the Corporation: A Manifesto for Business Revolution.* New York City: HarperCollins, 1993.

Hanson, R. B., and Sayers, B. *Work and Role Redesign: Tools and Techniques for the Health Care Setting.* Chicago: American Hospital Publishing, 1995.

Hatten, K., and Hatten, M. *Strategic Management: Analysis and Action.* Englewood Cliffs, NJ: Prentice-Hall, 1987.

Heimstra, R., and Sisco, B. *Individualizing Instruction: Making Learning Personal, Empowering and Successful.* San Francisco: Jossey-Bass, 1990.

Helgesen, S. *The Web of Inclusion: A New Architecture for Building Great Organizations.* New York City: Currency/Doubleday, 1995.

Hirsh, S. K. *MBTI Team Building Program: Leader's Resource Guide.* Stanford, CA: Consulting Psychologists Press, 1992.

Jacks, G., and Hunt, C. T. *Patient-Centered Care: Everyone's Business.* Washington, DC: District of Columbia General Hospital, 1994.

Joiner, B. L. *Fourth Generation Management.* New York City: McGraw-Hill, 1994.

Joyce, B., and Showers, B. *Student Achievement Through Staff Development.* White Plains, NY: Longman, Inc., 1995.

Kaiser, L. R. *Lifework Planning.* Brighton, CO: Brighton Books, 1989.

Kanter, M. R. *The Change Masters: Innovation and Entrepreneurship in the American Corporation.* New York City: Simon and Schuster, 1983.

Kanter, M. R. *When Giants Learn to Dance.* New York City: Simon and Schuster, 1989.

Kaufman, R., and Zahn, D. *Quality Management Plus: The Continuous Improvement of Education.* Newbury Park, CA: Corwin Press, 1993.

Kilmann, R. H. *Making Organizations Competitive.* San Francisco: Jossey-Bass, 1991.

Kilmann, R. H. *Managing Beyond the Quick Fix.* San Francisco: Jossey-Bass, 1989.

Kilmann, R. H. *Workbook for Implementing the Five Tracks.* Vols. 1 and 2. Tuxedo, NY: XICOM, Sterling Forest, 1991.

Knowles, M. *The Adult Learner: A Neglected Species.* 3rd ed. Houston: Gulf Publishing, 1984.

Kohles, M. K., Baker, W. G., Jr., and Donaho, B. A. *Transformational Leadership: Renewing Fundamental Values and Achieving New Relationships in Health Care.* Chicago: American Hospital Publishing, 1995.

Kouzes, J. M., and Posner, B. Z. *The Leadership Challenge: How to Get Extraordinary Things Done in Organizations.* San Francisco: Jossey-Bass, 1987.

Kouzes, J. M., and Posner, B. Z. *Leadership Practices Inventory LPI.* San Diego, CA: Pfeiffer & Company, 1993.

Kram, B. I. *Mentoring at Work: Developmental Relationships in Organizational Life.* Glenview, IL, and London, England: Scott Foresman, 1985.

Kroeger, O., and Theusen, J. M. *Type Talk: The Sixteen Personality Types That Determine How We Live, Love and Work.* New York City: Dell Publishing, 1988.

Leebov, W., and Ersoz, C. J. *The Health Care Manager's Guide to Continuous Quality Improvement.* Chicago: American Hospital Publishing, 1991.

Leebov, W., and Scott, G. *Health Care Managers in Transition: Shifting Roles and Changing Organizations.* San Francisco: Jossey-Bass, 1990.

Leebov, W., and Scott, G. *Service Quality Improvement: The Customer Satisfaction Strategy for Health Care.* Chicago: American Hospital Publishing, 1994.

Lindberg, J., Hunter, M., and Kruszewski, A. *Skills Manual for Introduction to Person-Centered Nursing.* Philadelphia: J. B. Lippincott Co., 1983.

Lombardi, D. *Progressive Management Health Care Strategies.* Chicago: American Hospital Publishing, 1992.

Marszalek-Gaucher, E., and Coffey, R. *Transforming Healthcare Organizations: How to Achieve and Sustain Organizational Excellence.* San Francisco: Jossey-Bass, 1990.

Melum, M. M., and Collett, C. *Beakthrough Leadership: Achieving Organizational Alignment through Hoshin Planning.* Chicago: American Hospital Publishing, 1995.

Melum, M. M., and Sinioris, M. K. *Total Quality Management: The Health Care Pioneers.* Chicago: American Hospital Publishing, 1992.

Merriam, S. B., and Caffarella, R. S. *Learning in Adulthood.* San Francisco: Jossey-Bass, 1991.

Moore, N., and Komras, H. *Patient-Focused Healing: Integrating Caring and Curing in Health Care.* San Francisco: Jossey-Bass, 1993.

Morgan, G. *Imaginization: The Art of Creative Management.* Newbury Park, CA: Sage Publications, 1993.

Morgan, G. *Personal Communication.* Newbury Park, CA: Sage Publications, 1995.

National Program Office. *Strengthening Hospital Nursing: A Program to Improve Patient Care, Gaining Momentum: A Progress Report.* St. Petersburg, FL: Robert Wood Johnson Foundation and Pew Charitable Trusts, 1992.

Osborne, D., and Gaebler, T. *Reinventing Government: How the Entrepreneurial Spirit is Transforming the Public Sector.* Reading, MA: Addison-Wesley Longman Publishing, 1992.

Patton, M. Q. *Practical Evaluation.* Newbury Park, CA: Sage Publications, 1982.

Peck, M. S. *The Road Less Traveled.* New York City: Simon & Schuster, 1978.

Peck, M. S. *A World Waiting to Be Born: Civility Rediscovered.* New York City: Bantam Books, 1993.

Porter-O'Grady, T. *Creative Nursing Administration: Participative Management into the 21st Century.* Rockville, MD: Aspen Publishers, 1986.

Ray, M., and Rinzler, A., eds. *The New Paradigm in Business.* New York City: Jeremy P. Tarcher/Perigee Books, 1993.

Robinson, D. G., and Robinson, J. C. *Training for Impact: How to Link Training to Business Needs and Measure the Results.* San Francisco: Jossey-Bass, 1989.

Rogers, E. M. *Diffusion of Innovations.* New York City: The Free Press of Glencoe, 1962.

Rovin, S., and Ginsberg, L. *Managing Hospitals: Lessons from the Johnson & Johnson –Wharton Fellows Program in Management for Nurses.* San Francisco: Jossey-Bass, 1991.

Schmidt, W. H., and Finnigan, J. P. *The Race Without a Finish Line: America's Quest for Total Quality.* San Francisco: Jossey-Bass, 1992.

Schniedman, R. B., Lambert, S. S., and Wander, B. R. *Being a Nursing Assistant.* Upper Saddle River, NJ: Regents/Prentice Hall, 1991.

Scholtes, P. R. *The Team Handbook.* Madison, WI: Joiner Associates, 1992.

Schon, D. *Educating the Reflective Practitioner.* San Francisco: Jossey-Bass, 1987.

Senge, P. M. *The Fifth Discipline: The Art and Practice of the Learning Organization.* New York City: Doubleday, 1990.

Senge, P. M., Roberts, C., Ross, R. B., Smith, B. J., and Kleiner, A. *The Fifth Discipline Fieldbook: Strategies and Tools for Building a Learning Organization.* New York City: Doubleday, 1994.

Shortell, S. M., Morrison, E. M., and Friedman, B. *Strategic Choices for America's Hospitals: Managing Change in Turbulent Times.* San Francisco: Jossey-Bass, 1992.

Spath, P. L., ed. *Clinical Paths: Tools for Outcomes Management.* Chicago: American Hospital Publishing, 1994.

Stetler, C. B., and Charns, M. P. *Collaboration in Health Care: Hartford Hospital's Experience in Changing Management and Practice.* Chicago: American Hospital Publishing, 1995.

Watkins, K. E., and Marsick, V. J. *Sculpting the Learning Organization: Lessons in the Art and Science of Systemic Change.* San Francisco: Jossey-Bass, 1993.

Weisbord, M. *Discovering Common Ground.* San Francisco: Berrett-Koehler, 1992.

Weisbord, M. R. *Productive Workplaces: Organizing and Managing for Dignity, Meaning and Community.* San Francisco: Jossey-Bass, 1987.

Wheatley, M. J. *Leadership and the New Science: Learning about Organization from an Orderly Universe.* San Francisco: Berrett-Koehler, 1992.

Zander, K., ed. *Managing Outcomes Through Collaborative Care: The Application of CareMapping and Case Management.* Chicago: American Hospital Publishing, 1995.

Additional Books of Interest

Transformational Leadership: Renewing Fundamental Values and Achieving New Relationships in Health Care

by Mary K. Kohles, RN, MSW, William G. Baker, Jr., MD, and Barbara A. Donaho, RN, MA

This book carefully looks at the role of leaders in transforming an organization to meet the challenge of providing compassionate, effective care within the restraints of current and future economic environments. You'll explore the visioning process, the continuous value improvement strategy, interactive planning methods, and the human and system factors that challenge transformational leaders. The book also describes the characteristics and experiences of organizations and their leaders that have made successful transformations possible.

Catalog No. E99-001116 (must be included when ordering)
1995. 294 pages, 14 figures, 1 table, 3 appendixes.
$40.00 (AHA members, $32.00)

Breakthrough Leadership: Achieving Organizational Alignment through Hoshin Planning

by Mara Minerva Melum and Casey Collett
copublished by GOAL/QPC

This book introduces you to a strategy that can help you achieve lasting, organizationwide improvements. With hoshin planning, the full power of people throughout the organization is focused on achieving the organization's most important priorities. Employees at every level understand how they will contribute to those priorities. Progress through such collaboration is often made in quantum leaps.

Catalog No. E99-169108 (must be included when ordering)
1995. 344 pages, 125 figures, 3 appendixes, glossary, bibliography, index.
$69.00 (AHA members, $55.00)

Work and Role Redesign: Tools and Techniques for the Health Care Setting

by Ruth Bredlie Hanson, MS, RN, and Betty Sayers, MS

It's a struggle to redesign work roles and responsibilities to improve efficiency and effectiveness. This book helps ease that struggle by showing you how to tap into and take advantage of an underutilized resource — the vast knowledge and experience of your employees. By using the ideas in this book, you'll be able to unleash the creative problem-solving abilities of the people closest to the customer.

Catalog No. E99-067102 (must be included when ordering)
1995. 216 pages, 39 figures, 13 tables, 2 appendixes.
$49.00 (AHA members, $39.00)

To order, call TOLL FREE
1-800-AHA-2626